A Little History:
THE *SENGOKU JIDAI*

INUYASHA takes place in the *Sengoku Jidai*, approximately 1482-1558, also called the "Warlord Era," or "Era of the Warring States." The time period got its name from the constant civil wars that took place throughout Japan's 15th and 16th-centuries. The reasons for these conflicts were mostly economic. Feudal overlords, or *daimyo*, became increasingly powerful and wealthy, while the ruling *shogun* and his central government weakened. Regional *daimyo* fought among themselves for control of the land and its resources. Average working folk were mostly concerned with keeping their heads down and not ending up in the middle of the next great battlefield. It was an age of great battles, powerful samurai and mysterious ninja. With this as a backdrop, it's not hard to see why so much Japanese fiction takes place around this time. Many of the Akira Kurosawa's films, Stan Sakai's comic *USAGI YOJIMBO* (Based loosely on the tales of Miyomoto Musashi), Kazuo Koike and Goseki Kojima's samurai classic *LONE WOLF AND CUB* and many others are set in this time period.

In a 2001 interview with *ANIMERICA* magazine, Takahashi gave her reason for setting the story of *INUYASHA* during the *Sengoku Jidai* as because it was "relatively easier to draw out a ghost story from that time period...In the Sengoku Era, there was war, and lots of people died."

Additionally, the subtitle for the *INUYASHA* anime series, *Sengoku o-Togi Zôshi*, is a reference to a specific kind of popular pulp stories written during this tumultuous period.

Julie Davis
Editor, *INUYASHA*

VOL. 2
2nd Edition
Story and Art by
RUMIKO TAKAHASHI

English Adaptation by
Gerard Jones

Translation/Mari Morimoto
Touch-Up Art & Lettering/Wayne Truman
Cover Design/Hidemi Sahara
Graphics & Design/Sean Lee
Editor (1st Edition)/Trish Ledoux
Editor (2nd Edition)/Julie Davis

Editor in Chief, Books/Alvin Lu
Editor in Chief, Magazines/Marc Weidenbaum
VP of Publishing Licensing/Rika Inouye
VP of Sales/Gonzalo Ferreyra
Sr. VP of Marketing/Liza Coppola
Publisher/Hyoe Narita

© 1997 Rumiko TAKAHASHI/Shogakukan Inc. First published by Shogakukan Inc. in Japan as "Inuyasha."

Printed in the U.S.A.

Published by VIZ Media, LLC
P.O. Box 77010
San Francisco, CA 94107

1st English Edition published 1998

2nd Edition
13
Thirteenth printing, December 2007

www.viz.com   store.viz.com

INUYASHA

VOL. 2

2nd Edition

STORY AND ART BY
RUMIKO TAKAHASHI

CONTENTS

SCROLL ONE
YURA'S WEB

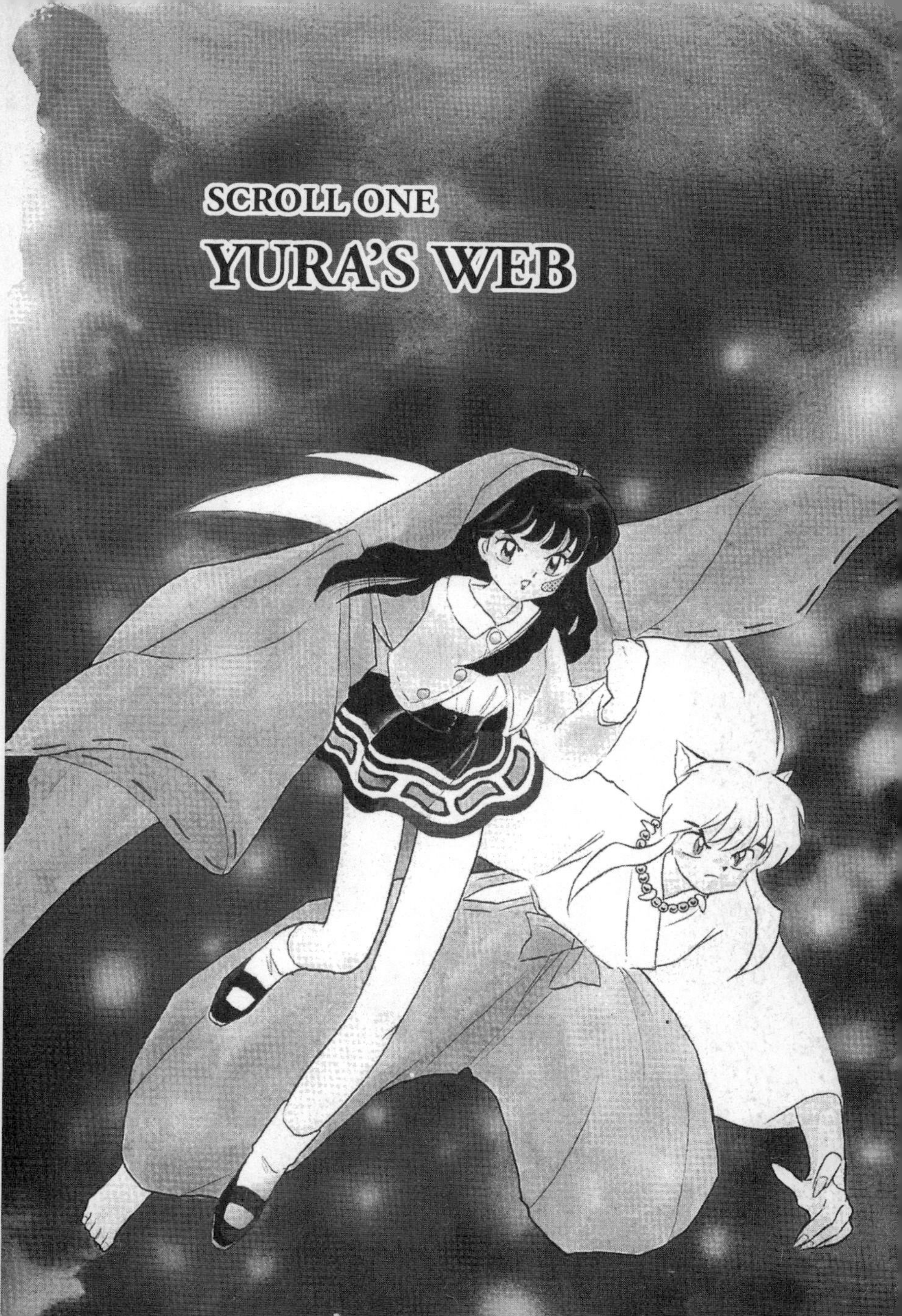

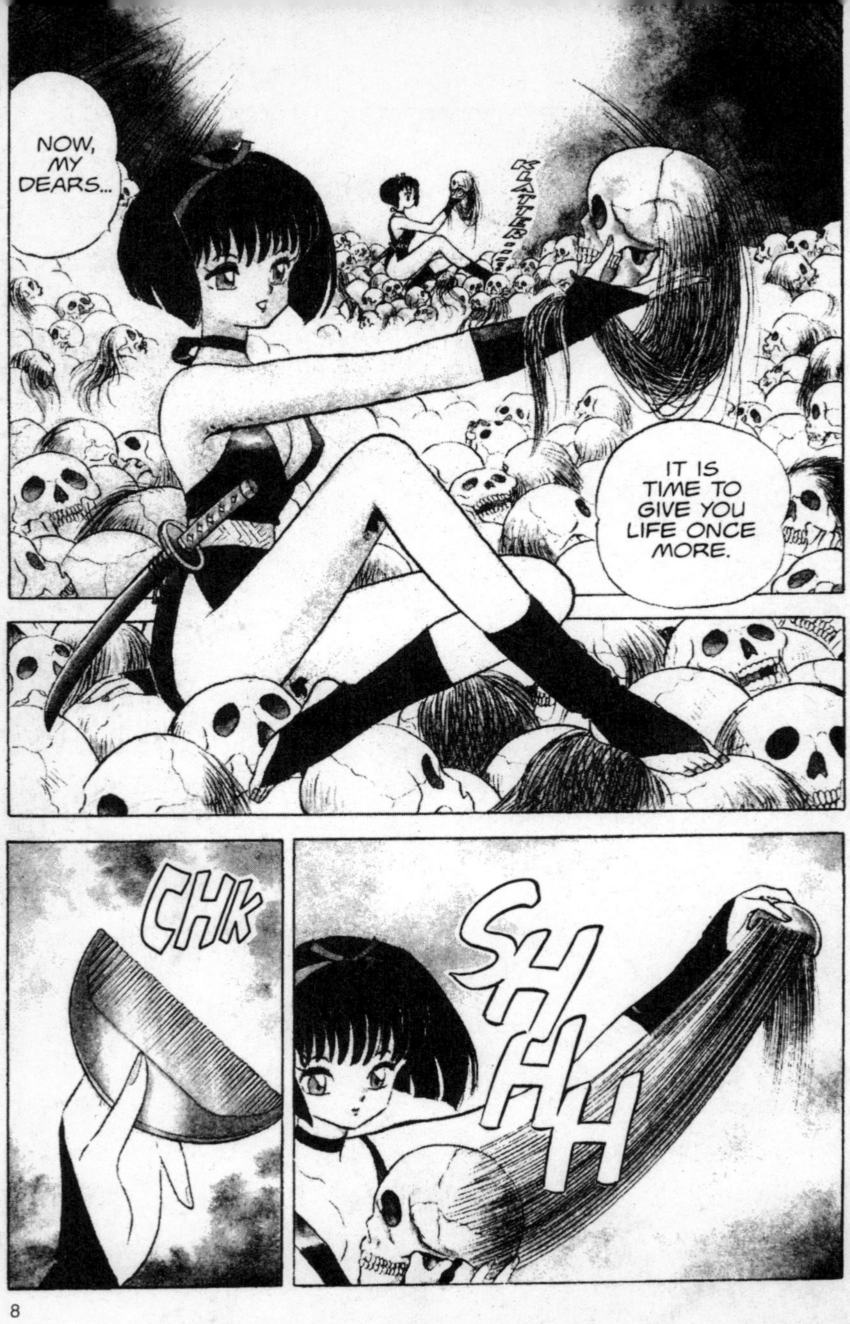
NOW, MY DEARS...
KLATTER...
IT IS TIME TO GIVE YOU LIFE ONCE MORE.
CHK
SHHHH

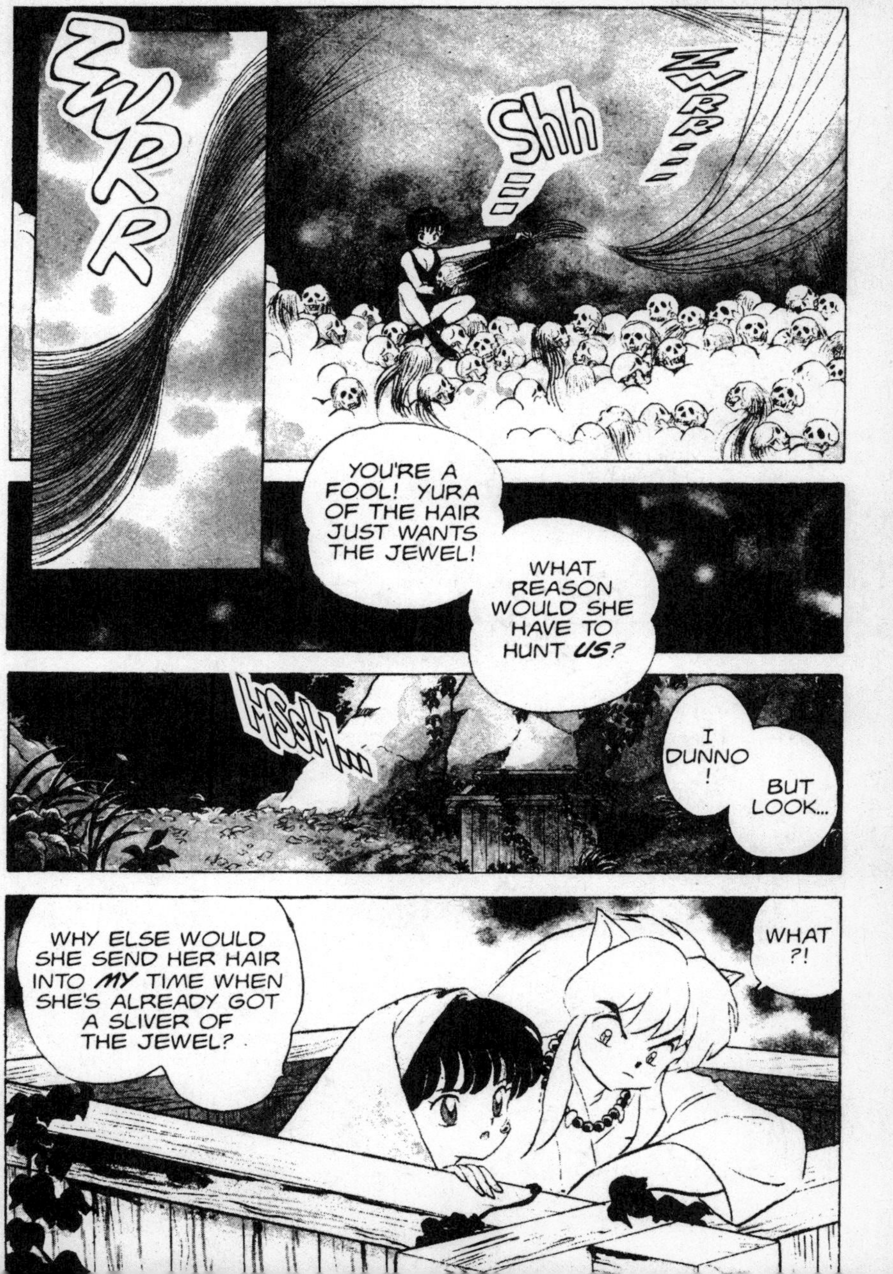
ZWRR
Shh...
ZWRR...
YOU'RE A FOOL! YURA OF THE HAIR JUST WANTS THE JEWEL!
WHAT REASON WOULD SHE HAVE TO HUNT *US*?
HSSH...
I DUNNO!
BUT LOOK...
WHY ELSE WOULD SHE SEND HER HAIR INTO *MY* TIME WHEN SHE'S ALREADY GOT A SLIVER OF THE JEWEL?
WHAT?!

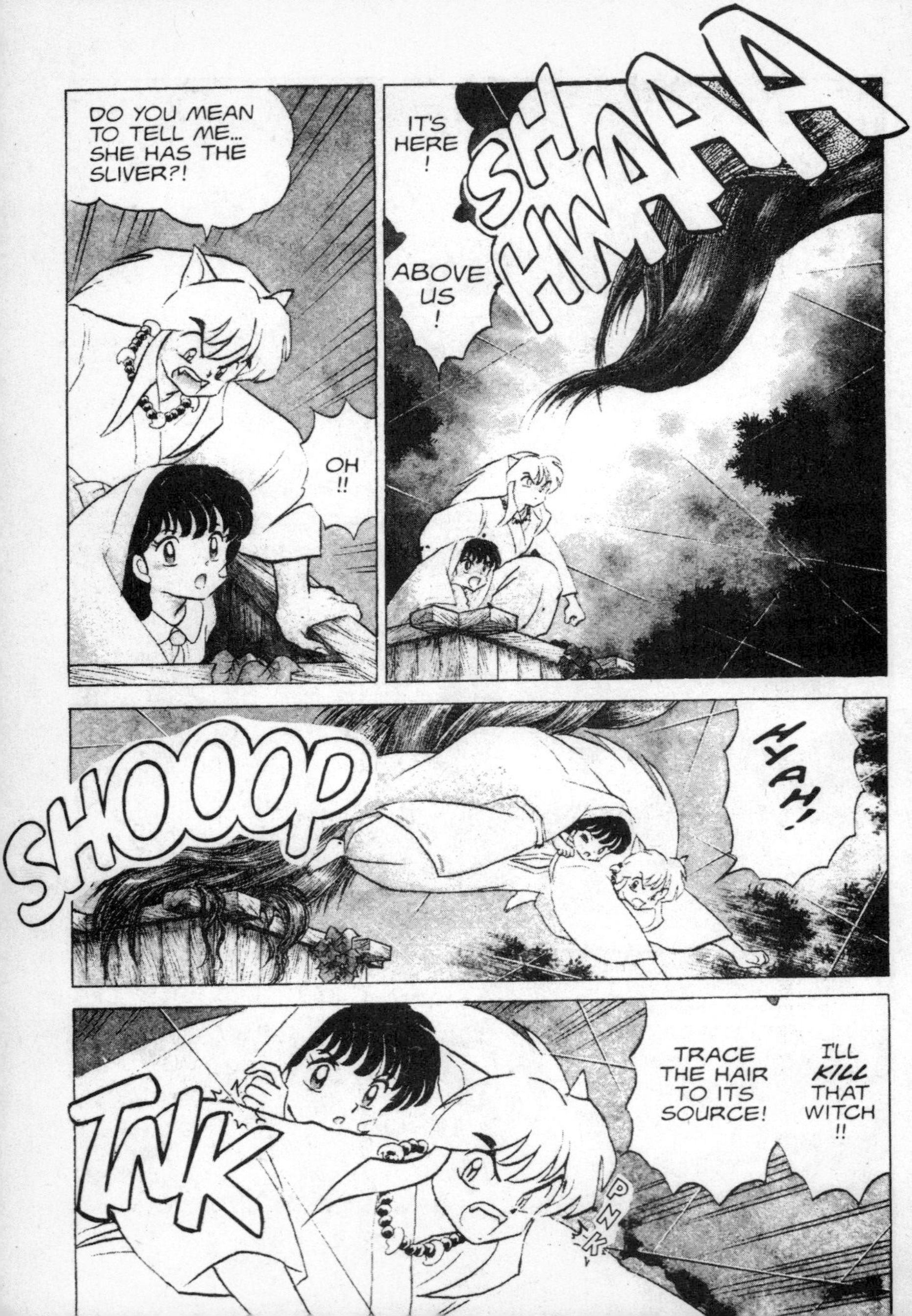
DO YOU MEAN TO TELL ME... SHE HAS THE SLIVER?!
OH !!
IT'S HERE !
ABOVE US !
SHHWAAA
SHOOOP
HYAH!
TNK
TRACE THE HAIR TO ITS SOURCE!
I'LL KILL THAT WITCH !!
PNK

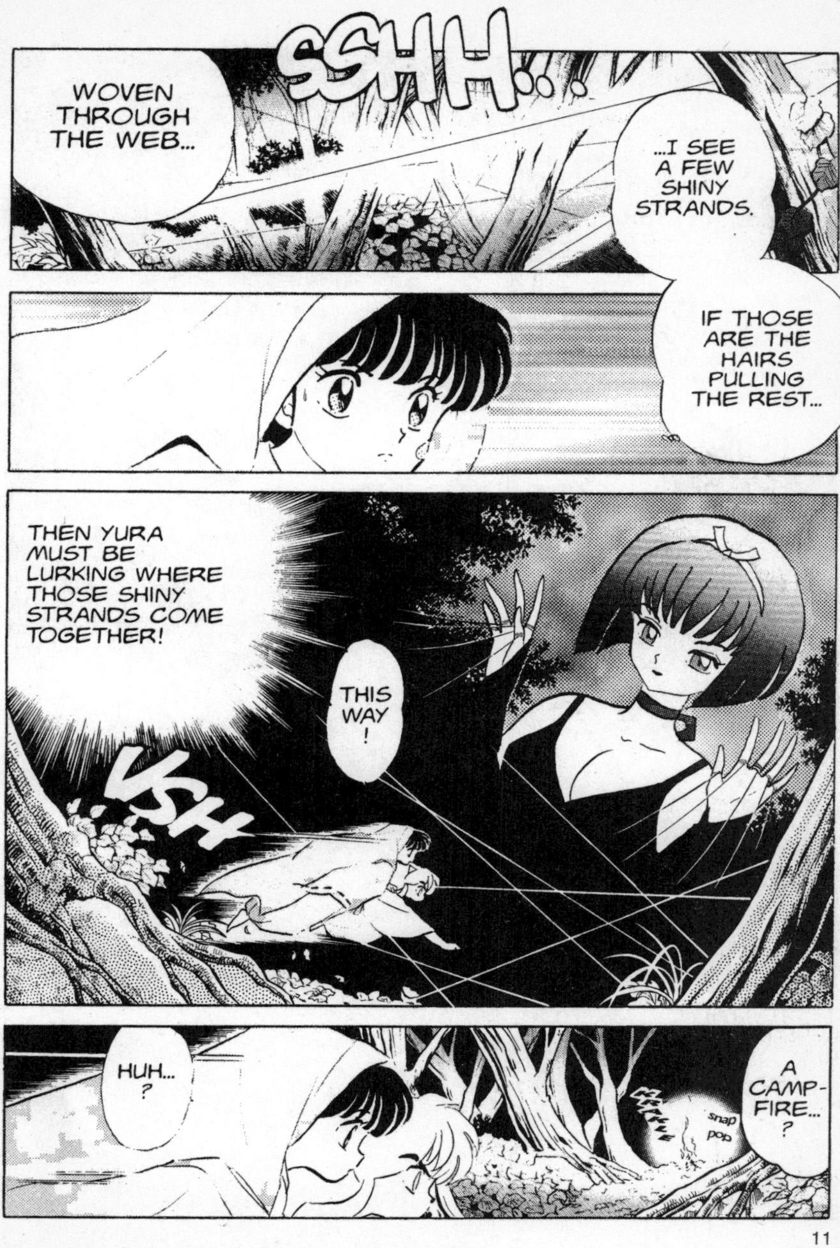
WOVEN THROUGH THE WEB...
SSHH...
...I SEE A FEW SHINY STRANDS.
IF THOSE ARE THE HAIRS PULLING THE REST...
THEN YURA MUST BE LURKING WHERE THOSE SHINY STRANDS COME TOGETHER!
THIS WAY!
VSH
HUH...?
snap
pop
A CAMP-FIRE...?

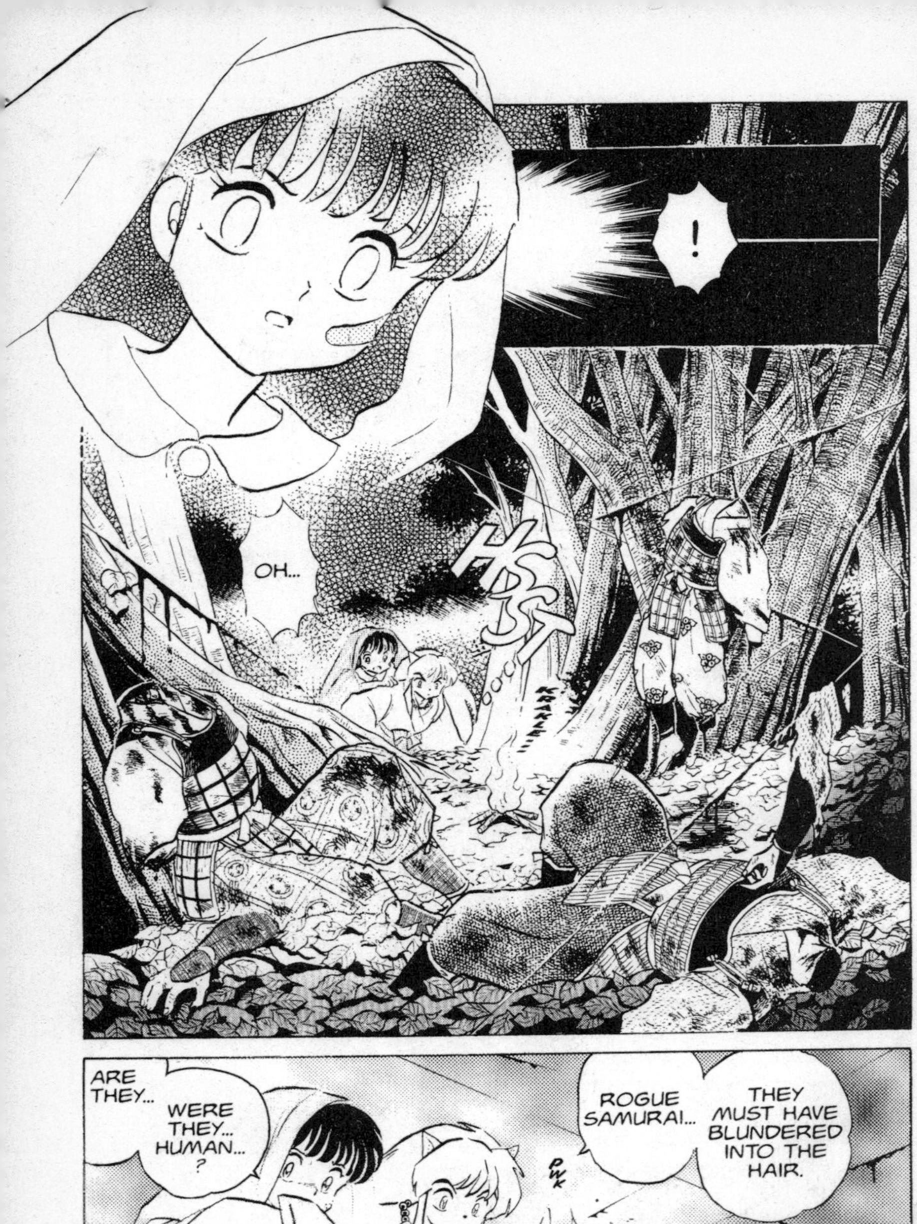

!
OH...
HSST
KRAKKLE...
ARE THEY...
WERE THEY... HUMAN...?
PWK
ROGUE SAMURAI...
THEY MUST HAVE BLUNDERED INTO THE HAIR.

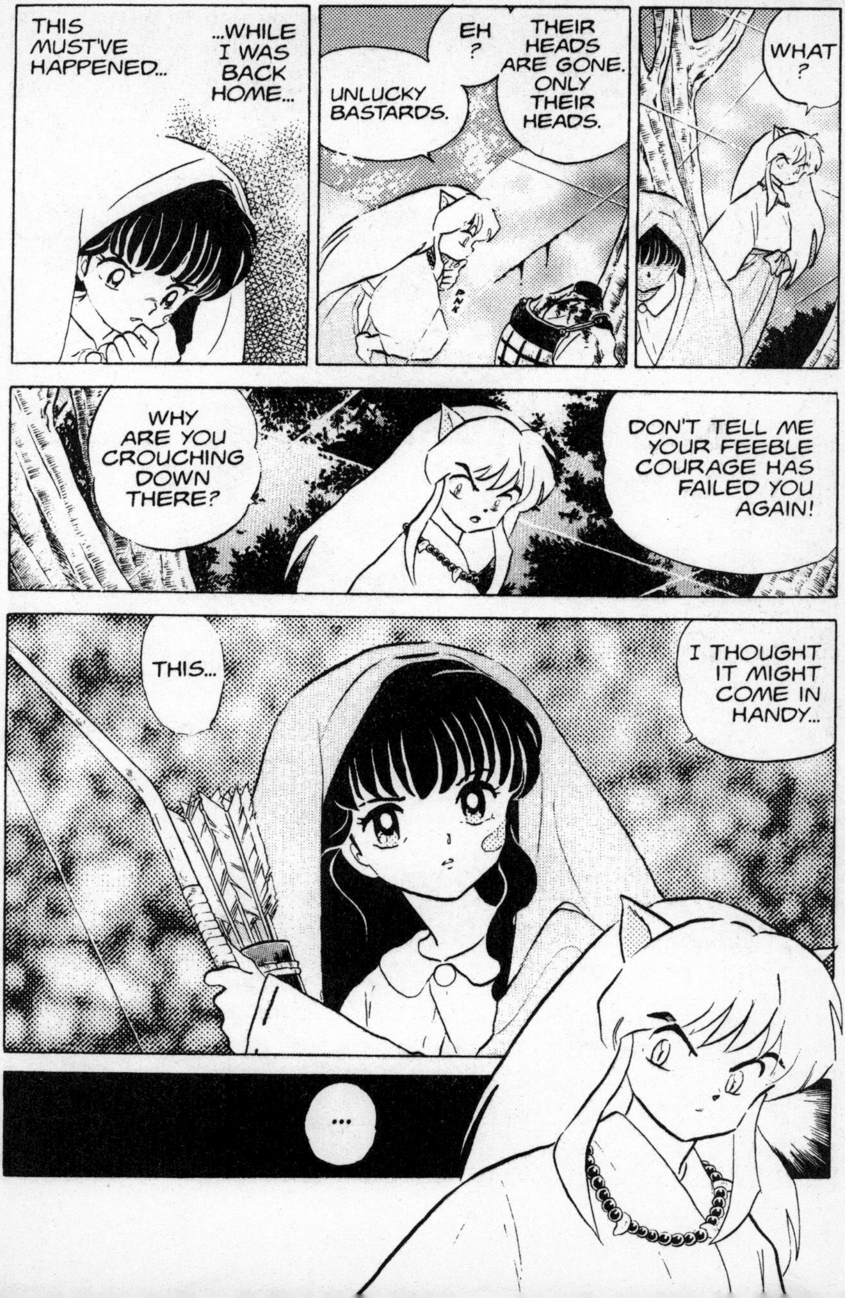
THIS MUST'VE HAPPENED...
...WHILE I WAS BACK HOME...
UNLUCKY BASTARDS.
EH ?
THEIR HEADS ARE GONE. ONLY THEIR HEADS.
WHAT ?
WHY ARE YOU CROUCHING DOWN THERE?
DON'T TELL ME YOUR FEEBLE COURAGE HAS FAILED YOU AGAIN!
THIS...
I THOUGHT IT MIGHT COME IN HANDY...
...

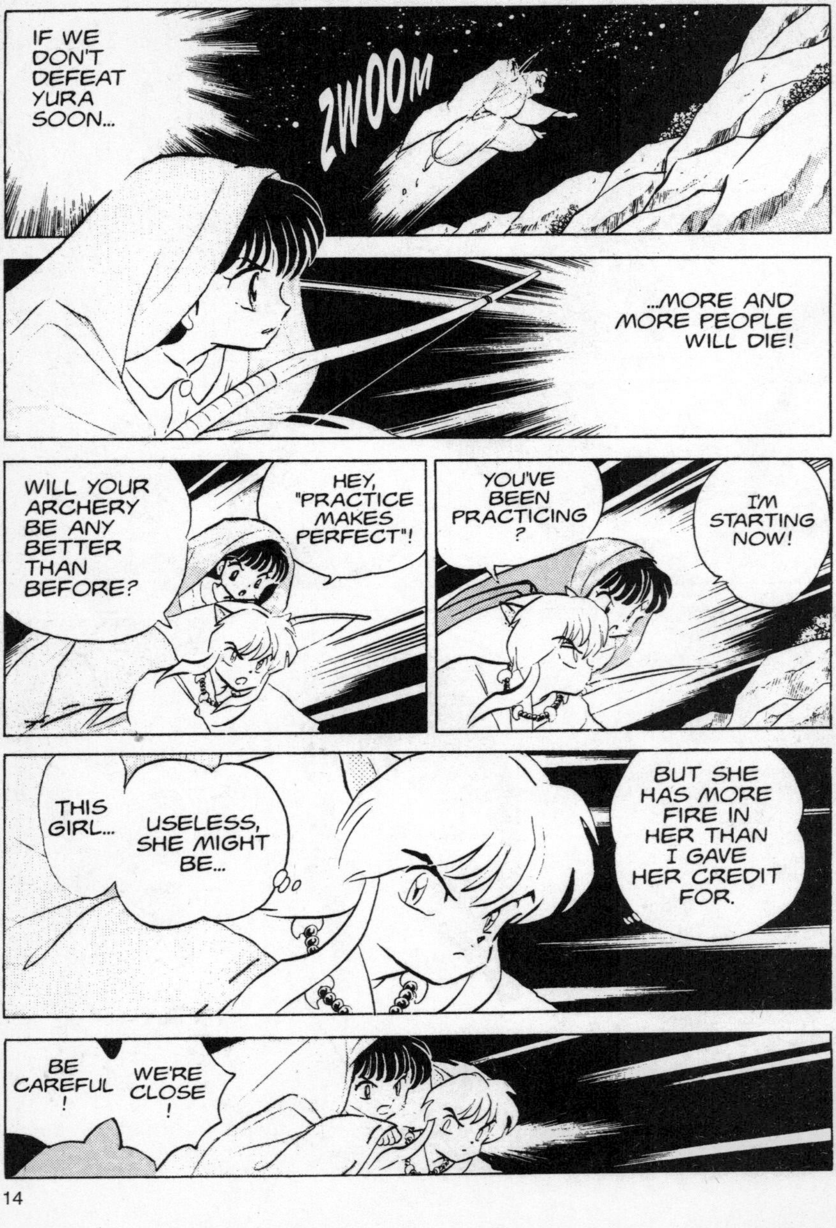
IF WE DON'T DEFEAT YURA SOON...
ZWOOM
...MORE AND MORE PEOPLE WILL DIE!
WILL YOUR ARCHERY BE ANY BETTER THAN BEFORE?
HEY, "PRACTICE MAKES PERFECT"!
YOU'VE BEEN PRACTICING?
I'M STARTING NOW!
THIS GIRL...
USELESS, SHE MIGHT BE...
BUT SHE HAS MORE FIRE IN HER THAN I GAVE HER CREDIT FOR.
BE CAREFUL!
WE'RE CLOSE!

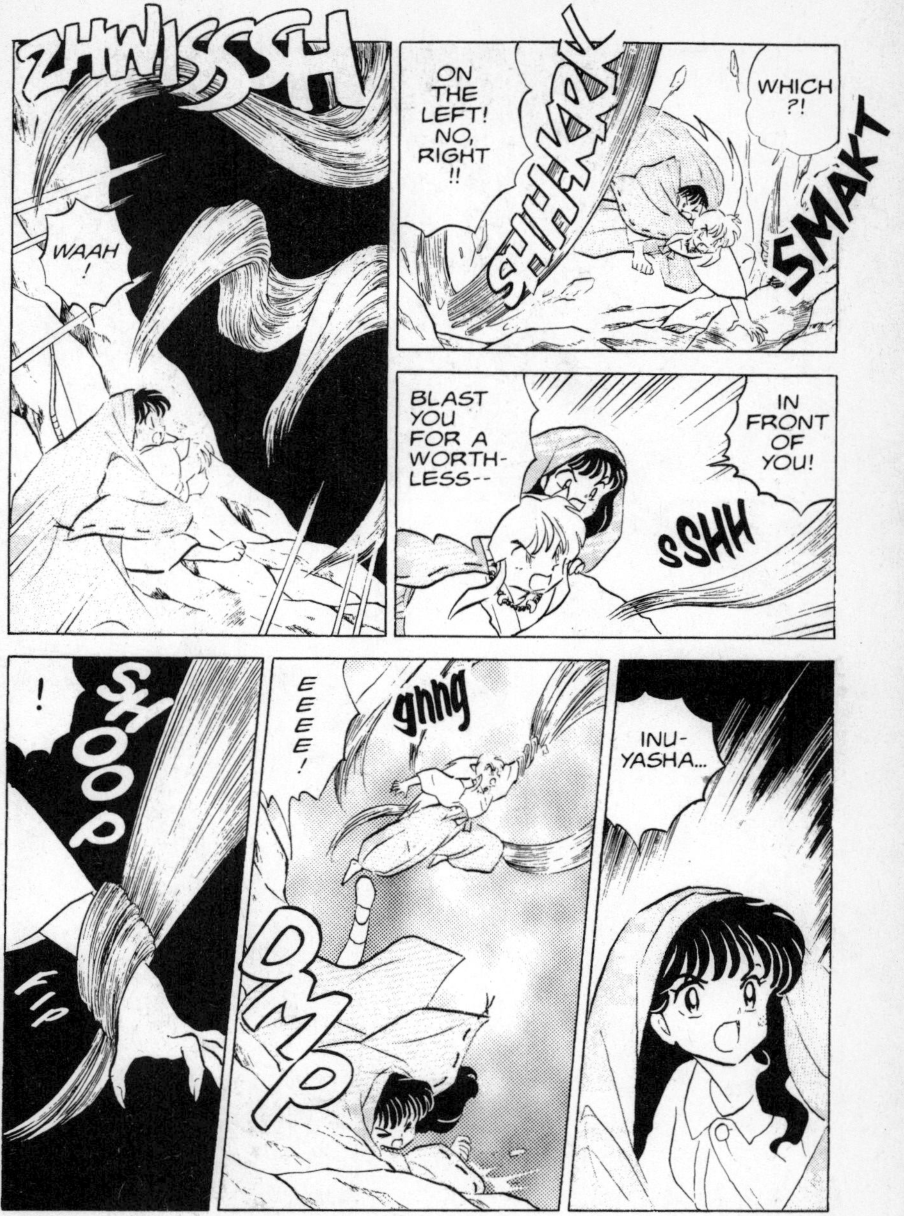
ZHWISSCH
WAAH!
ON THE LEFT! NO, RIGHT!!
SHHKARK
WHICH?!
SMAKT
BLAST YOU FOR A WORTHLESS--
IN FRONT OF YOU!
SSHH
!
SHOOP
FLIP
EEEE!
gnng
DMP
INU-YASHA...

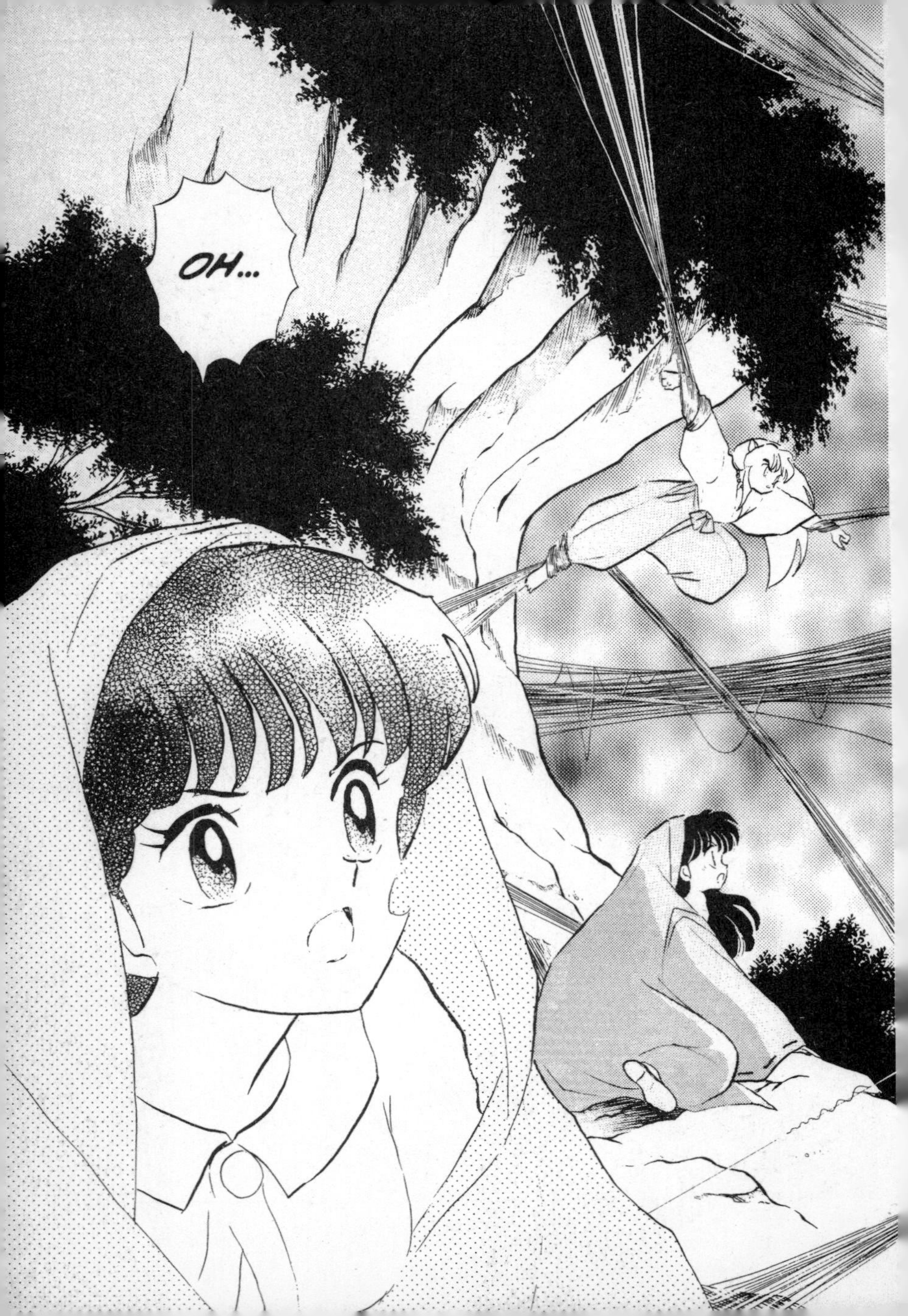
OH...

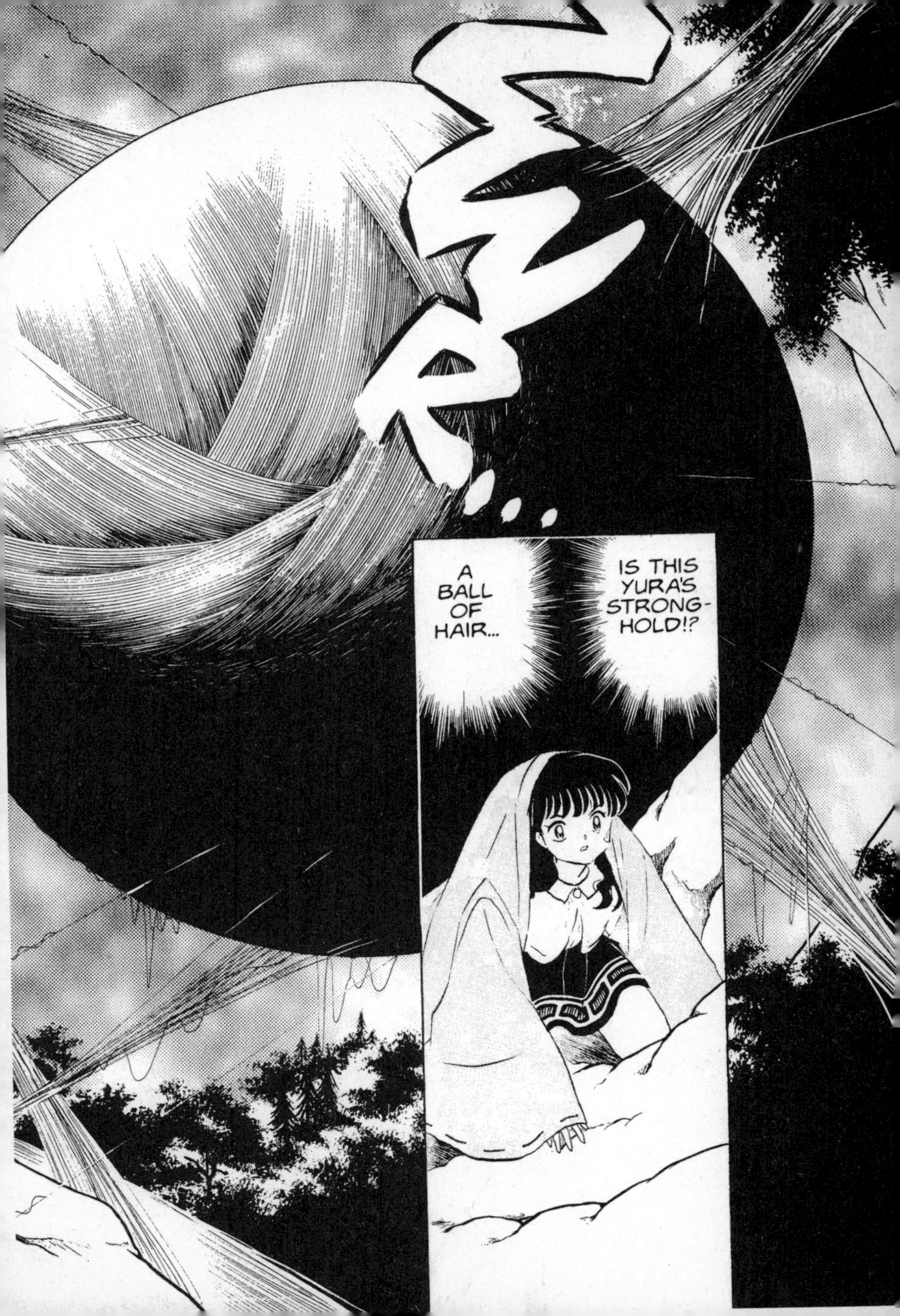
A BALL OF HAIR...
IS THIS YURA'S STRONGHOLD!?

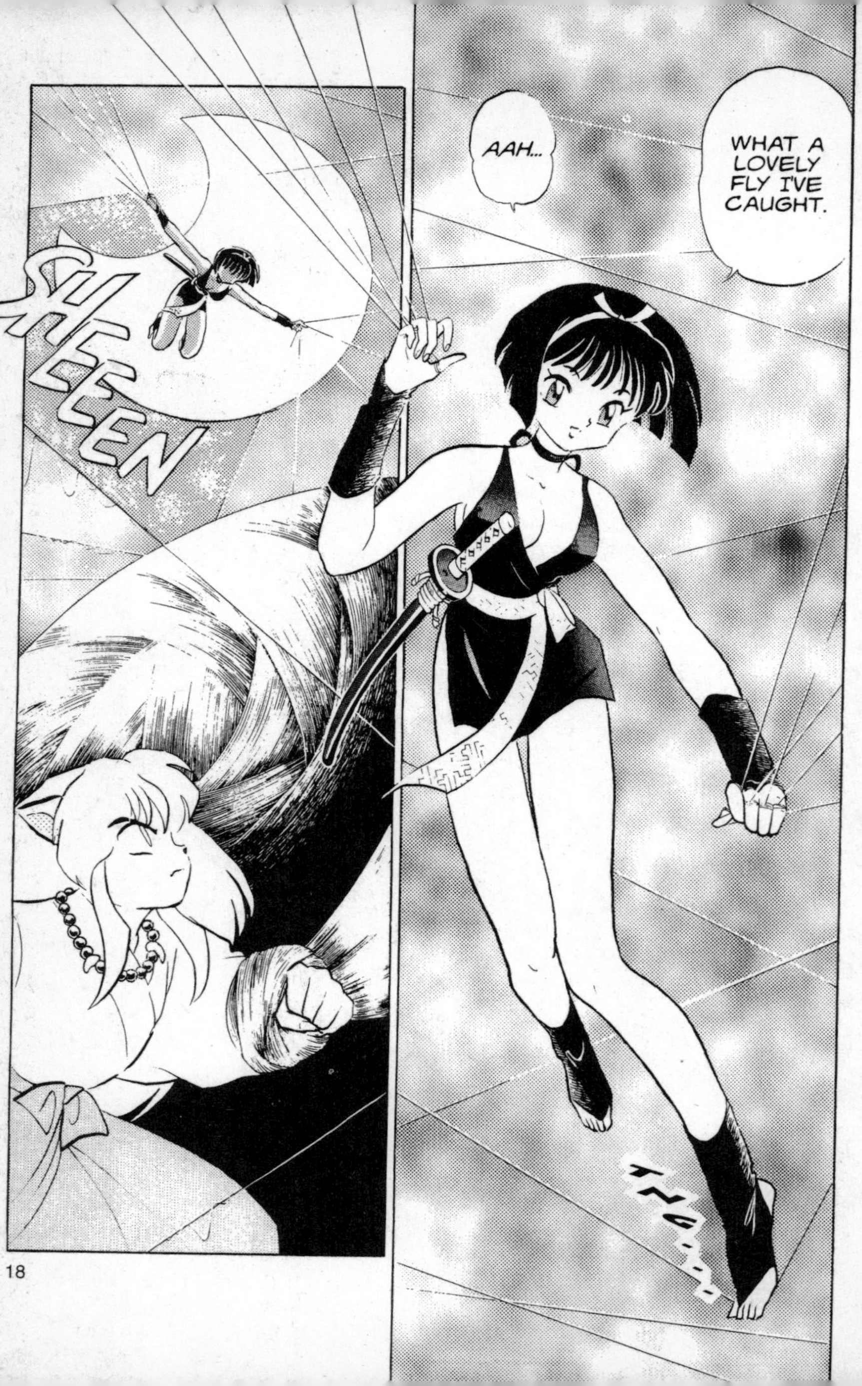
SHEEEN
AAH...
WHAT A LOVELY FLY I'VE CAUGHT.
TNG...

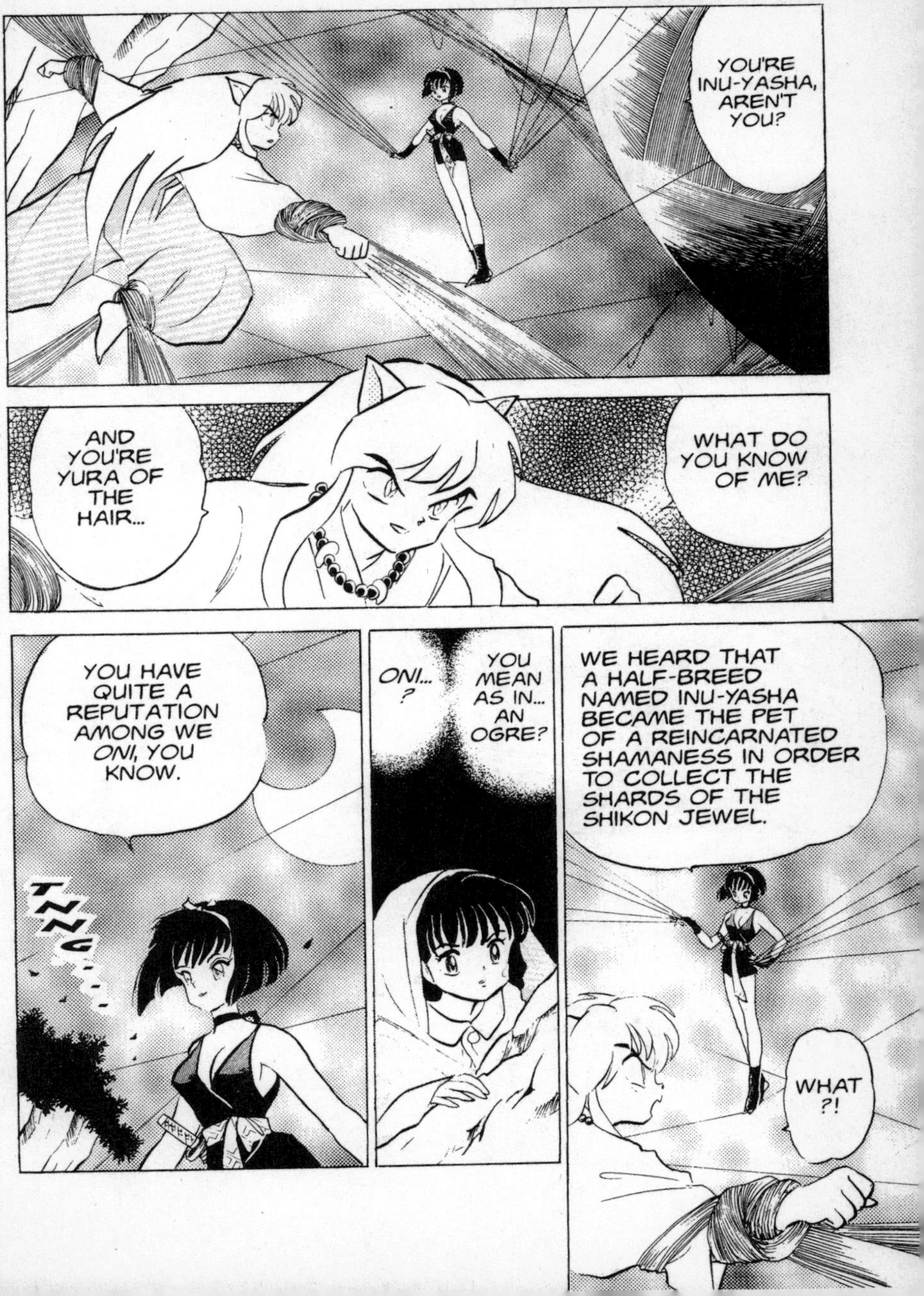
YOU'RE INU-YASHA, AREN'T YOU?
AND YOU'RE YURA OF THE HAIR...
WHAT DO YOU KNOW OF ME?
YOU HAVE QUITE A REPUTATION AMONG WE *ONI*, YOU KNOW.
TNNG...
ONI...?
YOU MEAN AS IN... AN OGRE?
WE HEARD THAT A HALF-BREED NAMED INU-YASHA BECAME THE PET OF A REINCARNATED SHAMANESS IN ORDER TO COLLECT THE SHARDS OF THE SHIKON JEWEL.
WHAT?!

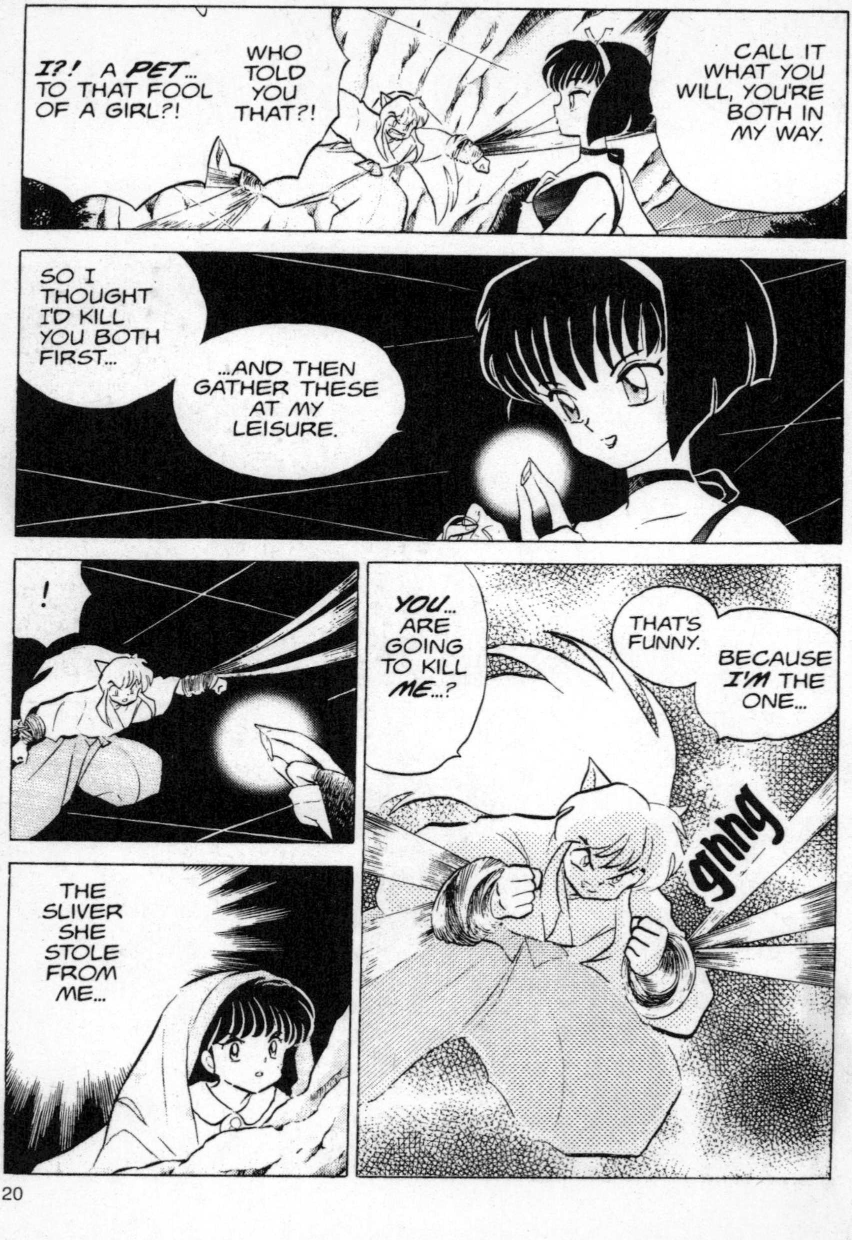
I?! A PET... TO THAT FOOL OF A GIRL?!
WHO TOLD YOU THAT?!
CALL IT WHAT YOU WILL, YOU'RE BOTH IN MY WAY.
SO I THOUGHT I'D KILL YOU BOTH FIRST...
...AND THEN GATHER THESE AT MY LEISURE.
!
THE SLIVER SHE STOLE FROM ME...
YOU... ARE GOING TO KILL ME...?
THAT'S FUNNY.
BECAUSE I'M THE ONE...
gnng

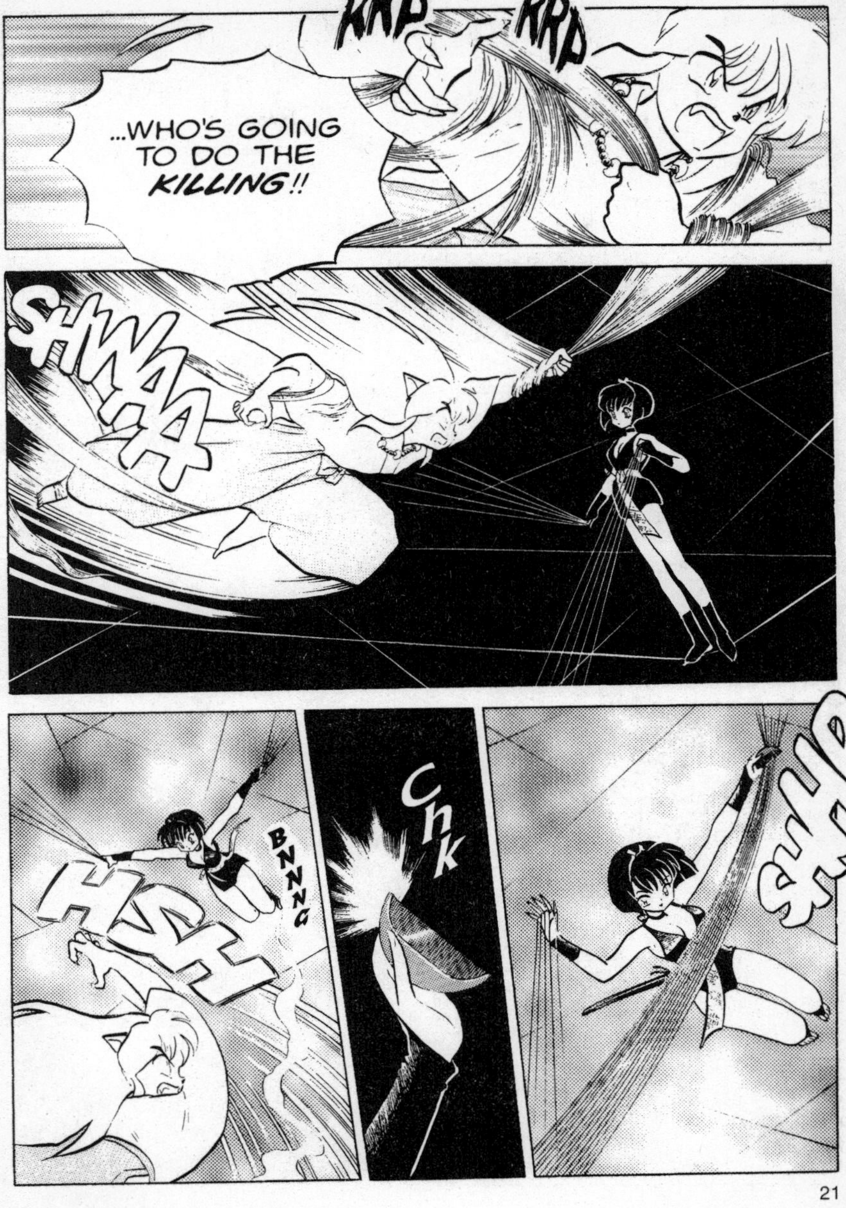
RRP
RRP
...WHO'S GOING TO DO THE *KILLING*!!
SHWAA
HSH
BNNNG
Chk
SHUP

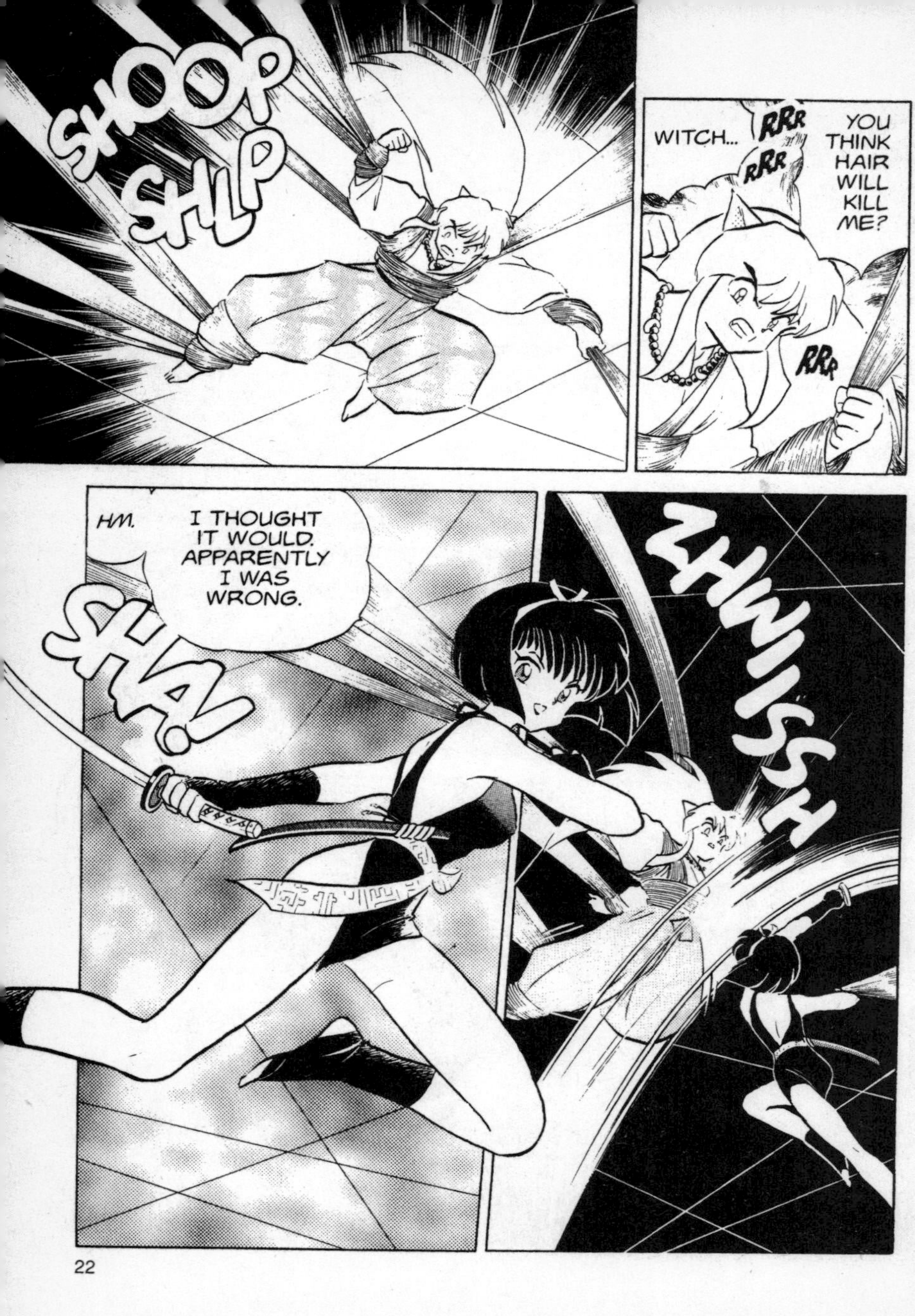
SHOOP
SHLIP
WITCH...
RRR
RRR
YOU THINK HAIR WILL KILL ME?
RRR
HM.
I THOUGHT IT WOULD. APPARENTLY I WAS WRONG.
SHA!
ZHWISSH

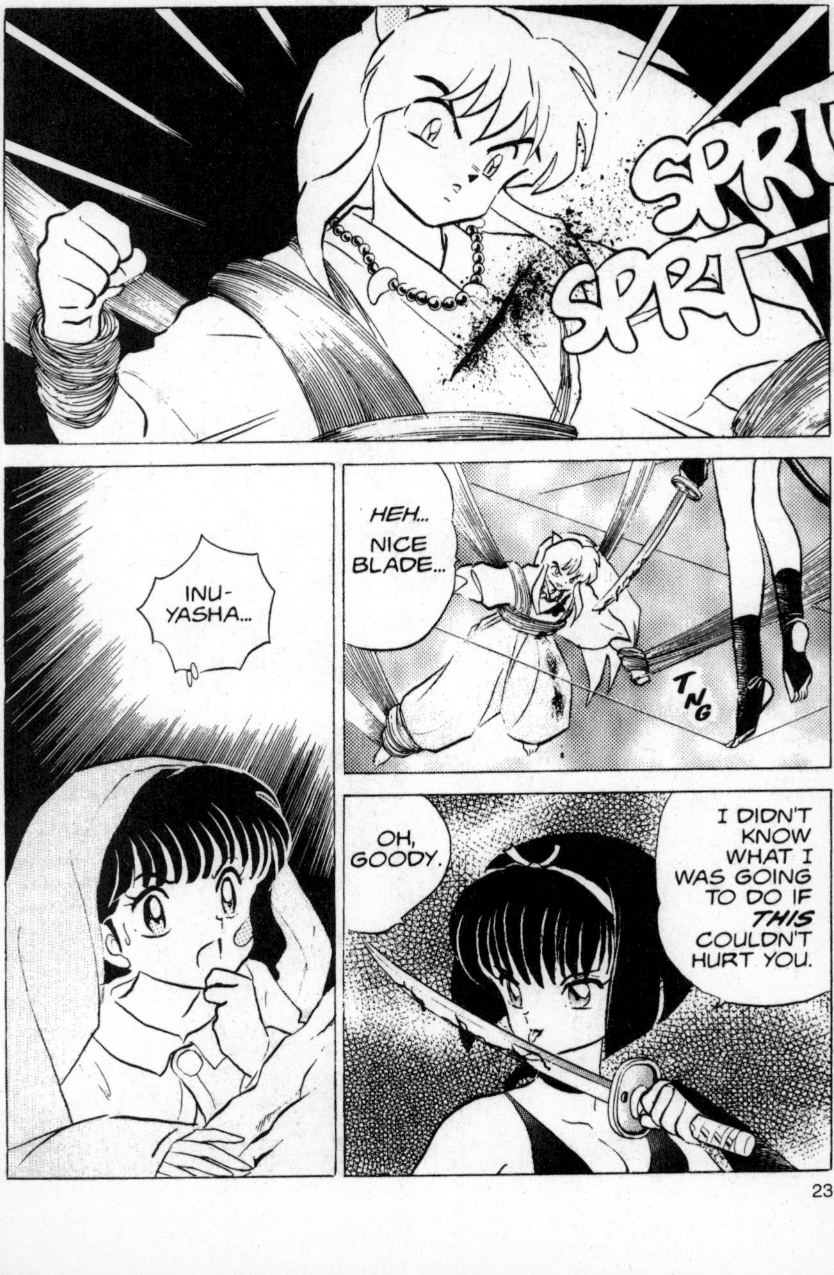
SPRT
SPRT
INU-YASHA...
HEH... NICE BLADE...
TNG
OH, GOODY.
I DIDN'T KNOW WHAT I WAS GOING TO DO IF *THIS* COULDN'T HURT YOU.

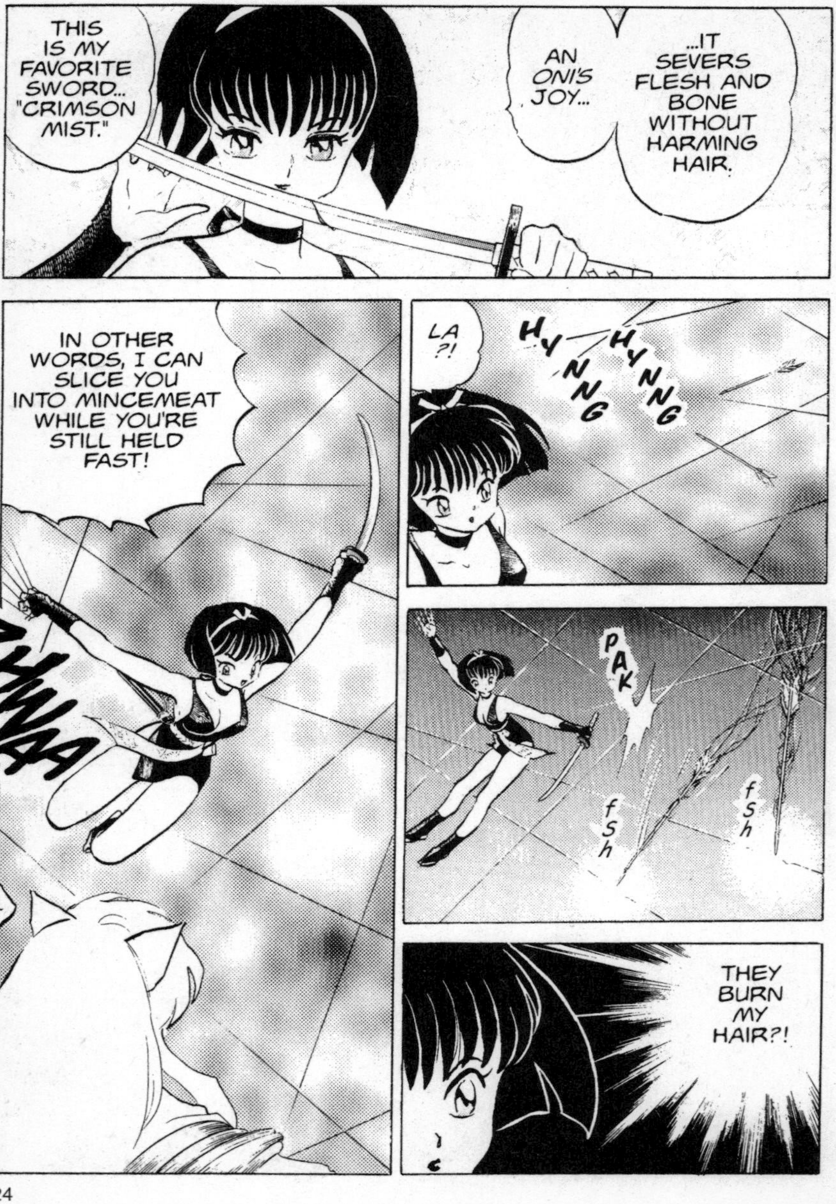
THIS IS MY FAVORITE SWORD... "CRIMSON MIST."
AN ONI'S JOY...
...IT SEVERS FLESH AND BONE WITHOUT HARMING HAIR.
IN OTHER WORDS, I CAN SLICE YOU INTO MINCEMEAT WHILE YOU'RE STILL HELD FAST!
ZHWAA
LA?!
HYNNG HYNNG
PAK
fsh
fsh
THEY BURN MY HAIR?!

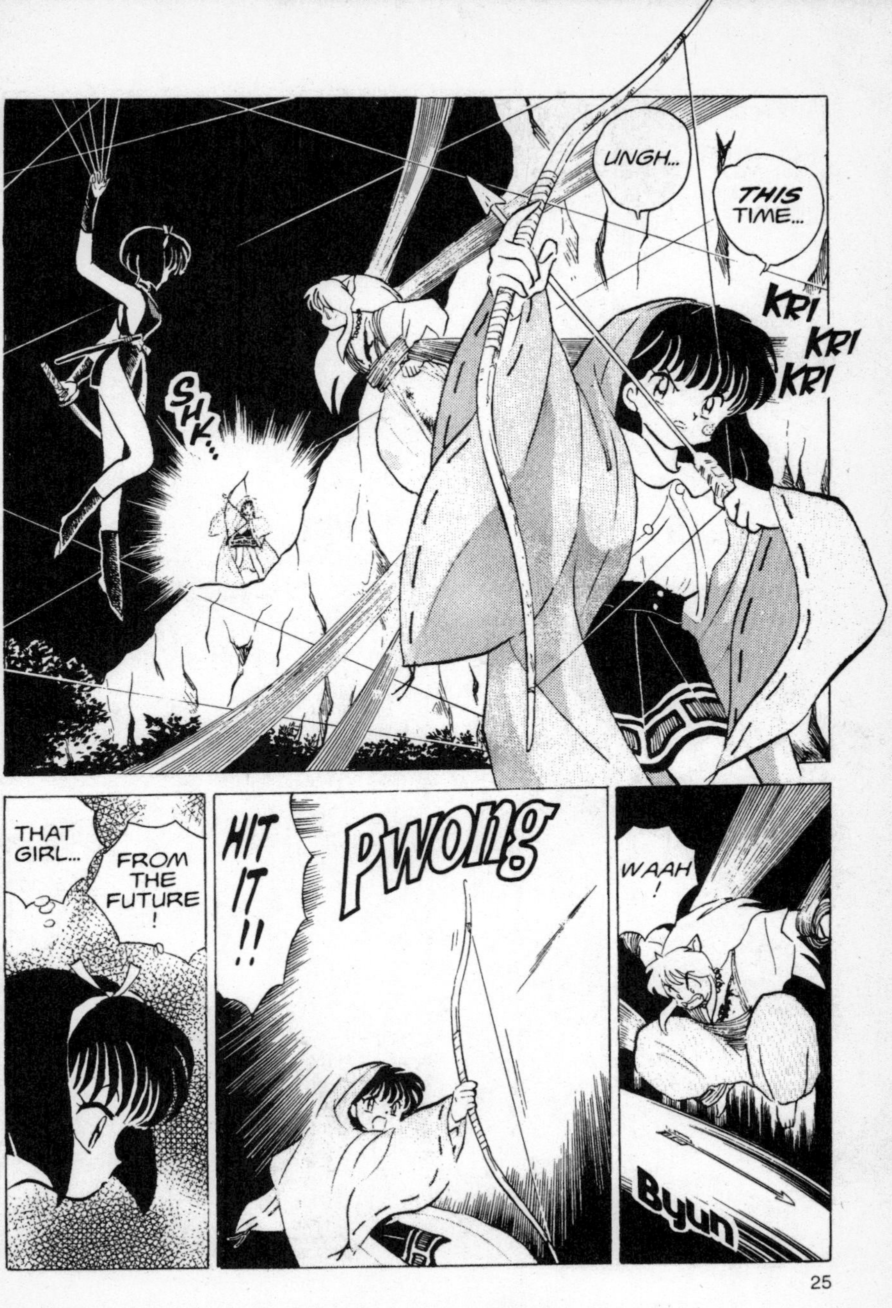
UNGH...
THIS TIME...
KRI KRI KRI
SHK...
THAT GIRL...
FROM THE FUTURE!
HIT IT!!
Pwong
WAAH!
Byun

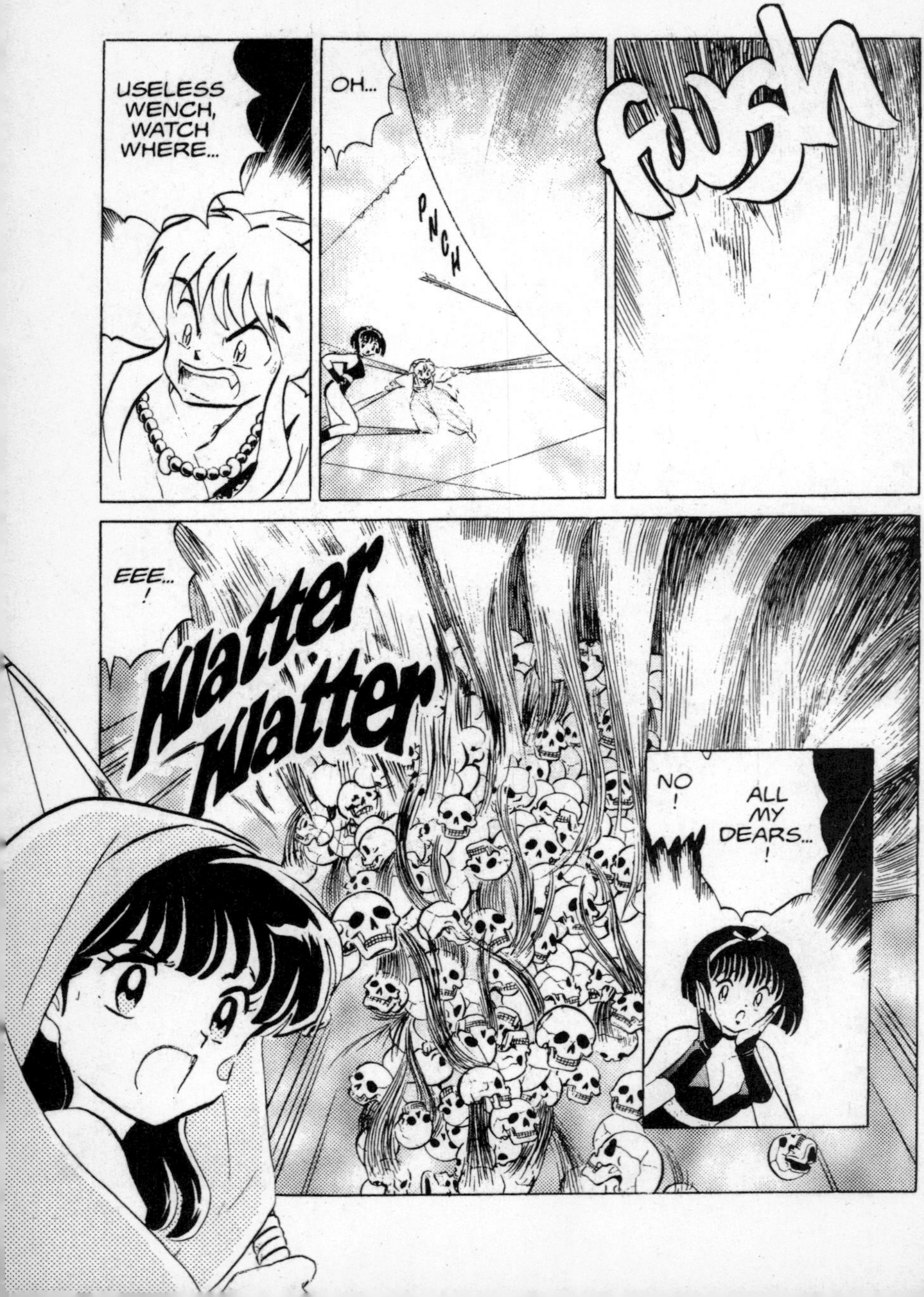
USELESS WENCH, WATCH WHERE...
OH...
PNCH
EEE...!
Klatter Klatter
NO!
ALL MY DEARS...!

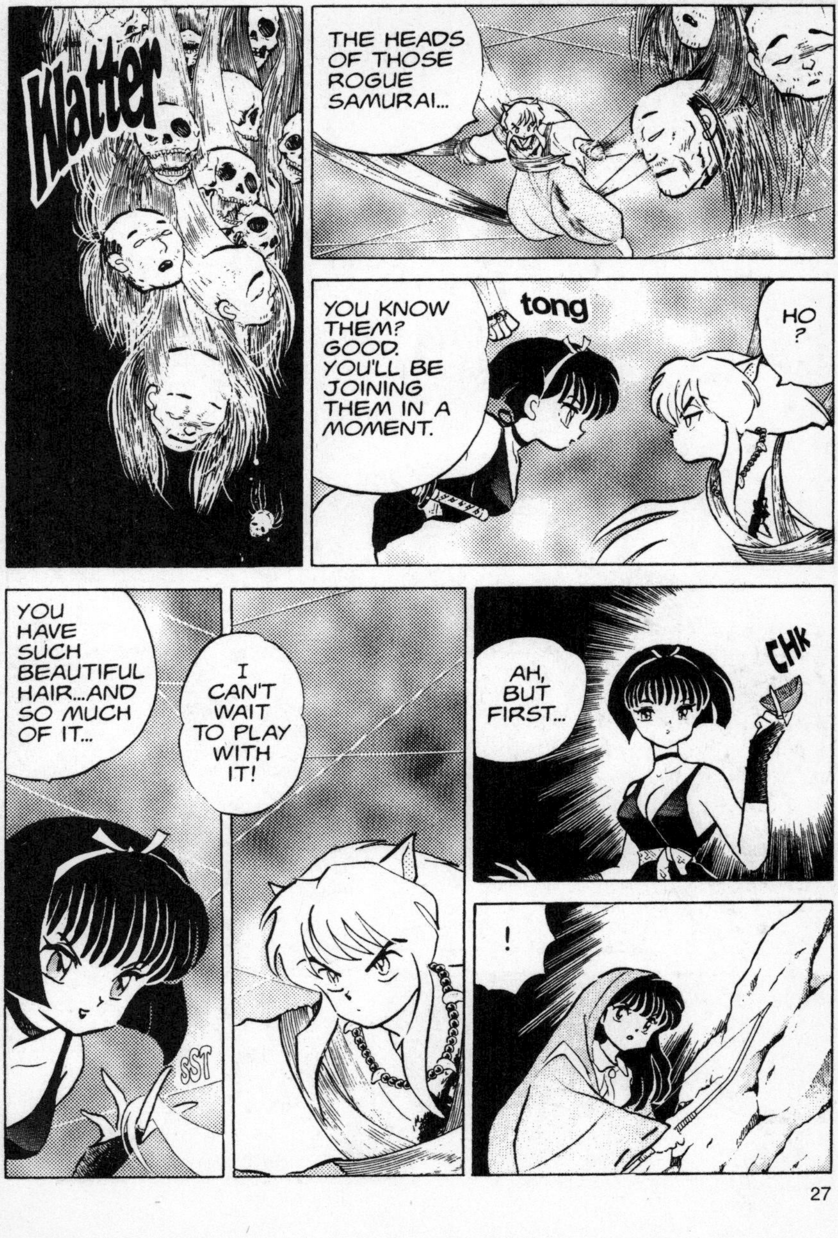
Klatter
THE HEADS OF THOSE ROGUE SAMURAI...
YOU KNOW THEM? GOOD. YOU'LL BE JOINING THEM IN A MOMENT.
tong
HO?
YOU HAVE SUCH BEAUTIFUL HAIR...AND SO MUCH OF IT...
I CAN'T WAIT TO PLAY WITH IT!
SST
AH, BUT FIRST...
CHK
!

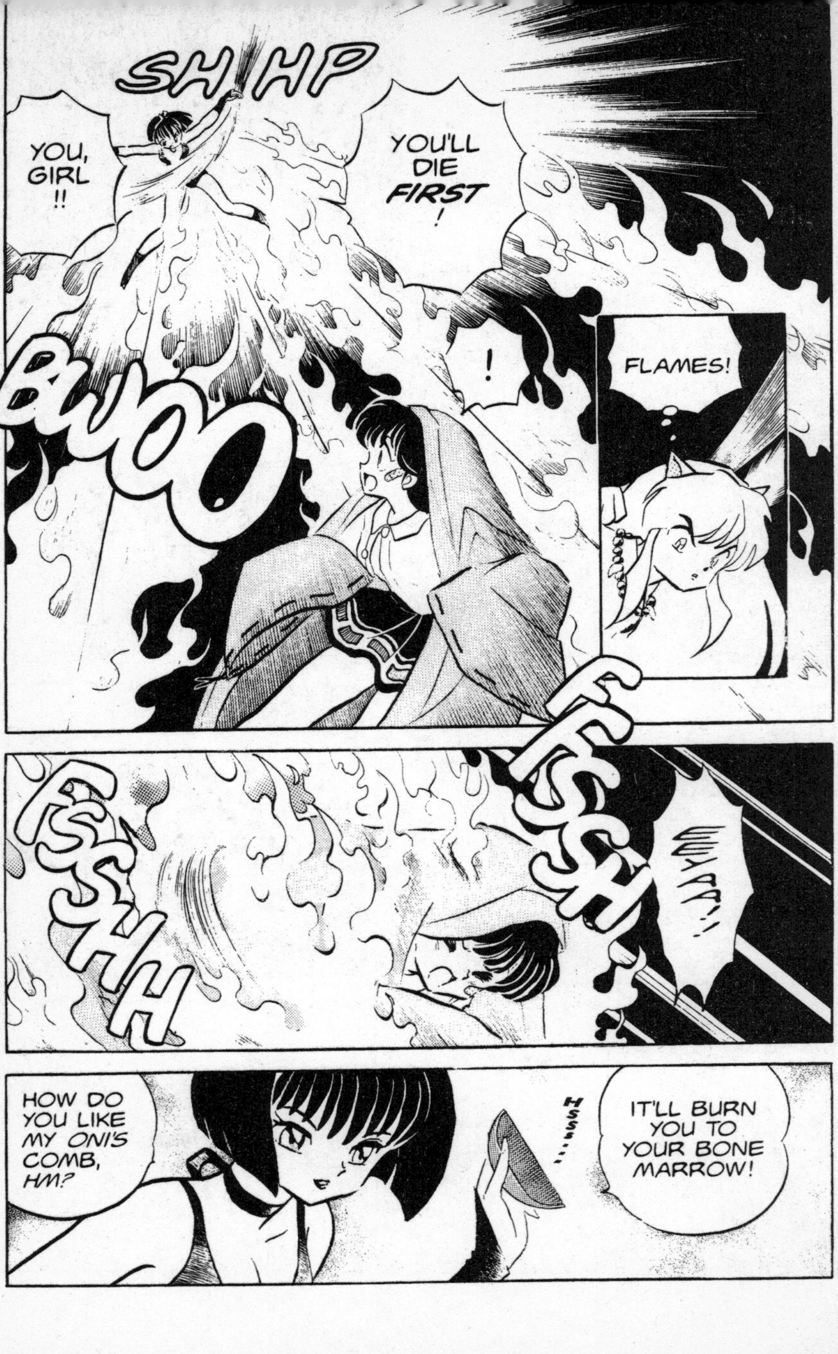
SHHP
YOU, GIRL!!
YOU'LL DIE *FIRST*!
BUOO
!
FLAMES!
FSSHH
FSSH
WEYAA!!
HOW DO YOU LIKE MY *ONI'S* COMB, HM?
HSSS...
IT'LL BURN YOU TO YOUR BONE MARROW!

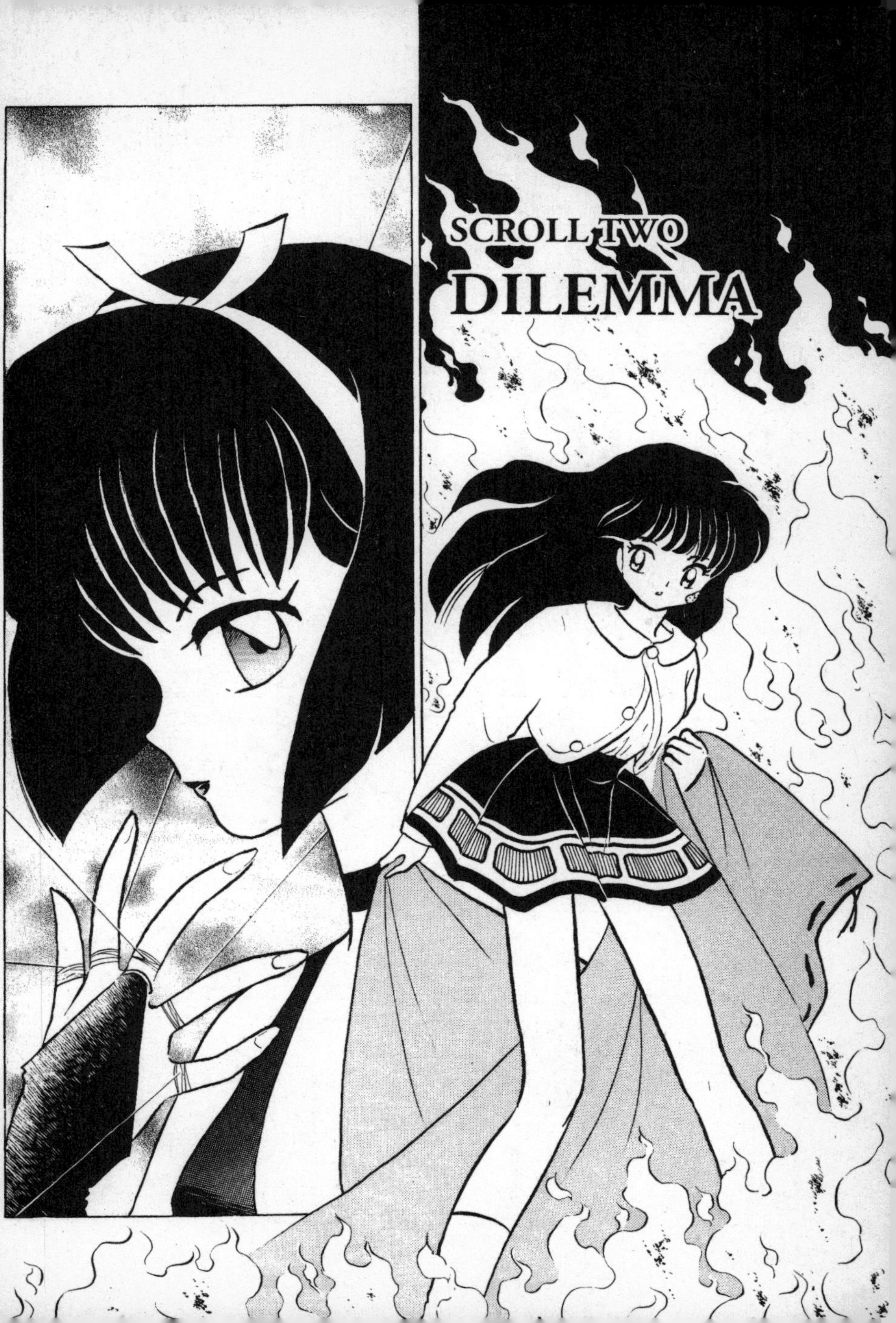
SCROLL TWO
DILEMMA

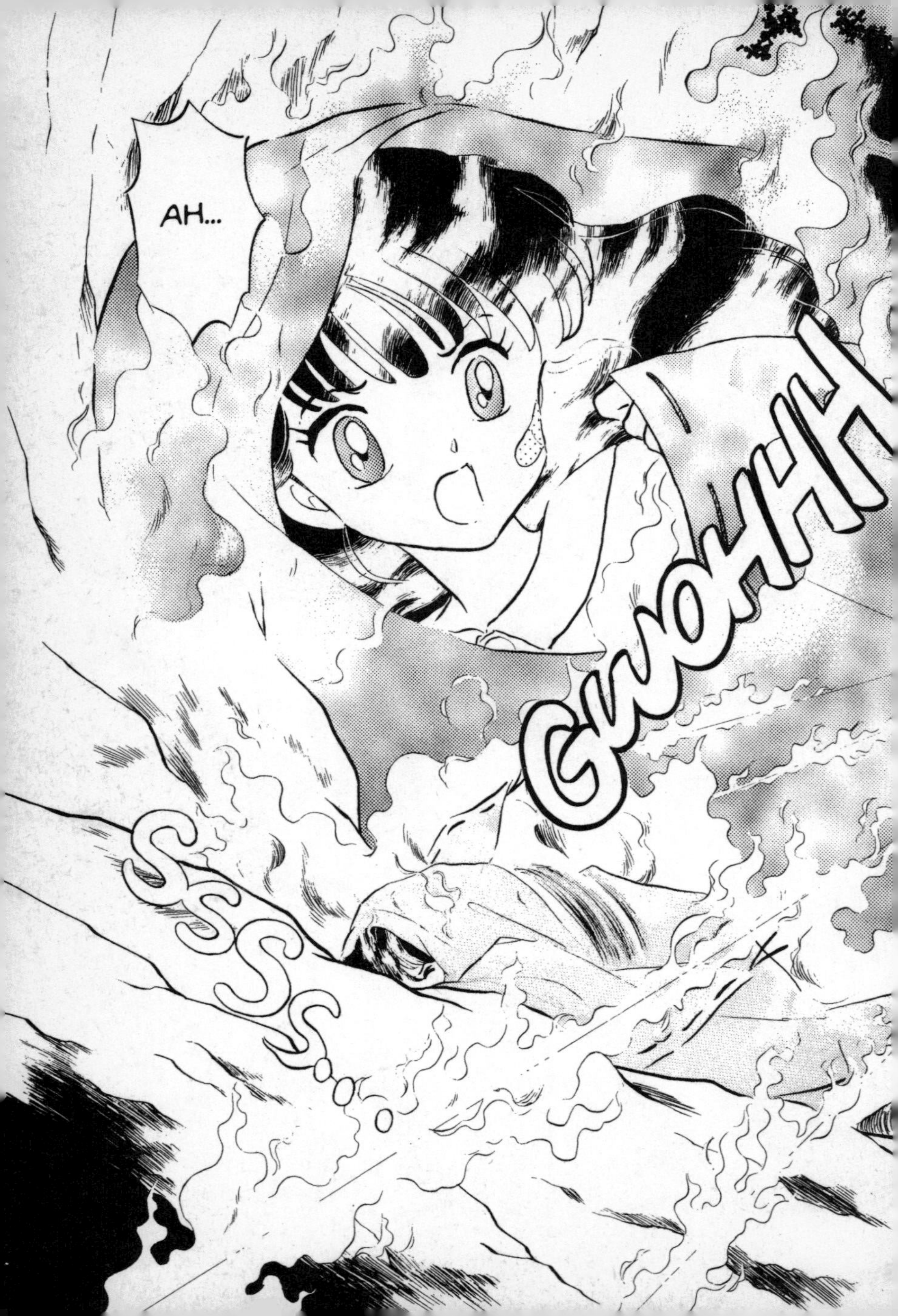
AH...
GWOHH
SSSS...

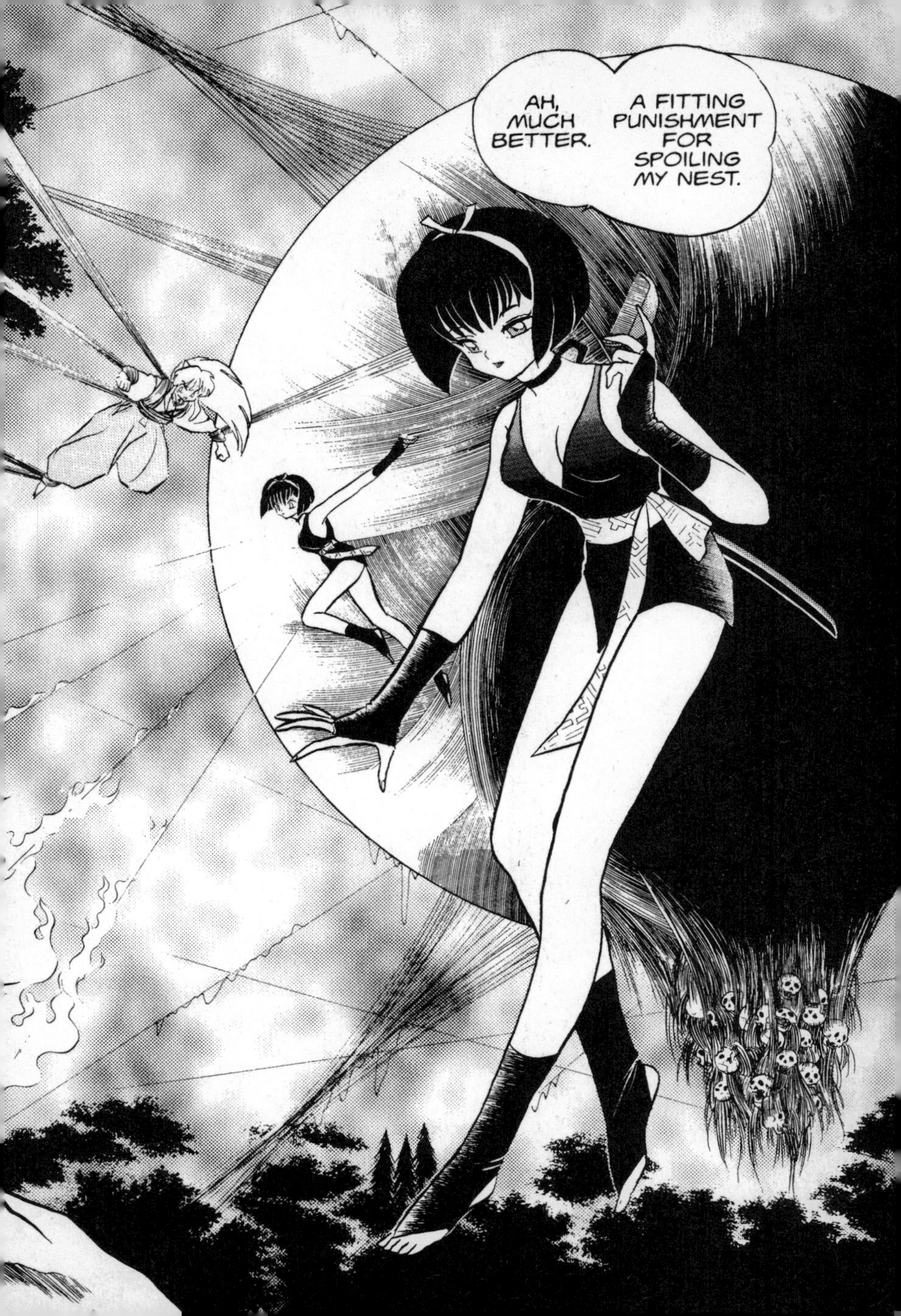
AH, MUCH BETTER.
A FITTING PUNISHMENT FOR SPOILING MY NEST.

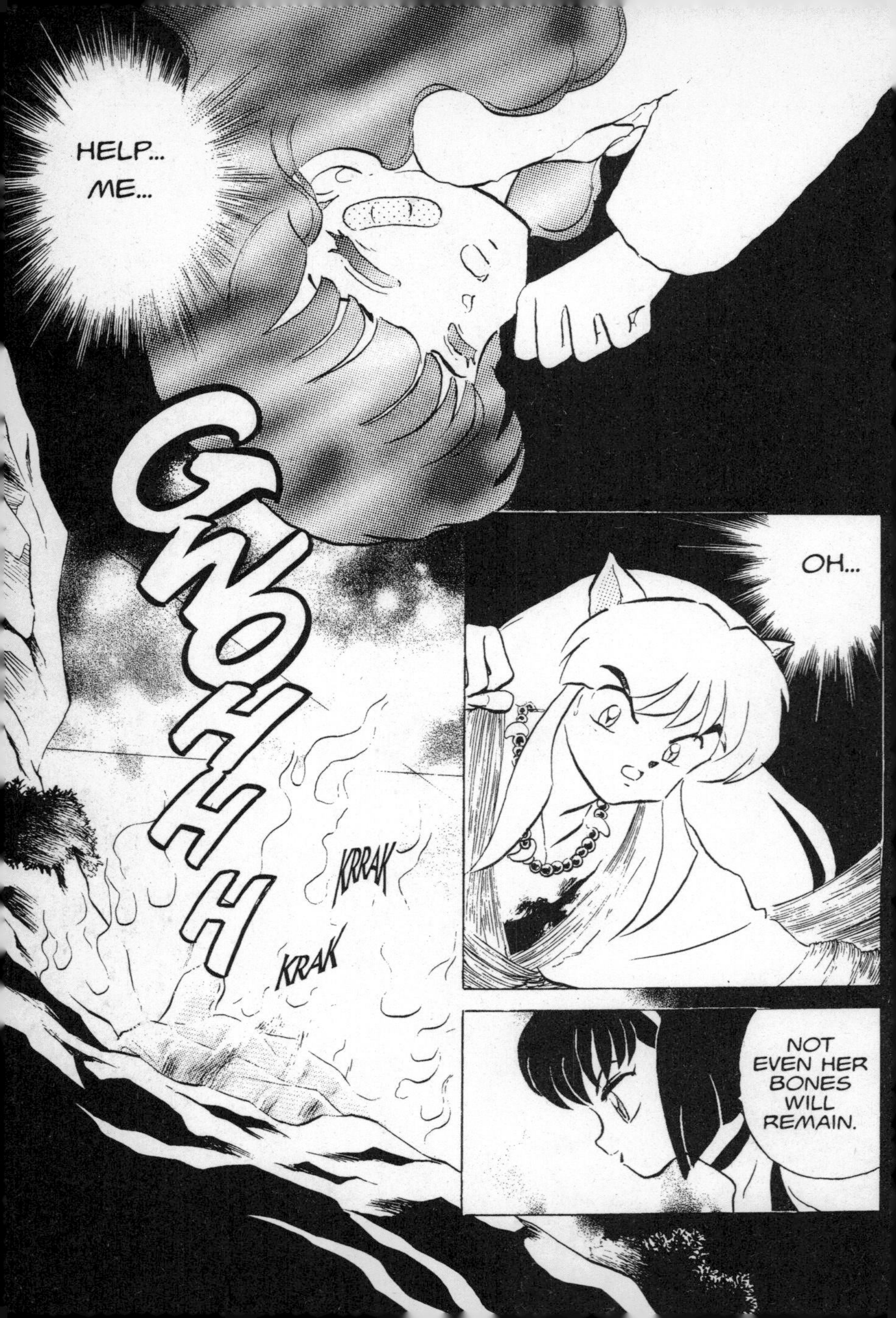
HELP... ME...
GWOHHHH
KRRAK
KRAK
OH...
NOT EVEN HER BONES WILL REMAIN.

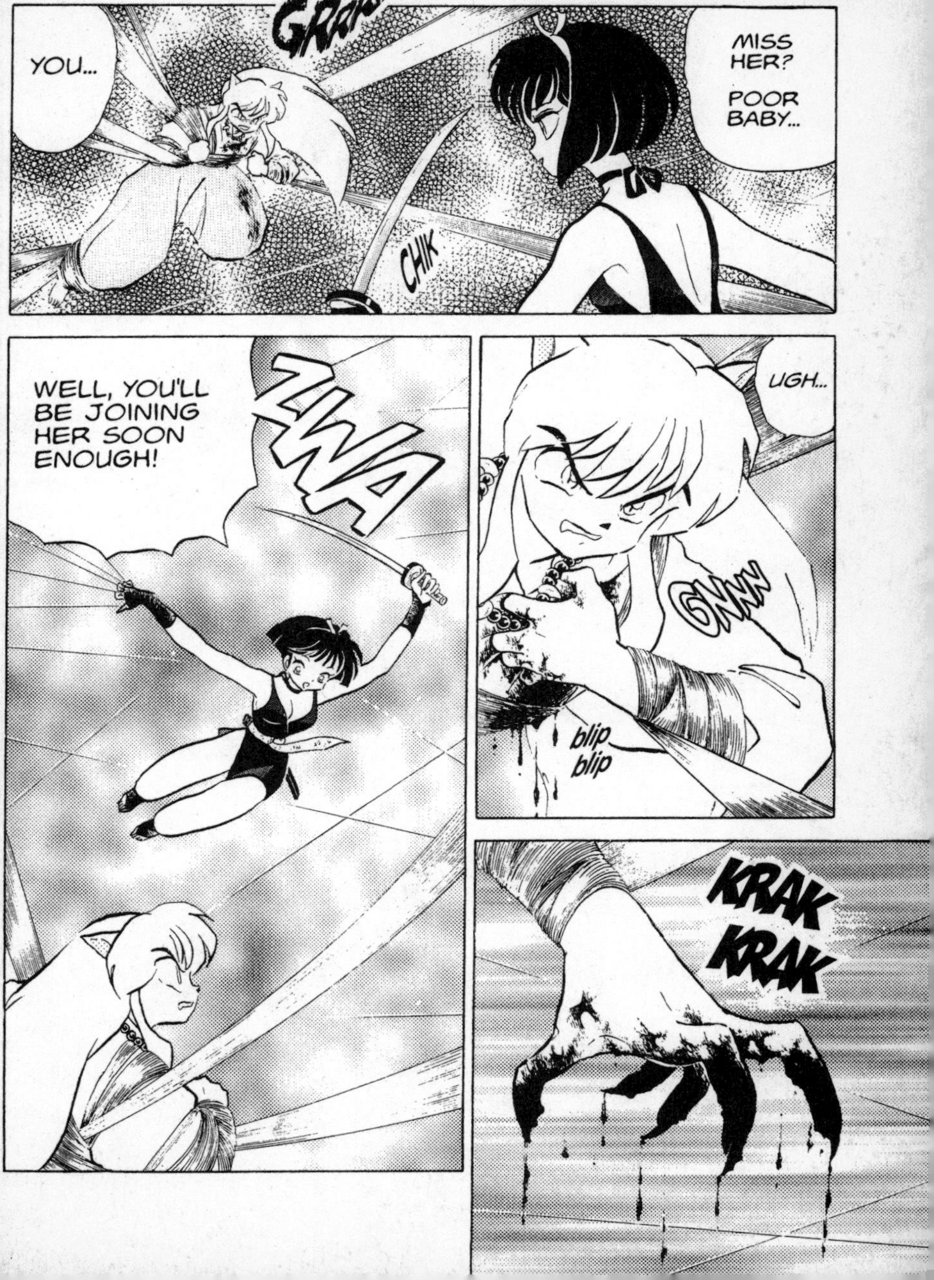
YOU...
GRRR...
CHIK
MISS HER?
POOR BABY...
WELL, YOU'LL BE JOINING HER SOON ENOUGH!
ZWA
UGH...
GNNN
blip blip
KRAK KRAK

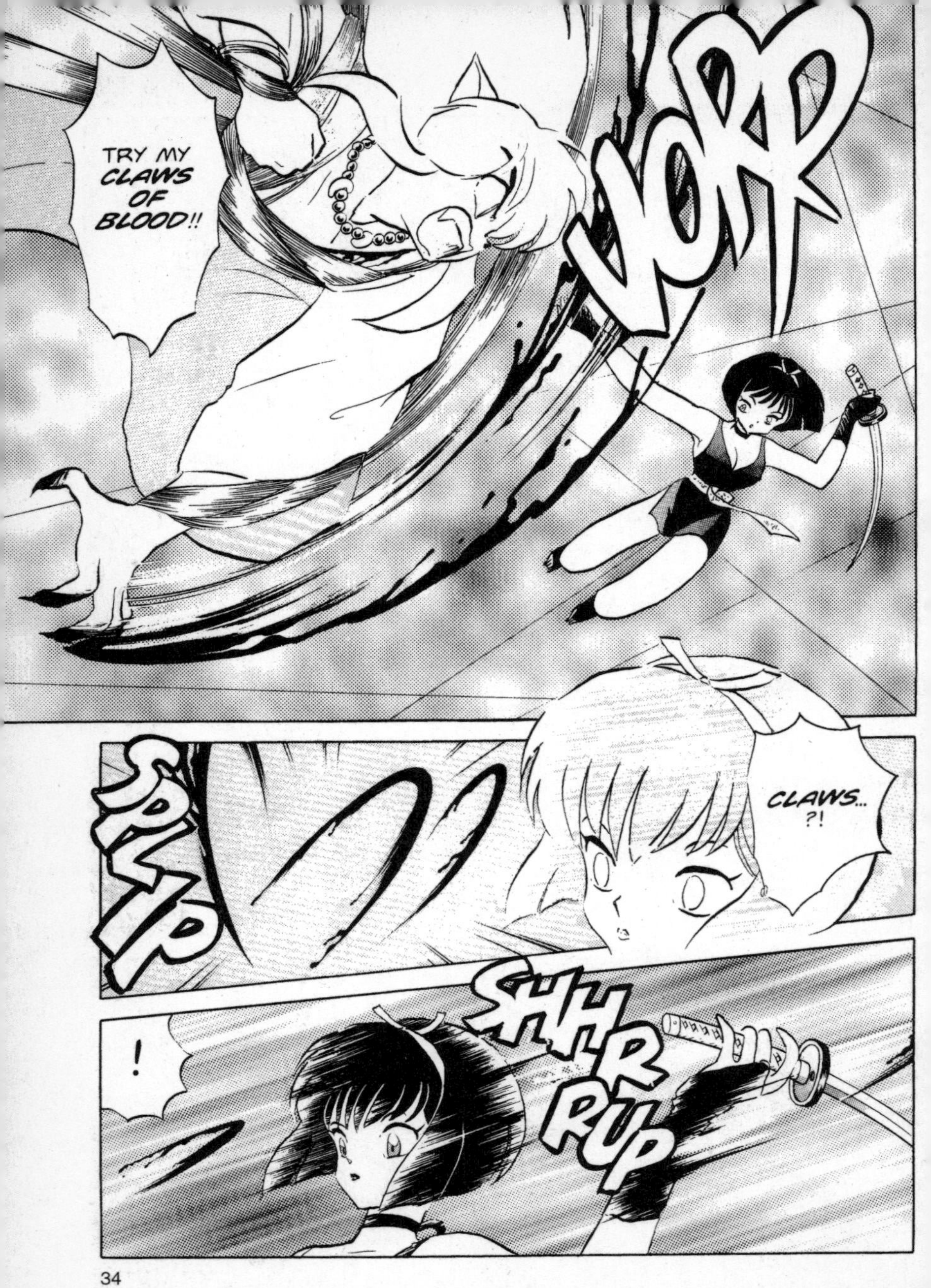
TRY MY *CLAWS OF BLOOD*!!
VOOP
SPLIP
CLAWS... ?!
!
SHHRRUP

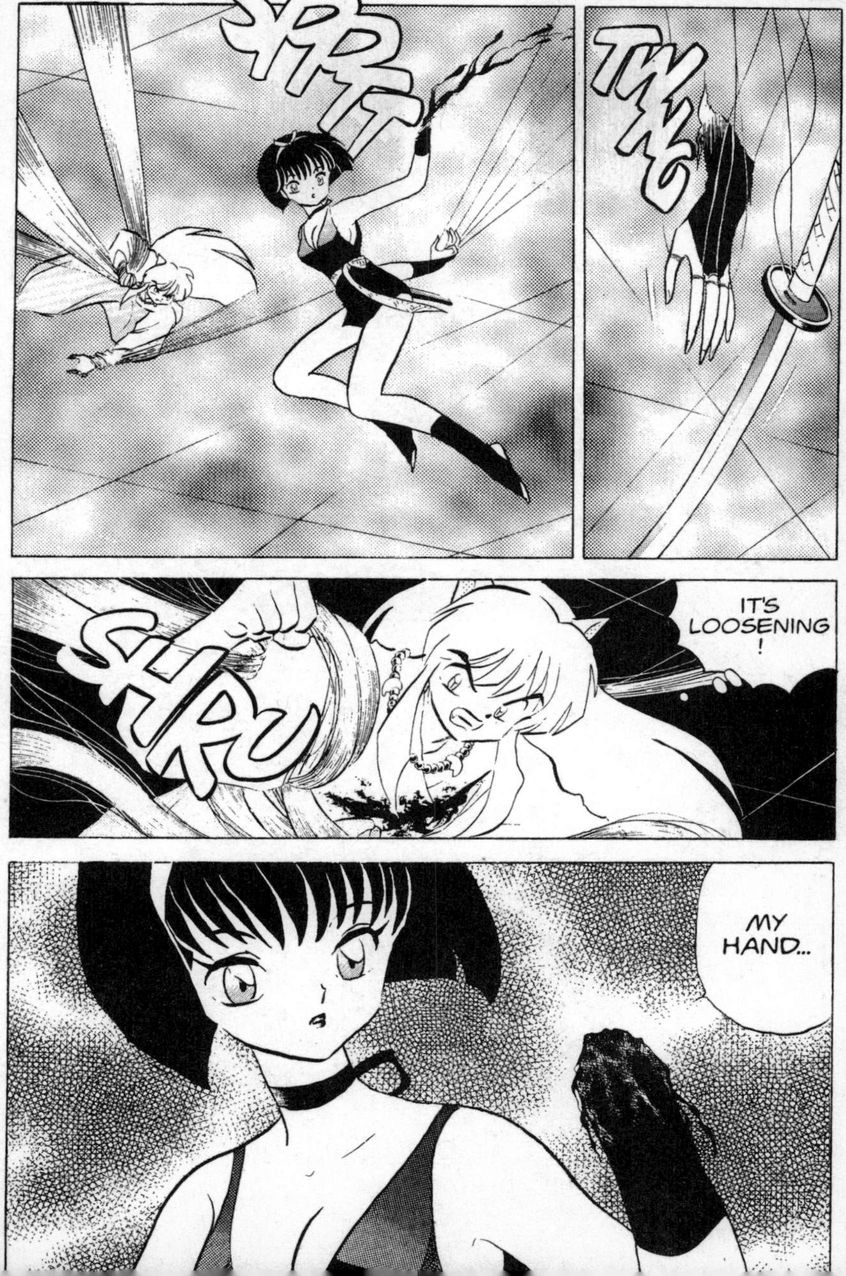
SPRT
TWING
SHRU
IT'S LOOSENING !
MY HAND...

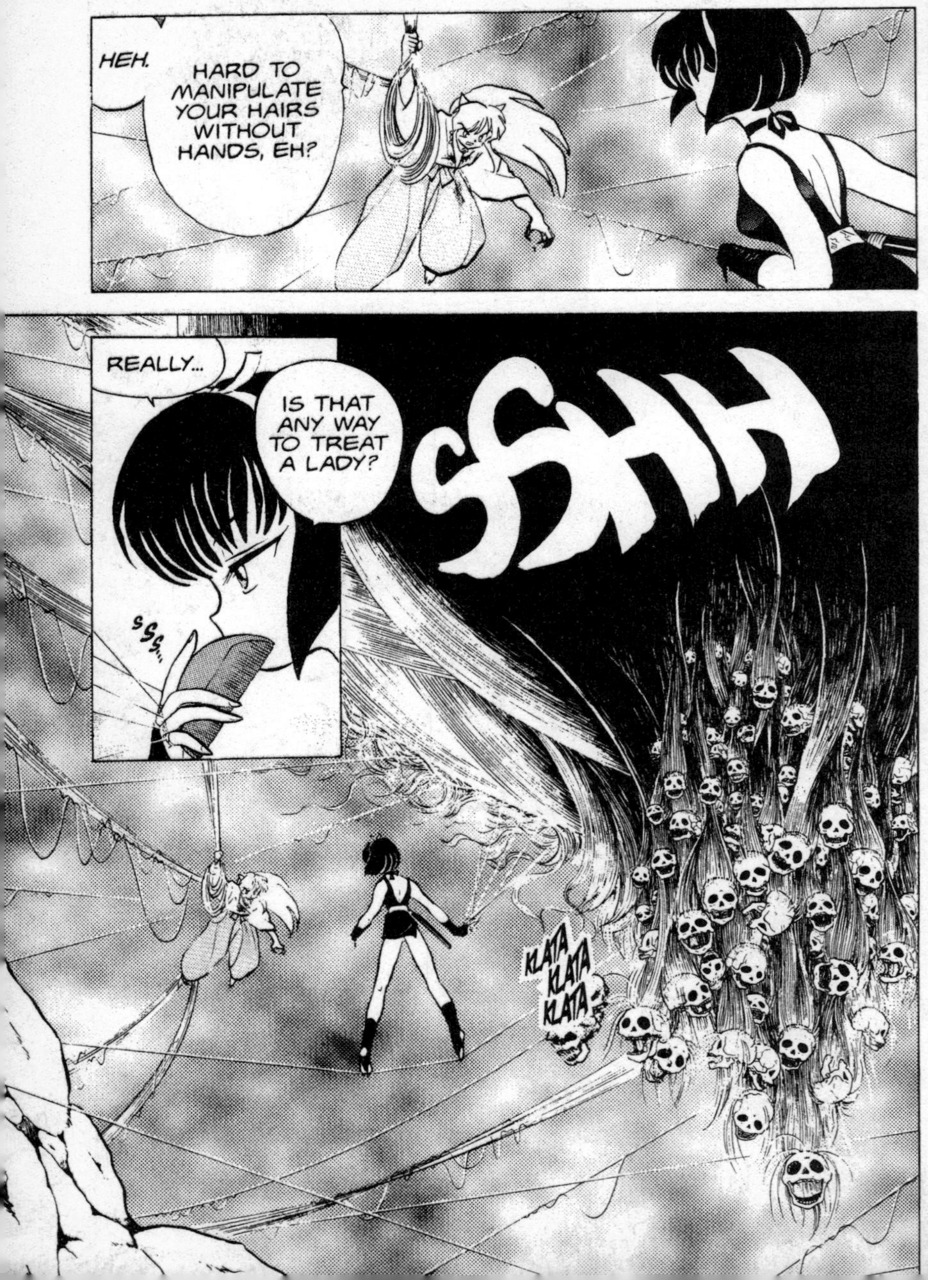
HEH.
HARD TO MANIPULATE YOUR HAIRS WITHOUT HANDS, EH?
REALLY...
IS THAT ANY WAY TO TREAT A LADY?
SSS...
SSHH
KLATA KLATA KLATA

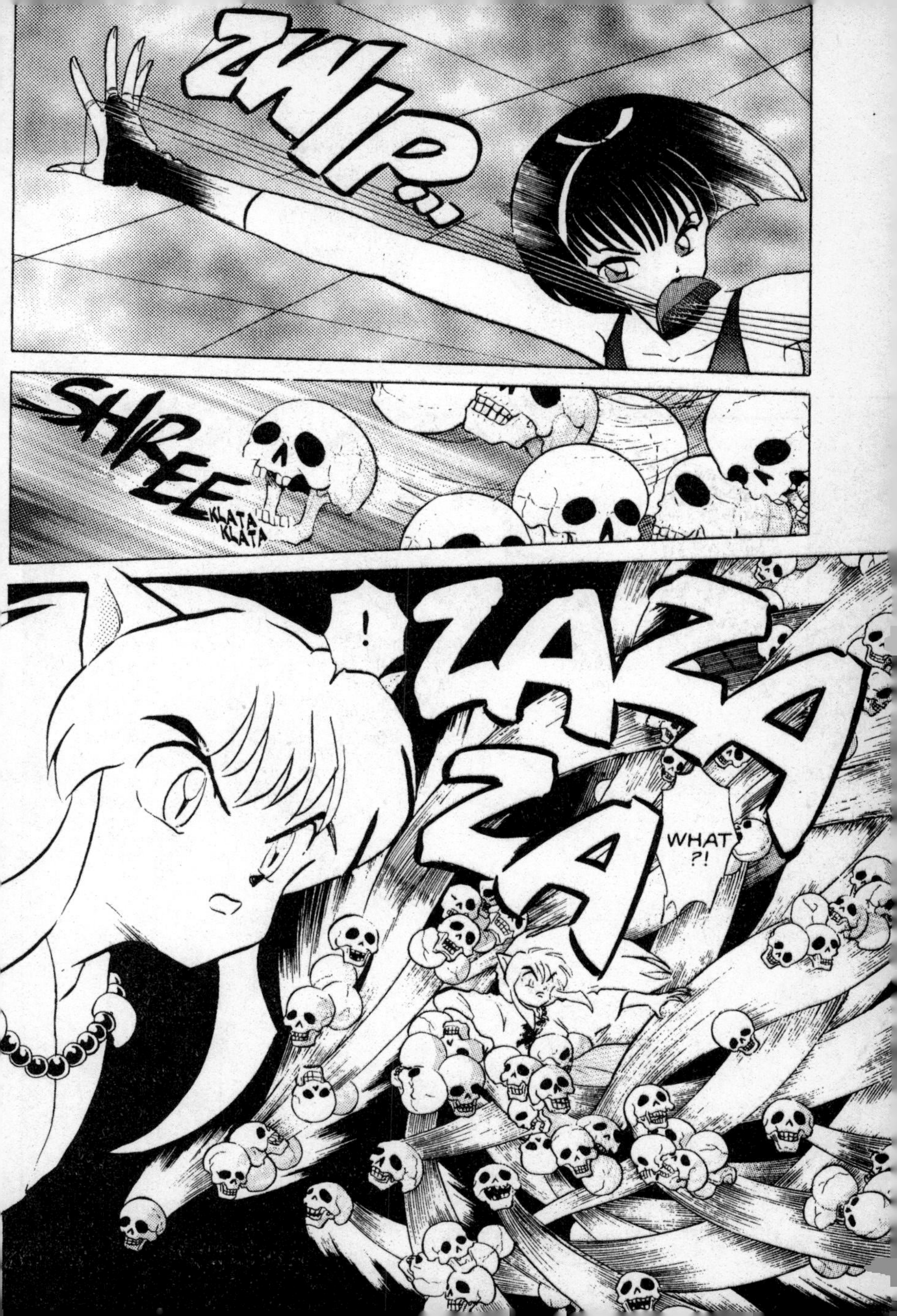
ZWIP...
SHREE
KLATA KLATA
!
ZAZAZA
WHAT?!

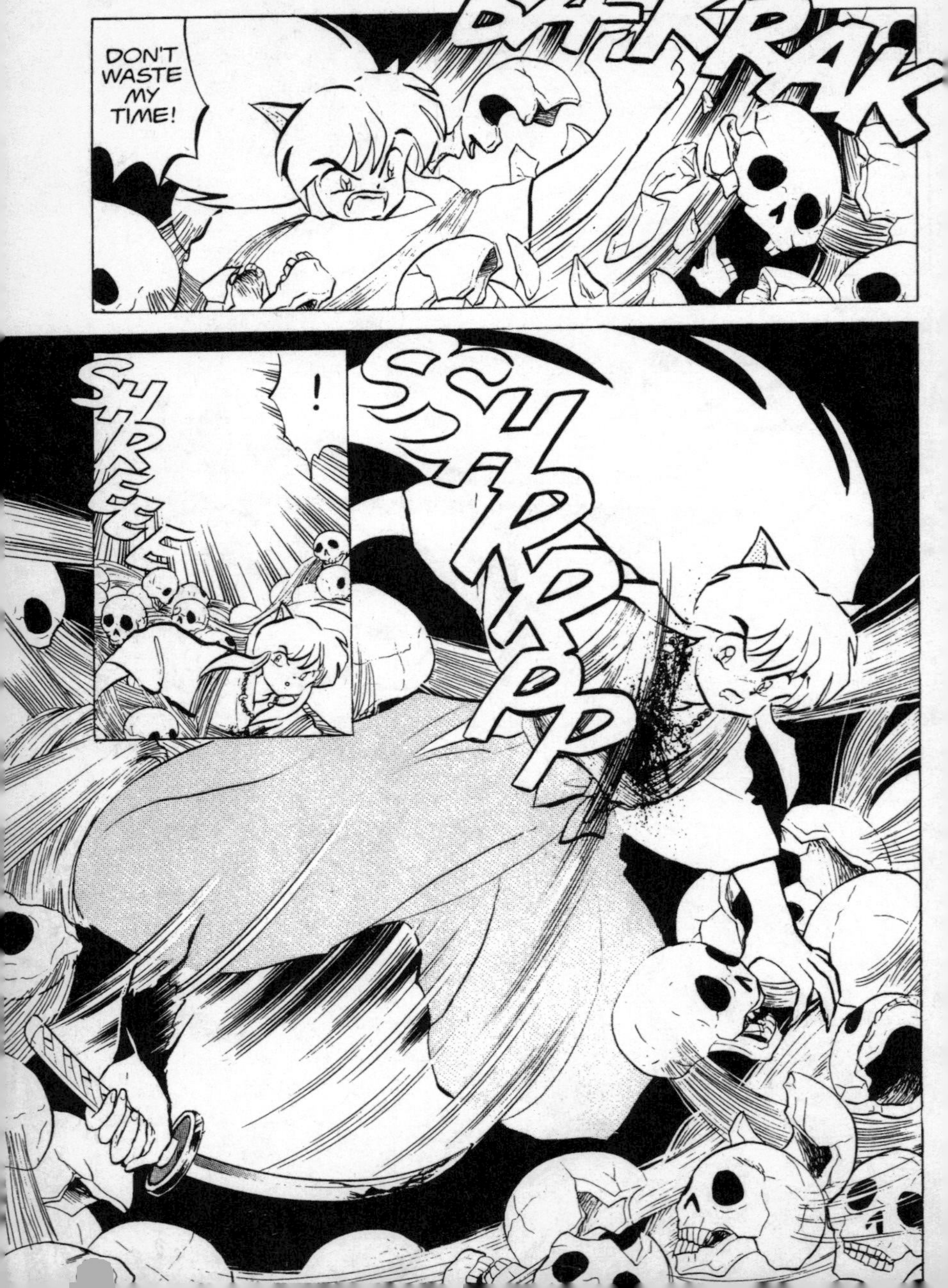

DON'T WASTE MY TIME!
BAKRAK
SHREEE
!
SSHRRPP

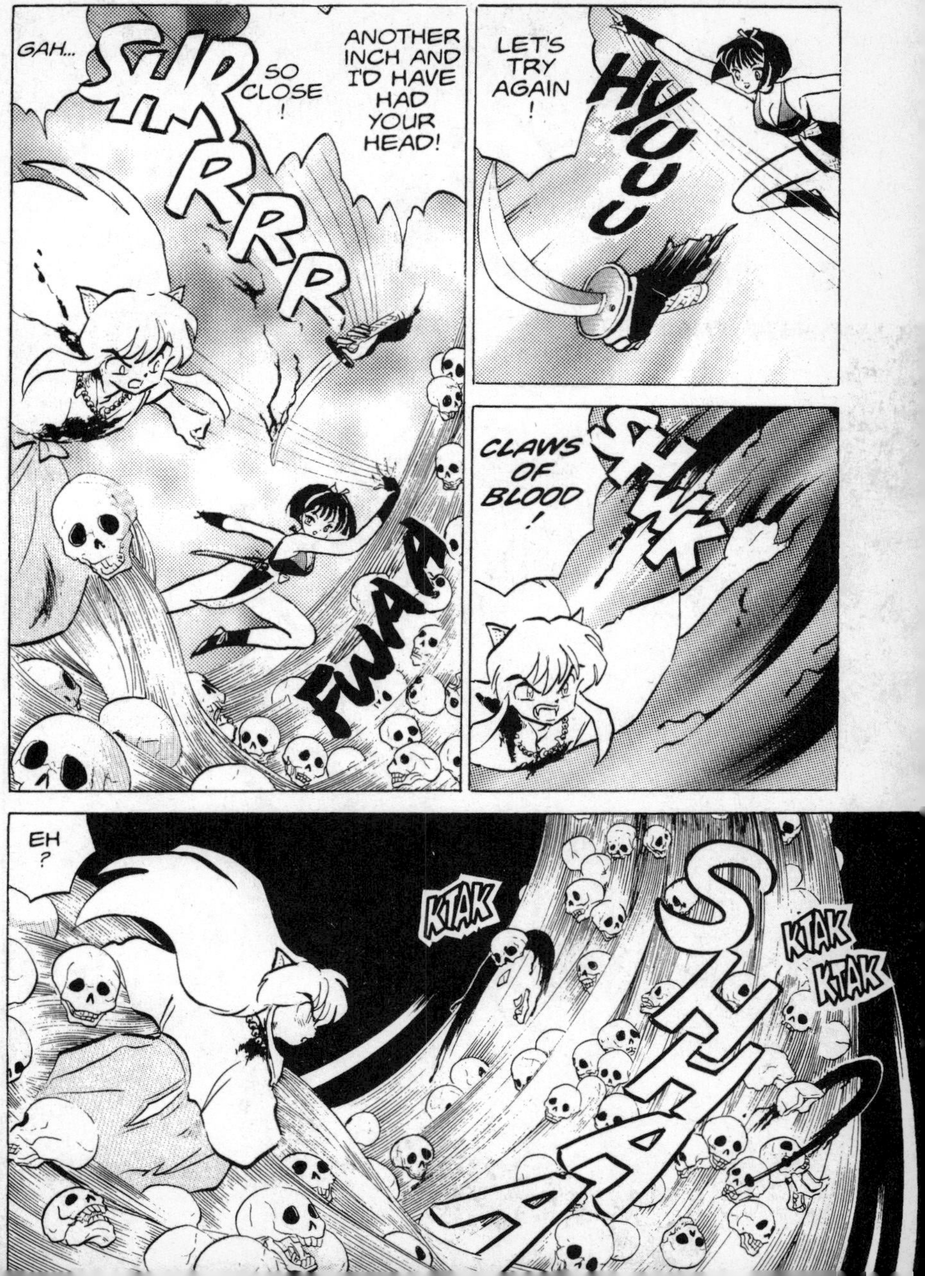
GAH...
SHRRRRR
SO CLOSE!
ANOTHER INCH AND I'D HAVE HAD YOUR HEAD!
FWAP
LET'S TRY AGAIN!
HYUUU
CLAWS OF BLOOD!
SHWK
EH?
KTAK
STHAAA
KTAK KTAK

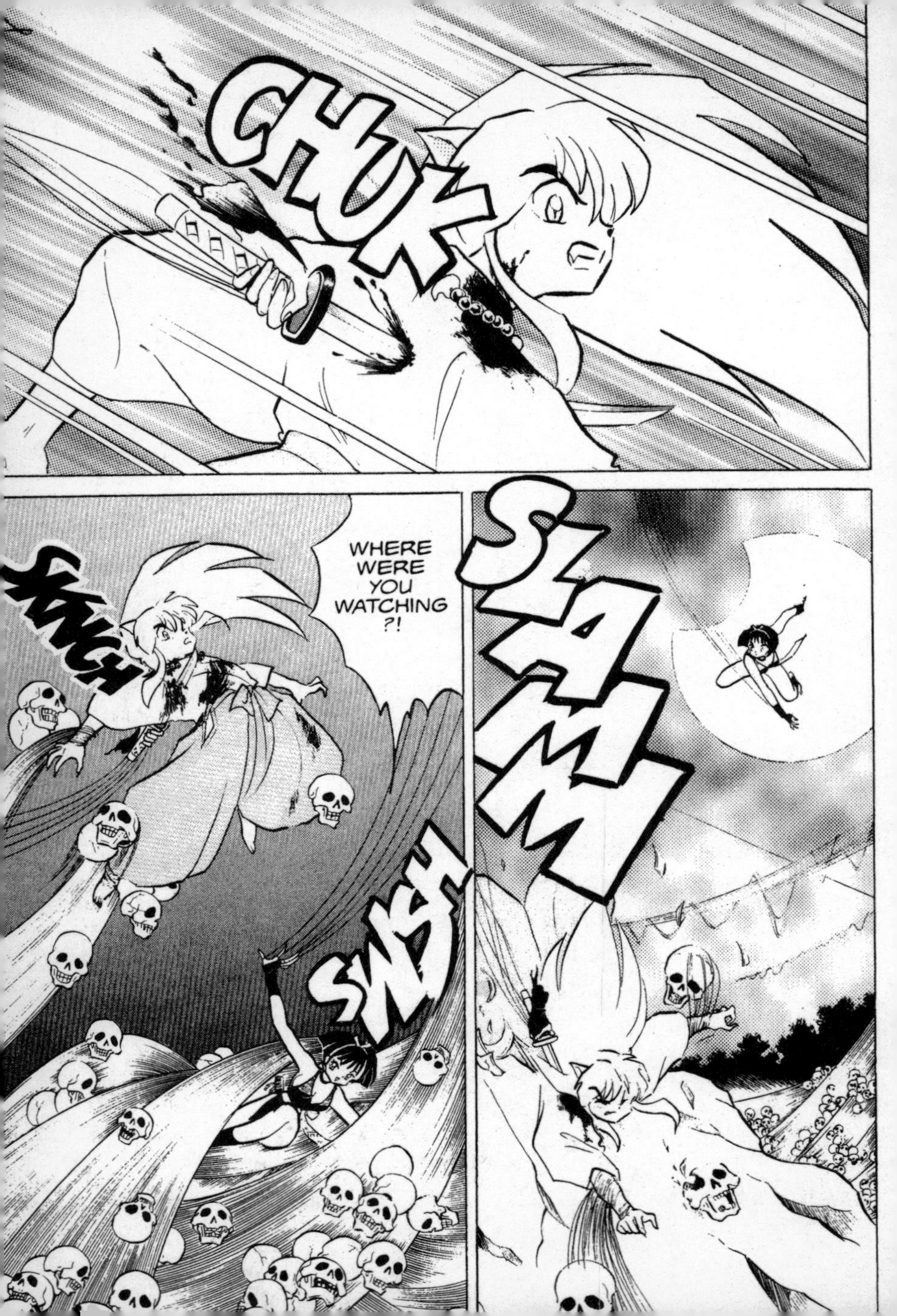
CHUK
SKNCH
WHERE WERE YOU WATCHING?!
SWSH
SLAMM

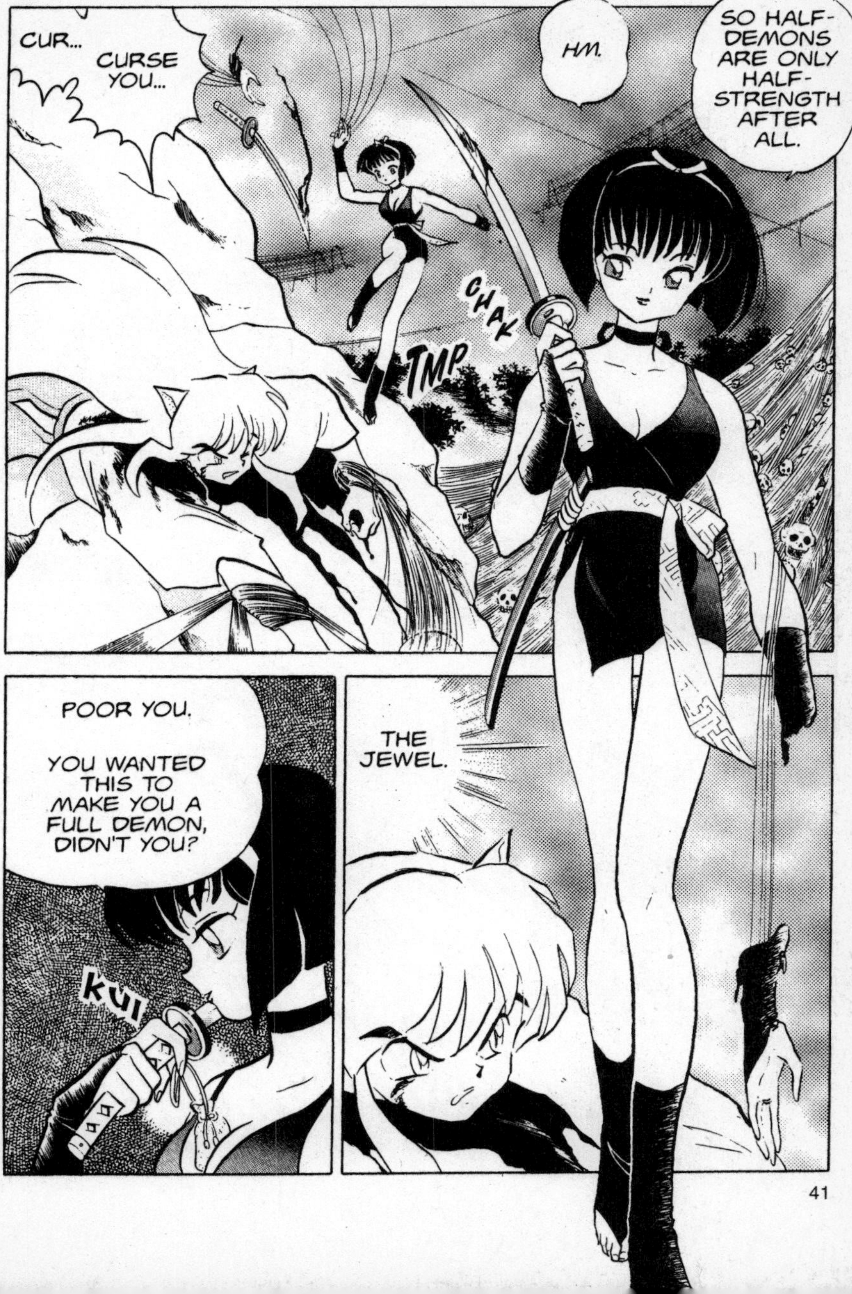
CUR... CURSE YOU...
HM.
SO HALF-DEMONS ARE ONLY HALF-STRENGTH AFTER ALL.
CHAK
TMP
POOR YOU.
YOU WANTED THIS TO MAKE YOU A FULL DEMON, DIDN'T YOU?
KUI
THE JEWEL.

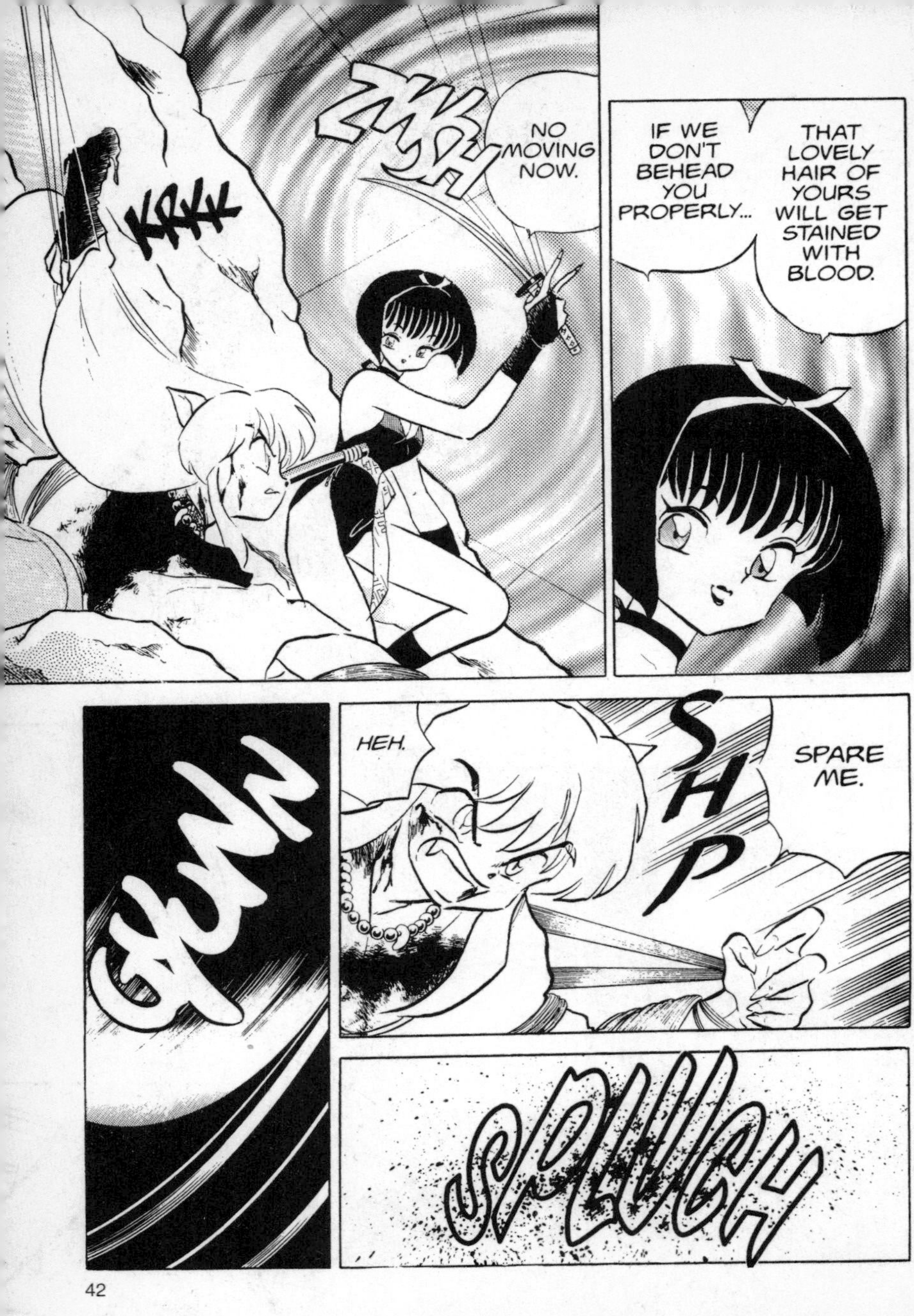
ZASH
KRKK
NO MOVING NOW.
IF WE DON'T BEHEAD YOU PROPERLY...
THAT LOVELY HAIR OF YOURS WILL GET STAINED WITH BLOOD.
HEH.
SHP
SPARE ME.

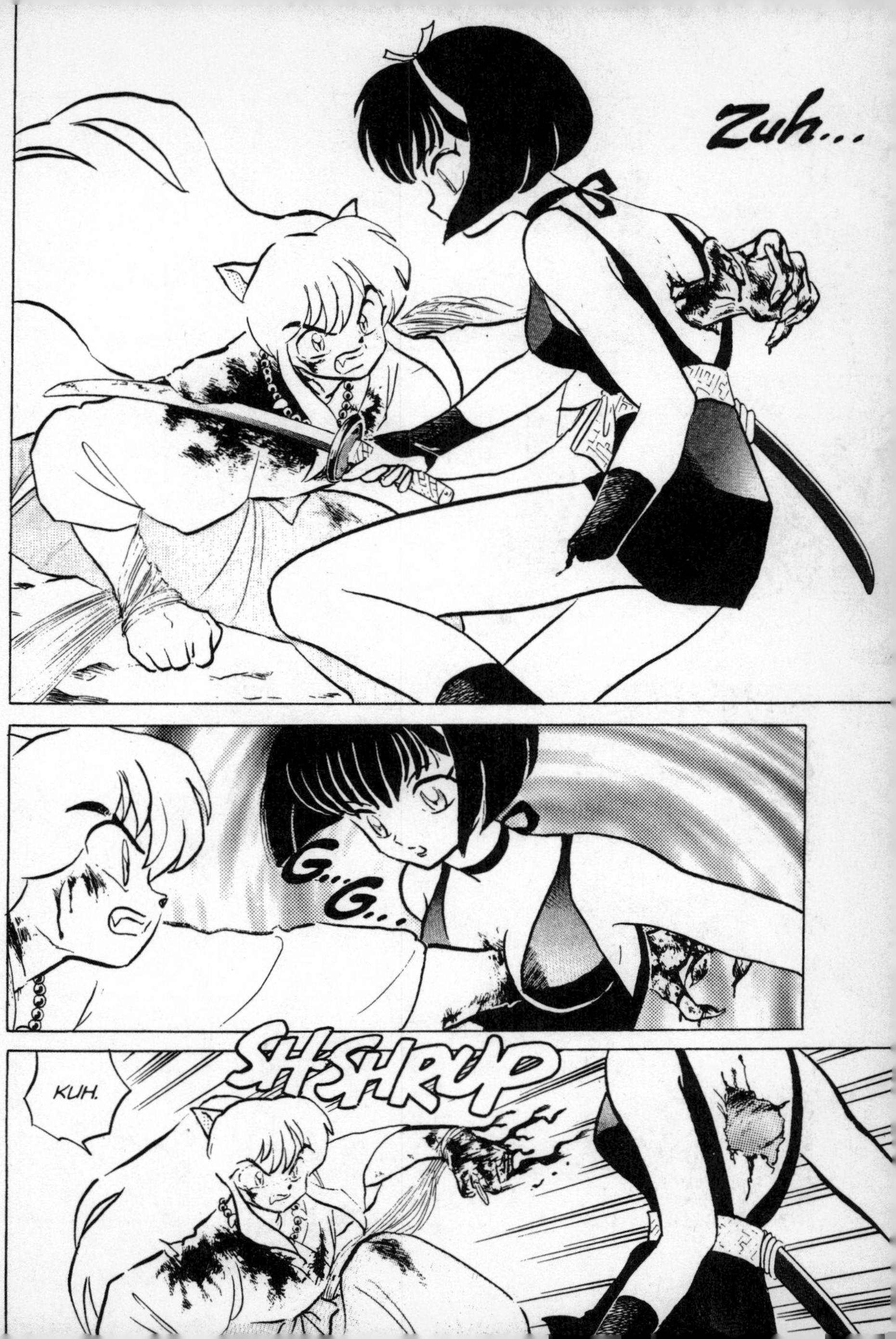
Zuh...
G...G...
SHSHRUP
KUH.

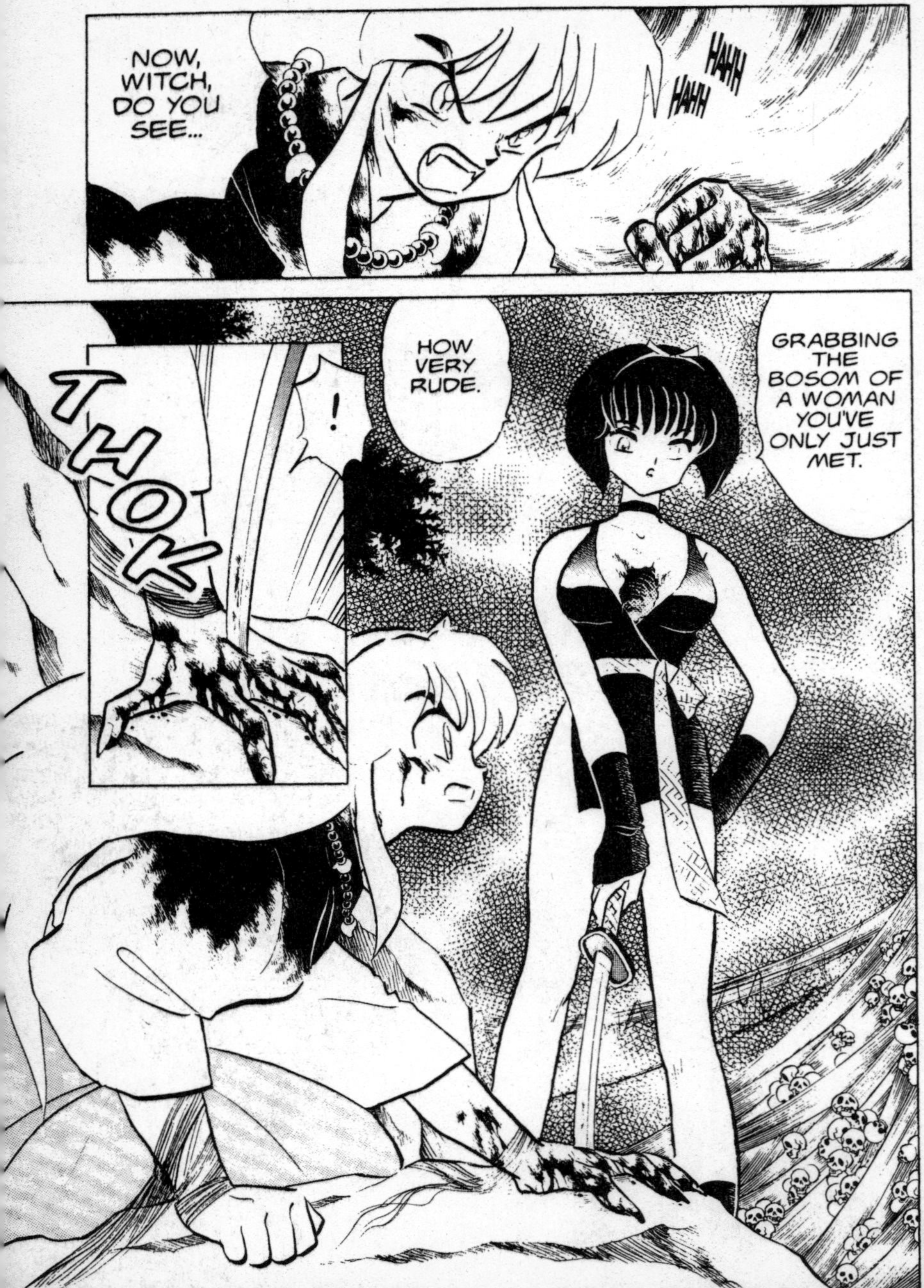
NOW, WITCH, DO YOU SEE...
HAHH
HAHH
THOK
!
HOW VERY RUDE.
GRABBING THE BOSOM OF A WOMAN YOU'VE ONLY JUST MET.

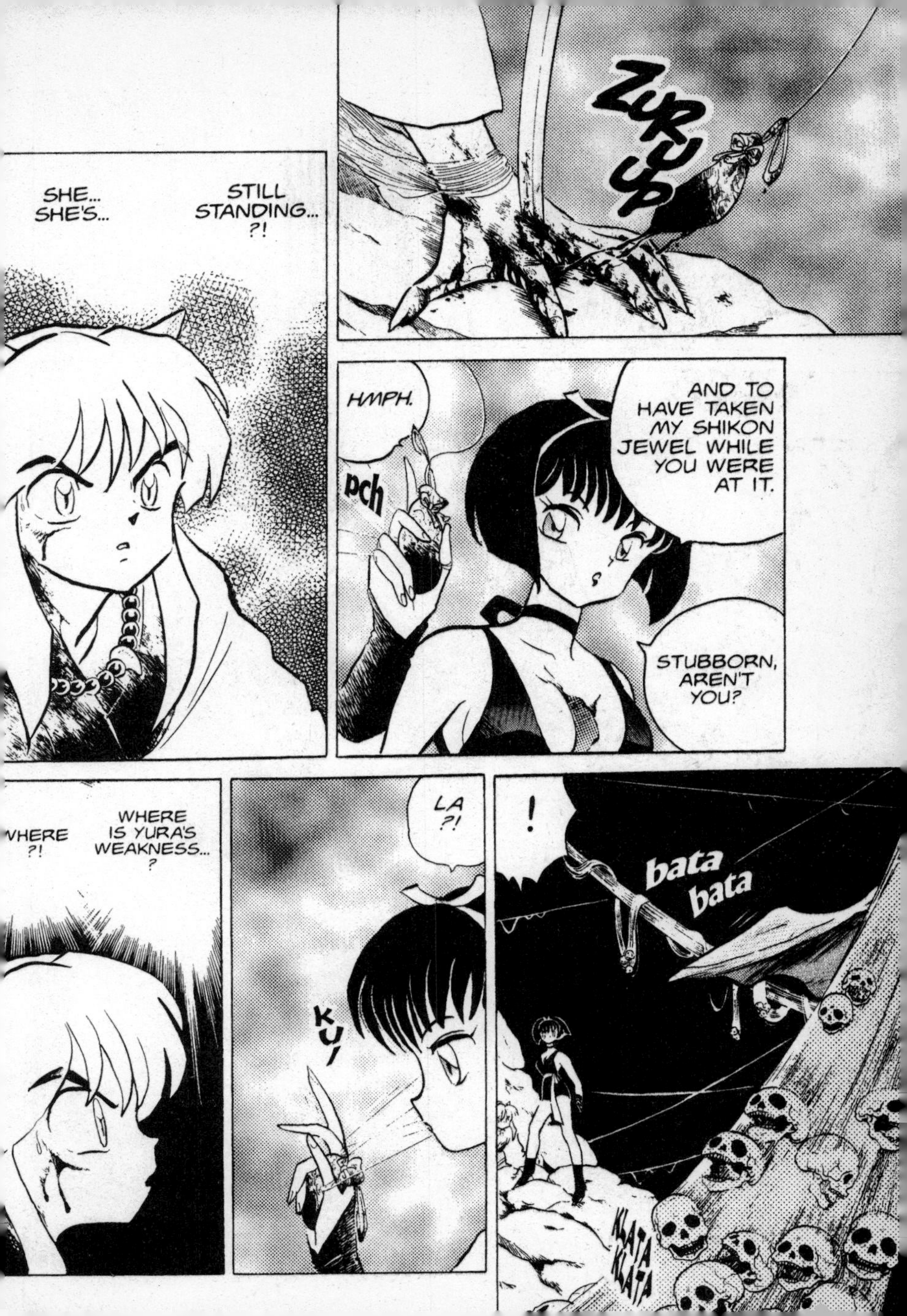
SHE... SHE'S...
STILL STANDING... ?!
ZURUUP
HMPH.
AND TO HAVE TAKEN MY SHIKON JEWEL WHILE YOU WERE AT IT.
pch
STUBBORN, AREN'T YOU?
WHERE ?!
WHERE IS YURA'S WEAKNESS... ?
LA ?!
KUI
!
bata bata
KLATA KLATA

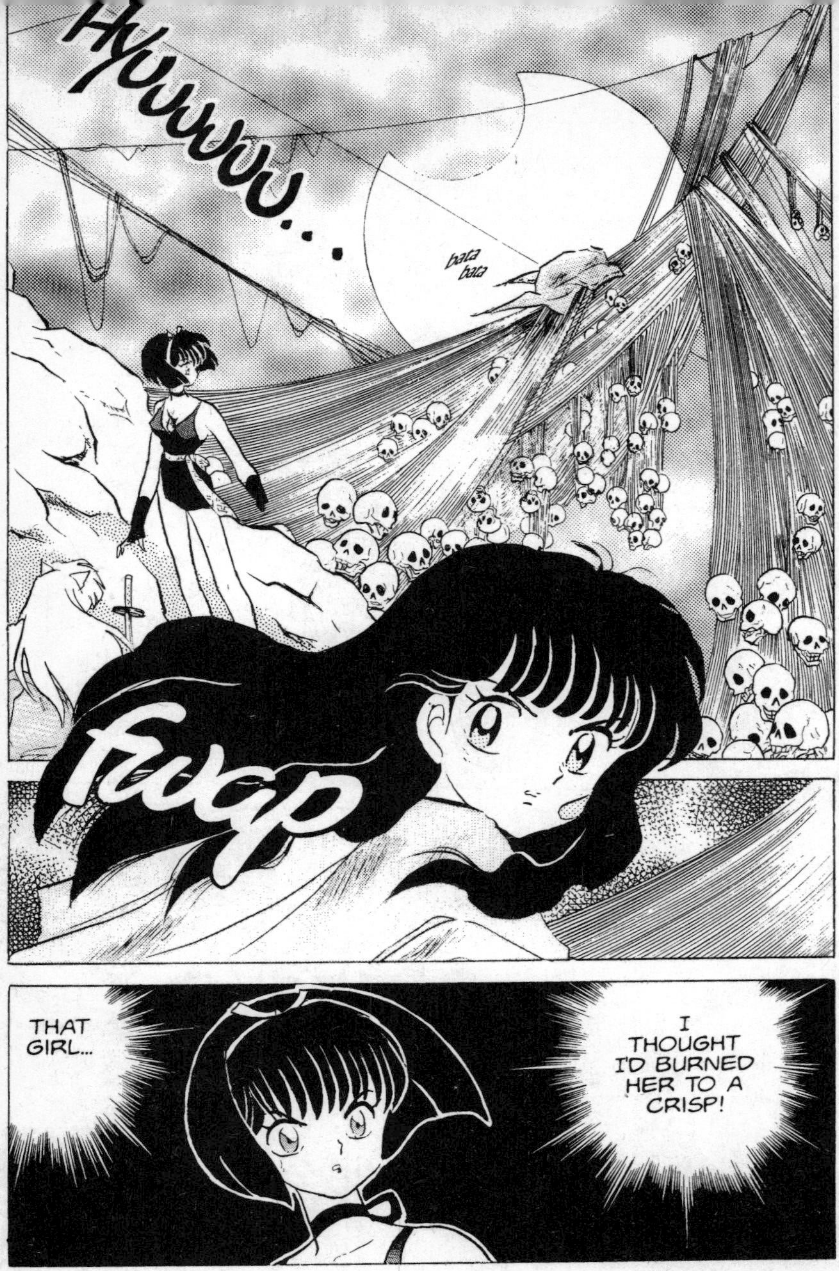
HYUUUUU...
bata bata
fwap
THAT GIRL...
I THOUGHT I'D BURNED HER TO A CRISP!

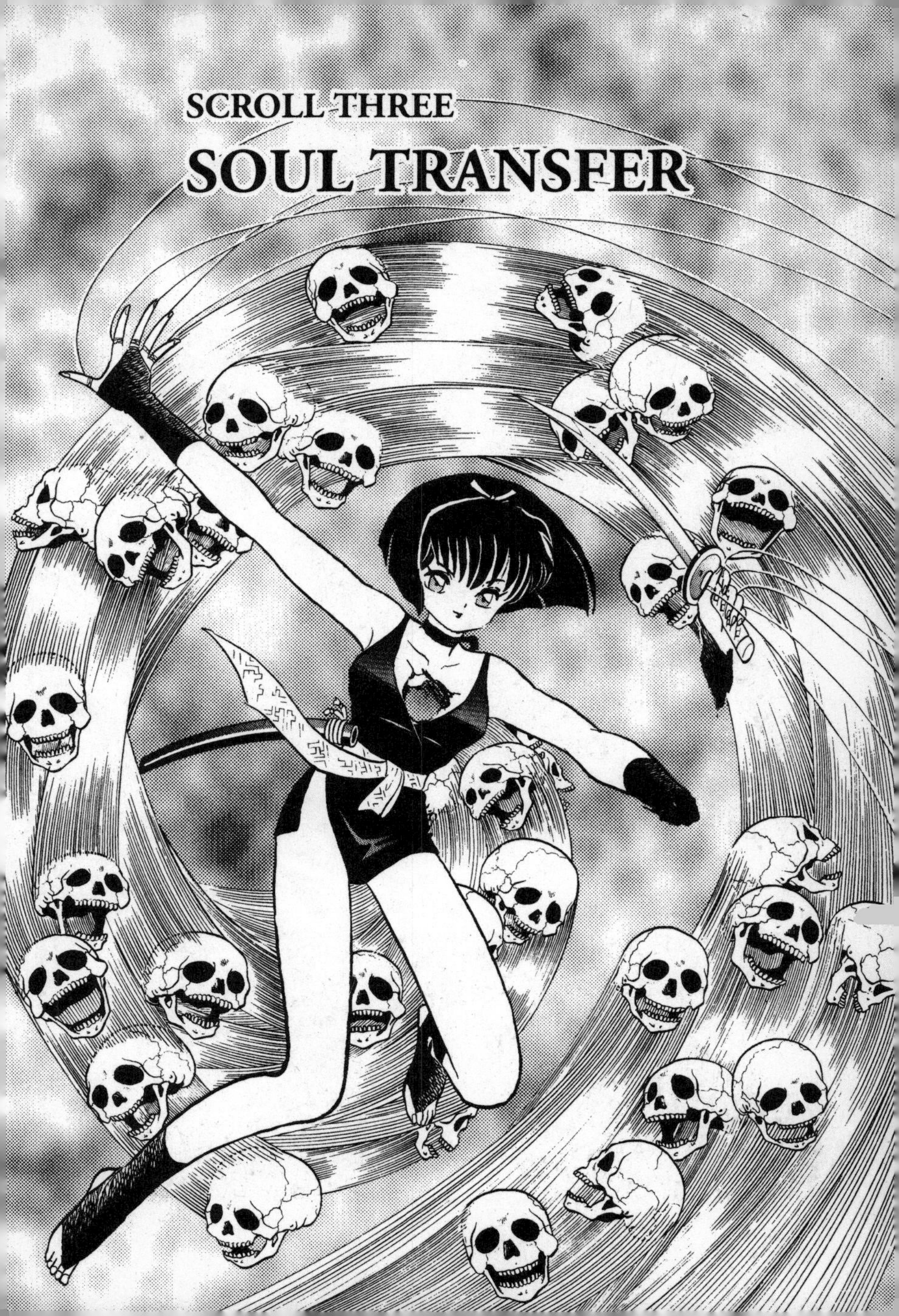
SCROLL THREE
SOUL TRANSFER

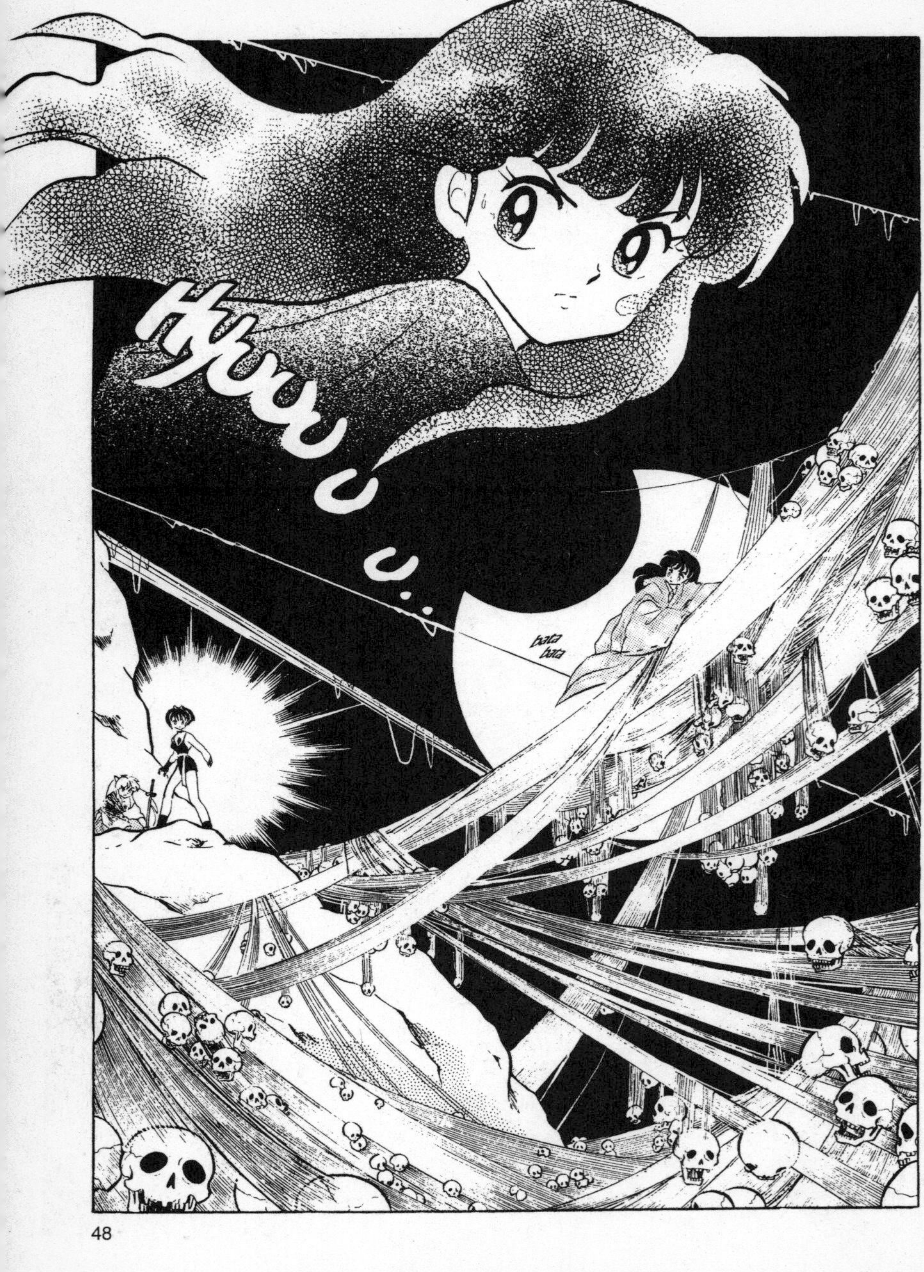
Hyuuu...
bata bata

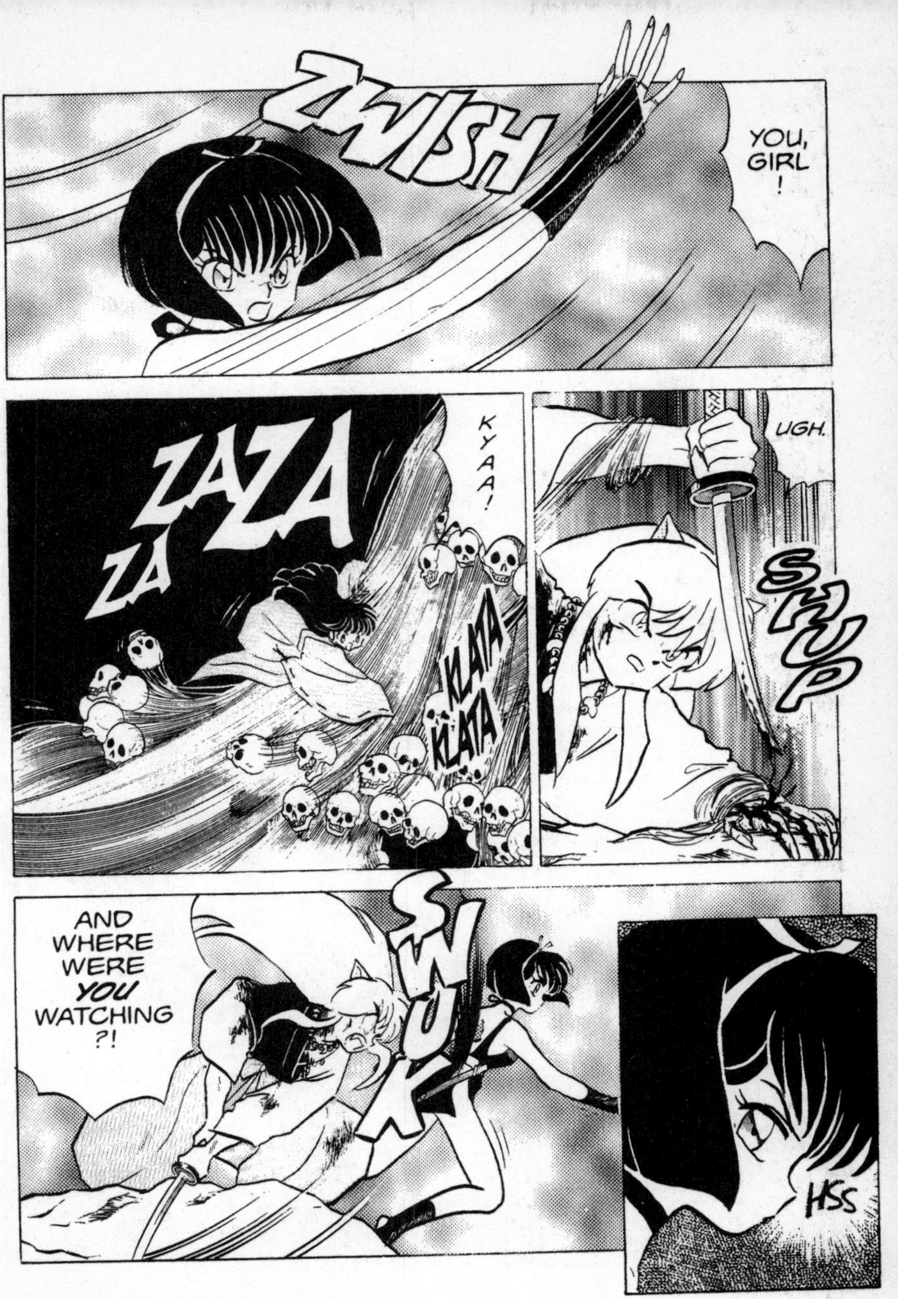

ZWISH
YOU, GIRL!
ZA ZA ZA
KYAAA!
KLATA KLATA
UGH.
SHUP
AND WHERE WERE *YOU* WATCHING?!
SWUK
HSS

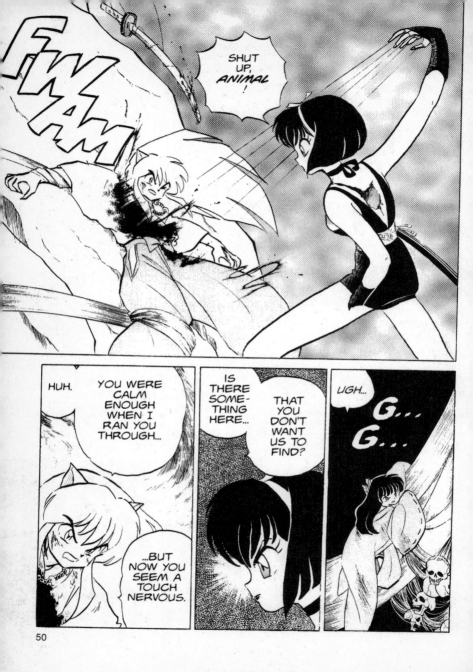

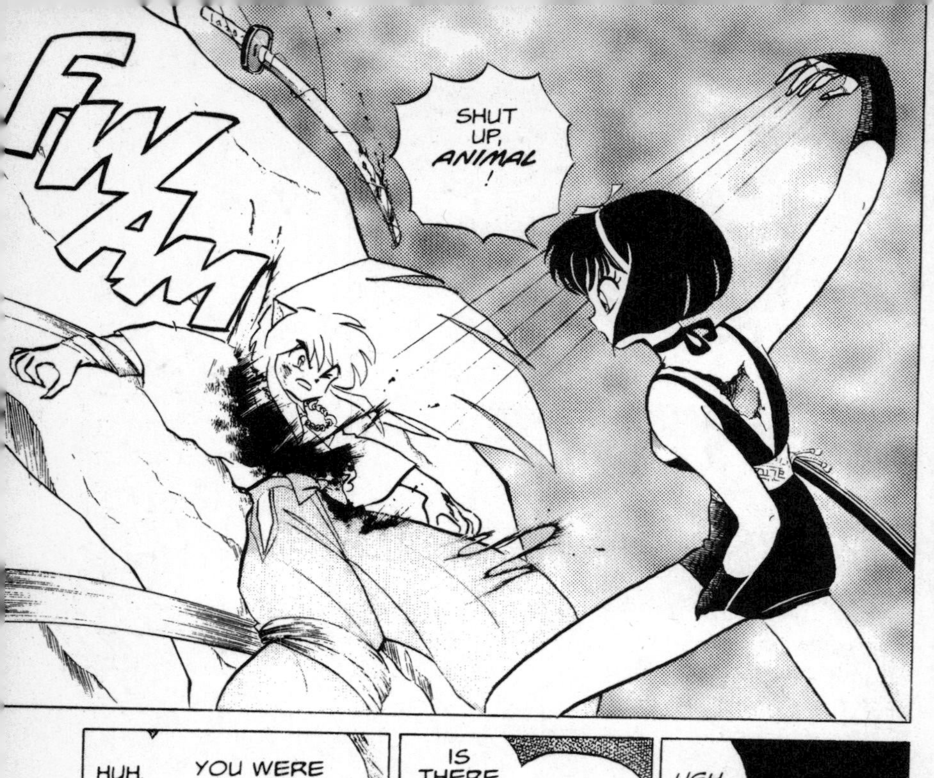
FWAM
SHUT UP, ANIMAL!
HUH.
YOU WERE CALM ENOUGH WHEN I RAN YOU THROUGH...
...BUT NOW YOU SEEM A TOUCH NERVOUS.
IS THERE SOME-THING HERE...
THAT YOU DON'T WANT US TO FIND?
UGH...
G...
G...

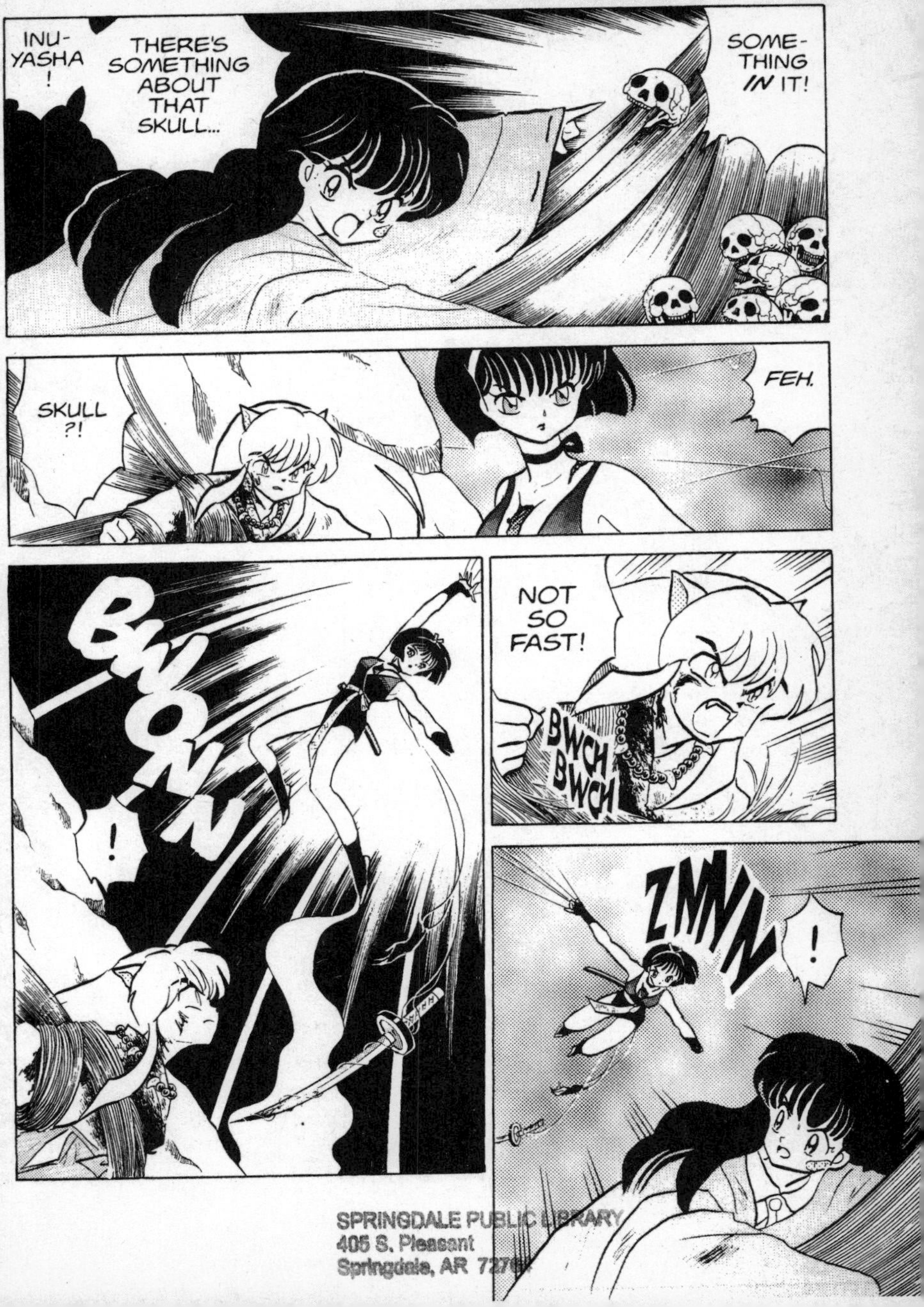
INU-YASHA!
THERE'S SOMETHING ABOUT THAT SKULL...
SOMETHING IN IT!
SKULL?!
FEH.
BWOMN
!
NOT SO FAST!
BWCH BWCH
ZMMN
!

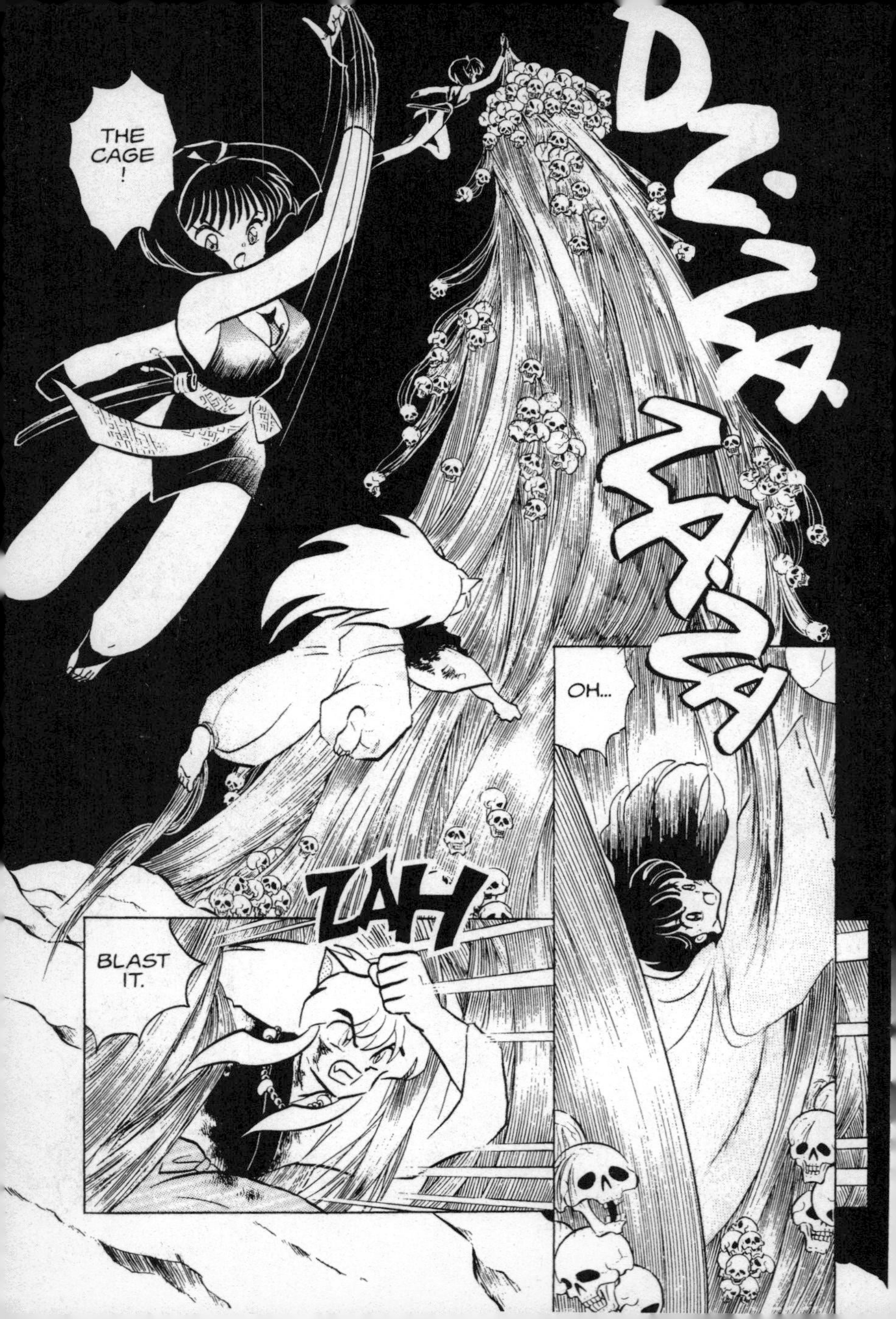
THE CAGE!
DZZA ZAZA
ZAH
BLAST IT.
OH...

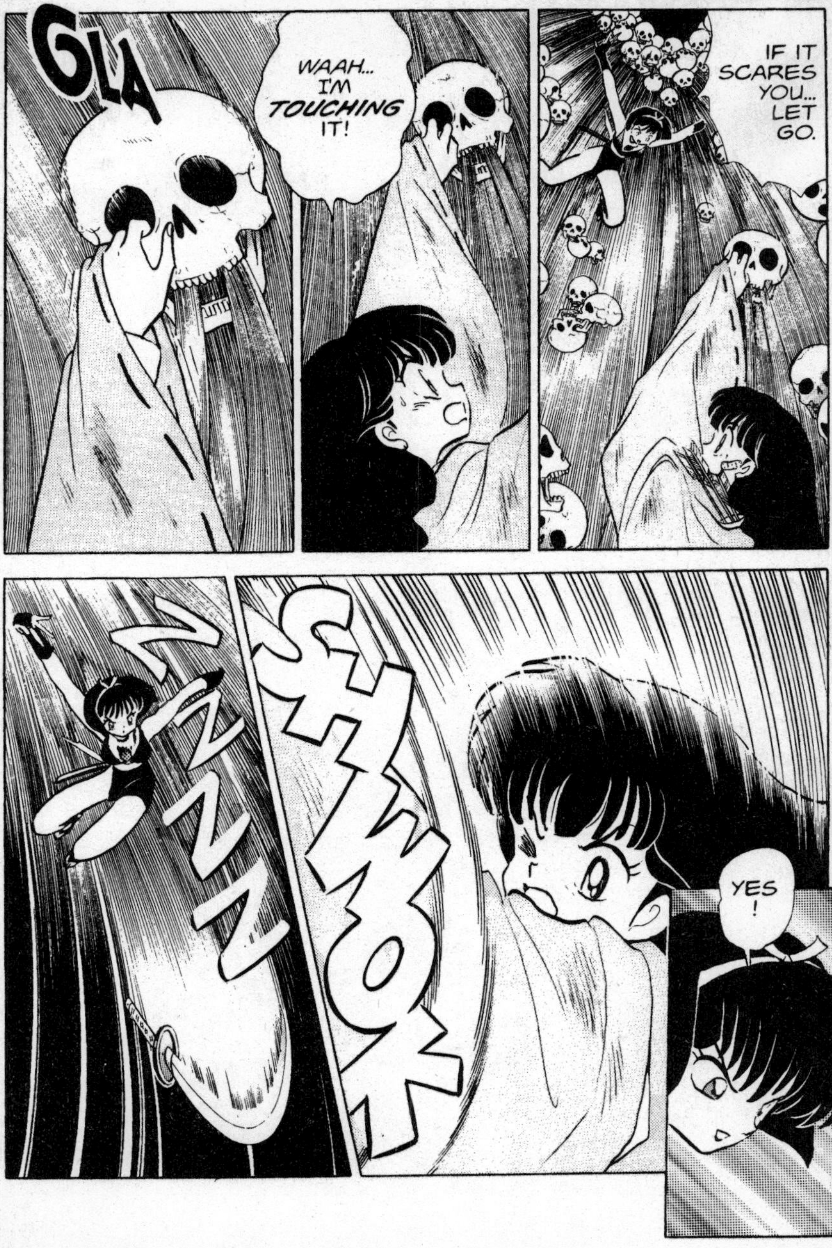
IF IT SCARES YOU... LET GO.
WAAH... I'M TOUCHING IT!
GLA
YES!
SHWOK
ZNNN

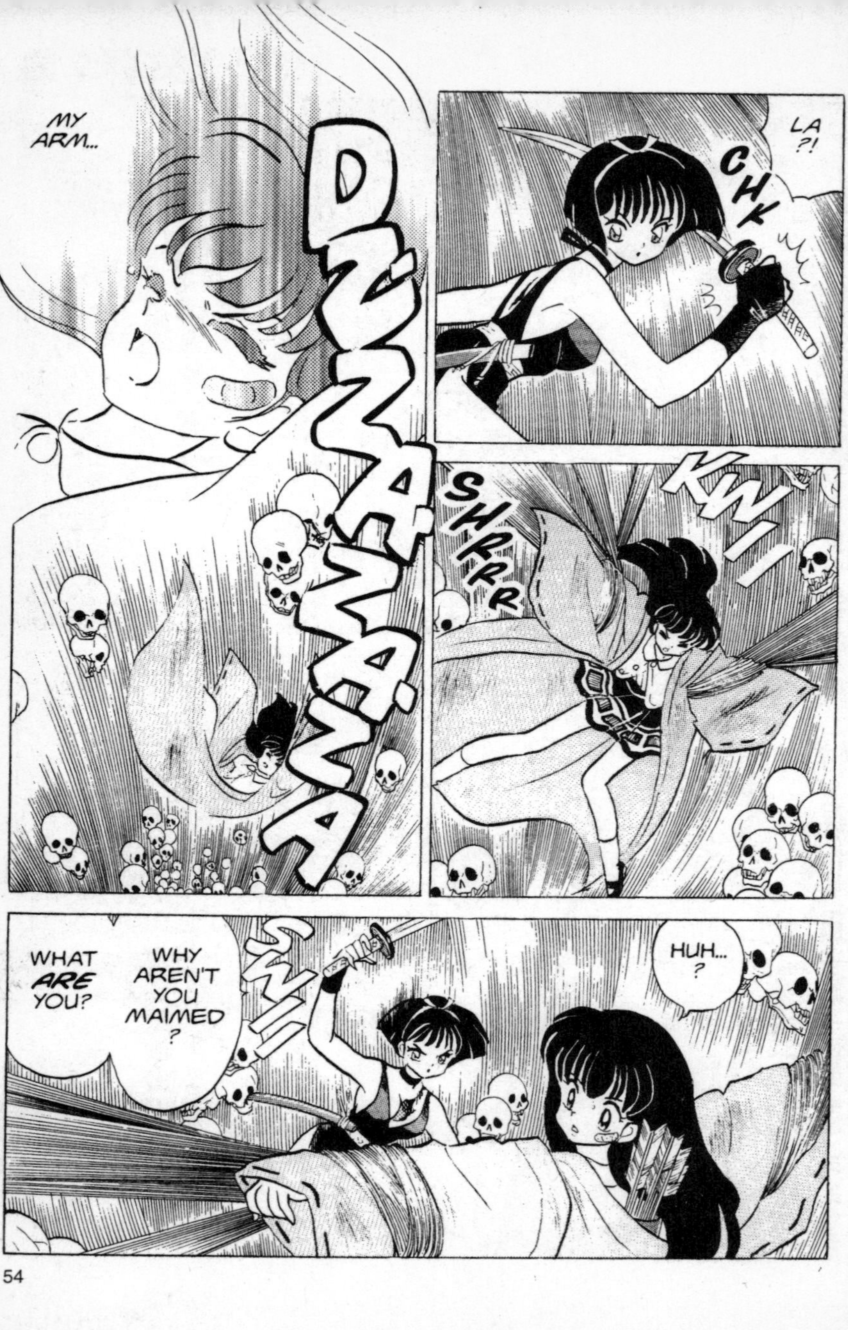
MY ARM...
LA ?!
CHK
SHRRR
KWIII
WHAT *ARE* YOU?
WHY AREN'T YOU MAIMED ?
SWIII
HUH... ?

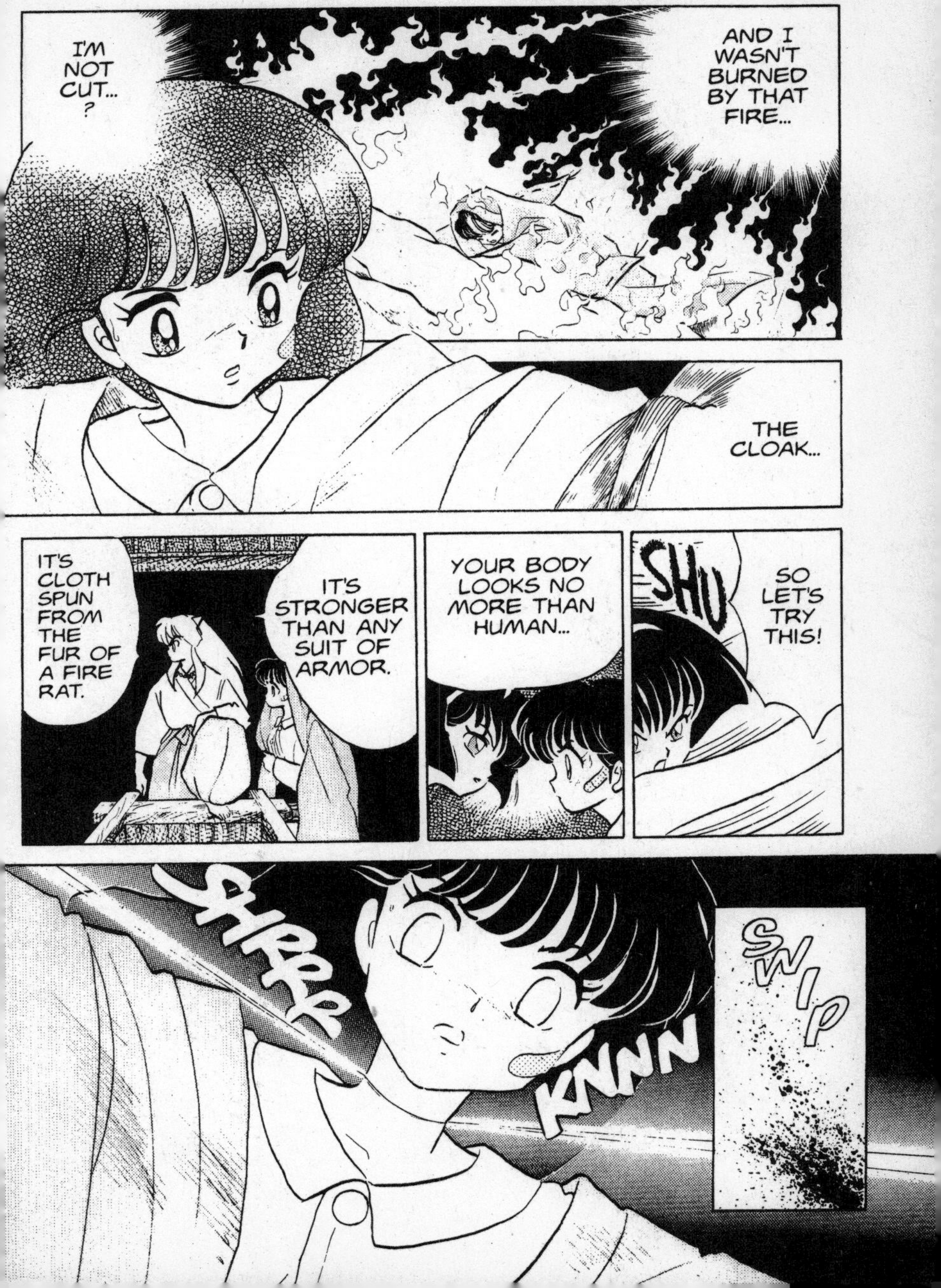
I'M NOT CUT... ?
AND I WASN'T BURNED BY THAT FIRE...
THE CLOAK...
IT'S CLOTH SPUN FROM THE FUR OF A FIRE RAT.
IT'S STRONGER THAN ANY SUIT OF ARMOR.
YOUR BODY LOOKS NO MORE THAN HUMAN...
SHU
SO LET'S TRY THIS!
SHRRR
KNNN
SWIP

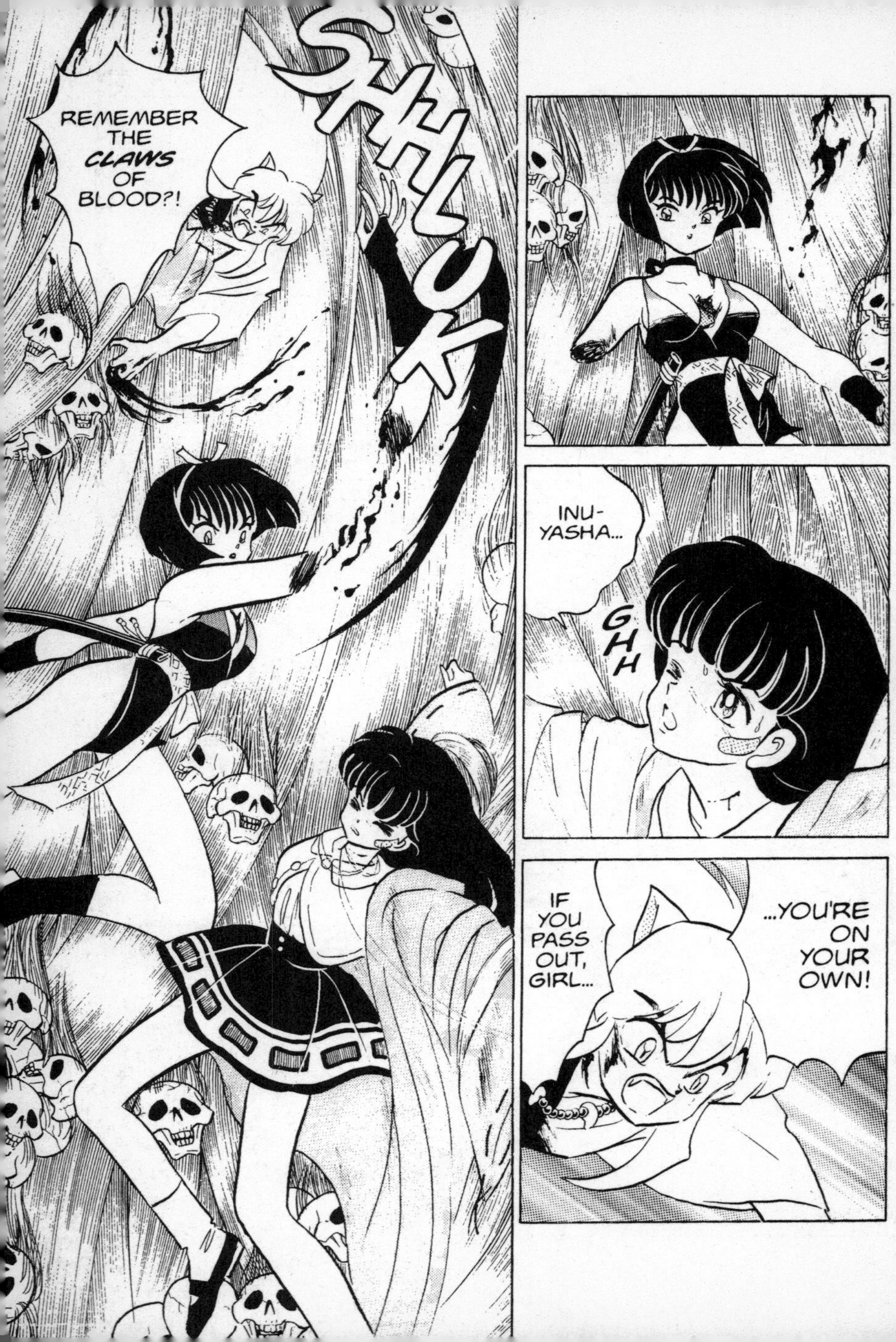
REMEMBER THE CLAWS OF BLOOD?!
SHHLUK
INU-YASHA...
GHH
IF YOU PASS OUT, GIRL...
...YOU'RE ON YOUR OWN!

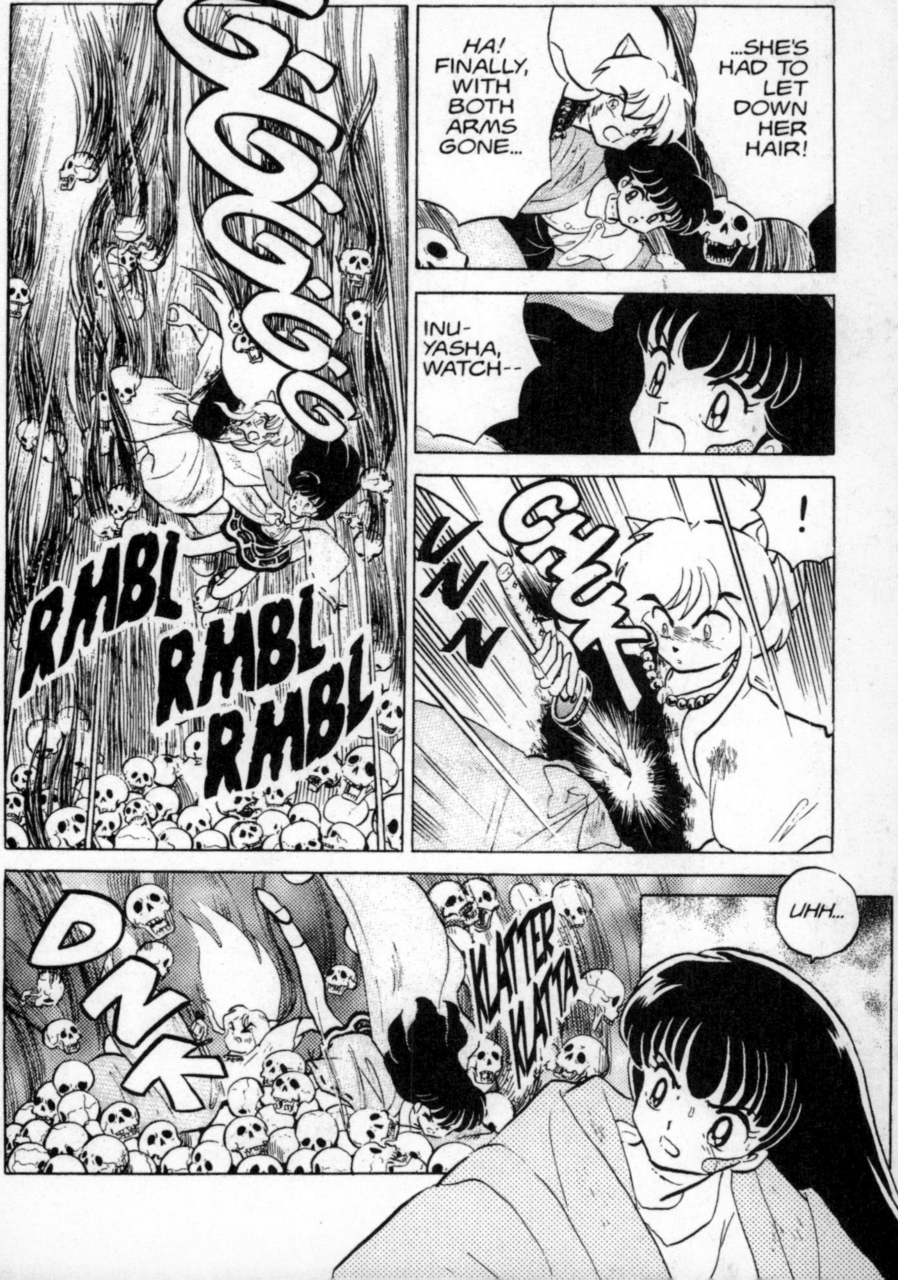
HA! FINALLY, WITH BOTH ARMS GONE...
...SHE'S HAD TO LET DOWN HER HAIR!
INU-YASHA, WATCH--
CHUNK
VNN
!
GGGGGG
RMBL RMBL RMBL RMBL RMBL
UHH...
KLATTER KLATTA
DNK

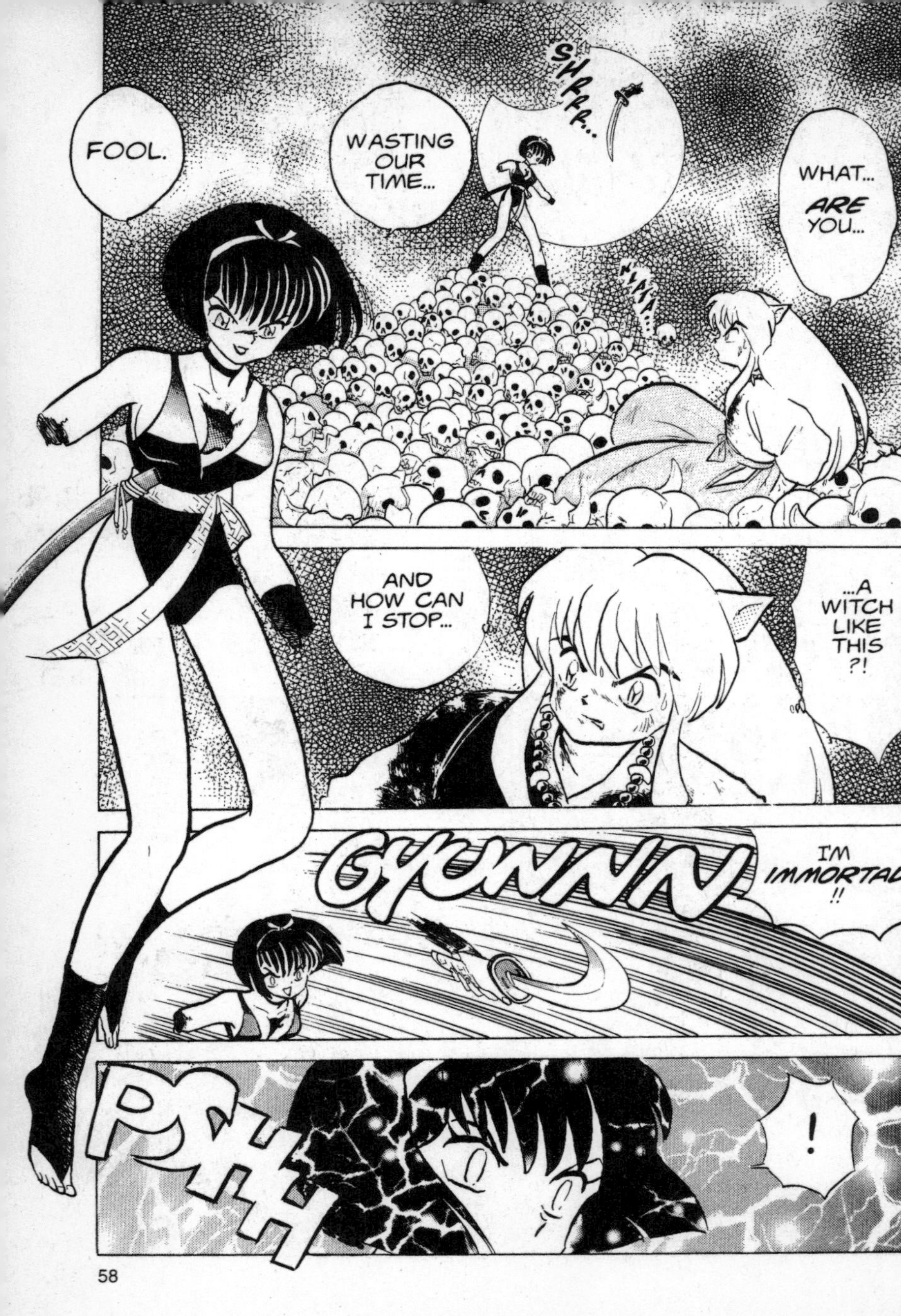
FOOL.
WASTING OUR TIME...
SHRRR...
WHAT... ARE YOU...
AND HOW CAN I STOP...
...A WITCH LIKE THIS ?!
GYUNNN
I'M IMMORTAL !!
PSHH
!

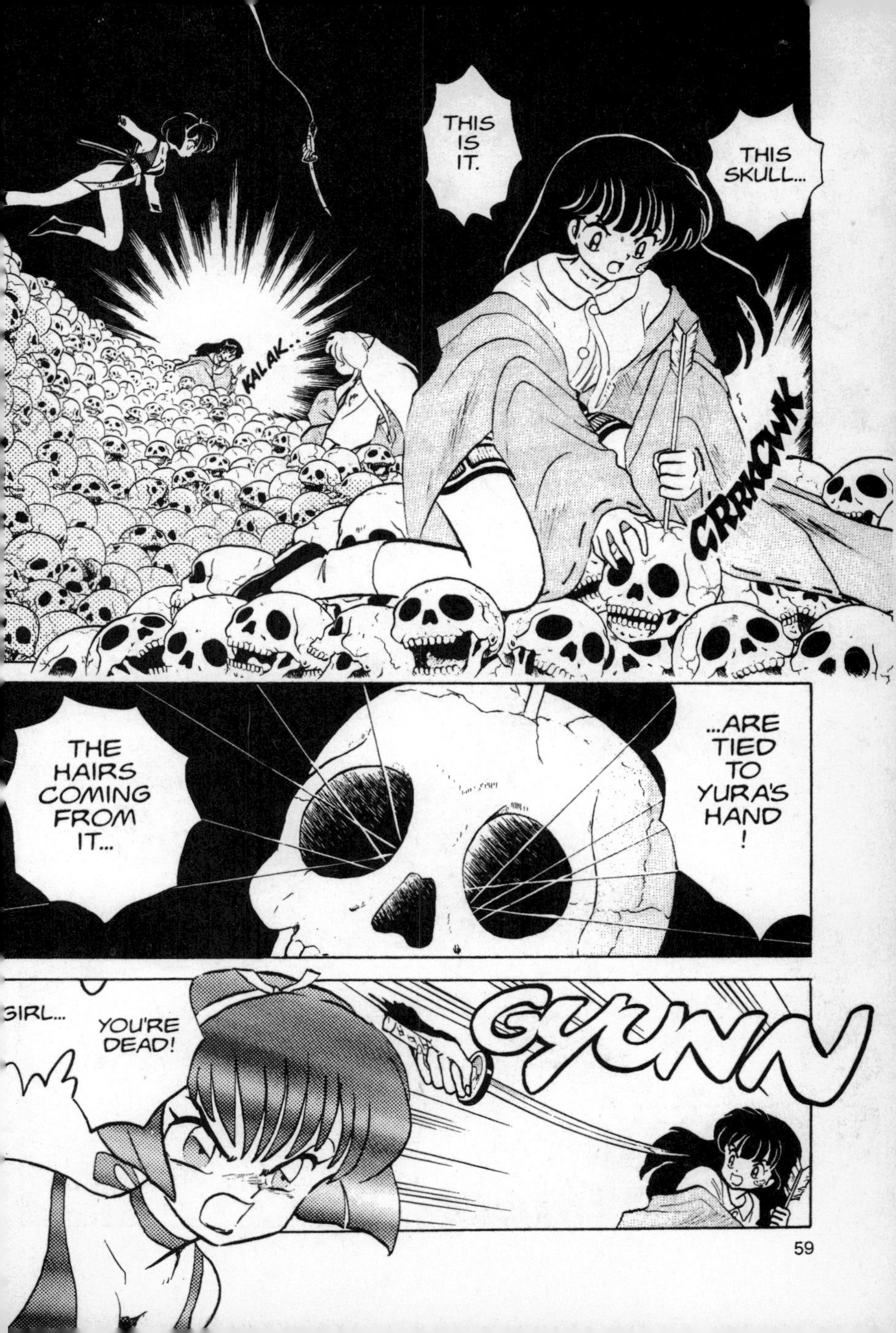
KALAK...
THIS IS IT.
THIS SKULL...
CRRKOWK
THE HAIRS COMING FROM IT...
...ARE TIED TO YURA'S HAND !
GIRL...
YOU'RE DEAD!
GYUNN

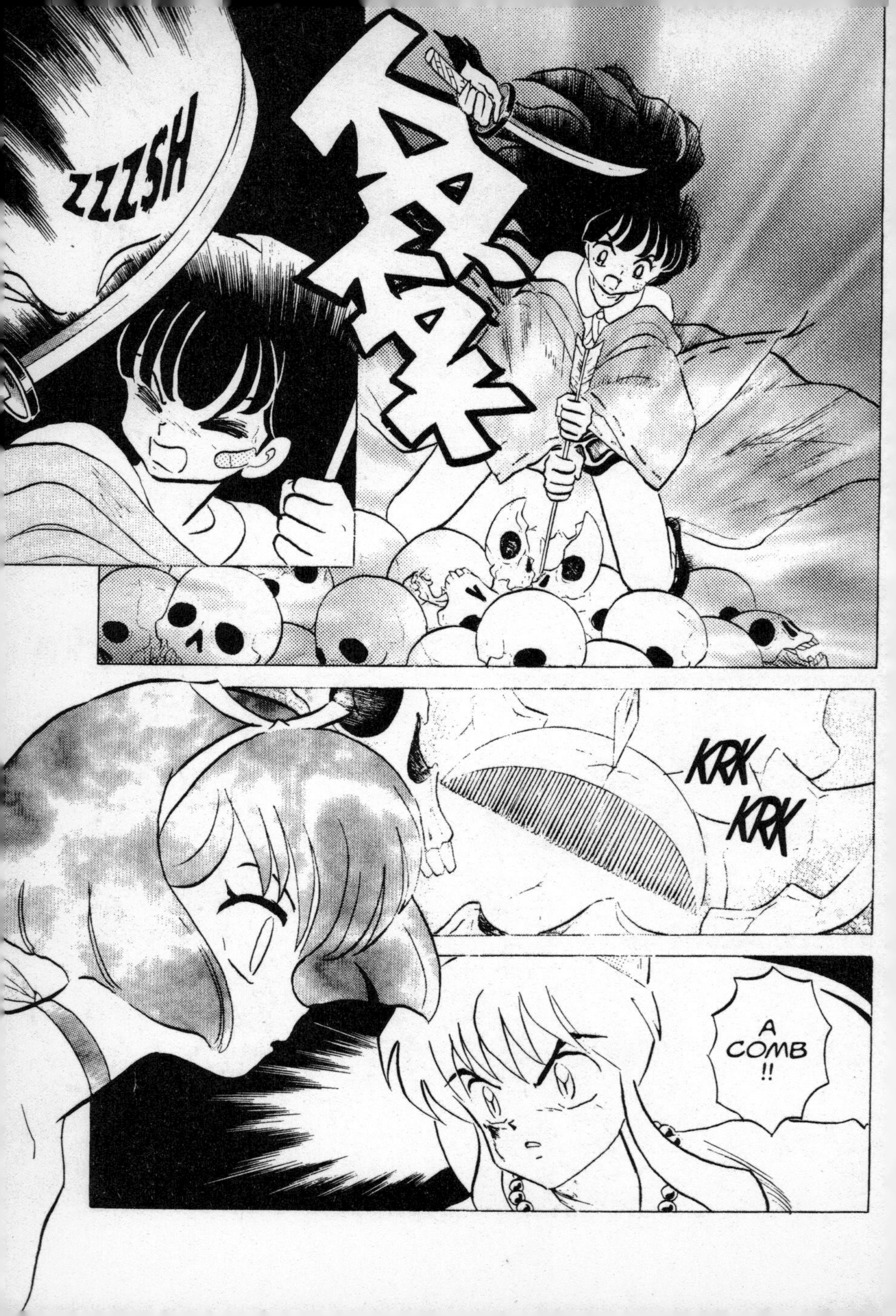
ZZZSH
KRK
KRK
A COMB!!

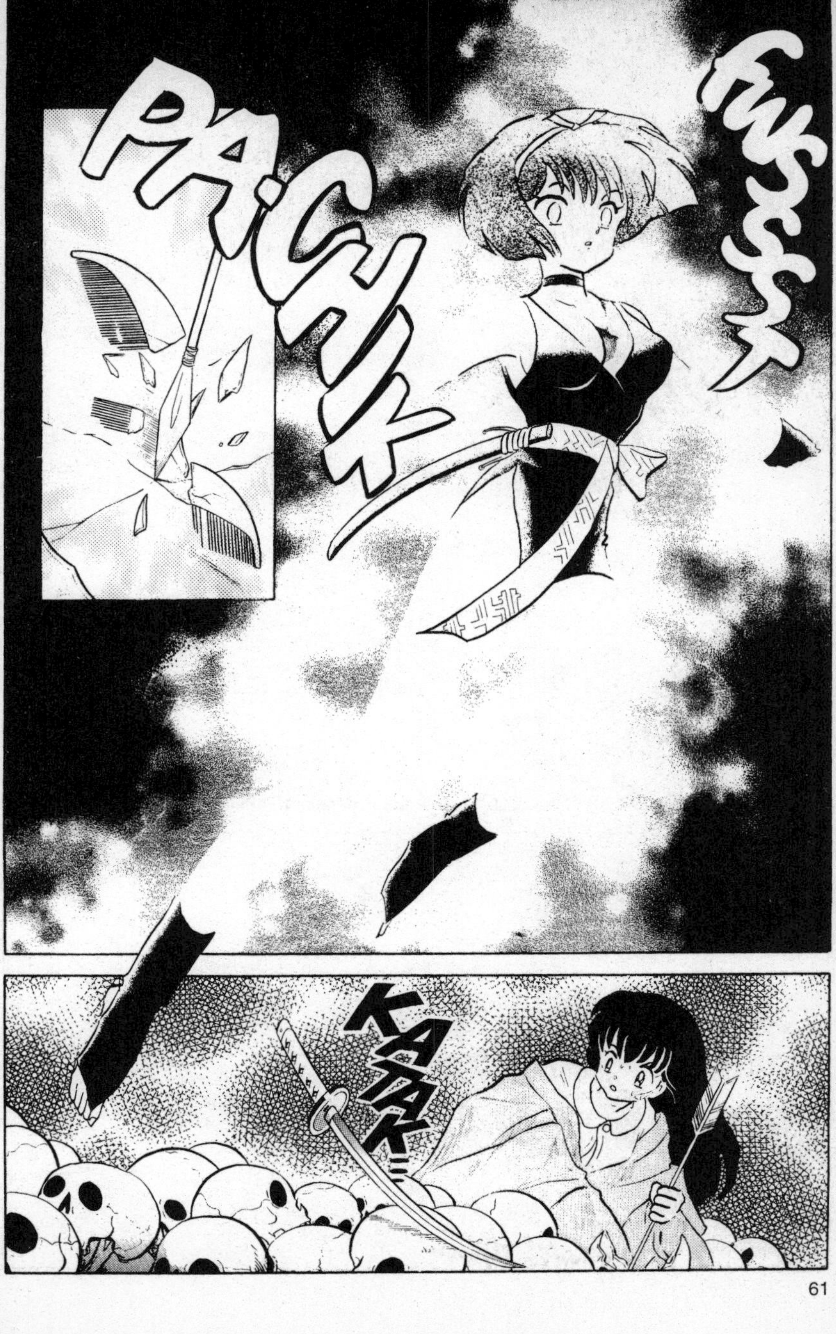
PA-CHIK
FWSSSST
KATAK

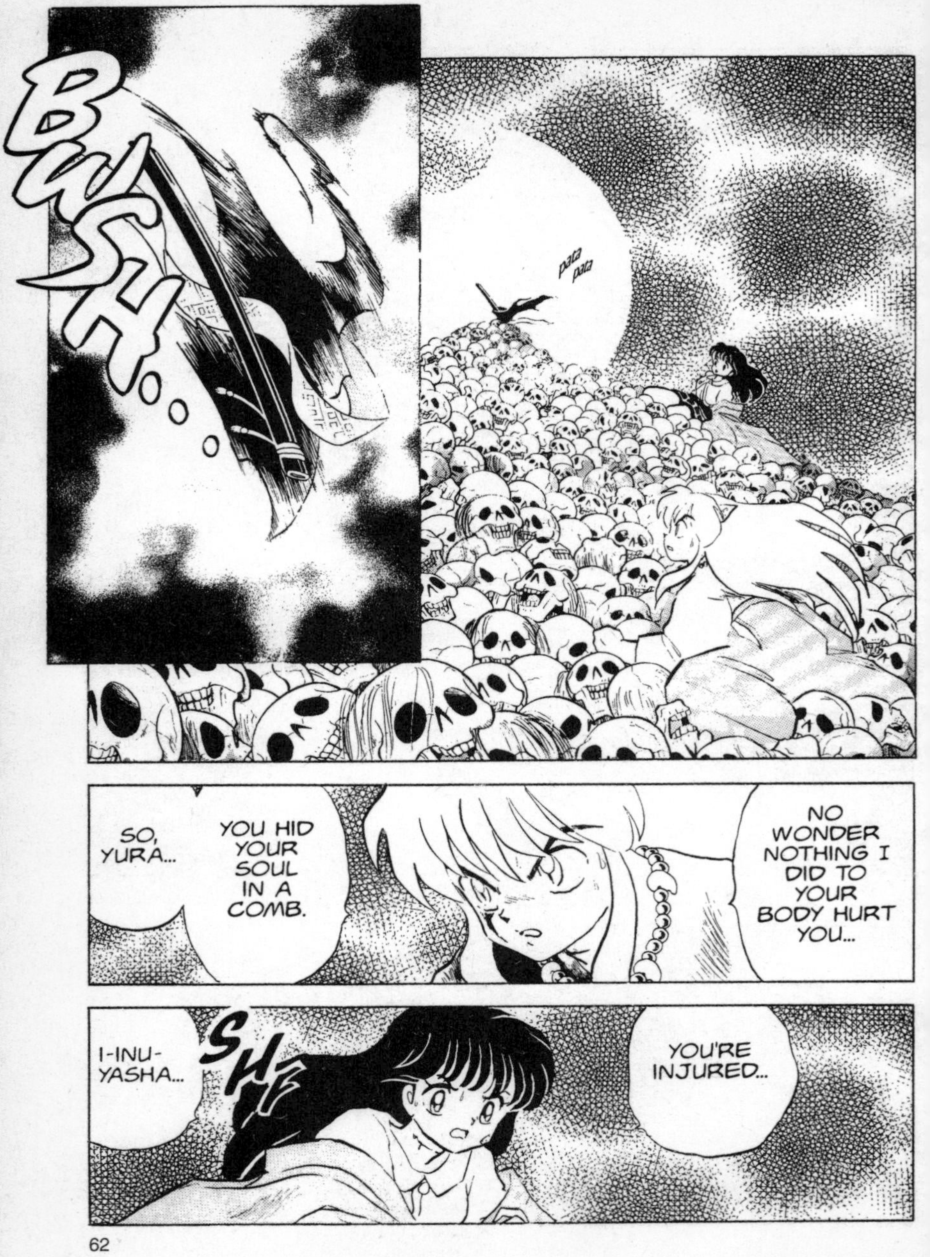
BUSH...
pata pata
SO, YURA...
YOU HID YOUR SOUL IN A COMB.
NO WONDER NOTHING I DID TO YOUR BODY HURT YOU...
I-INU-YASHA...
SHF
YOU'RE INJURED...

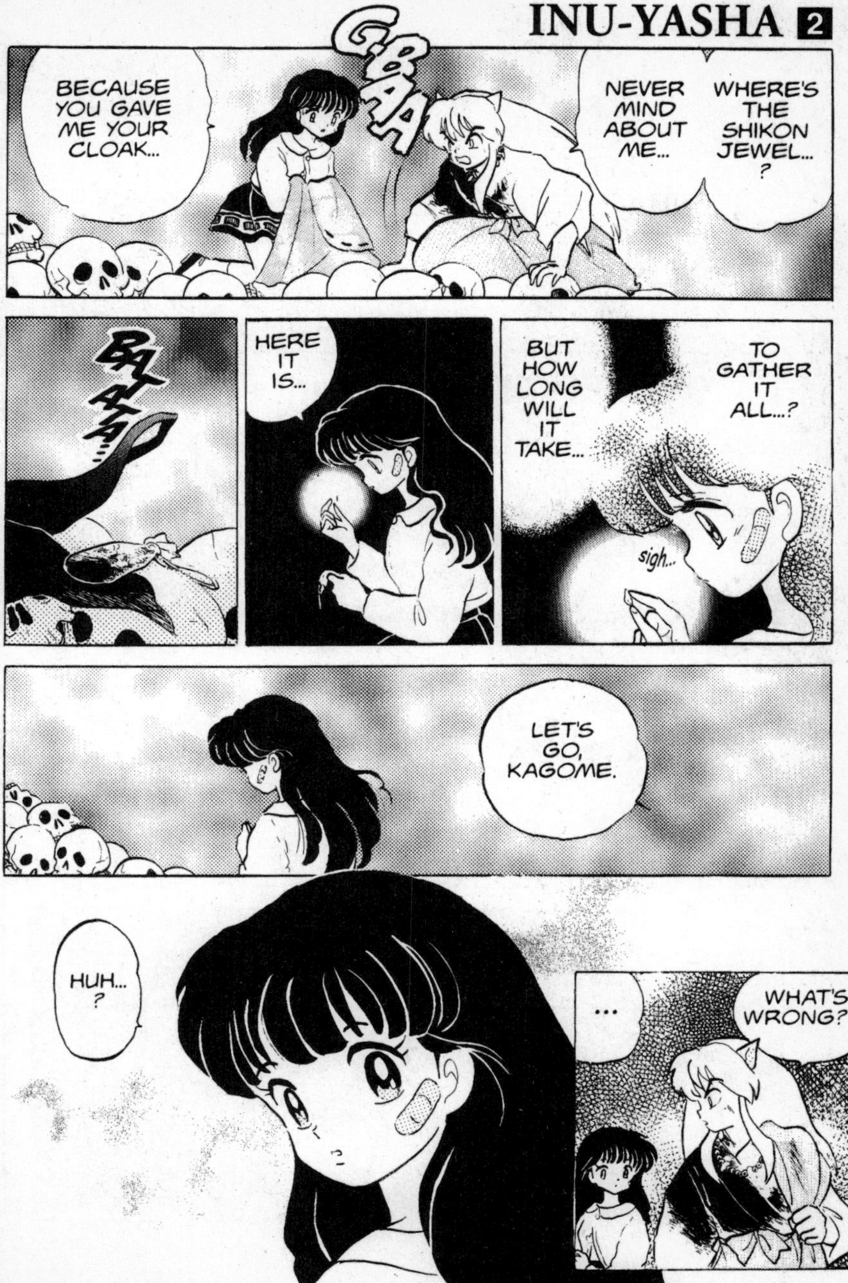
BECAUSE YOU GAVE ME YOUR CLOAK...
NEVER MIND ABOUT ME...
WHERE'S THE SHIKON JEWEL...?
HERE IT IS...
BUT HOW LONG WILL IT TAKE...
TO GATHER IT ALL...?
sigh...
LET'S GO, KAGOME.
HUH...?
...
WHAT'S WRONG?

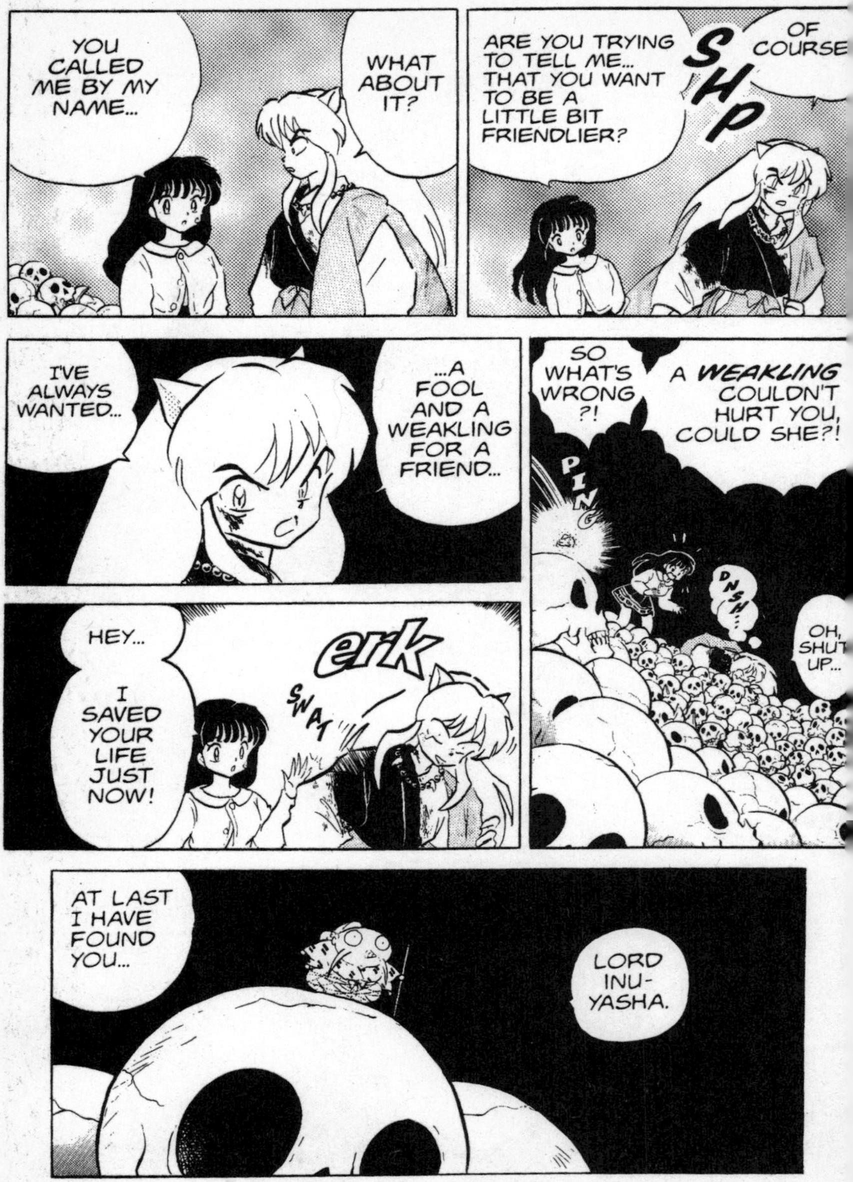
YOU CALLED ME BY MY NAME...
WHAT ABOUT IT?
ARE YOU TRYING TO TELL ME... THAT YOU WANT TO BE A LITTLE BIT FRIENDLIER?
SHP
OF COURSE
I'VE ALWAYS WANTED...
...A FOOL AND A WEAKLING FOR A FRIEND...
SO WHAT'S WRONG ?!
A WEAKLING COULDN'T HURT YOU, COULD SHE?!
PIN
DNSH...
OH, SHUT UP...
HEY...
I SAVED YOUR LIFE JUST NOW!
erk
SWAT
AT LAST I HAVE FOUND YOU...
LORD INU-YASHA.

SCROLL FOUR

HALF-BREED

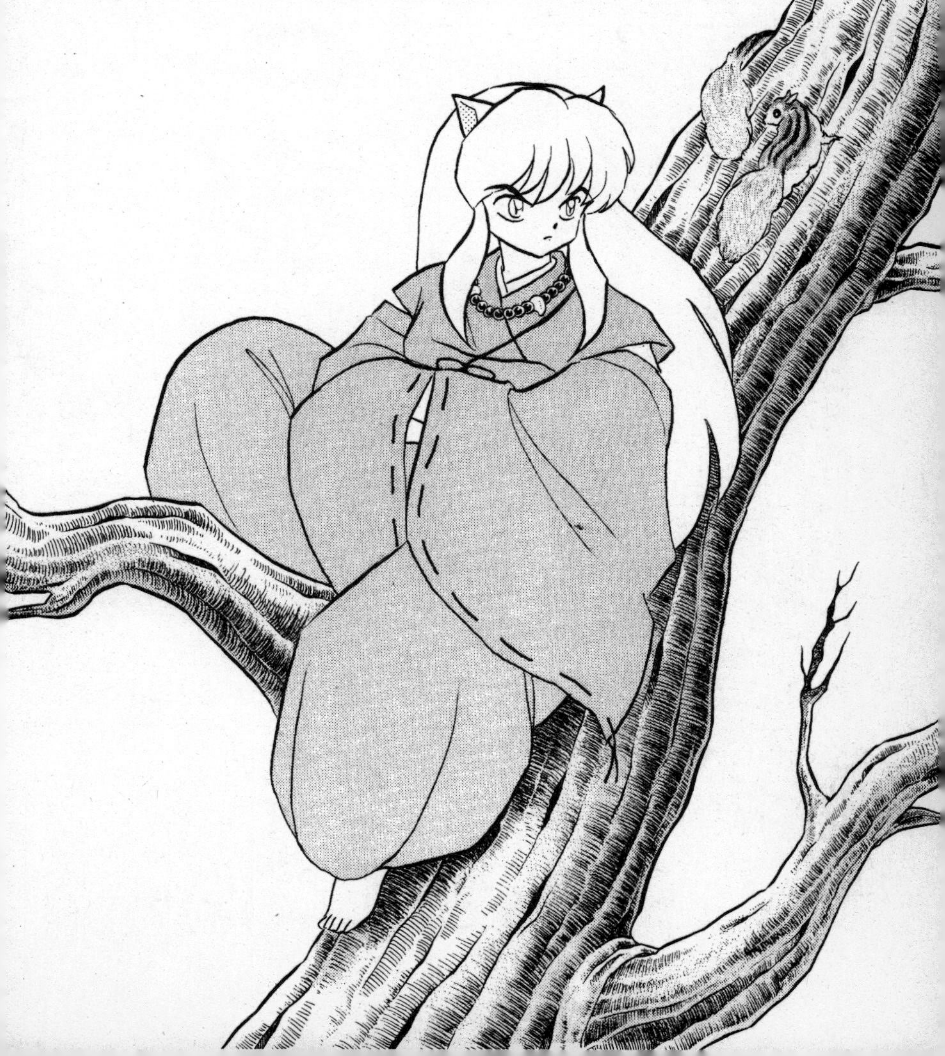

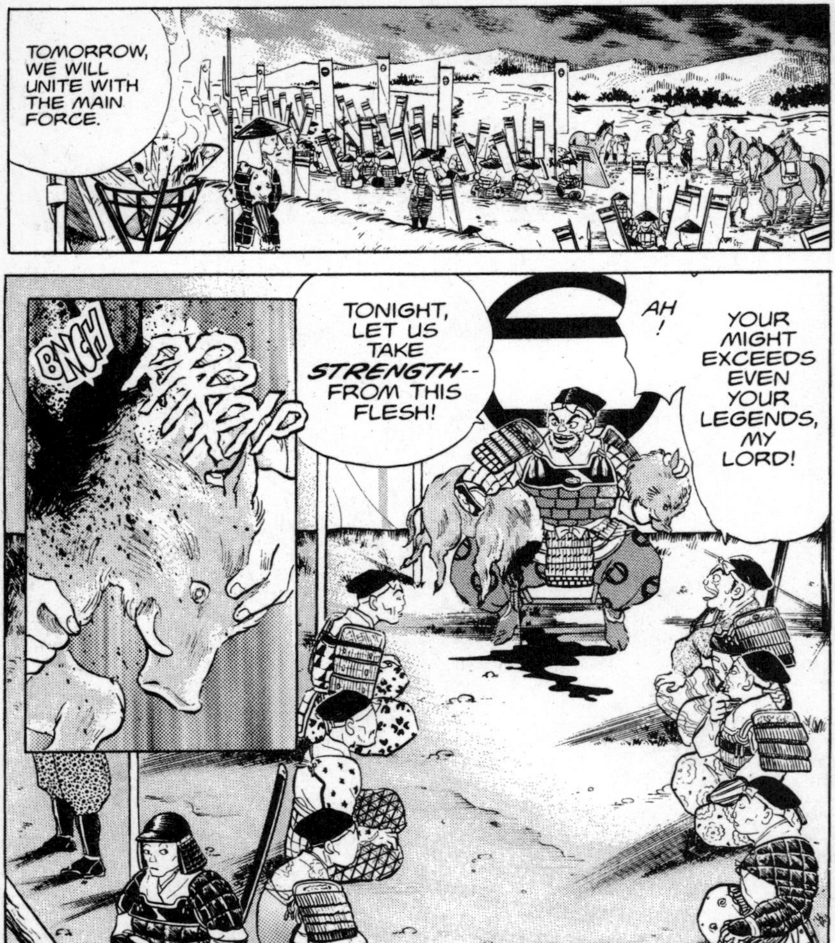
TOMORROW, WE WILL UNITE WITH THE MAIN FORCE.
BNCH
TONIGHT, LET US TAKE *STRENGTH*-- FROM THIS FLESH!
AH!
YOUR MIGHT EXCEEDS EVEN YOUR LEGENDS, MY LORD!
WITH YOU, WE CANNOT FAIL!
GNF GNF
WAHAHAHA! WATCH ME WRENCH THE ENEMY'S HEAD OFF LIKE THIS PIG'S!

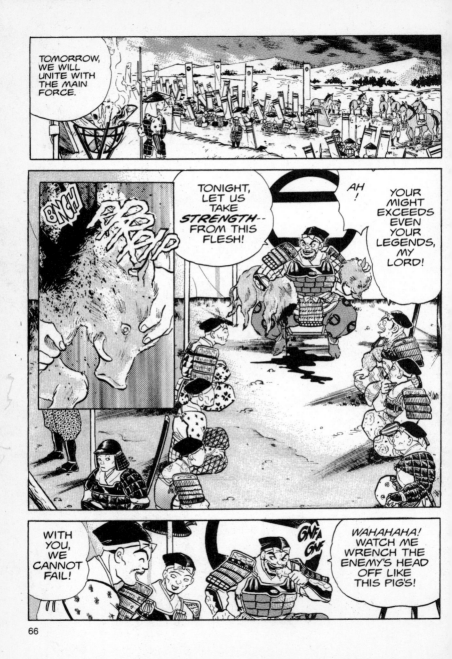

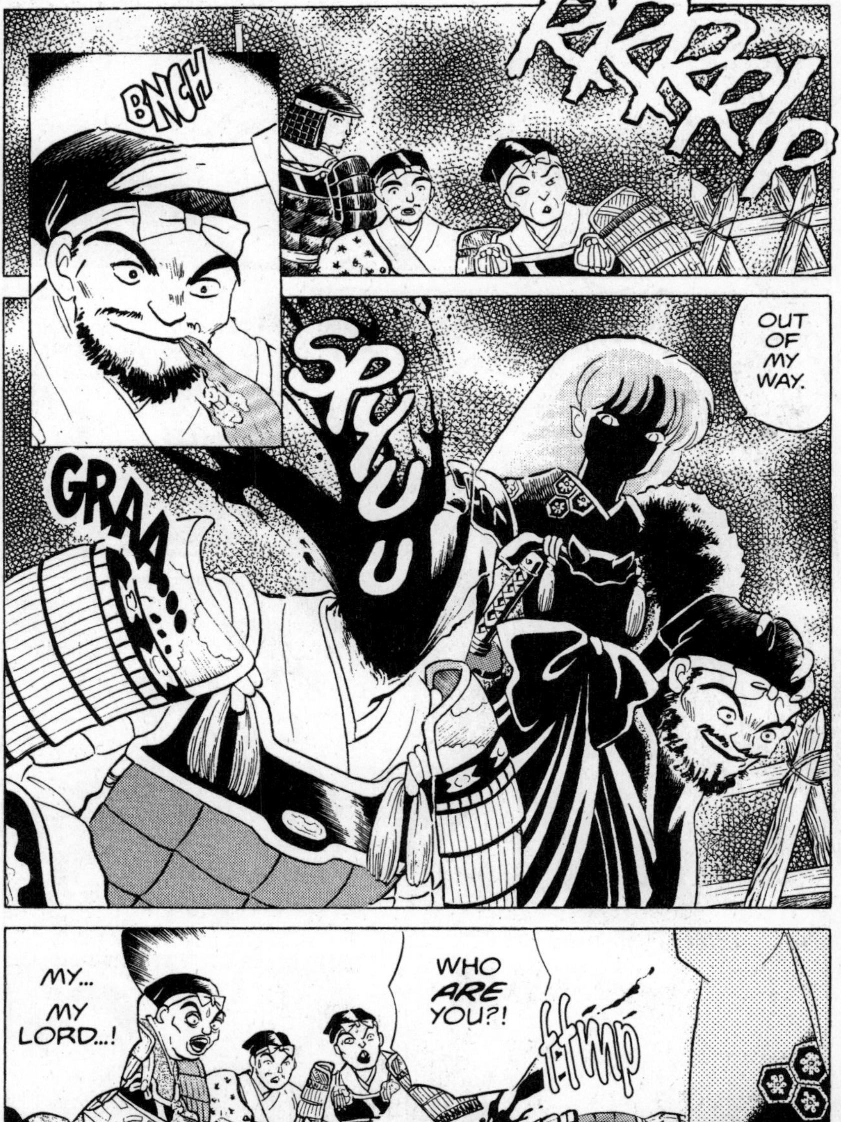
BNCH
RRRRRIP
SPYUU
GRAA...
OUT OF MY WAY.
MY... MY LORD...!
WHO *ARE* YOU?!
ffmp

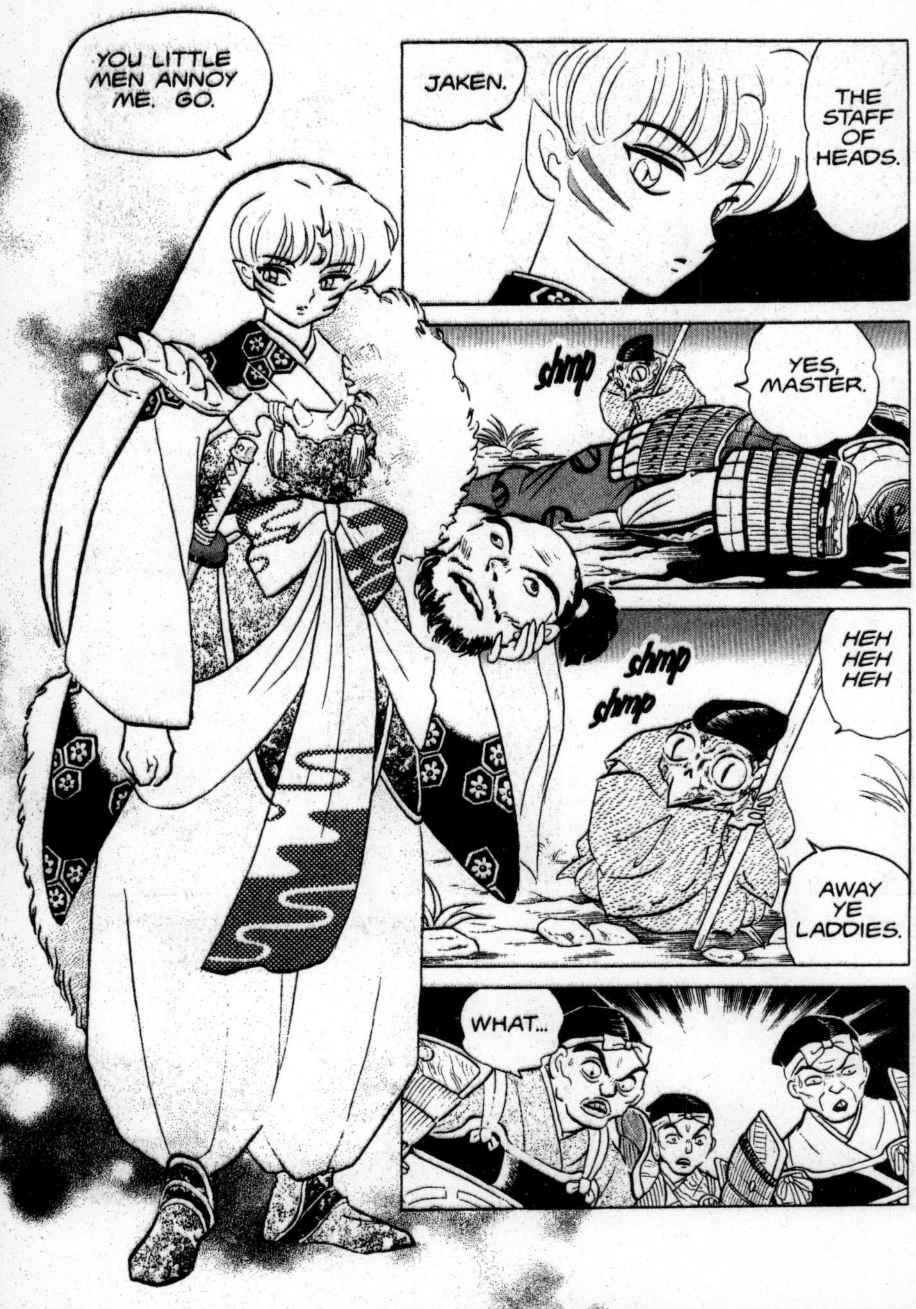
YOU LITTLE MEN ANNOY ME. GO.
JAKEN.
THE STAFF OF HEADS.
schmp
YES, MASTER.
schmp
schmp
HEH HEH HEH
AWAY YE LADDIES.
WHAT...

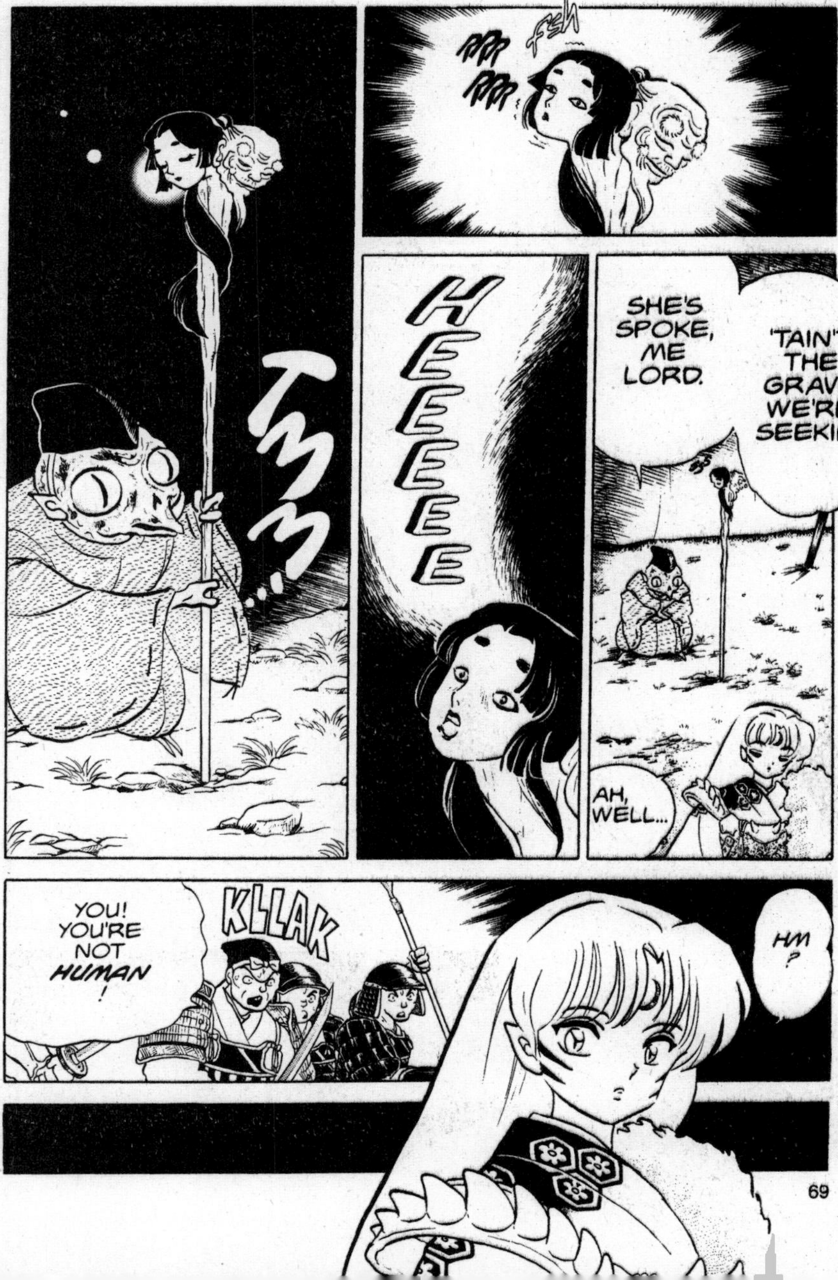
TMMM...
RRR
RRR
fsh
HEEEEEE
SHE'S SPOKE, ME LORD.
'TAIN'T THE GRAVE WE'RE SEEKIN'.
AH, WELL...
YOU! YOU'RE NOT *HUMAN*!
KLLAK
HM ?

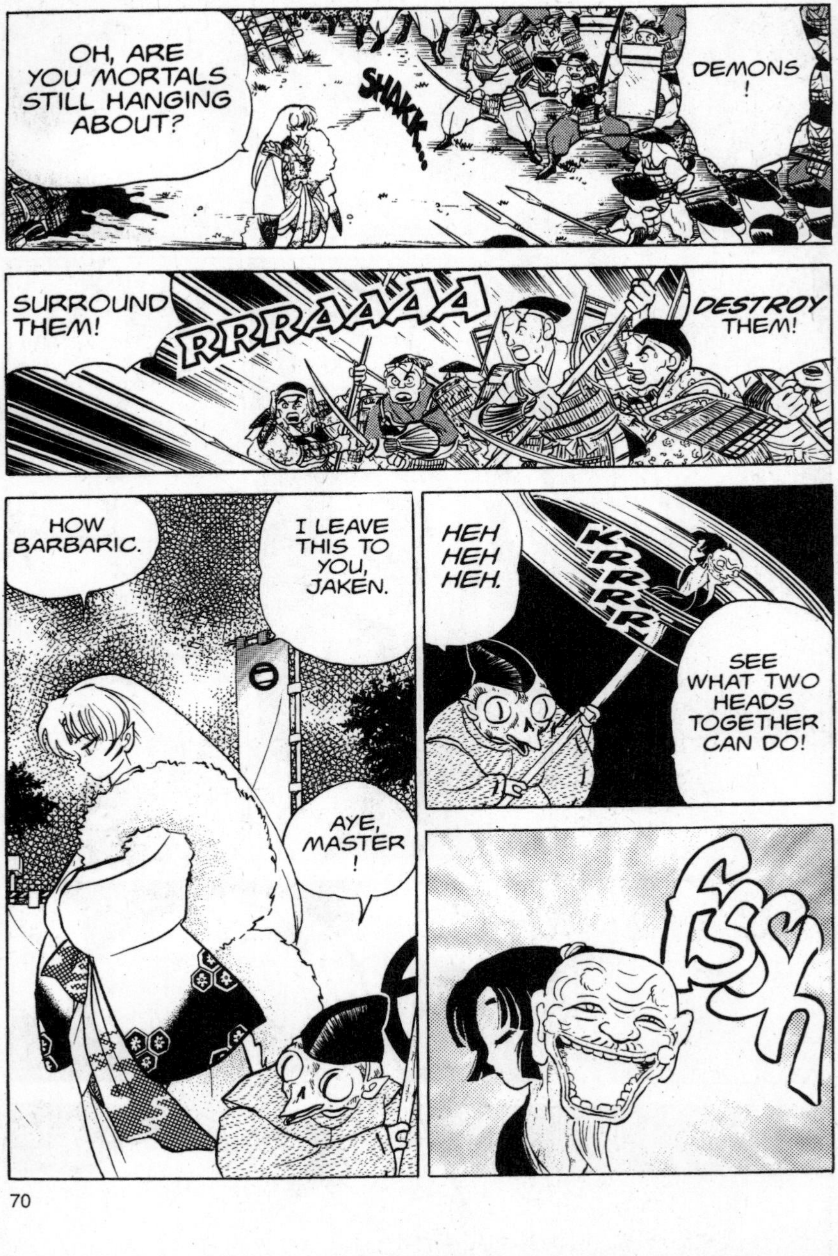
OH, ARE YOU MORTALS STILL HANGING ABOUT?
SHAKK...
DEMONS!
SURROUND THEM!
RRRAAAAA
DESTROY THEM!
HOW BARBARIC.
I LEAVE THIS TO YOU, JAKEN.
AYE, MASTER!
HEH HEH HEH.
KRRRRR
SEE WHAT TWO HEADS TOGETHER CAN DO!
fssh

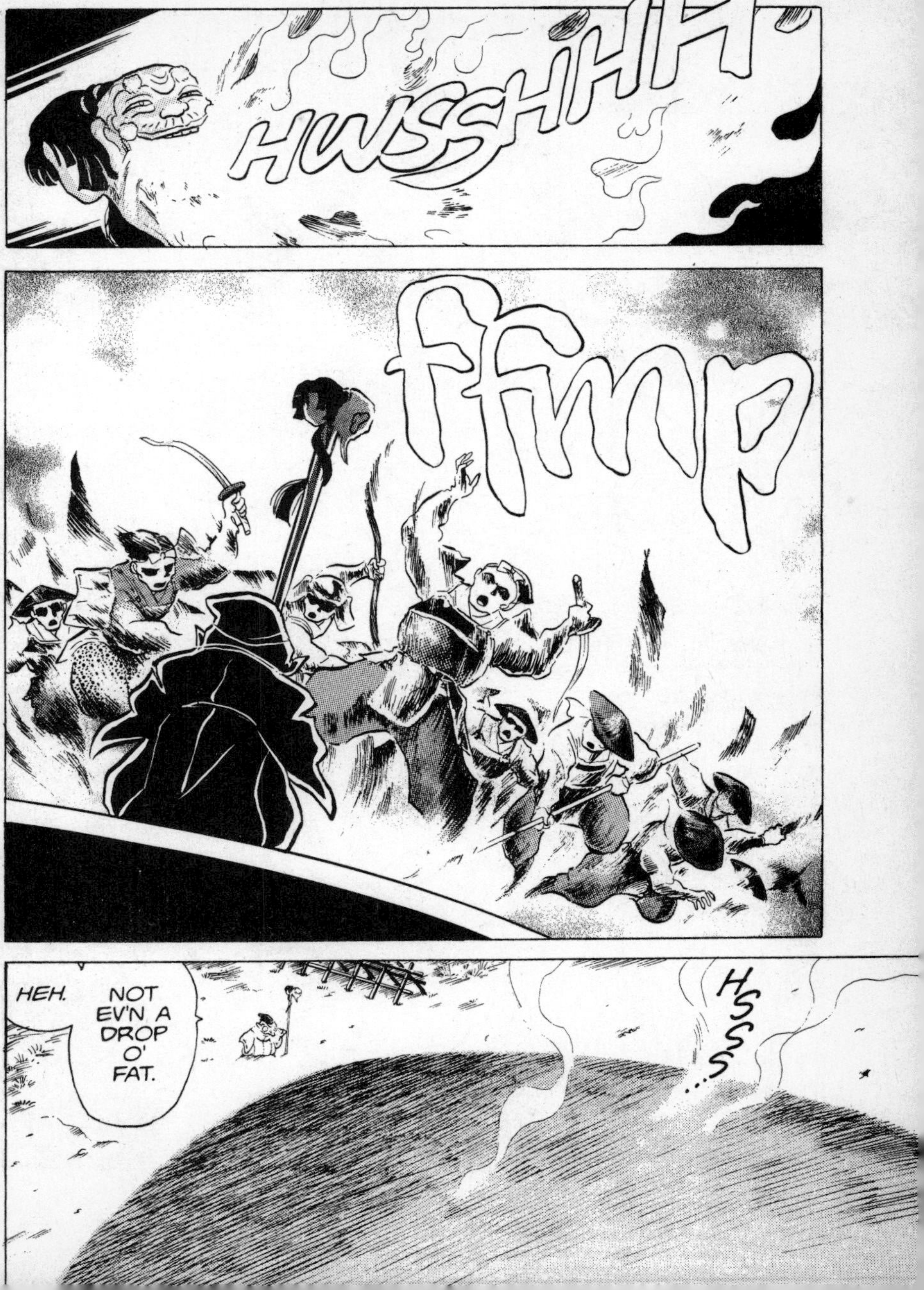
HWSSHHH
ffmp
HEH.
NOT EV'N A DROP O' FAT.
HSSS...

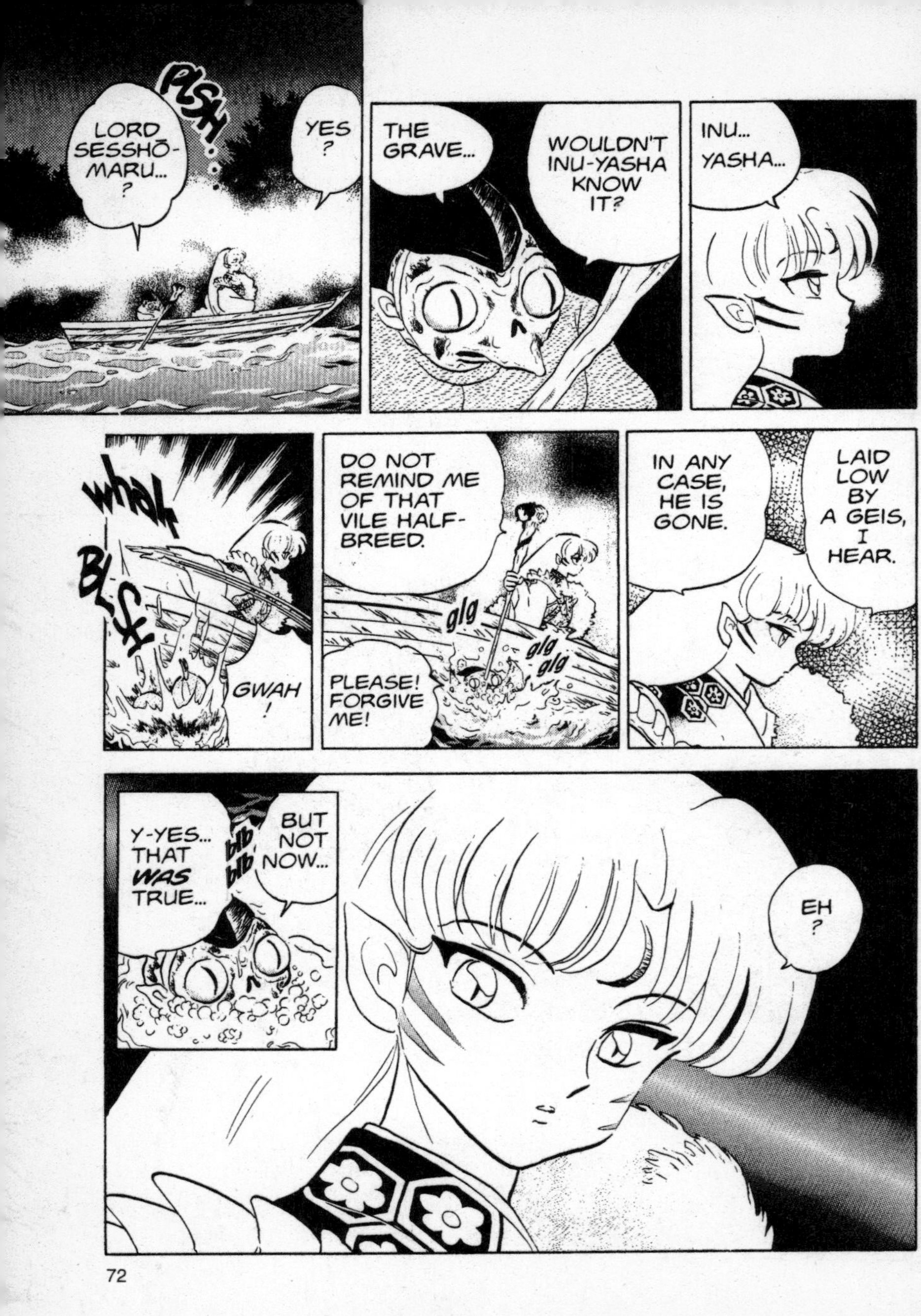
LORD SESSHŌ-MARU...?
PLSH...
YES?
THE GRAVE...
WOULDN'T INU-YASHA KNOW IT?
INU... YASHA...
whak
BL-FT
GWAH!
DO NOT REMIND ME OF THAT VILE HALF-BREED.
glg
PLEASE! FORGIVE ME!
glg glg
IN ANY CASE, HE IS GONE.
LAID LOW BY A GEIS, I HEAR.
Y-YES... THAT WAS TRUE...
blb blb
BUT NOT NOW...
EH?

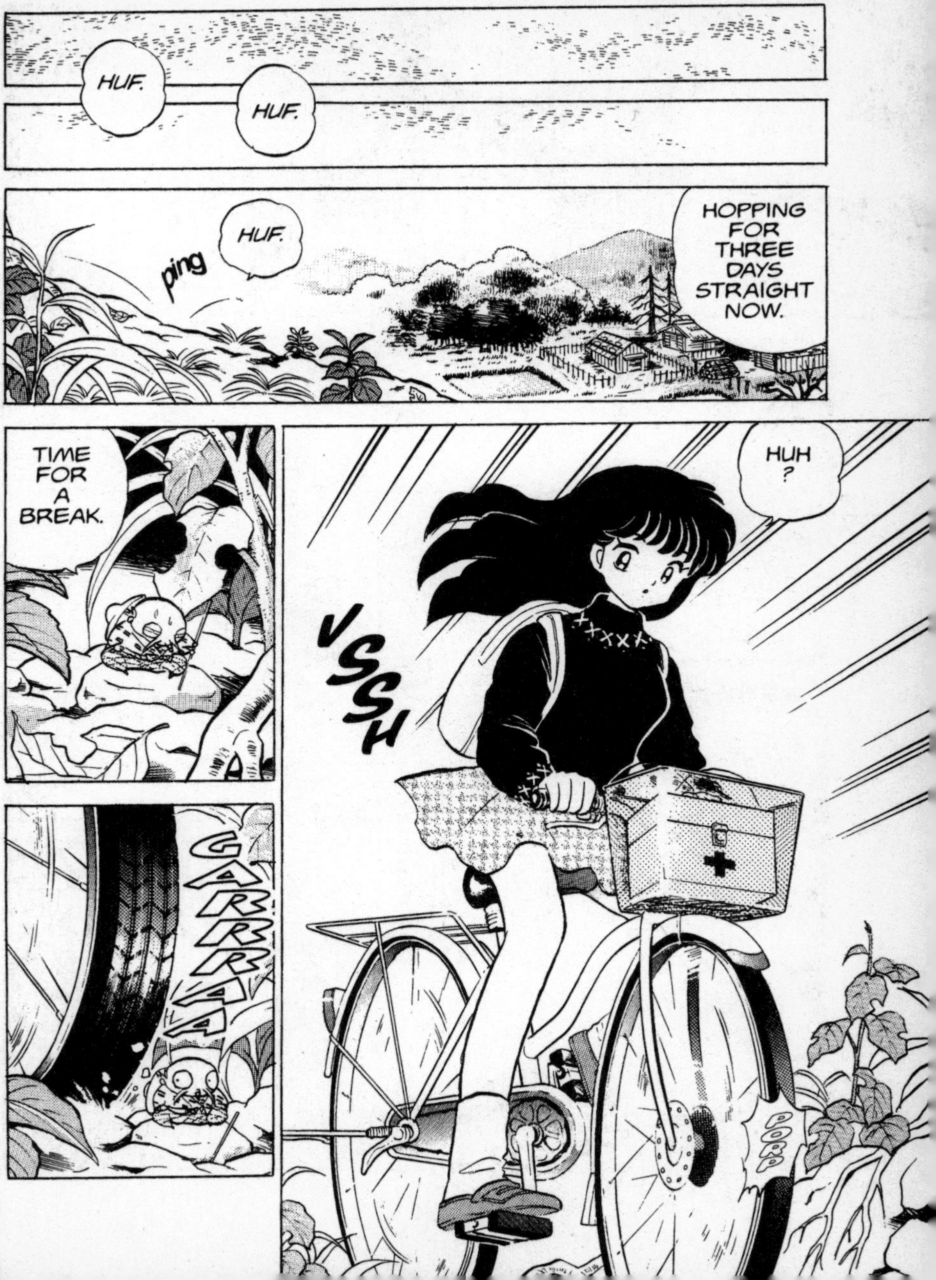
HUF.
HUF.
ping
HUF.
HOPPING FOR THREE DAYS STRAIGHT NOW.
TIME FOR A BREAK.
GARRRAAA
HUH?
VSSH
PORP

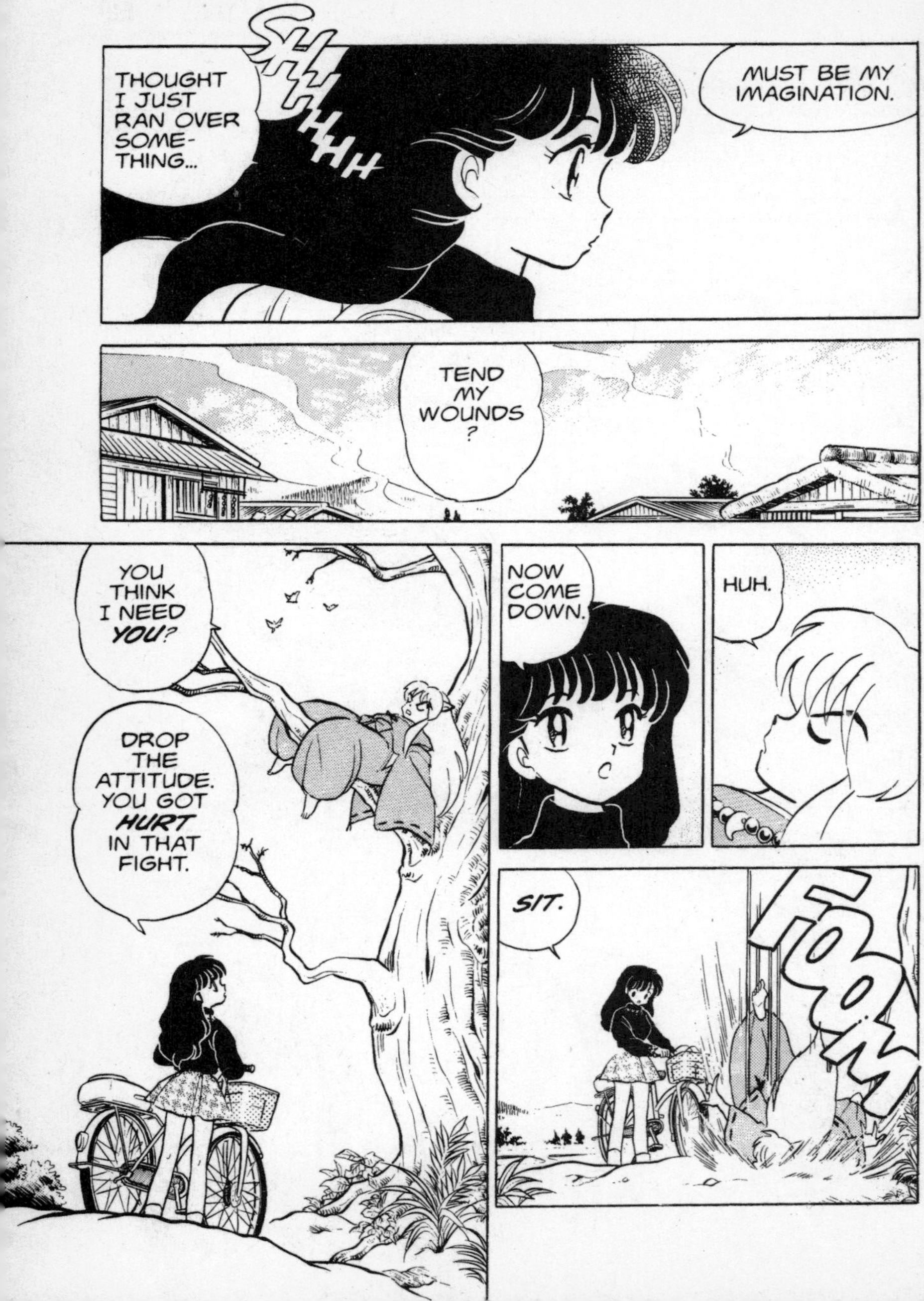
SHHHHH
THOUGHT I JUST RAN OVER SOME-THING...
MUST BE MY IMAGINATION.
TEND MY WOUNDS?
YOU THINK I NEED YOU?
DROP THE ATTITUDE. YOU GOT HURT IN THAT FIGHT.
NOW COME DOWN.
HUH.
SIT.
FOOM

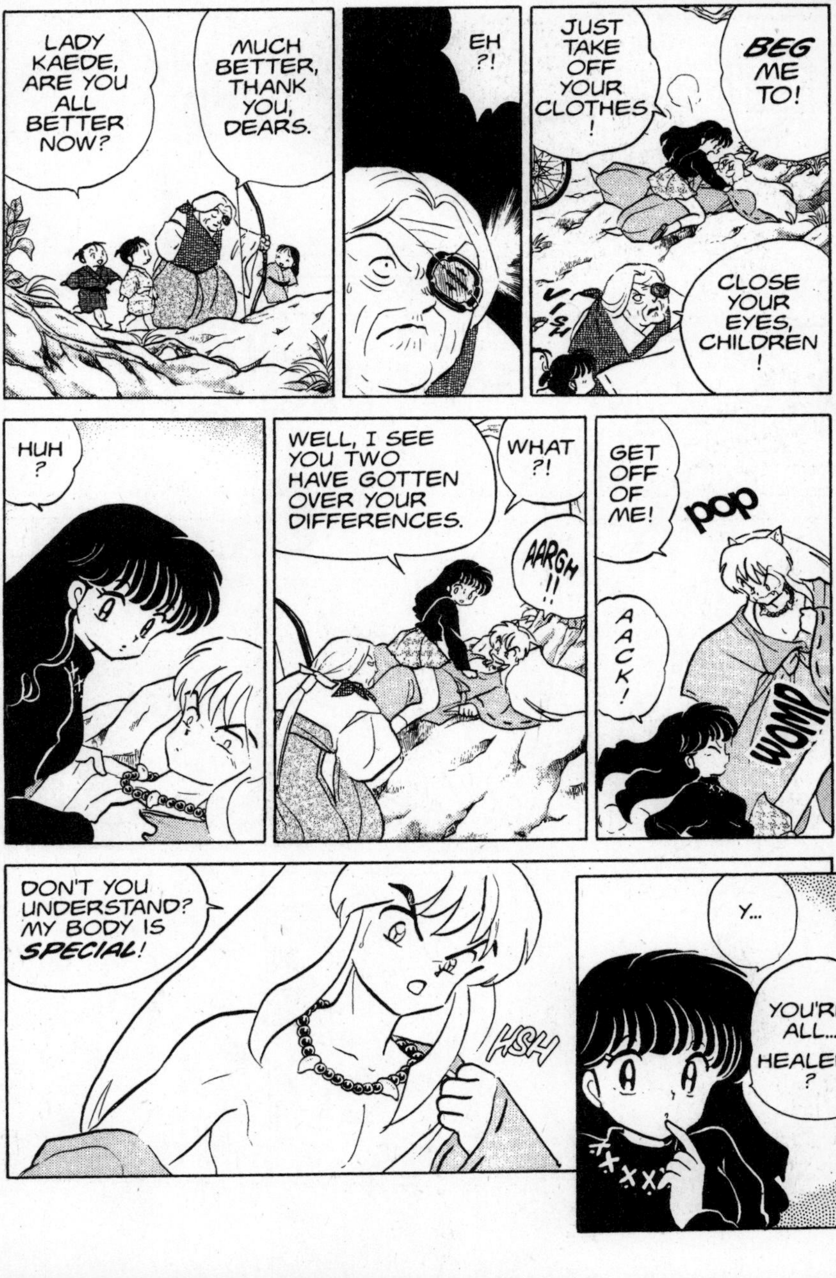
LADY KAEDE, ARE YOU ALL BETTER NOW?
MUCH BETTER, THANK YOU, DEARS.
EH ?!
JUST TAKE OFF YOUR CLOTHES!
BEG ME TO!
CLOSE YOUR EYES, CHILDREN!
HUH ?
WELL, I SEE YOU TWO HAVE GOTTEN OVER YOUR DIFFERENCES.
WHAT ?!
AARGH !!
GET OFF OF ME!
POP
AACK!
WOMP
DON'T YOU UNDERSTAND? MY BODY IS **SPECIAL**!
HSH
Y...
YOU'RE ALL... HEALED... ?

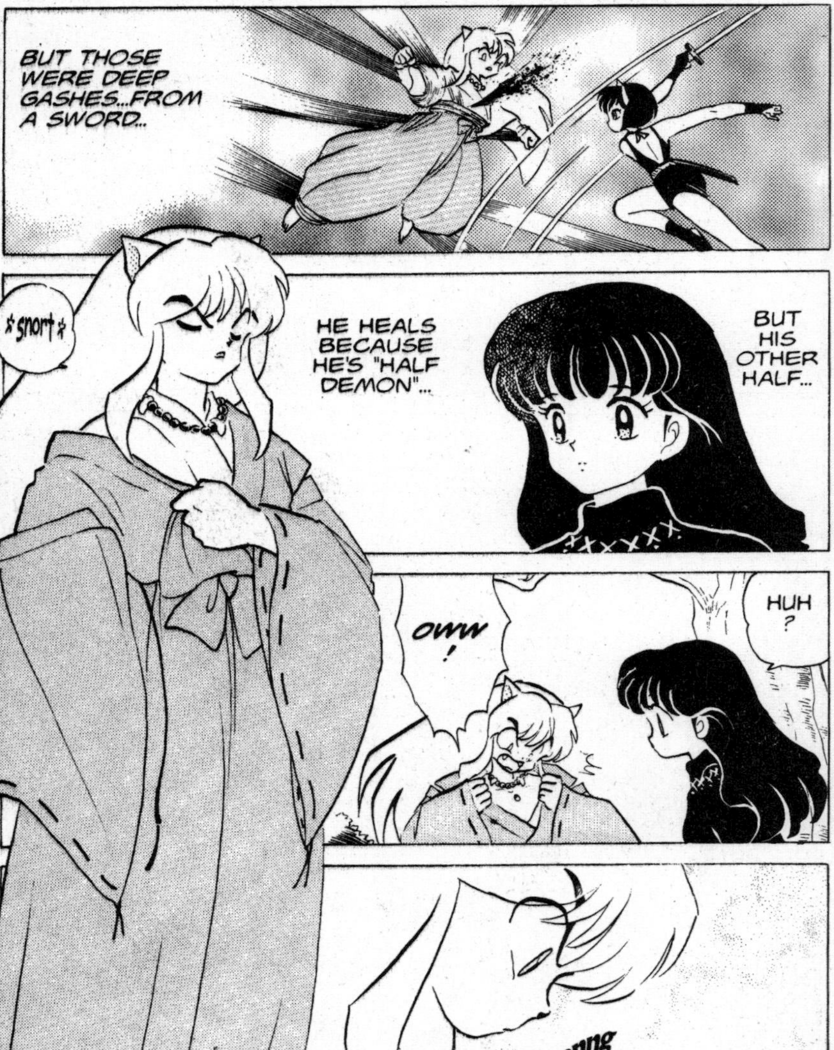
BUT THOSE WERE DEEP GASHES...FROM A SWORD...
snort
HE HEALS BECAUSE HE'S "HALF DEMON"...
BUT HIS OTHER HALF...
OWW!
HUH?
pwonng
SUCK SUCK SUCK

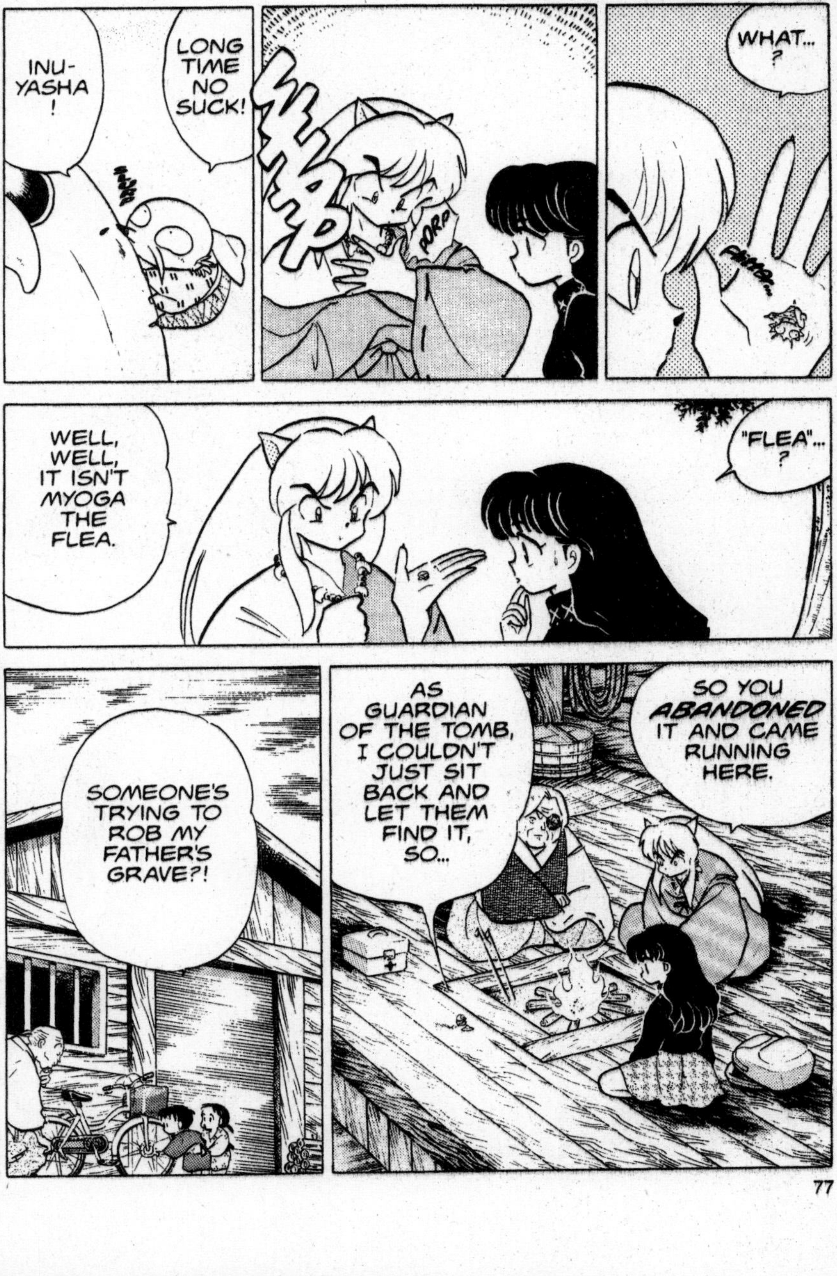
INU-YASHA!
LONG TIME NO SUCK!
SMAP
PORP
WHAT...?
WELL, WELL, IT ISN'T MYOGA THE FLEA.
"FLEA"...?
SOMEONE'S TRYING TO ROB MY FATHER'S GRAVE?!
AS GUARDIAN OF THE TOMB, I COULDN'T JUST SIT BACK AND LET THEM FIND IT, SO...
SO YOU *ABANDONED* IT AND CAME RUNNING HERE.

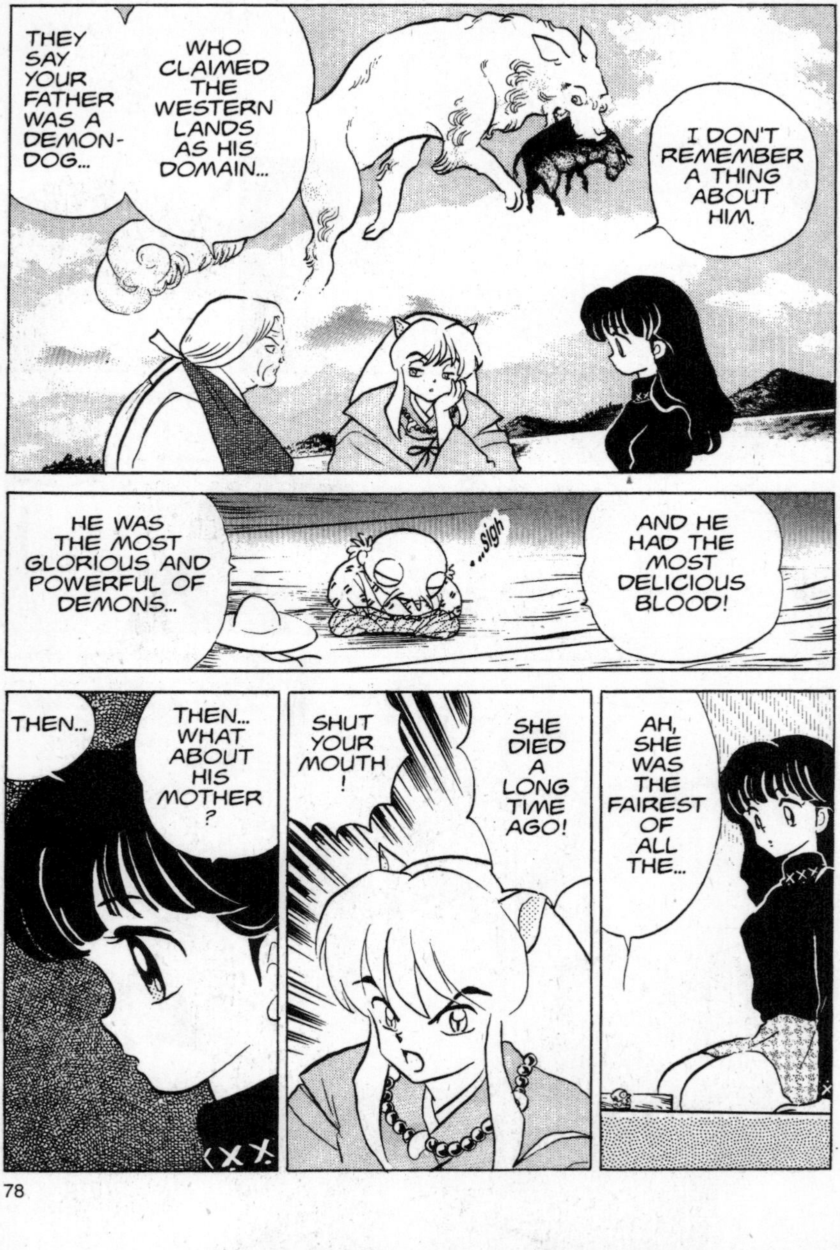
THEY SAY YOUR FATHER WAS A DEMON-DOG...
WHO CLAIMED THE WESTERN LANDS AS HIS DOMAIN...
I DON'T REMEMBER A THING ABOUT HIM.
HE WAS THE MOST GLORIOUS AND POWERFUL OF DEMONS...
...sigh
AND HE HAD THE MOST DELICIOUS BLOOD!
THEN...
THEN... WHAT ABOUT HIS MOTHER?
SHUT YOUR MOUTH!
SHE DIED A LONG TIME AGO!
AH, SHE WAS THE FAIREST OF ALL THE...

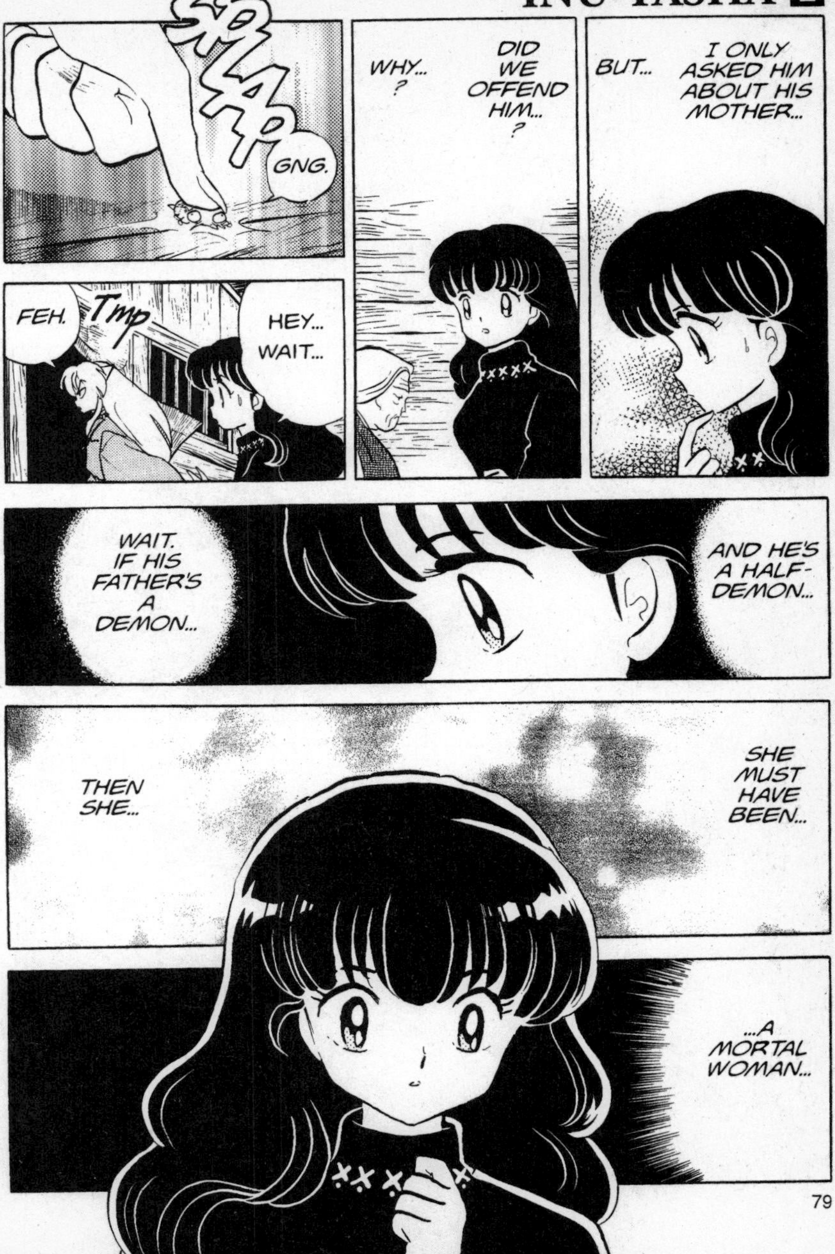
SPLAP
GNG.
FEH.
Tmp
HEY... WAIT...
WHY... ?
DID WE OFFEND HIM... ?
BUT...
I ONLY ASKED HIM ABOUT HIS MOTHER...
WAIT. IF HIS FATHER'S A DEMON...
AND HE'S A HALF-DEMON...
THEN SHE...
SHE MUST HAVE BEEN...
...A MORTAL WOMAN...

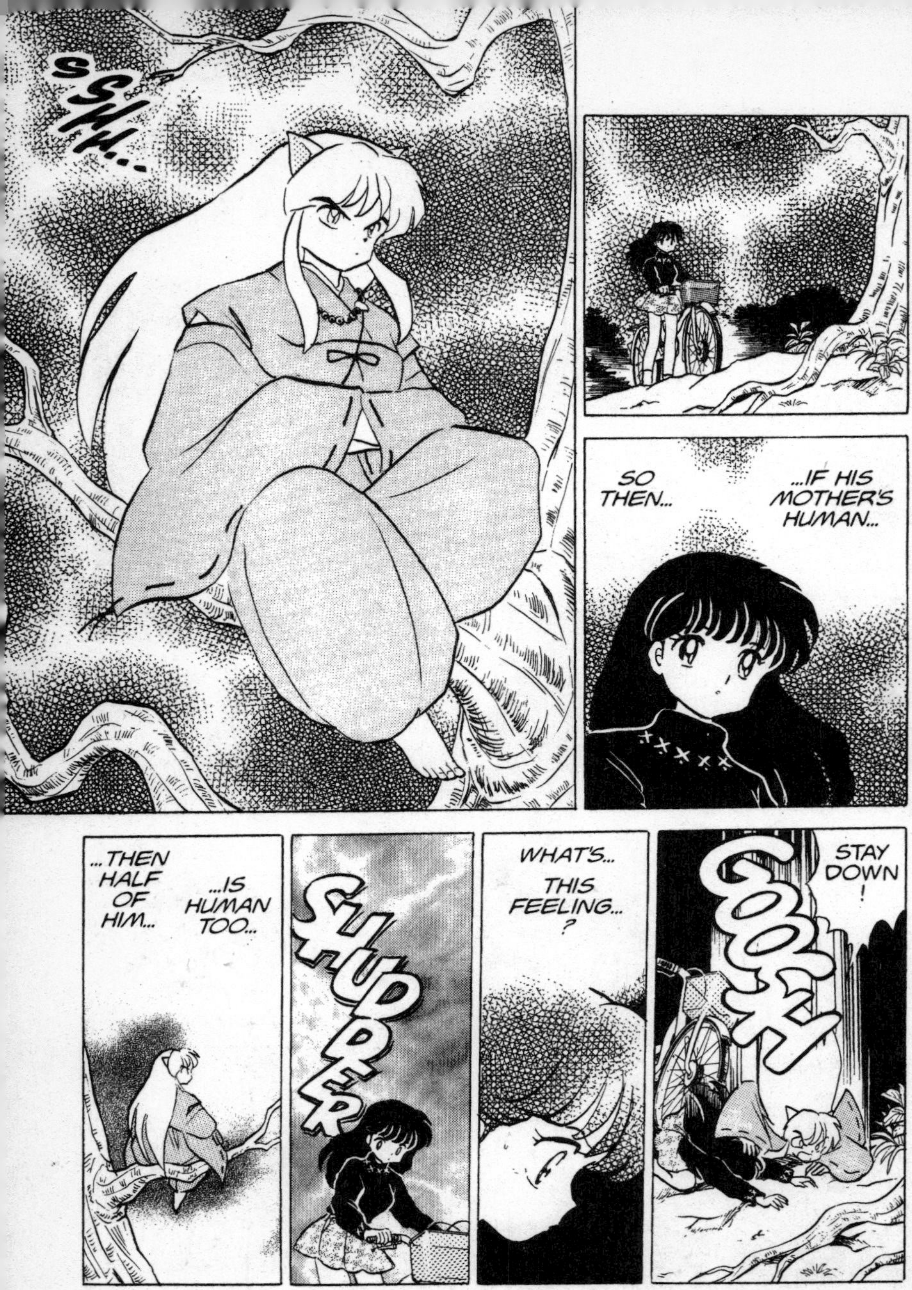
SSHH...
SO THEN...
...IF HIS MOTHER'S HUMAN...
...THEN HALF OF HIM...
...IS HUMAN TOO...
SHUDDER
WHAT'S...
THIS FEELING...?
GOOSH
STAY DOWN!

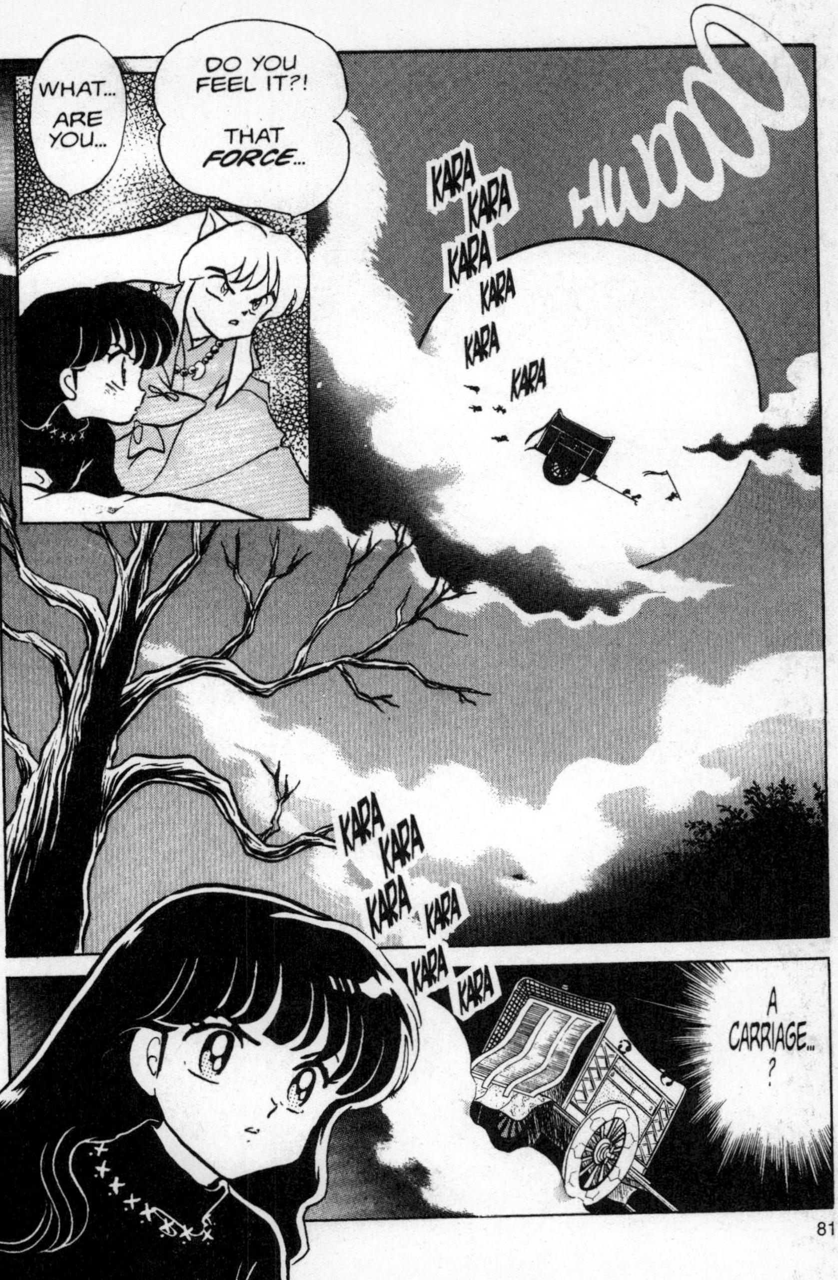
WHAT... ARE YOU...
DO YOU FEEL IT?!
THAT FORCE...
HWOOOO
KARA KARA KARA KARA KARA KARA
KARA KARA KARA KARA KARA KARA
A CARRIAGE...?

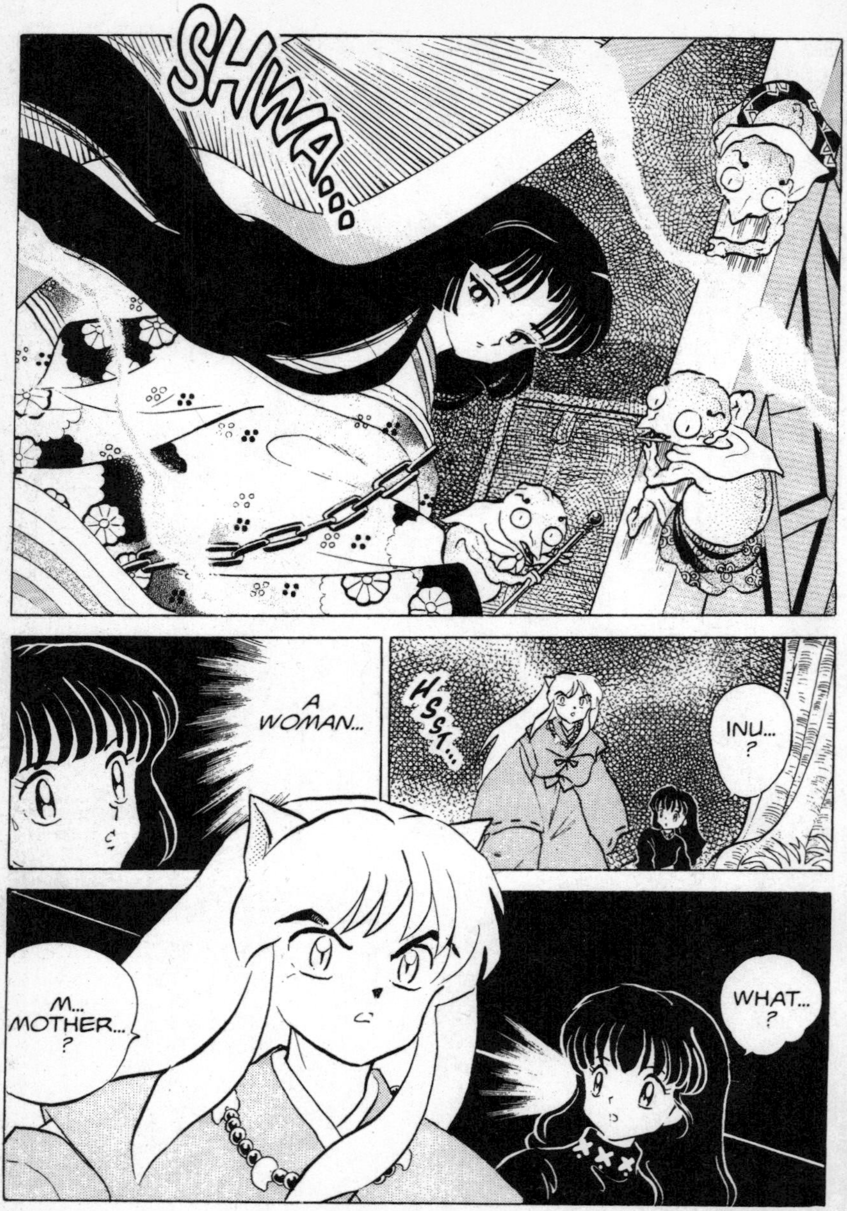
SHWA...
A WOMAN...
HSS1...
INU...?
M... MOTHER...?
WHAT...?

SCROLL FIVE

A MOTHER'S FACE

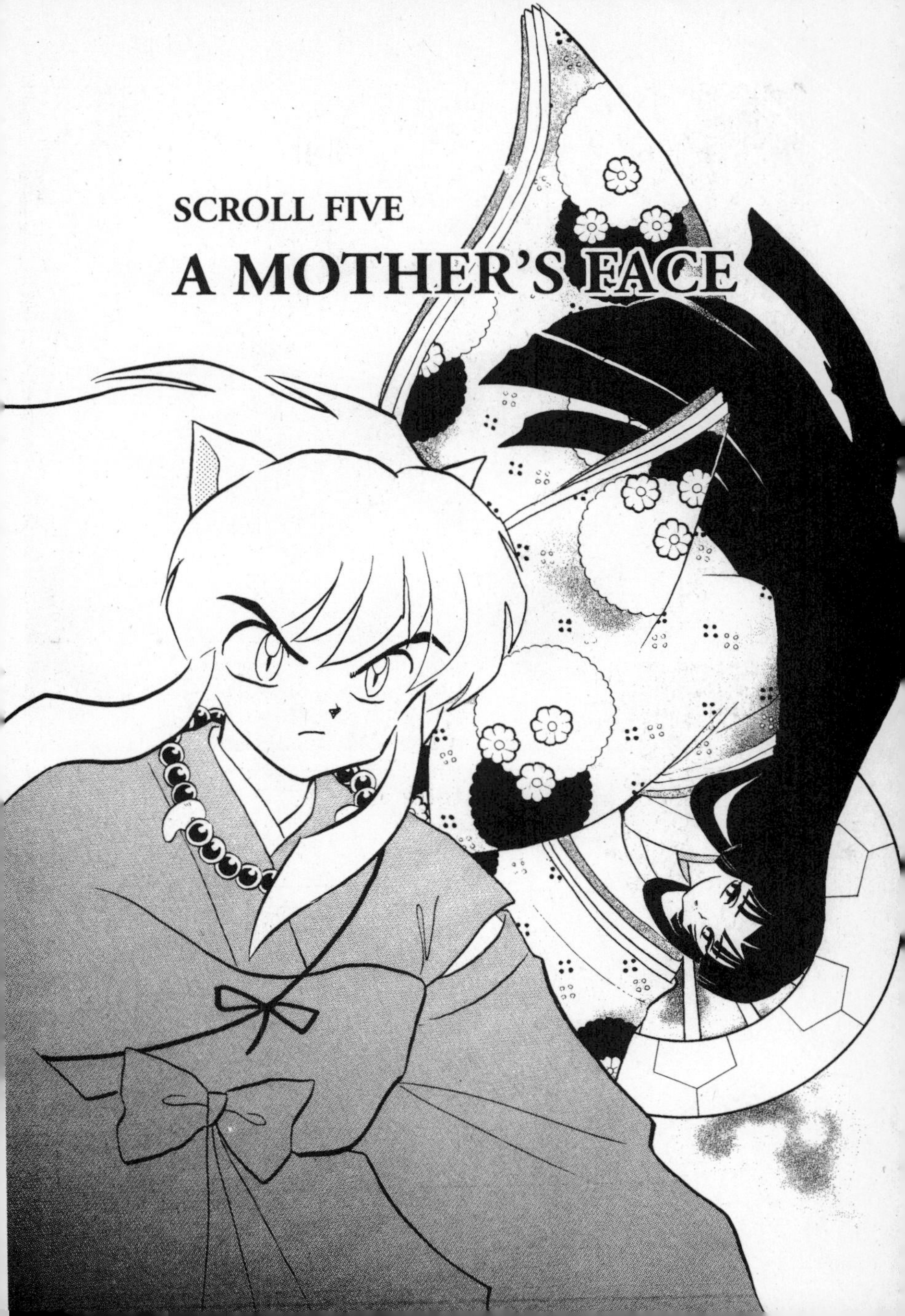

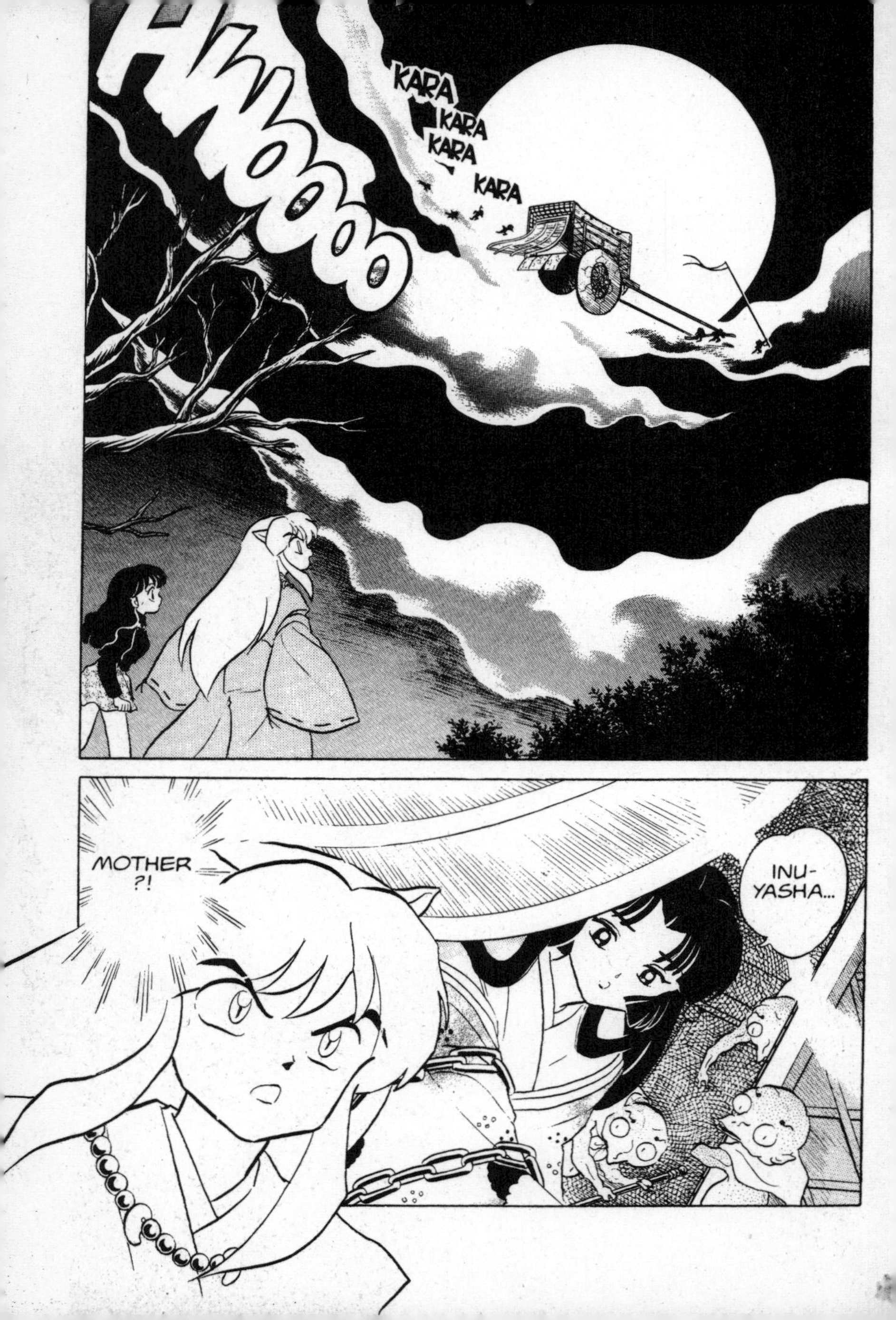
HWOOOO
KARA
KARA
KARA
KARA
MOTHER ?!
INU-YASHA...

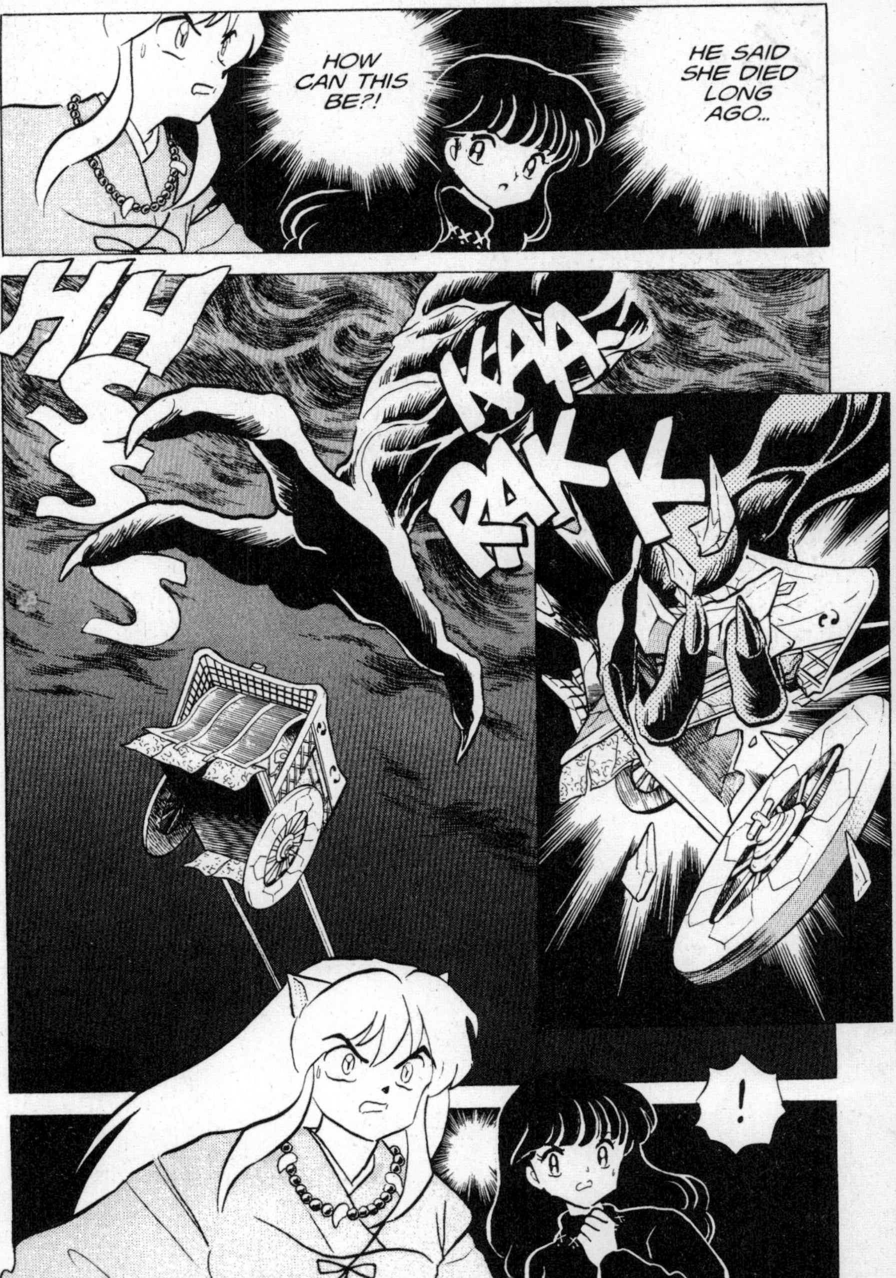
HOW CAN THIS BE?!
HE SAID SHE DIED LONG AGO...
HHSS
KAA-RAKK
!

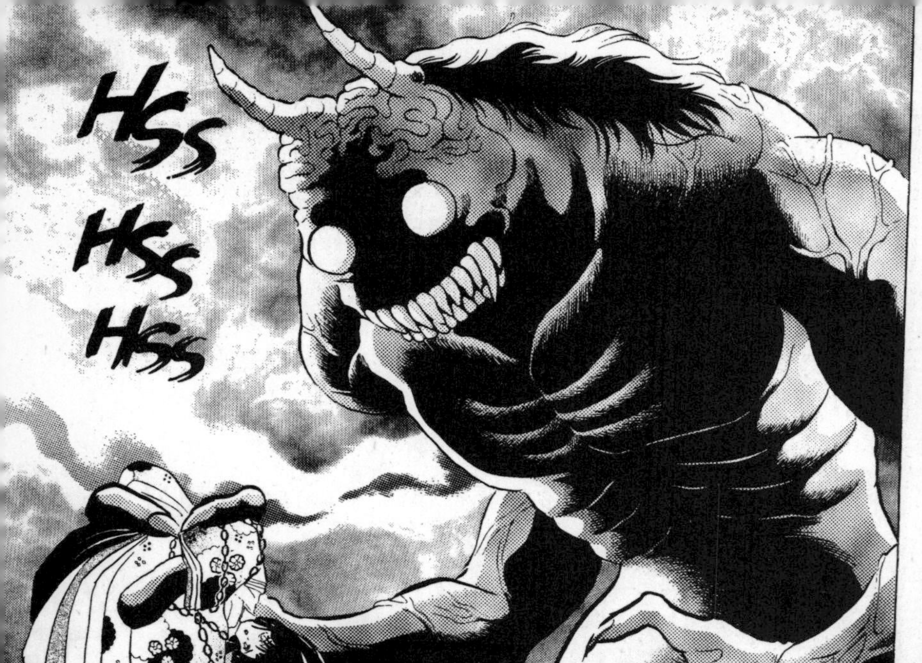
HSS
HSS
HSS
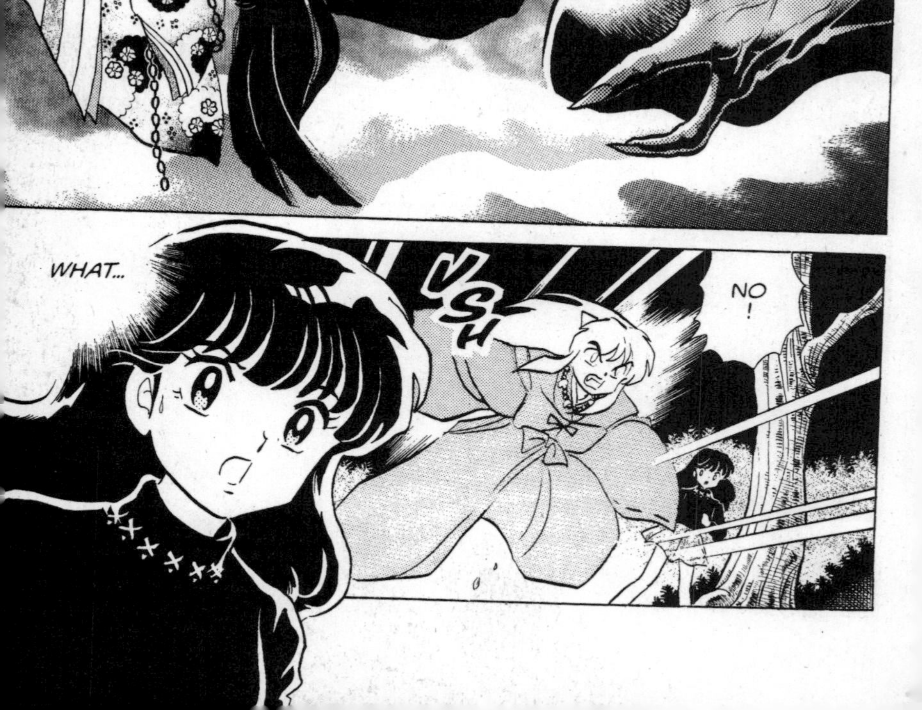
WHAT...
VSH
NO!

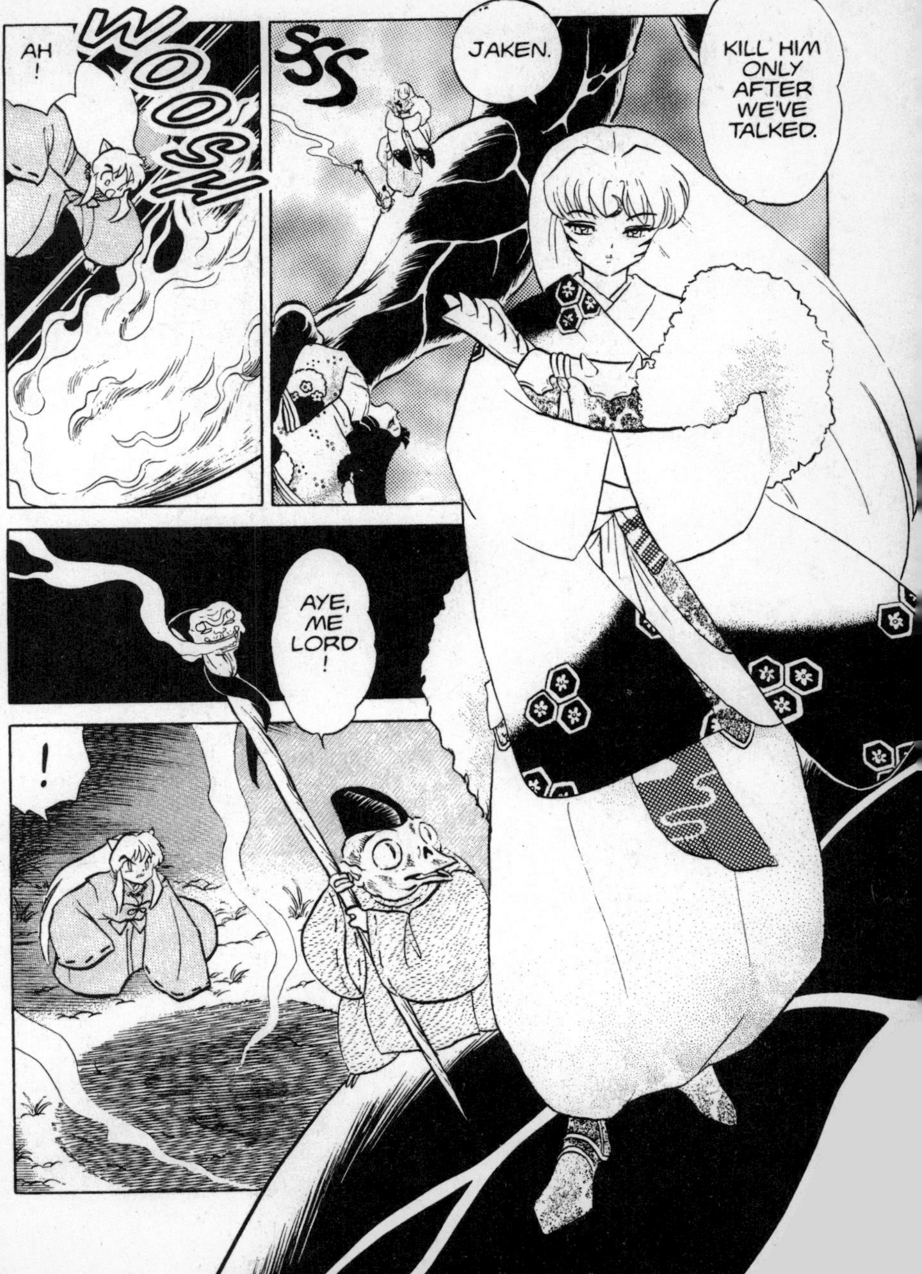
AH!
WOOSH
SSS
JAKEN.
KILL HIM ONLY AFTER WE'VE TALKED.
AYE, ME LORD!
!

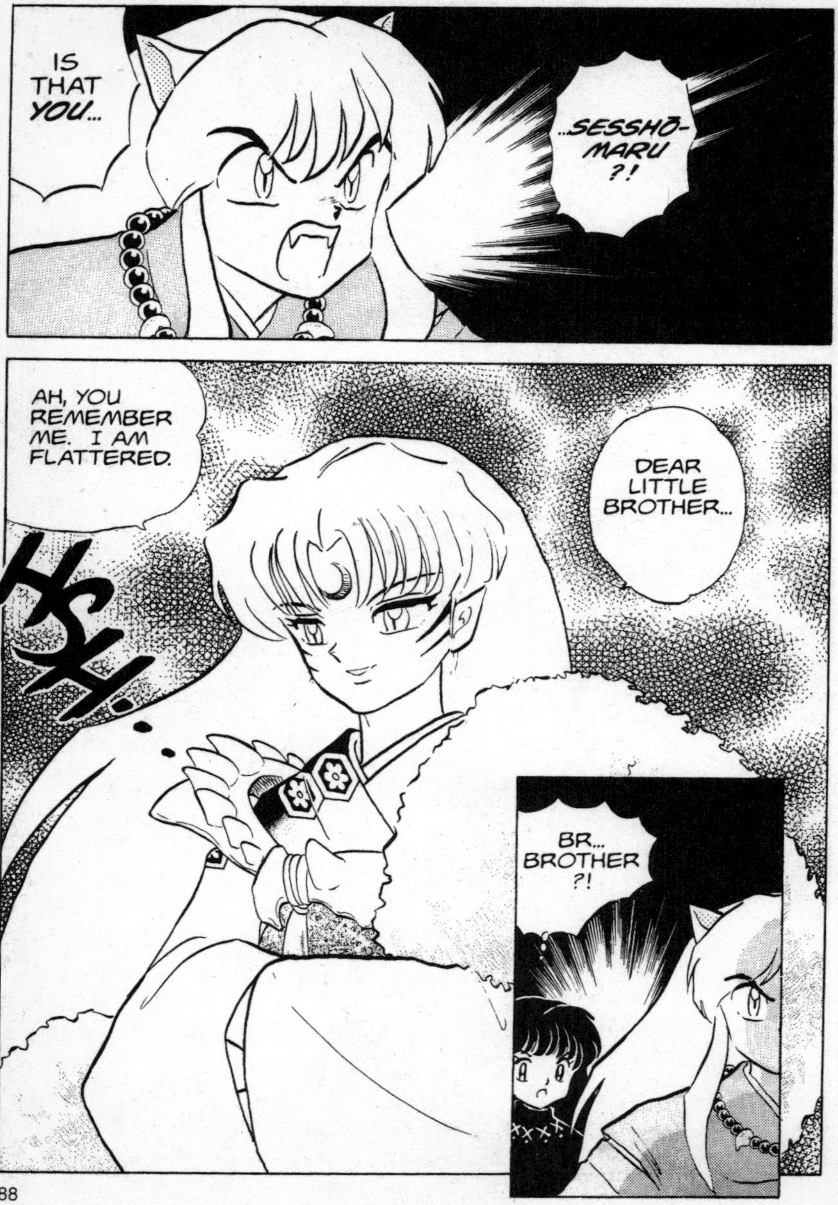
IS THAT YOU...
...SESSHŌ-MARU ?!
AH, YOU REMEMBER ME. I AM FLATTERED.
HSH!
DEAR LITTLE BROTHER...
BR... BROTHER ?!

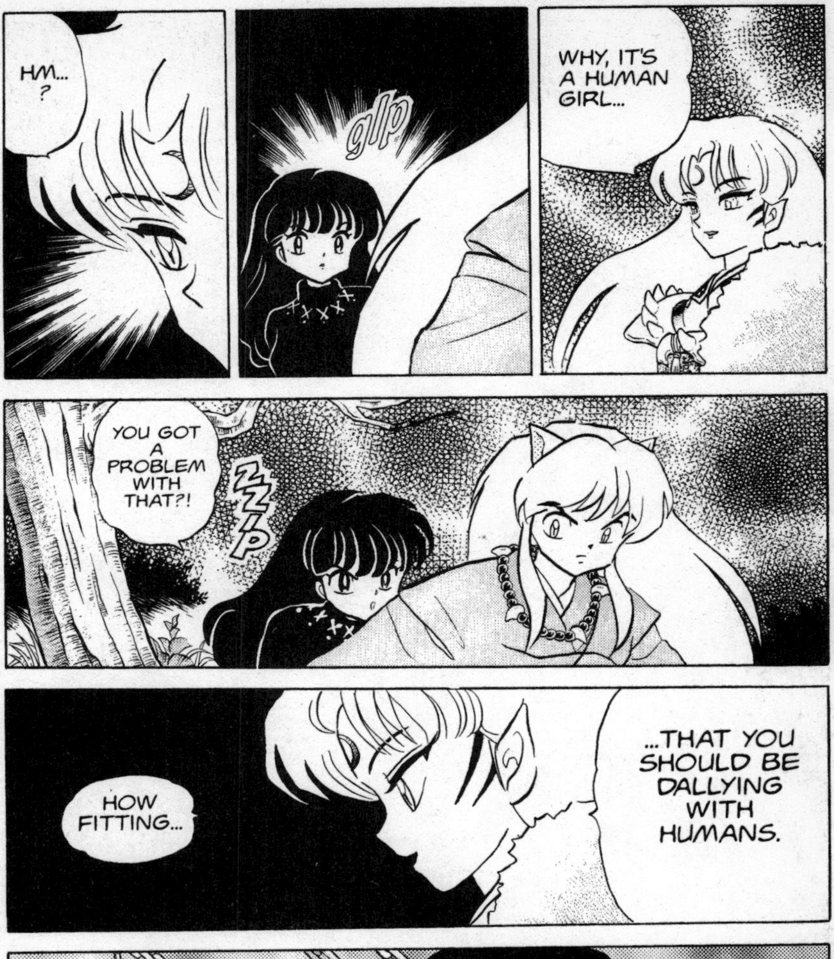
HM... ?
glp
WHY, IT'S A HUMAN GIRL...
YOU GOT A PROBLEM WITH THAT?!
ZZIP
HOW FITTING...
...THAT YOU SHOULD BE DALLYING WITH HUMANS.
gwi

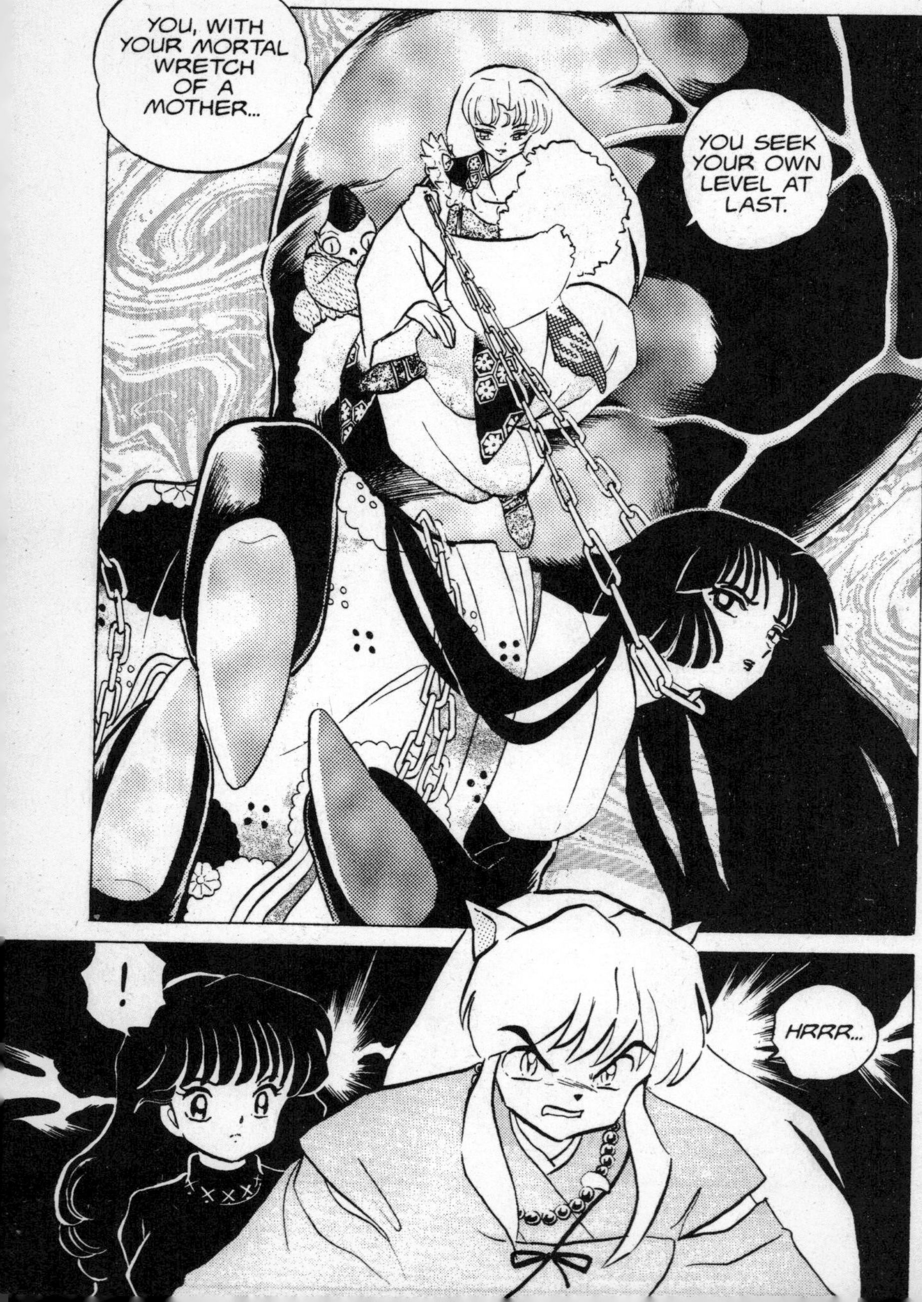
YOU, WITH YOUR MORTAL WRETCH OF A MOTHER...
YOU SEEK YOUR OWN LEVEL AT LAST.
!
HRRR...

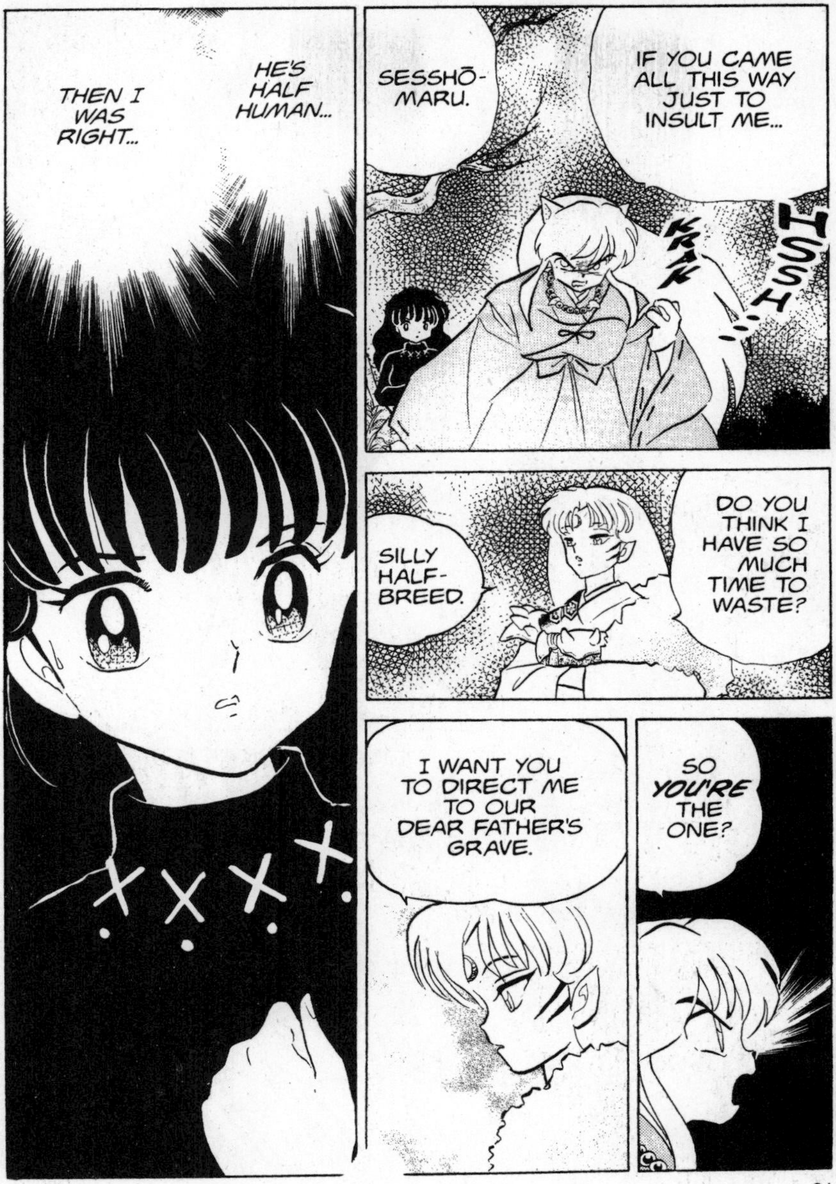
THEN I WAS RIGHT...
HE'S HALF HUMAN...
SESSHŌ-MARU.
IF YOU CAME ALL THIS WAY JUST TO INSULT ME...
KRAK
HSSH...
SILLY HALF-BREED.
DO YOU THINK I HAVE SO MUCH TIME TO WASTE?
I WANT YOU TO DIRECT ME TO OUR DEAR FATHER'S GRAVE.
SO *YOU'RE* THE ONE?

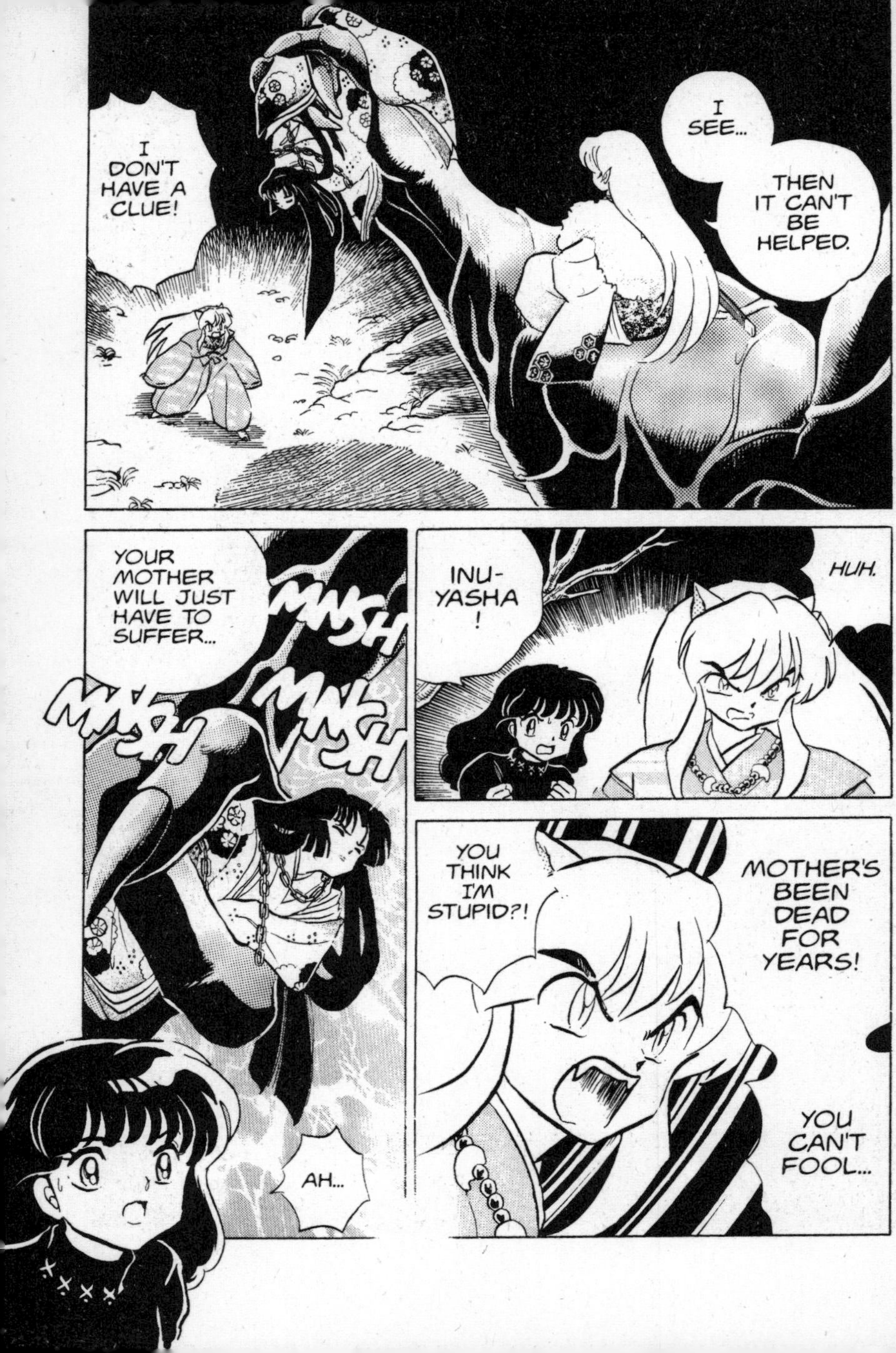
I DON'T HAVE A CLUE!
I SEE...
THEN IT CAN'T BE HELPED.
YOUR MOTHER WILL JUST HAVE TO SUFFER...
MNSH
MNCH
MNCH
AH...
INU-YASHA!
HUH.
YOU THINK I'M STUPID?!
MOTHER'S BEEN DEAD FOR YEARS!
YOU CAN'T FOOL...

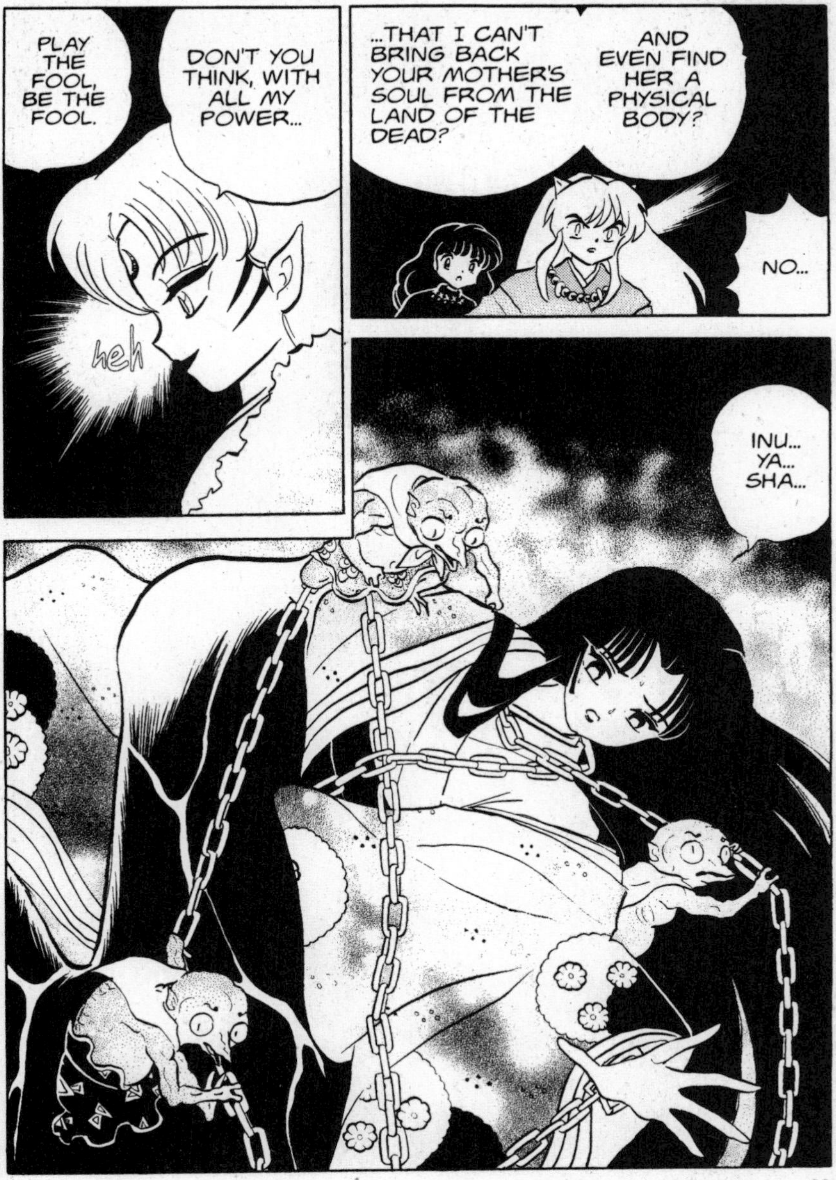
PLAY THE FOOL, BE THE FOOL.
DON'T YOU THINK, WITH ALL MY POWER...
heh
...THAT I CAN'T BRING BACK YOUR MOTHER'S SOUL FROM THE LAND OF THE DEAD?
AND EVEN FIND HER A PHYSICAL BODY?
NO...
INU... YA... SHA...

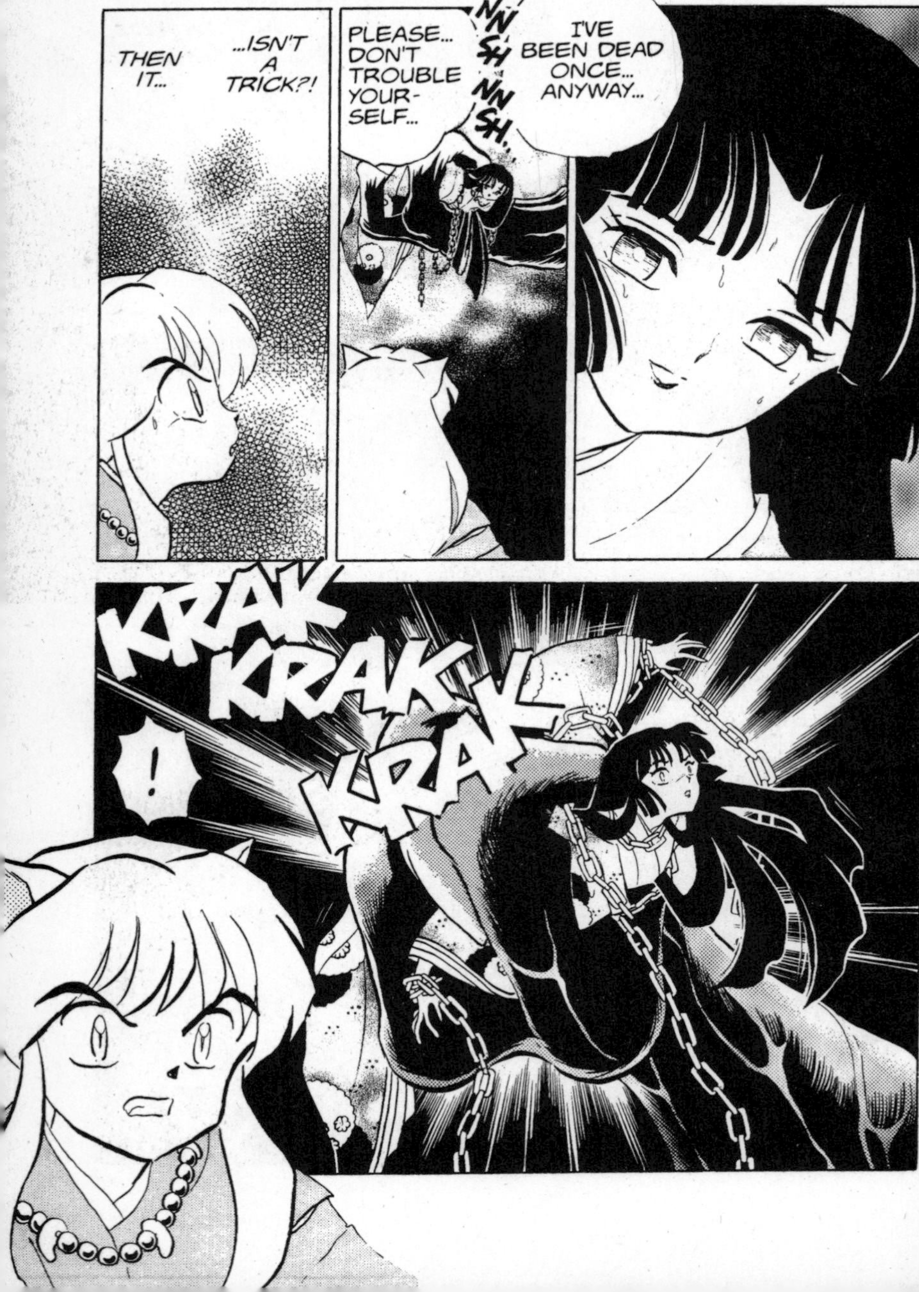
THEN IT...
...ISN'T A TRICK?!
PLEASE... DON'T TROUBLE YOUR-SELF...
NN SH NN SH...
I'VE BEEN DEAD ONCE... ANYWAY...
KRAK KRAK KRAK KRAK
!

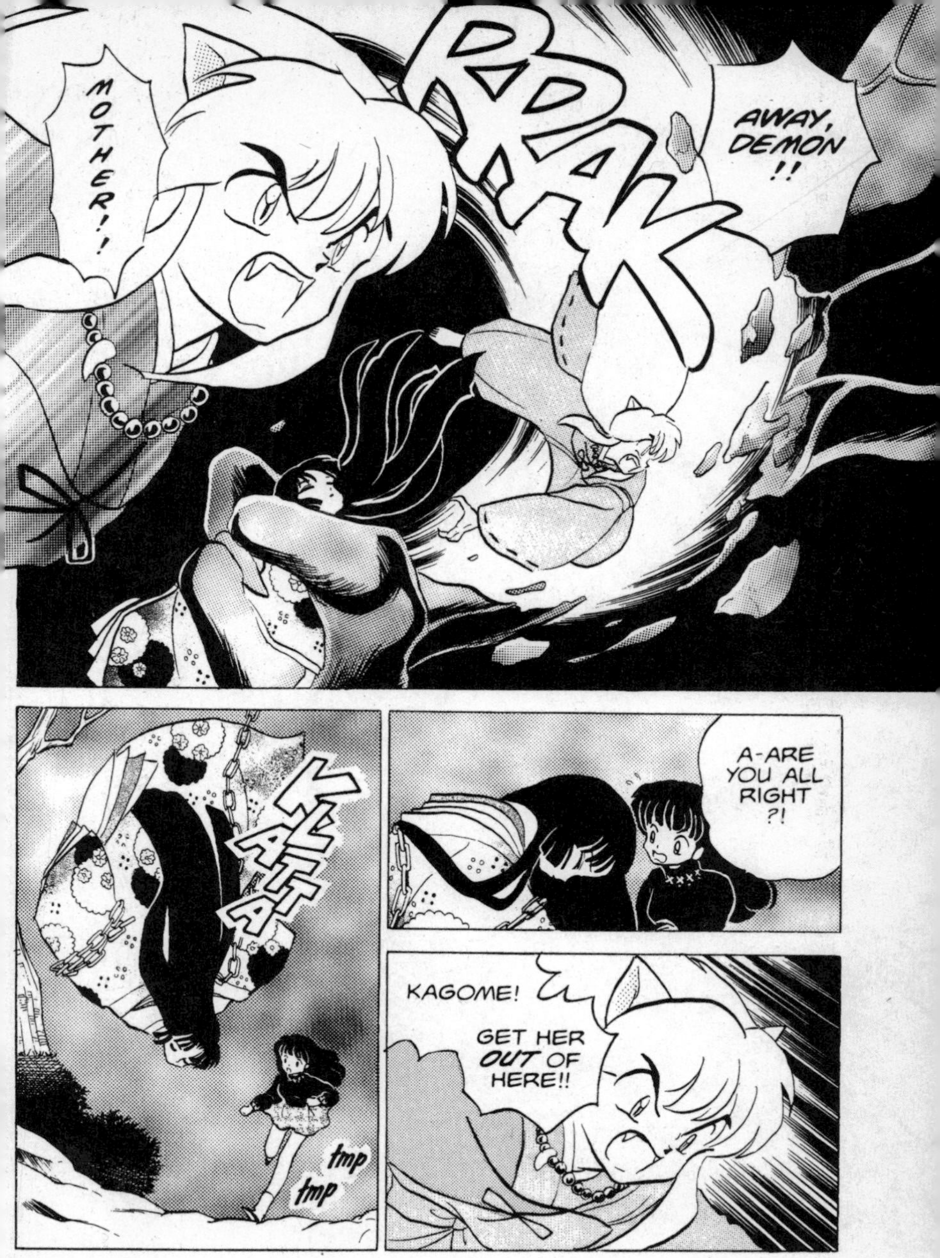
MOTHER!!
AWAY, DEMON!!
tmp
tmp
A-ARE YOU ALL RIGHT?!
KAGOME!
GET HER OUT OF HERE!!

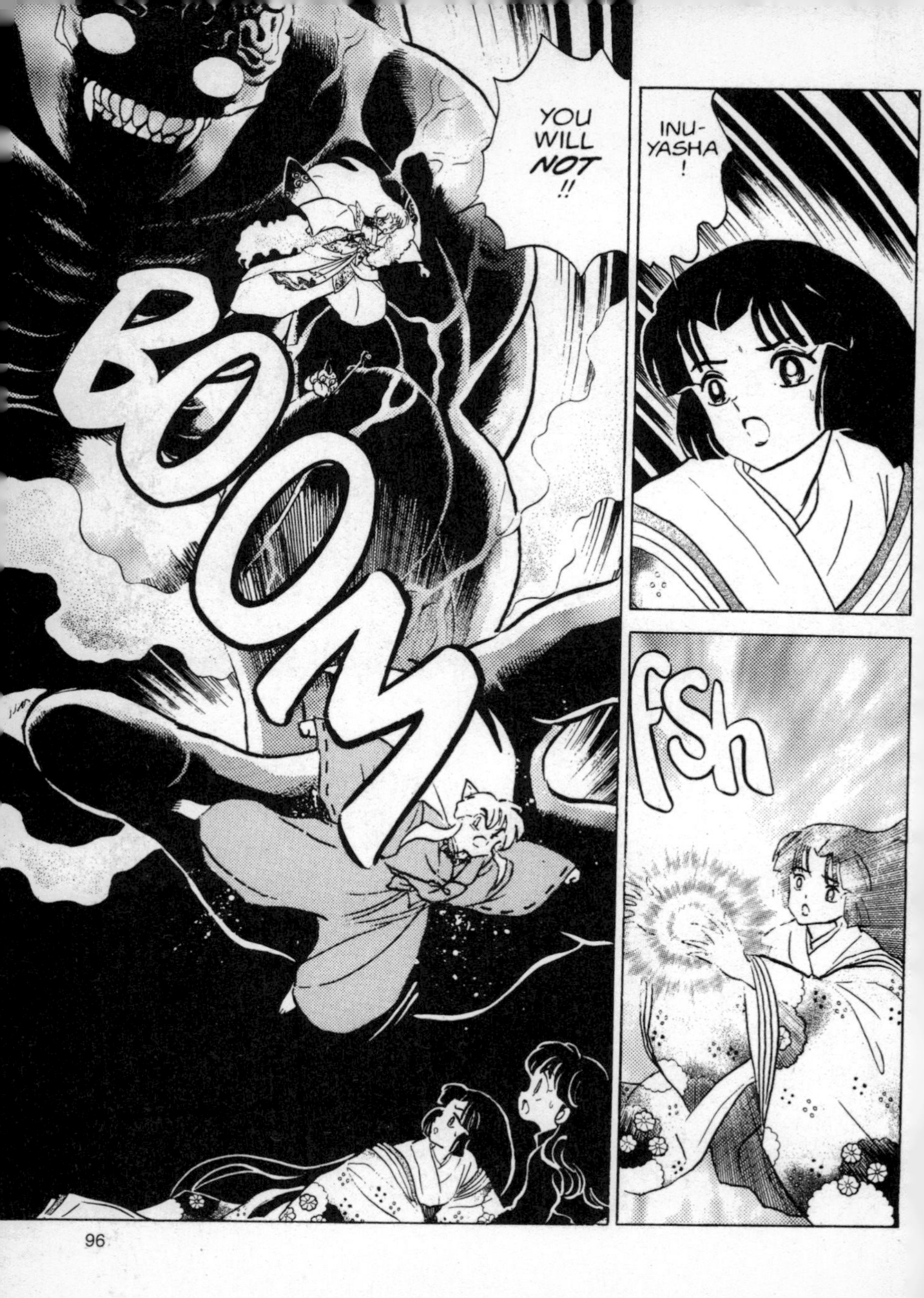
YOU WILL NOT !!
BOOM
INU-YASHA !
fsh

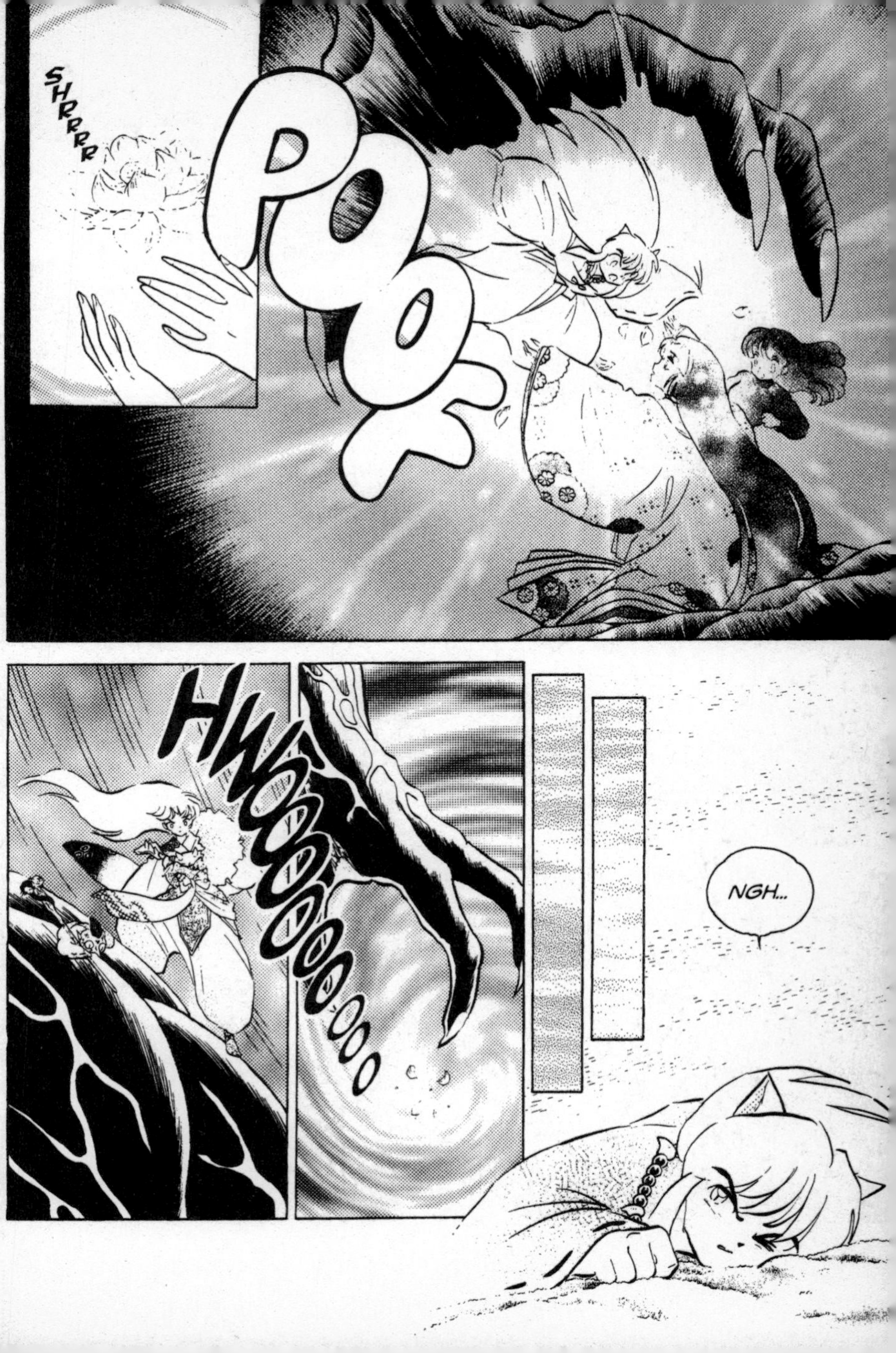
SHRRRR
POOF
HWOOOOOOOO
NGH...

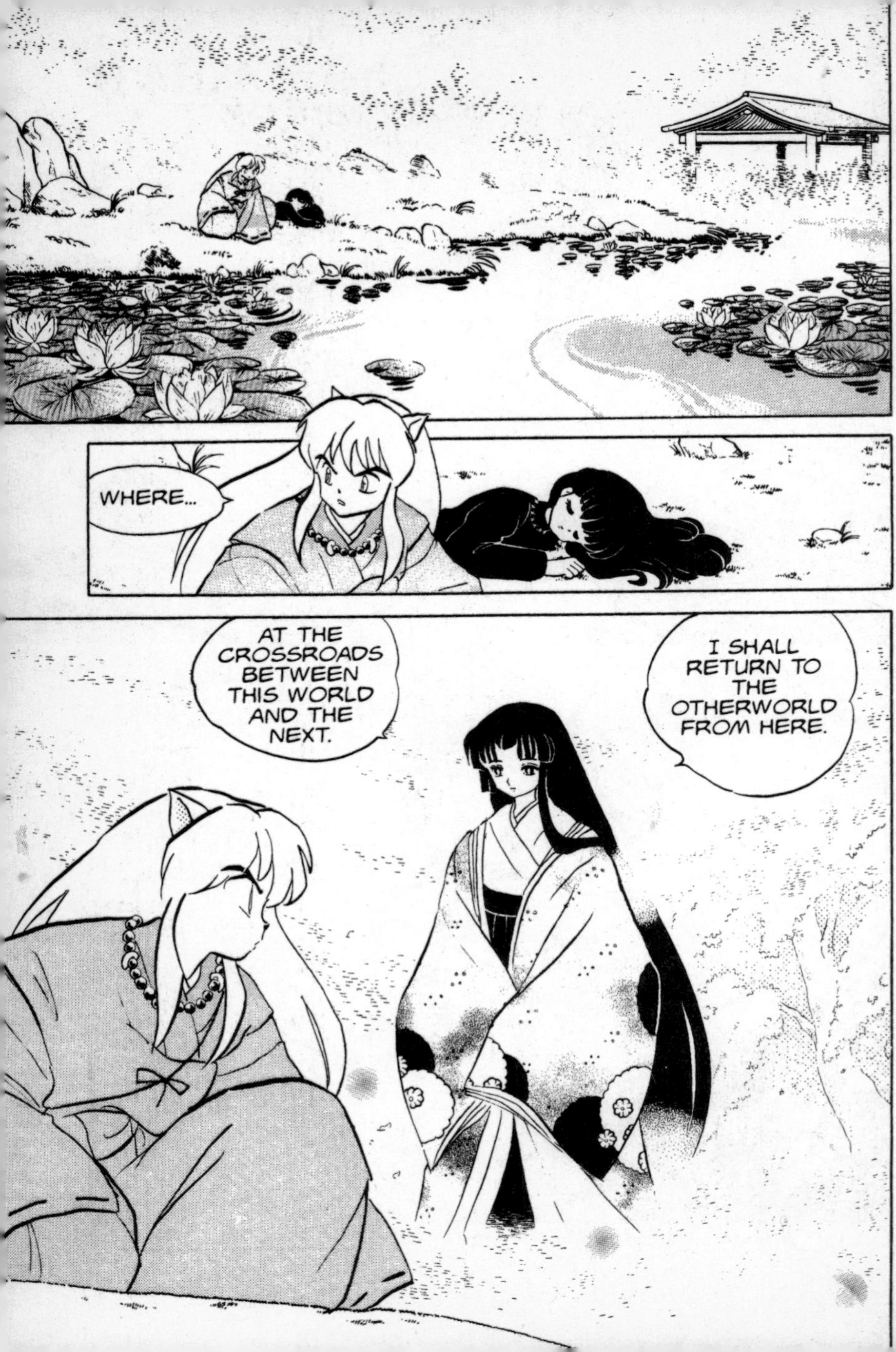
WHERE...
AT THE CROSSROADS BETWEEN THIS WORLD AND THE NEXT.
I SHALL RETURN TO THE OTHERWORLD FROM HERE.

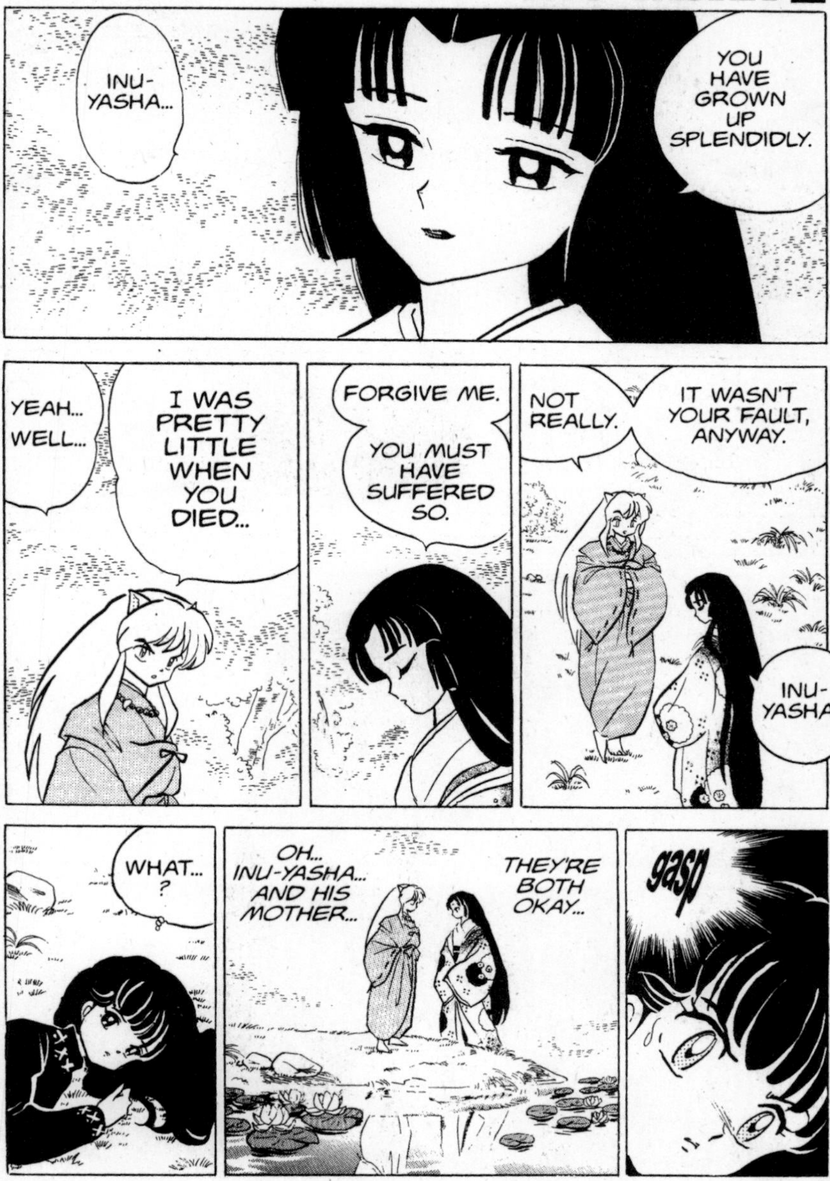
INU-YASHA...
YOU HAVE GROWN UP SPLENDIDLY.
YEAH... WELL...
I WAS PRETTY LITTLE WHEN YOU DIED...
FORGIVE ME.
YOU MUST HAVE SUFFERED SO.
NOT REALLY.
IT WASN'T YOUR FAULT, ANYWAY.
INU-YASHA...
WHAT...?
OH... INU-YASHA... AND HIS MOTHER...
THEY'RE BOTH OKAY...
gasp

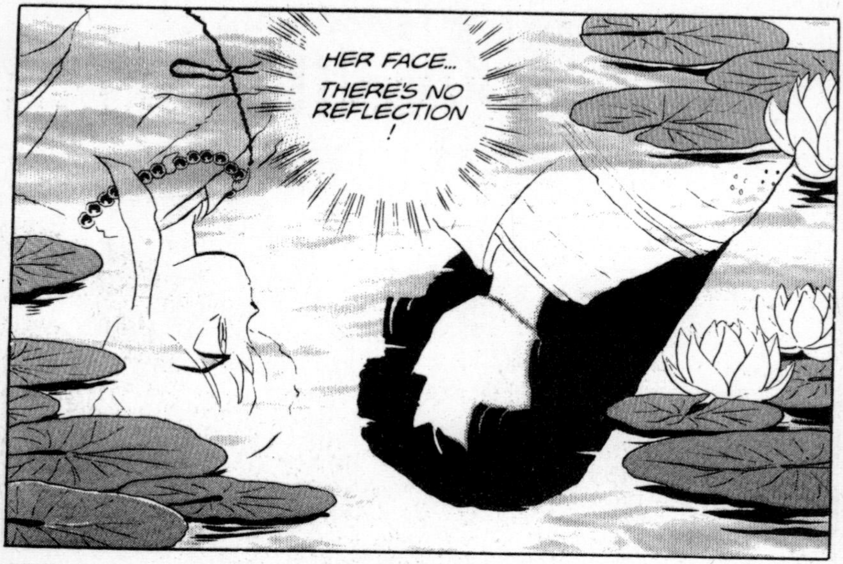
HER FACE...
THERE'S NO REFLECTION
!

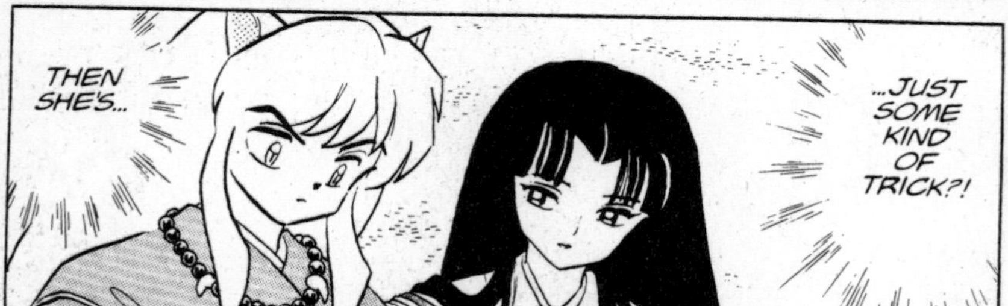
THEN SHE'S...
...JUST SOME KIND OF TRICK?!

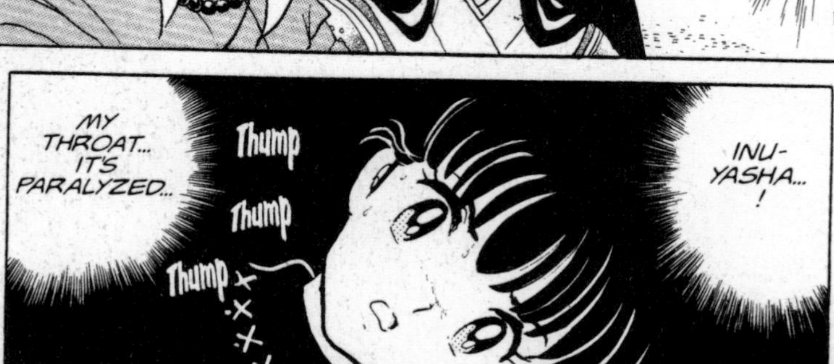
MY THROAT... IT'S PARALYZED...
Thump
Thump
Thump
INU-YASHA...
!

SCROLL SIX

THE NOTHING WOMAN

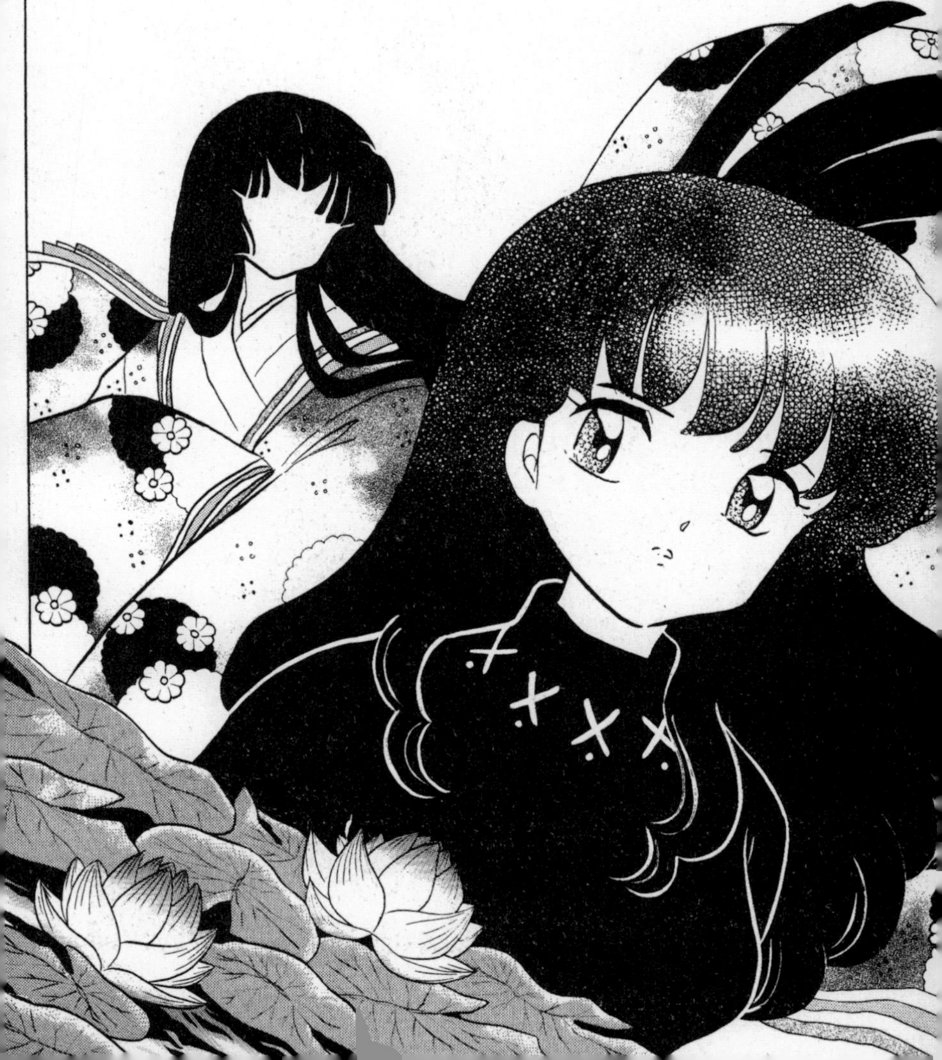

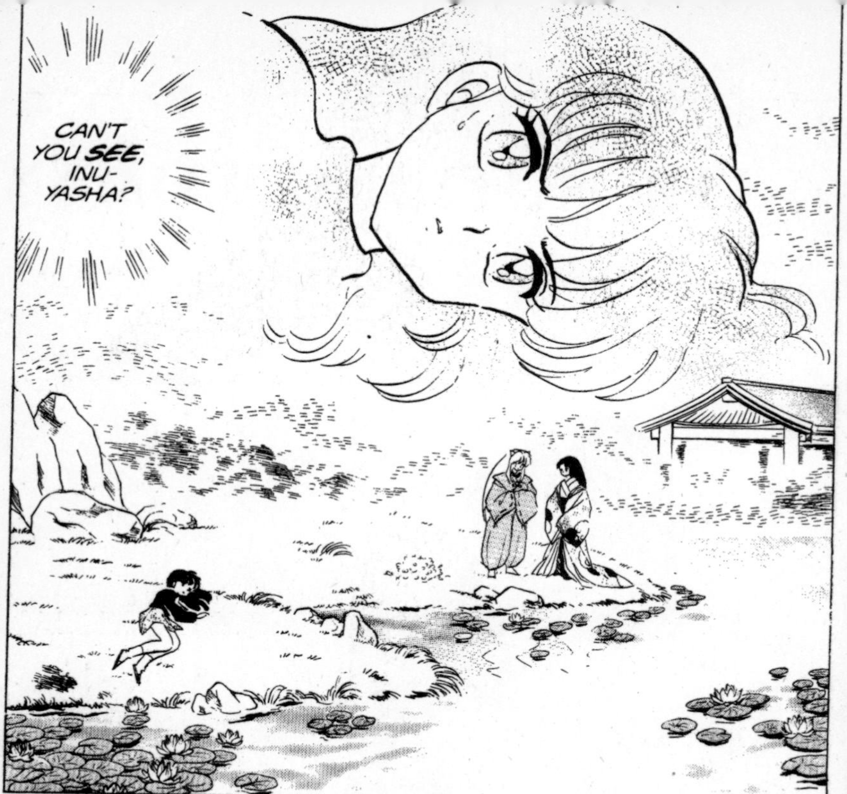
CAN'T YOU SEE, INU-YASHA?

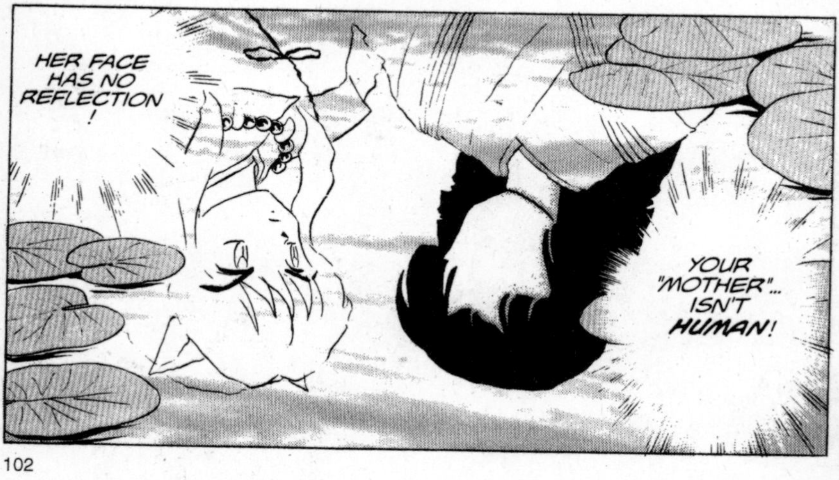
HER FACE HAS NO REFLECTION!
YOUR "MOTHER"... ISN'T HUMAN!

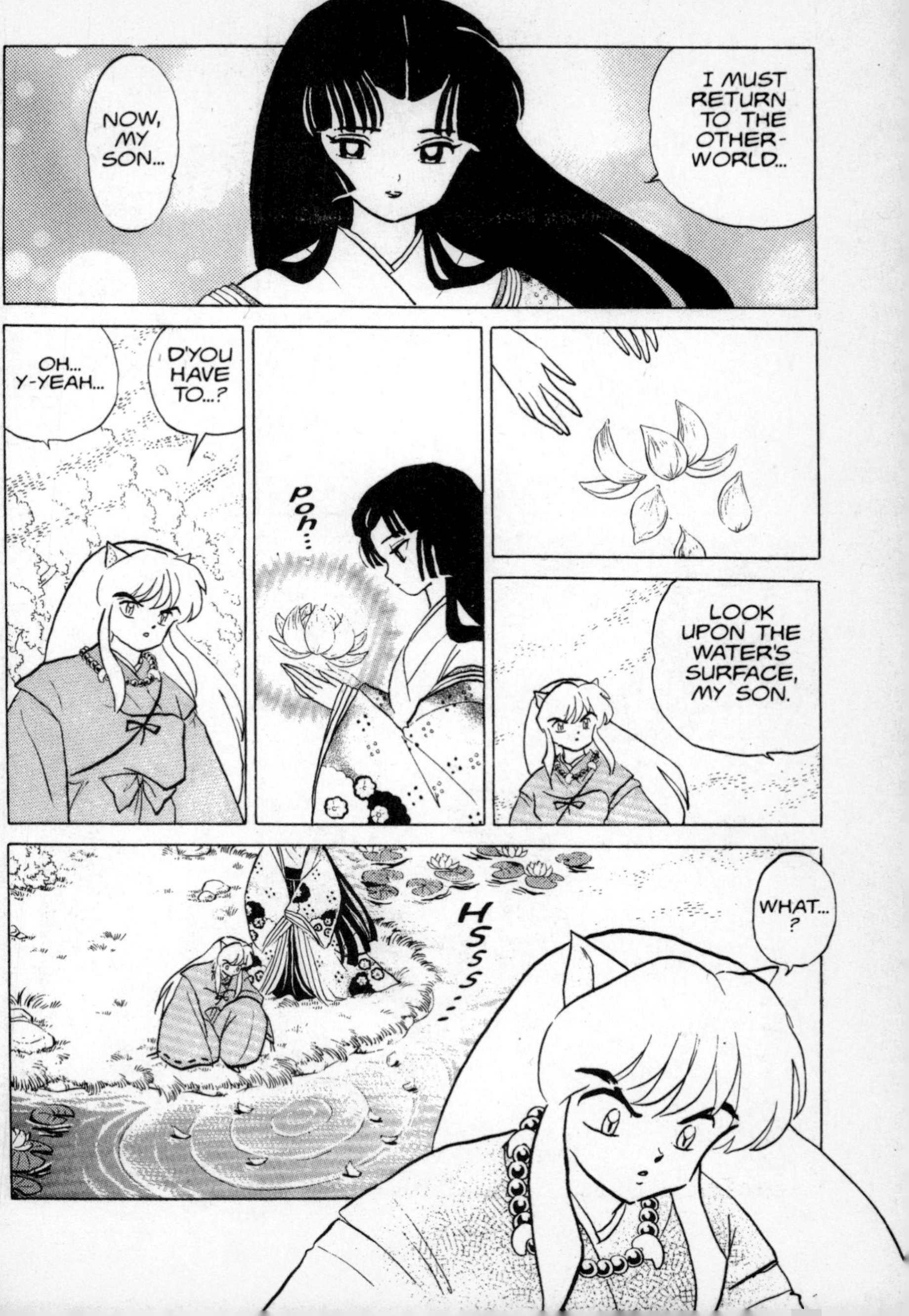
NOW, MY SON...
I MUST RETURN TO THE OTHER-WORLD...
OH... Y-YEAH...
D'YOU HAVE TO...?
poh...
LOOK UPON THE WATER'S SURFACE, MY SON.
HSSS...
WHAT...?

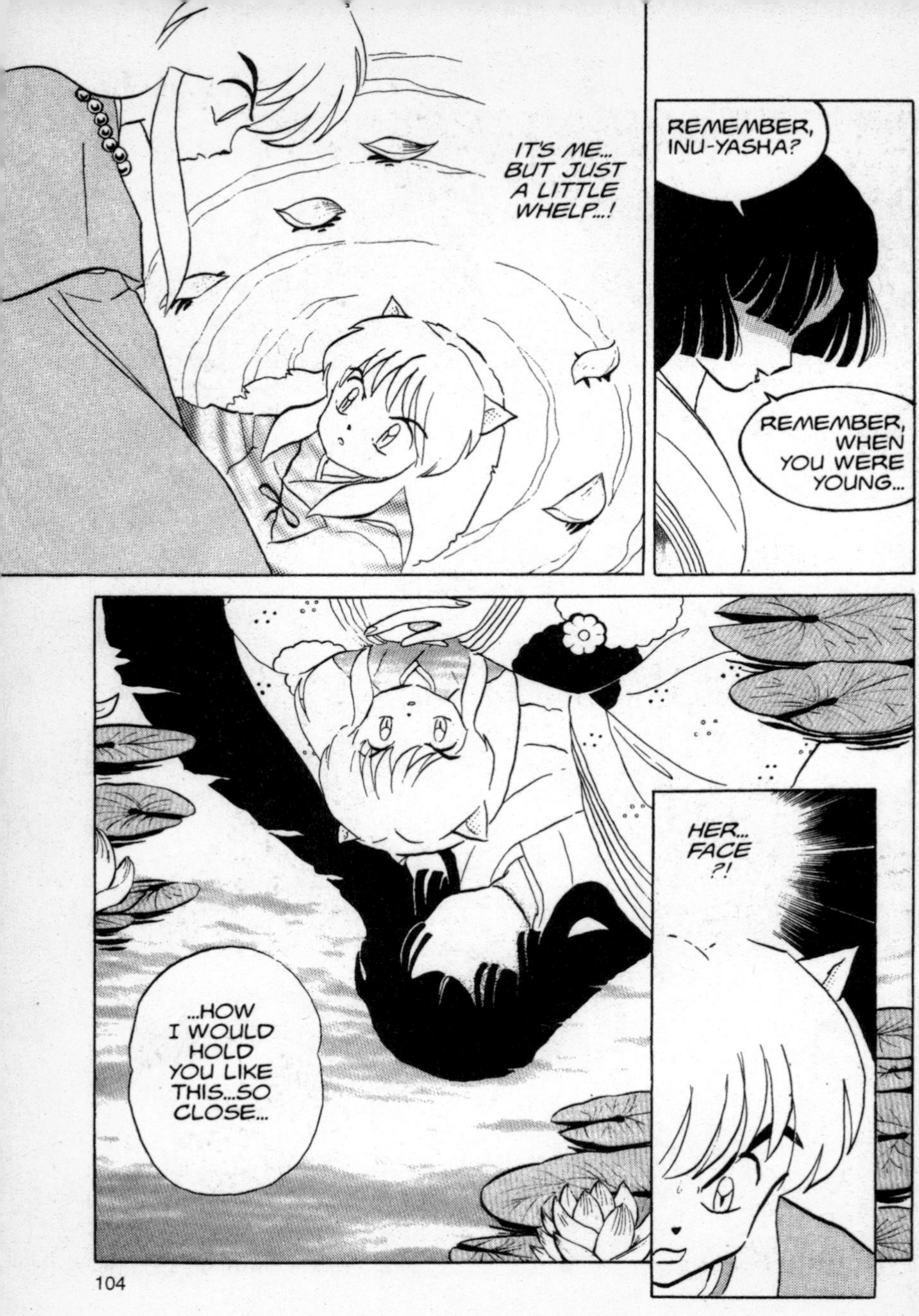
IT'S ME... BUT JUST A LITTLE WHELP...!
REMEMBER, INU-YASHA?
REMEMBER, WHEN YOU WERE YOUNG...
...HOW I WOULD HOLD YOU LIKE THIS...SO CLOSE...
HER... FACE ?!

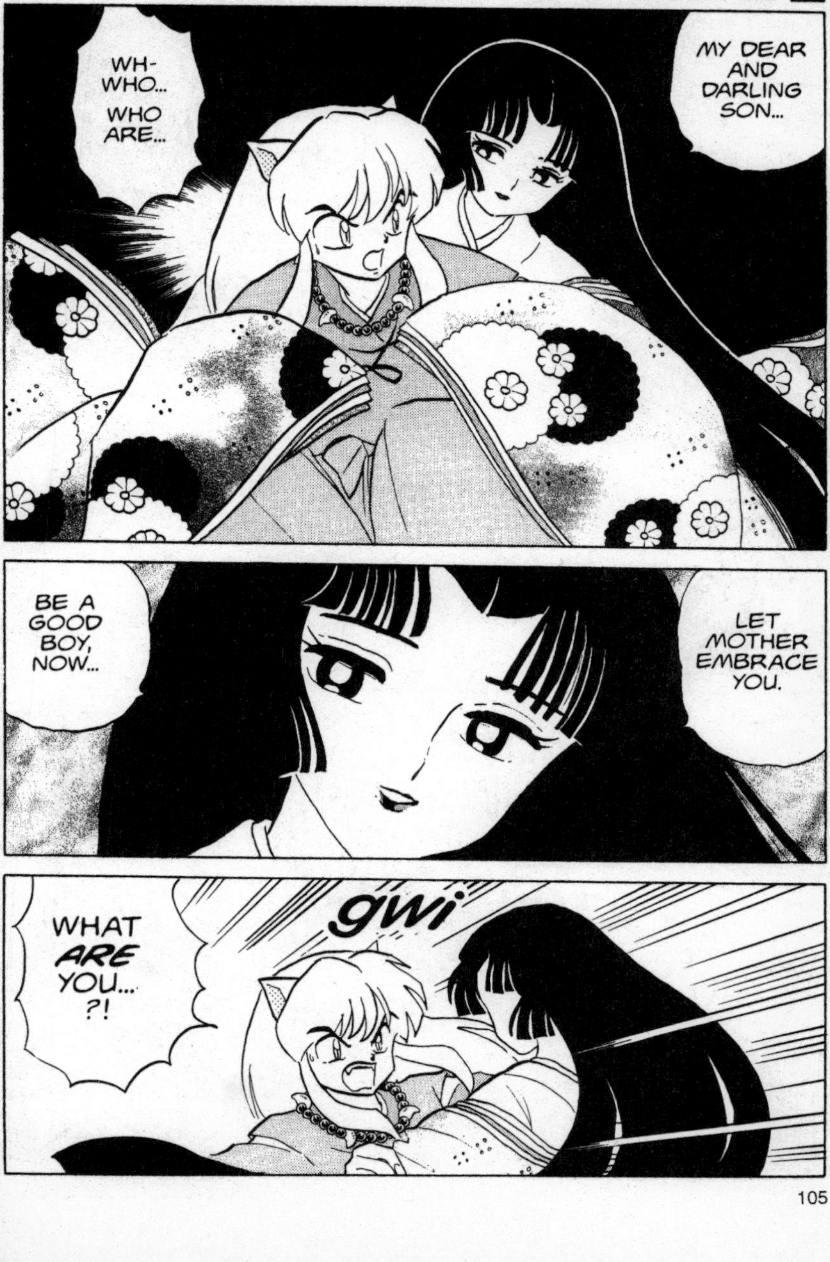
WH-
WHO...
WHO
ARE...
MY DEAR
AND
DARLING
SON...
BE A
GOOD
BOY,
NOW...
LET
MOTHER
EMBRACE
YOU.
WHAT
ARE
YOU...
?!
gwi

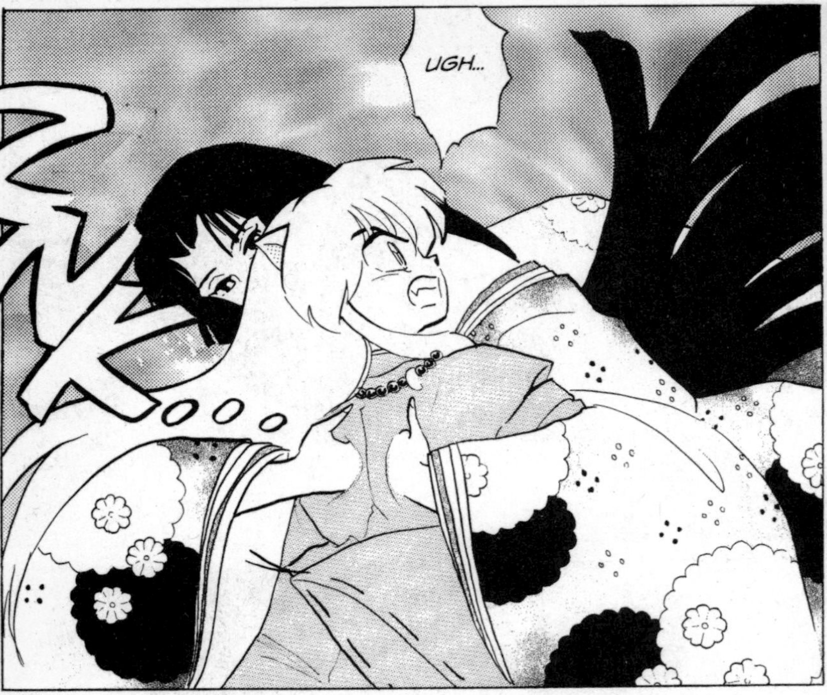
UGH...
I WILL NEVER LET YOU GO...
EVER AGAIN.
ZZG
ZZG
ZZG...
CURSE... THIS...
...WITCH...

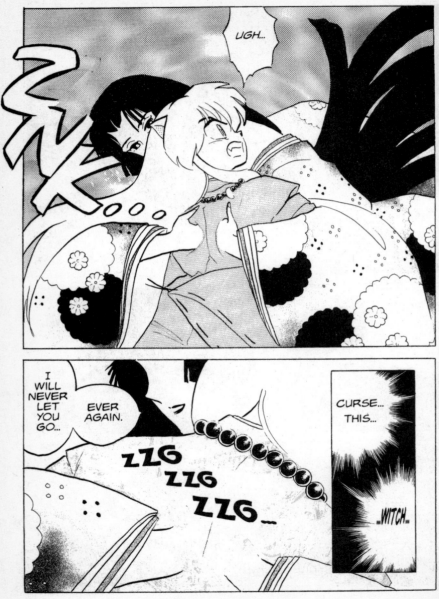

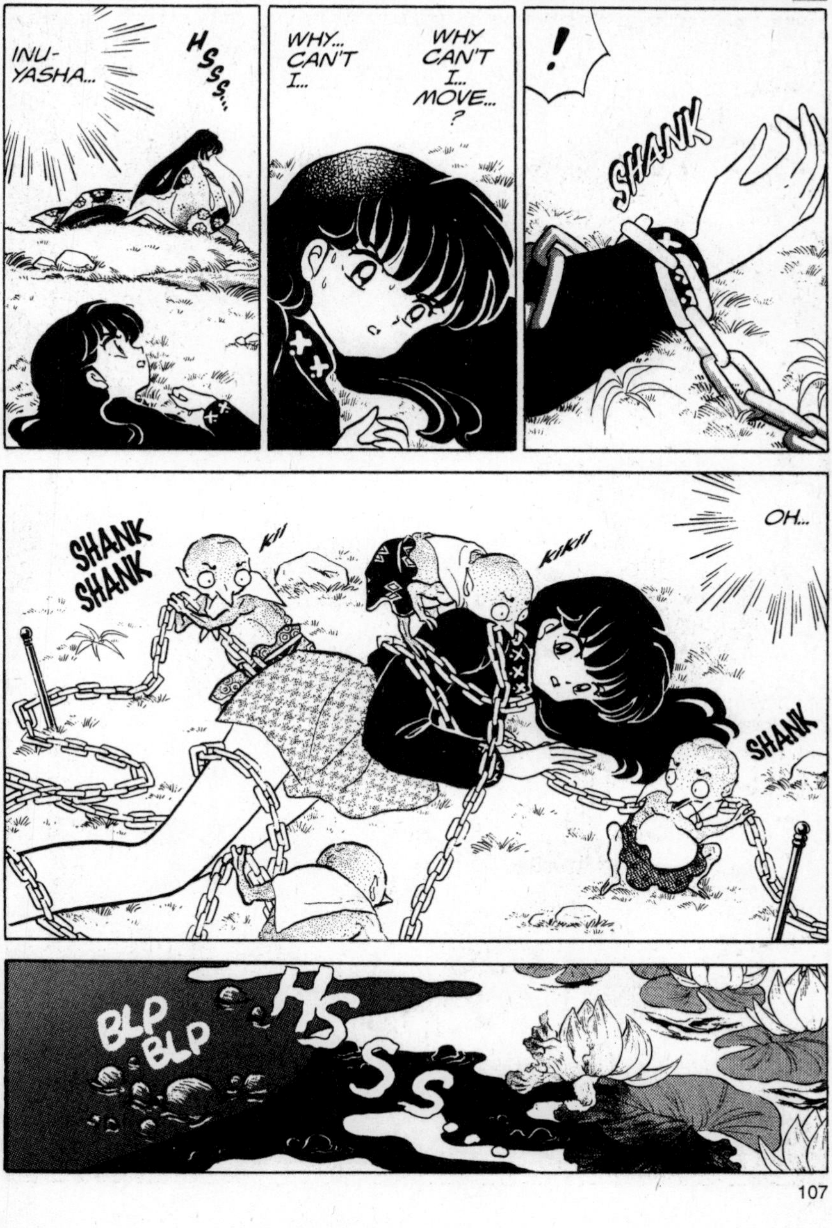
INU-YASHA...
HSSS...
WHY... CAN'T I...
WHY CAN'T I... MOVE...?
!
SHANK
SHANK SHANK
KII
KIKII
OH...
SHANK
BLP BLP
HSSS

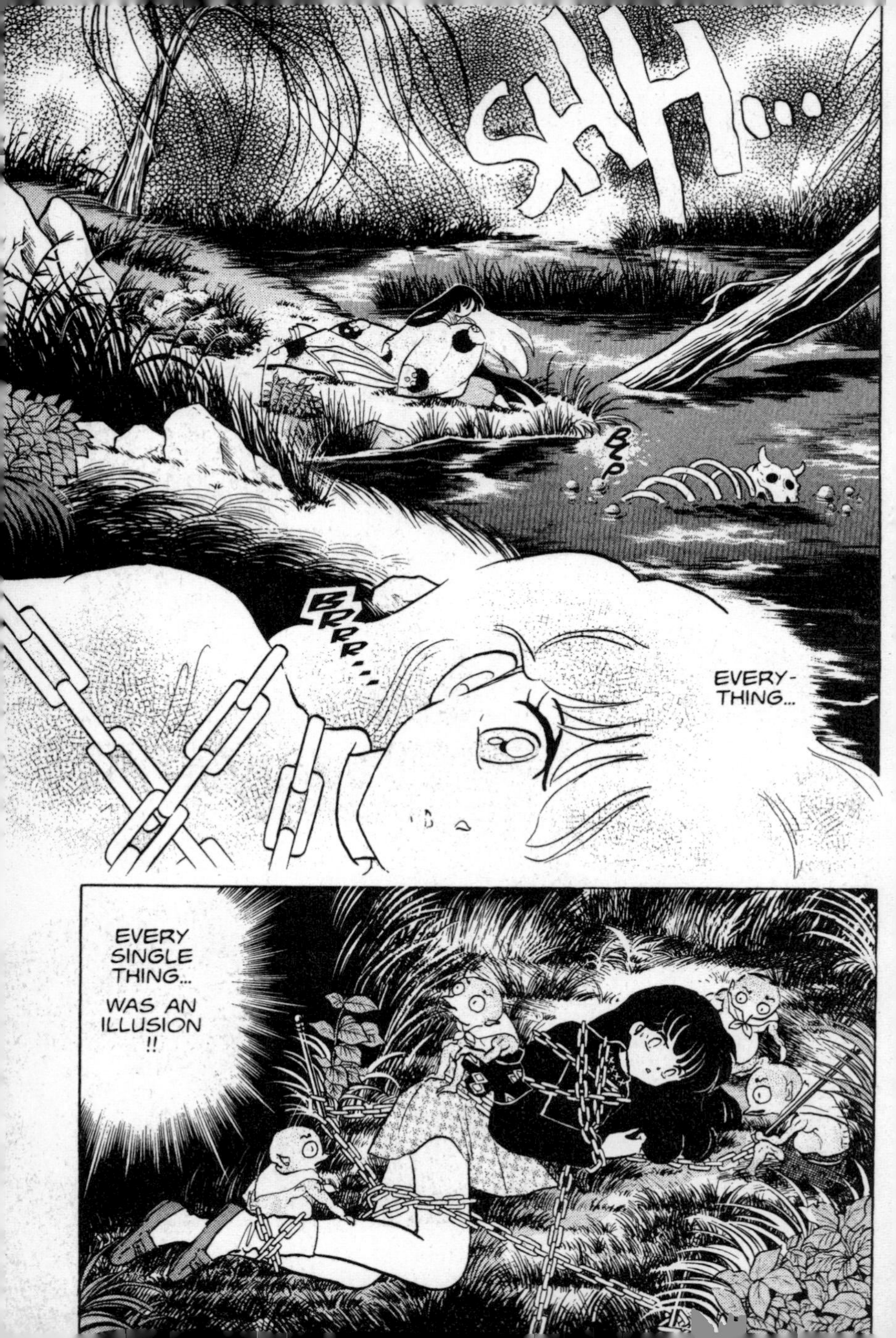
SHH...
BLP
BRRR...
EVERY-THING...
EVERY SINGLE THING...
WAS AN ILLUSION !!

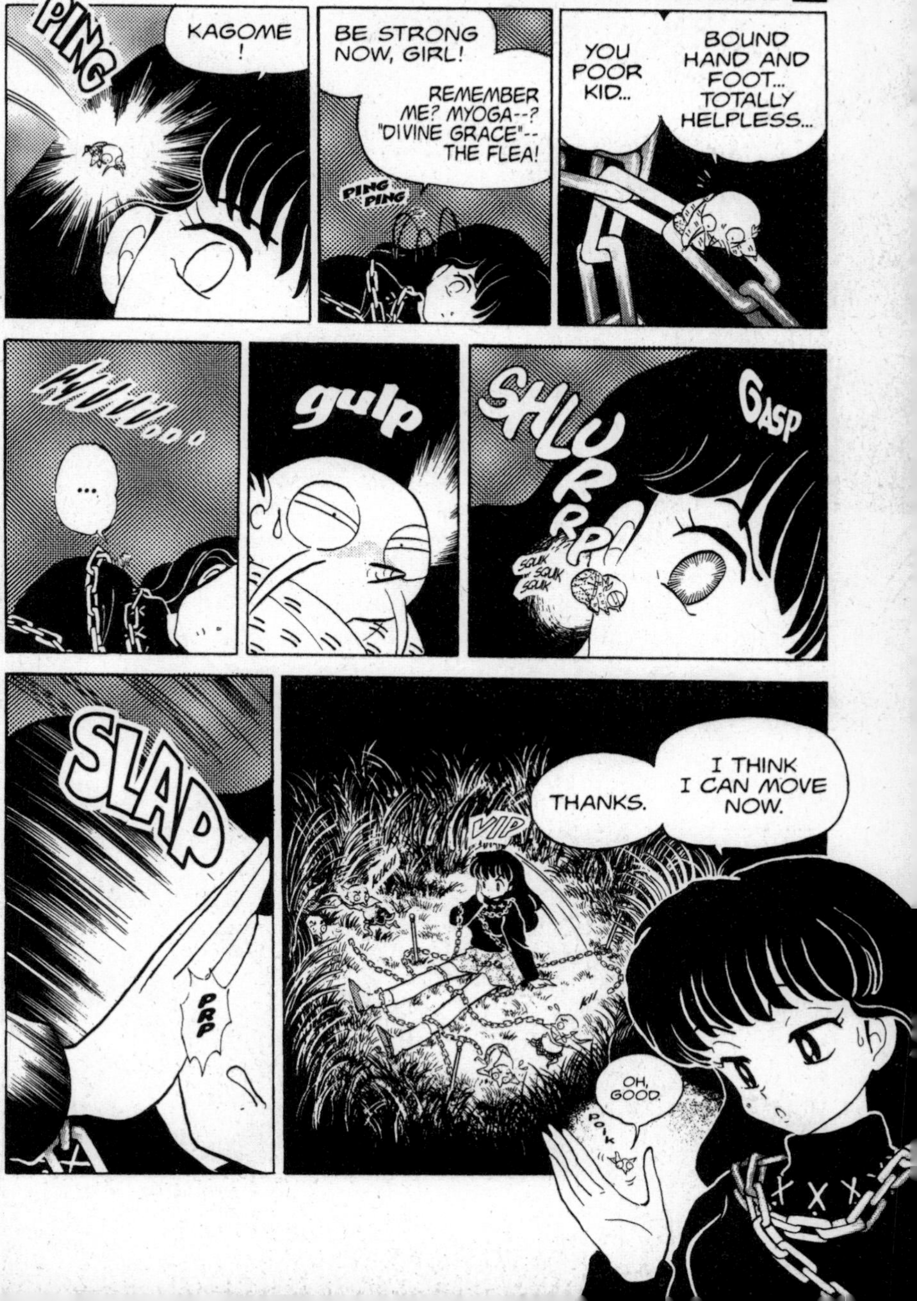
PING
KAGOME !
BE STRONG NOW, GIRL!
REMEMBER ME? MYOGA--? "DIVINE GRACE"-- THE FLEA!
PING PING
YOU POOR KID...
BOUND HAND AND FOOT... TOTALLY HELPLESS...
...
gulp
SHLURRP
GASP
SQUIK SQUIK SQUIK
SLAP
PRP
VIP
THANKS.
I THINK I CAN MOVE NOW.
OH, GOOD.
POIK

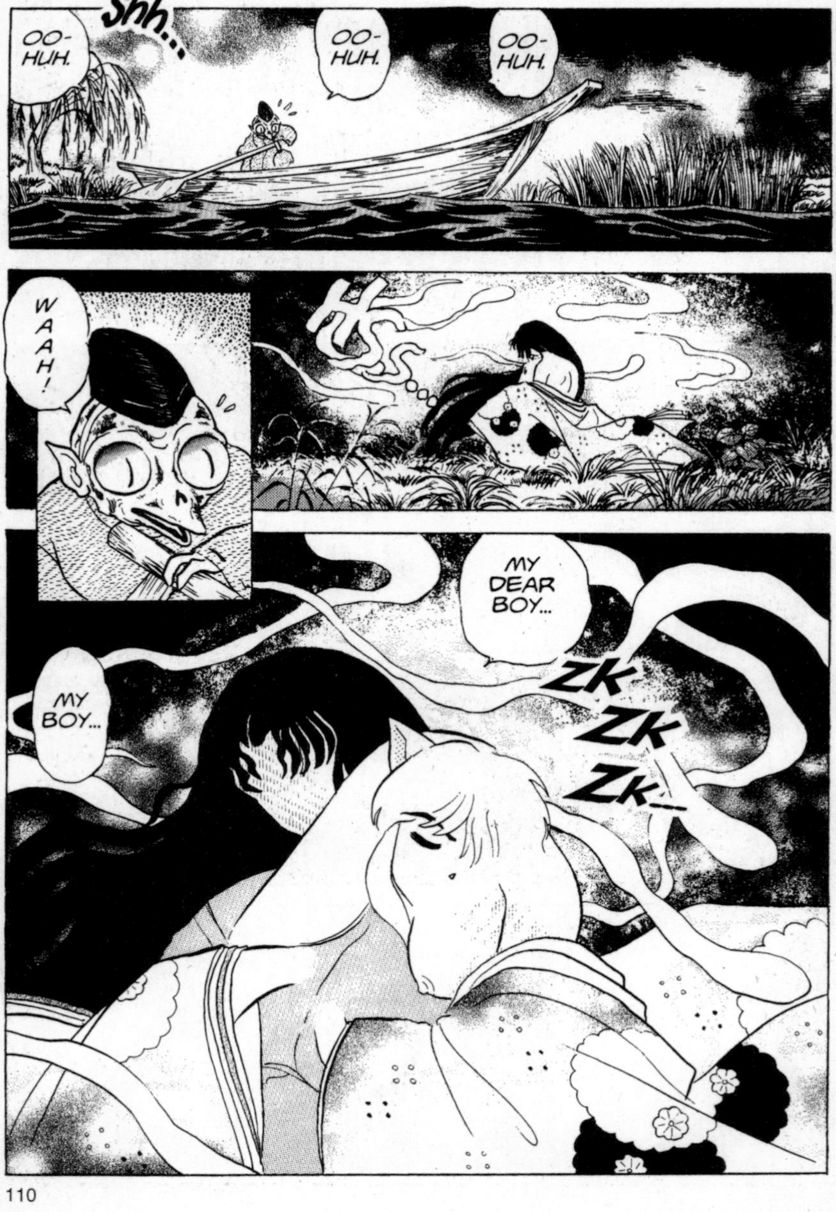
Shh...
OO-HUH.
OO-HUH.
OO-HUH.
WAAH!
MY DEAR BOY...
MY BOY...
Zk
Zk
Zk

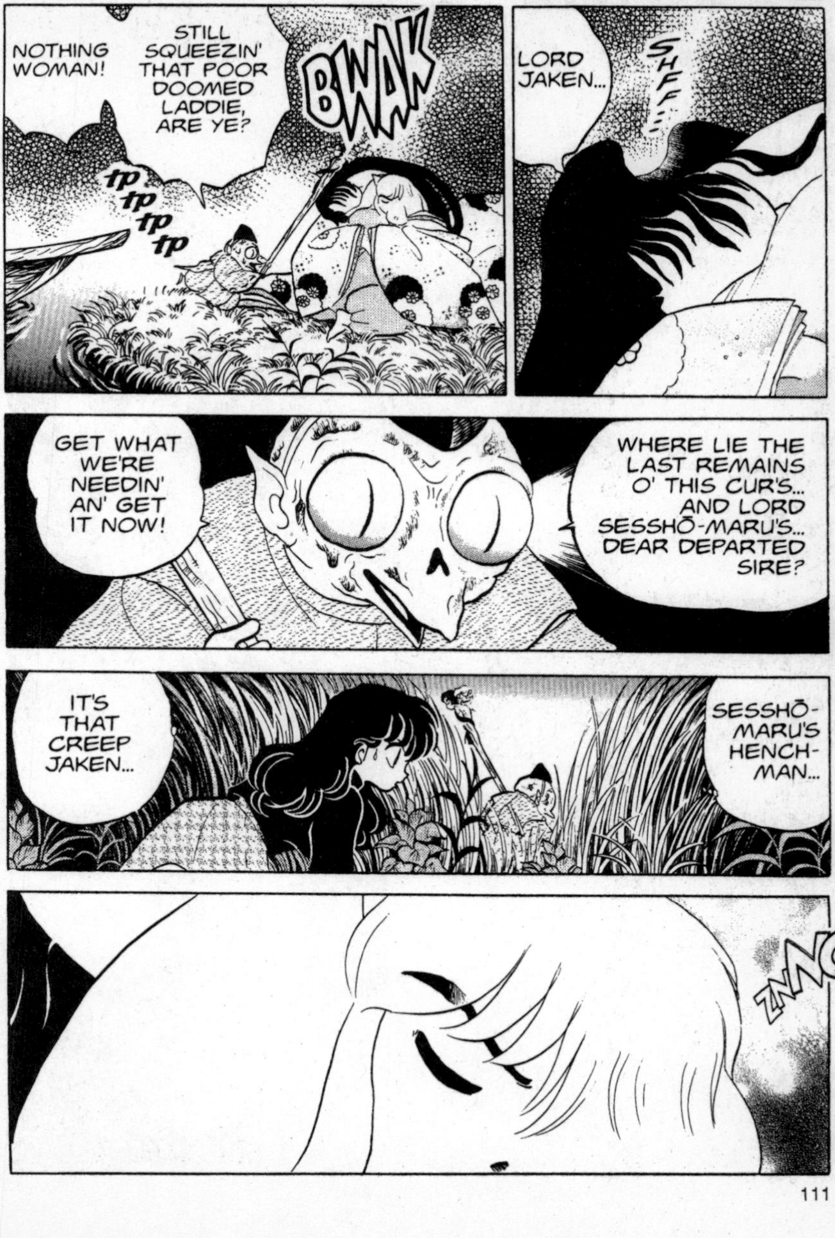
NOTHING WOMAN!
STILL SQUEEZIN' THAT POOR DOOMED LADDIE, ARE YE?
BWAK
tp tp tp tp
LORD JAKEN...
SHFF...
GET WHAT WE'RE NEEDIN' AN' GET IT NOW!
WHERE LIE THE LAST REMAINS O' THIS CUR'S... AND LORD SESSHŌ-MARU'S... DEAR DEPARTED SIRE?
IT'S THAT CREEP JAKEN...
SESSHŌ-MARU'S HENCHMAN...
ZNNG...

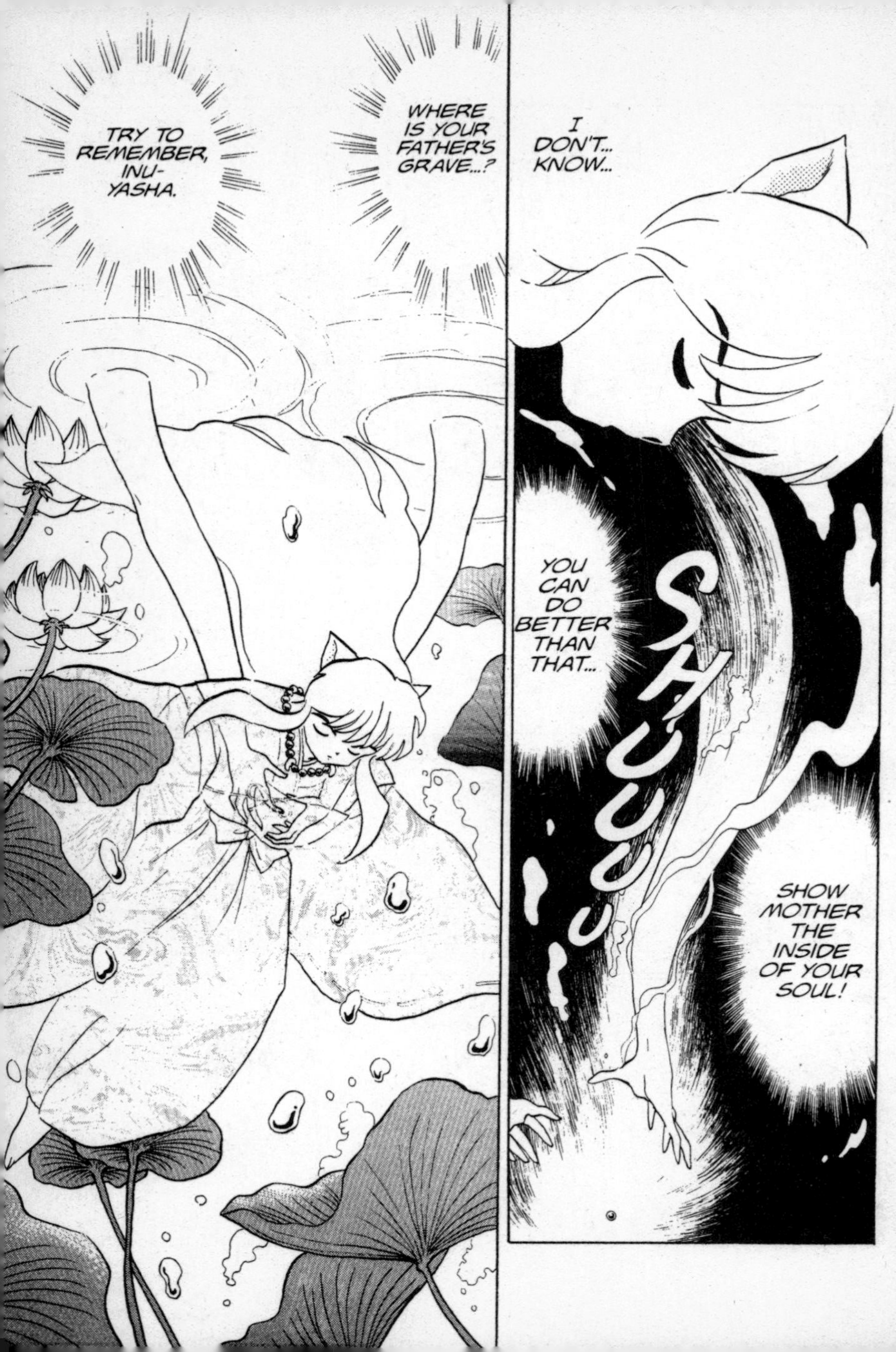
TRY TO REMEMBER, INU-YASHA.
WHERE IS YOUR FATHER'S GRAVE...?
I DON'T... KNOW...
YOU CAN DO BETTER THAN THAT...
SHUUUU
SHOW MOTHER THE INSIDE OF YOUR SOUL!

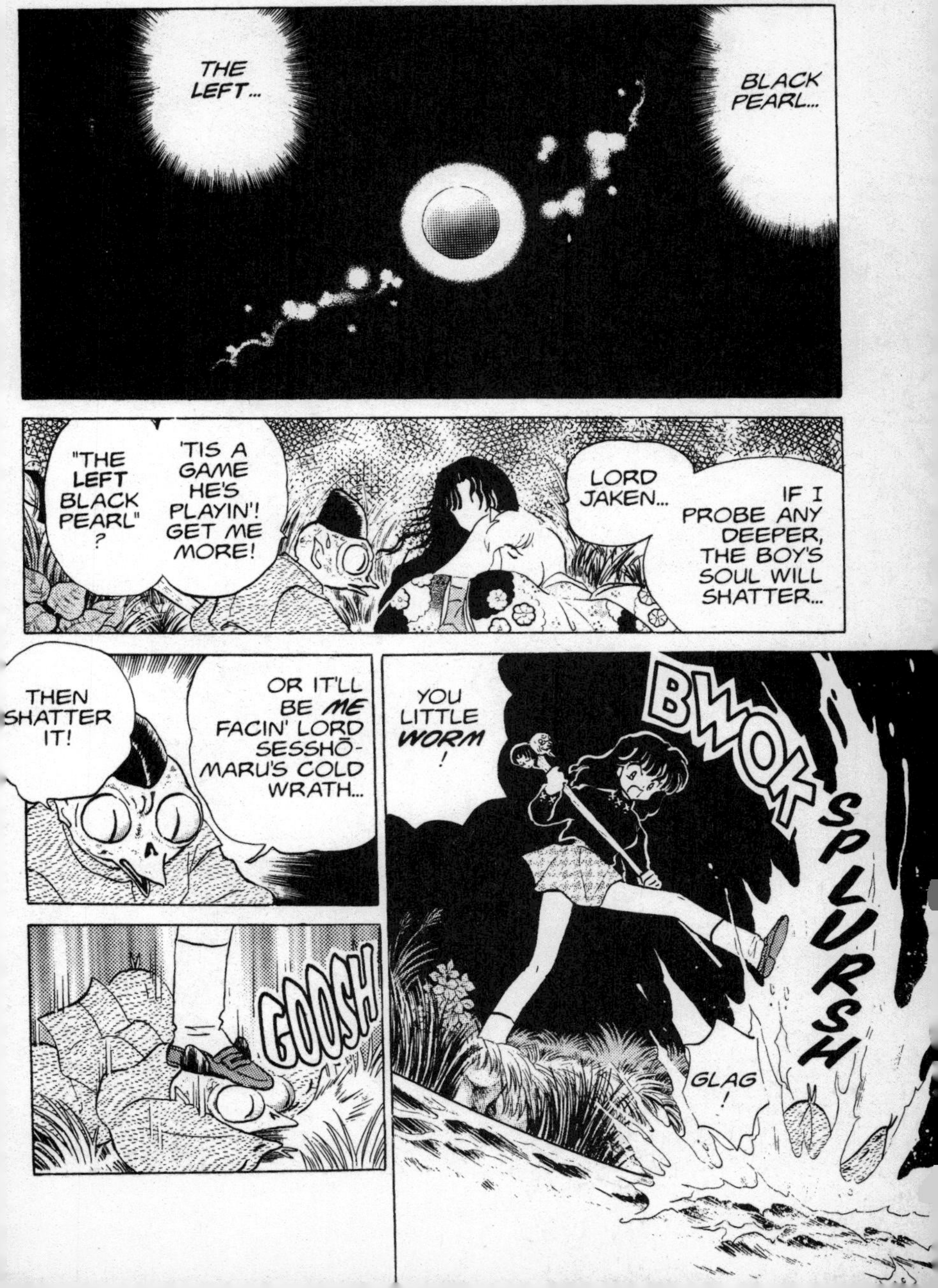
THE LEFT...
BLACK PEARL...
"THE LEFT BLACK PEARL" ?
'TIS A GAME HE'S PLAYIN'! GET ME MORE!
LORD JAKEN...
IF I PROBE ANY DEEPER, THE BOY'S SOUL WILL SHATTER...
THEN SHATTER IT!
OR IT'LL BE ME FACIN' LORD SESSHŌMARU'S COLD WRATH...
YOU LITTLE WORM!
BWOK
SPLURSH
GLAG!
GOOSH

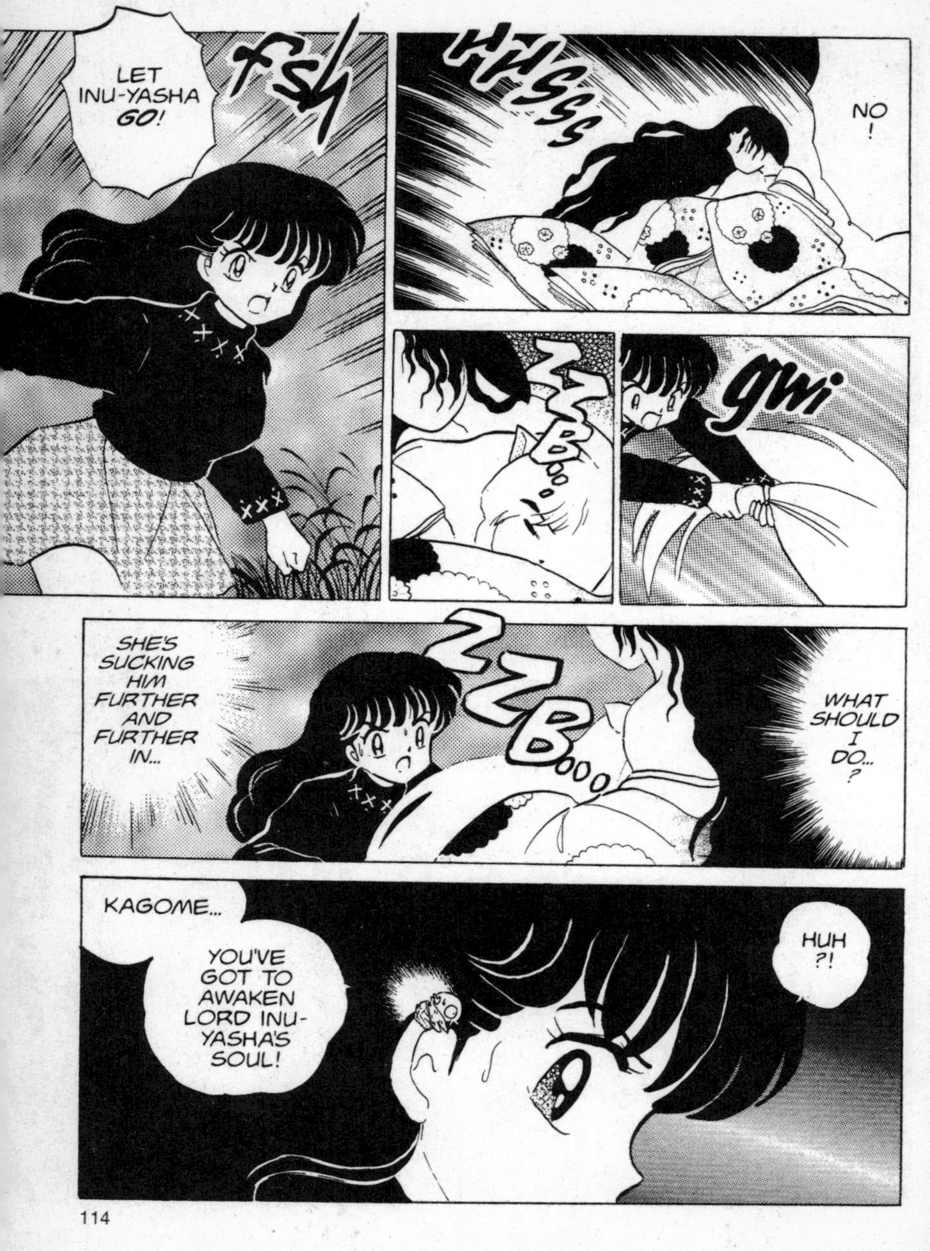
LET INU-YASHA GO!
fsh
NO!
gwi
SHE'S SUCKING HIM FURTHER AND FURTHER IN...
ZZBooo
WHAT SHOULD I DO...?
KAGOME...
YOU'VE GOT TO AWAKEN LORD INU-YASHA'S SOUL!
HUH?!

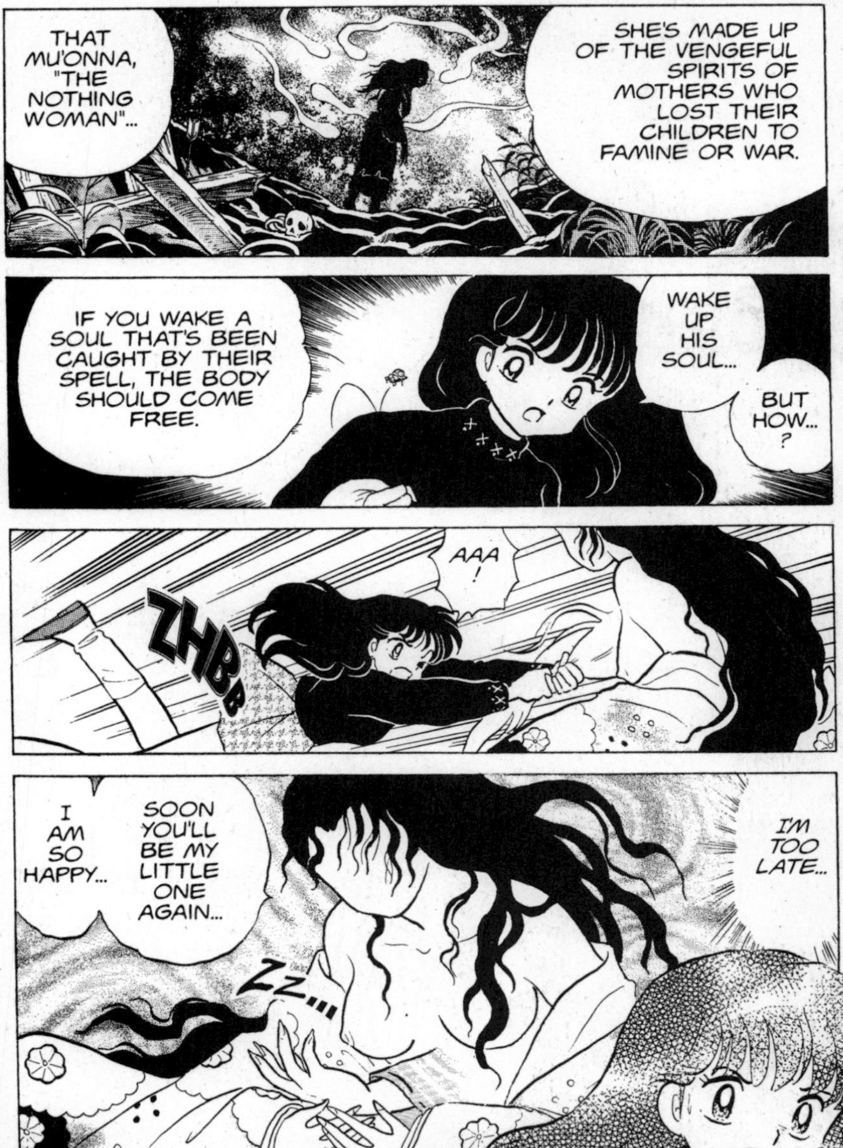
THAT MU'ONNA, "THE NOTHING WOMAN"...
SHE'S MADE UP OF THE VENGEFUL SPIRITS OF MOTHERS WHO LOST THEIR CHILDREN TO FAMINE OR WAR.
IF YOU WAKE A SOUL THAT'S BEEN CAUGHT BY THEIR SPELL, THE BODY SHOULD COME FREE.
WAKE UP HIS SOUL...
BUT HOW...?
AAA!
ZHBB
I AM SO HAPPY...
SOON YOU'LL BE MY LITTLE ONE AGAIN...
ZZ...
I'M TOO LATE...

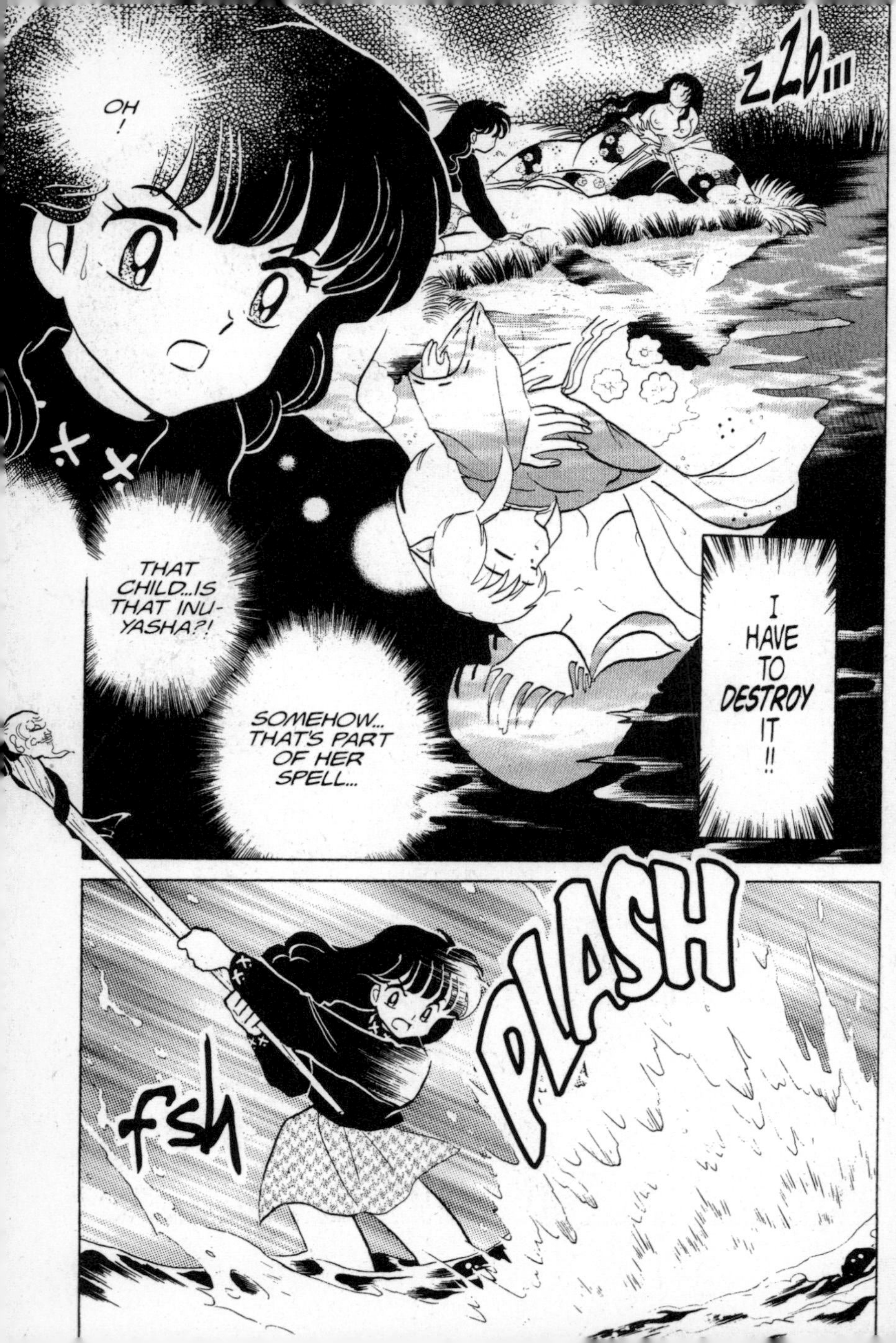
OH!
zzb...
THAT CHILD...IS THAT INU-YASHA?!
SOMEHOW... THAT'S PART OF HER SPELL...
I HAVE TO DESTROY IT!!
PLASH
fsh

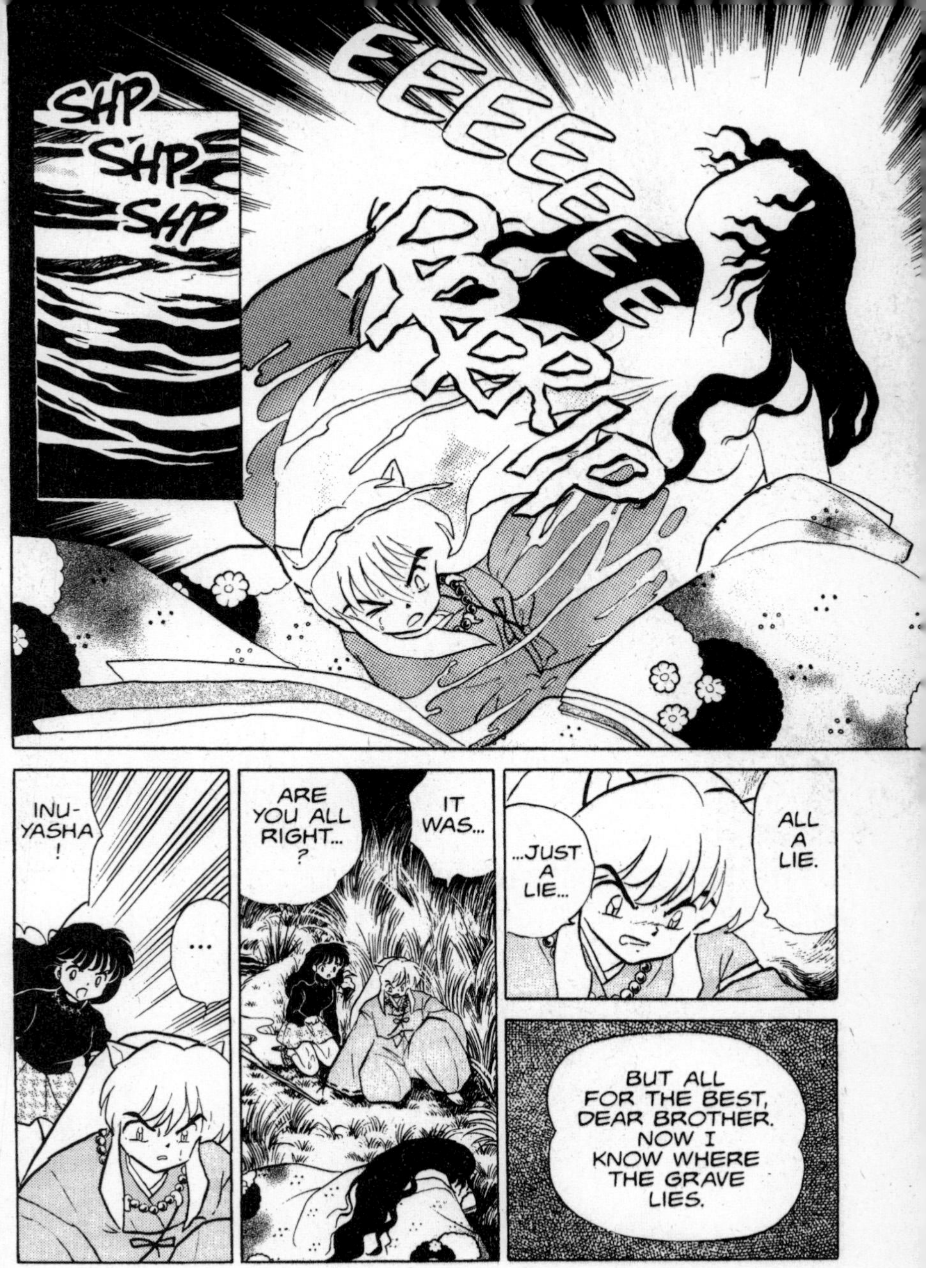
SHP SHP SHP
EEEEEEE
DRRRIP
INU-YASHA!
...
ARE YOU ALL RIGHT...?
IT WAS...
...JUST A LIE...
ALL A LIE.
BUT ALL FOR THE BEST, DEAR BROTHER. NOW I KNOW WHERE THE GRAVE LIES.

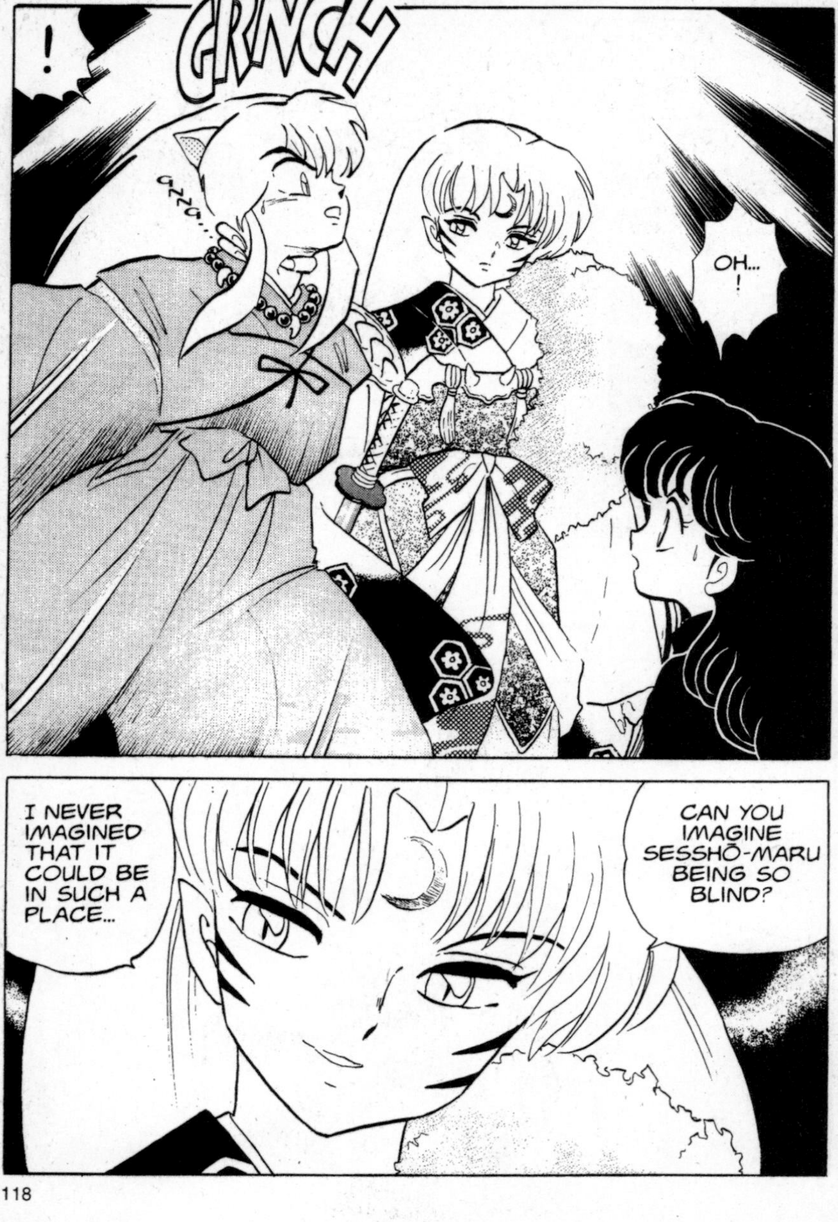
!
GRNCH
GNNG...
OH... !
I NEVER IMAGINED THAT IT COULD BE IN SUCH A PLACE...
CAN YOU IMAGINE SESSHŌ-MARU BEING SO BLIND?

SCROLL SEVEN

THE BLACK PEARL

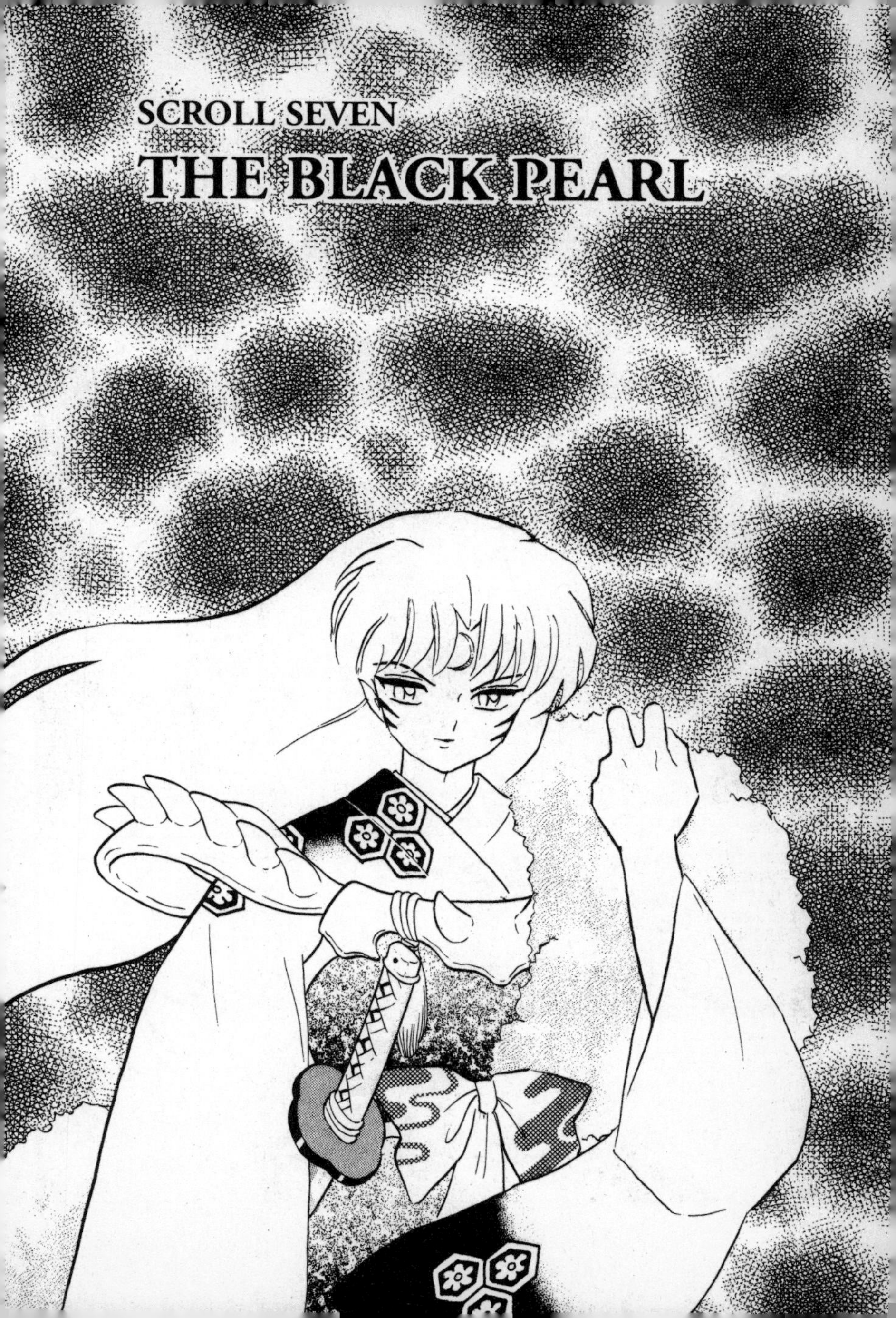

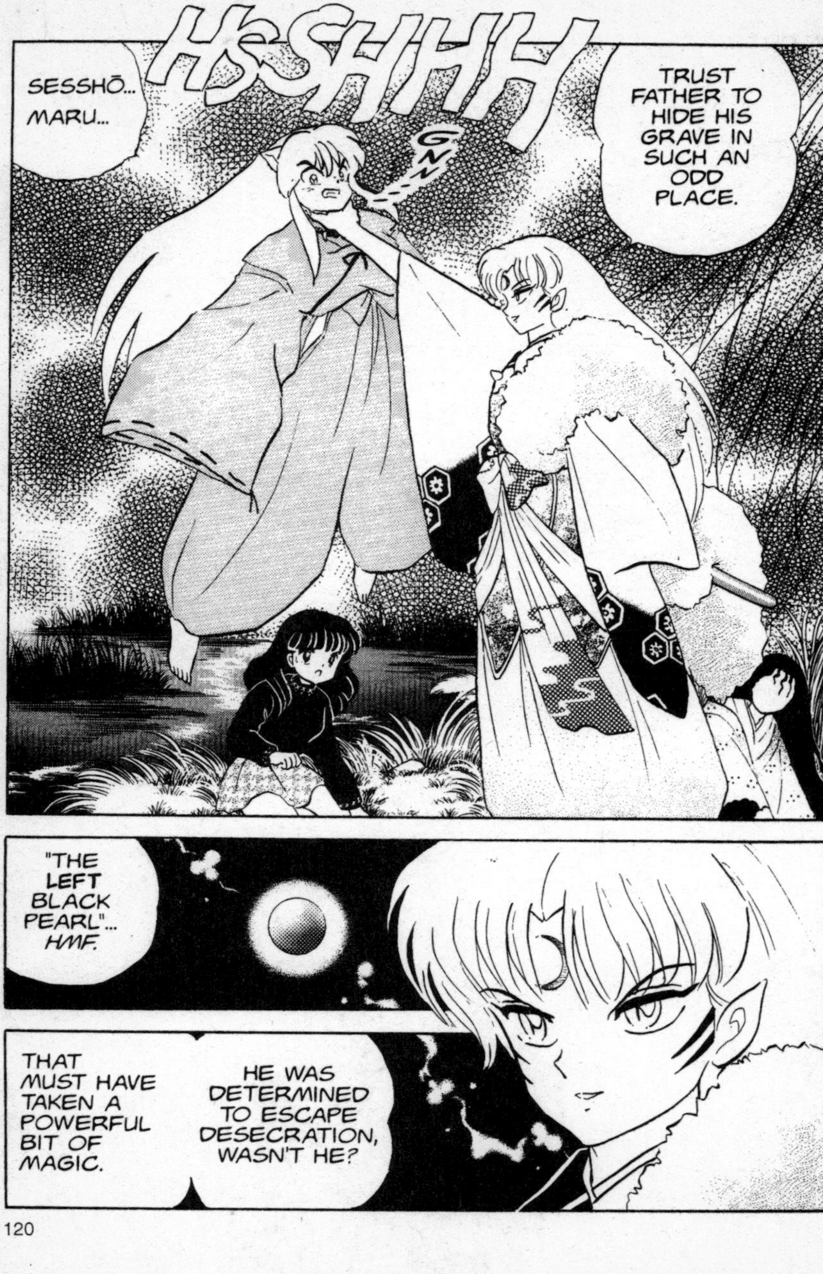
SESSHŌ... MARU...
HSSHHHH
GNN
TRUST FATHER TO HIDE HIS GRAVE IN SUCH AN ODD PLACE.
"THE LEFT BLACK PEARL"... HMF.
THAT MUST HAVE TAKEN A POWERFUL BIT OF MAGIC.
HE WAS DETERMINED TO ESCAPE DESECRATION, WASN'T HE?

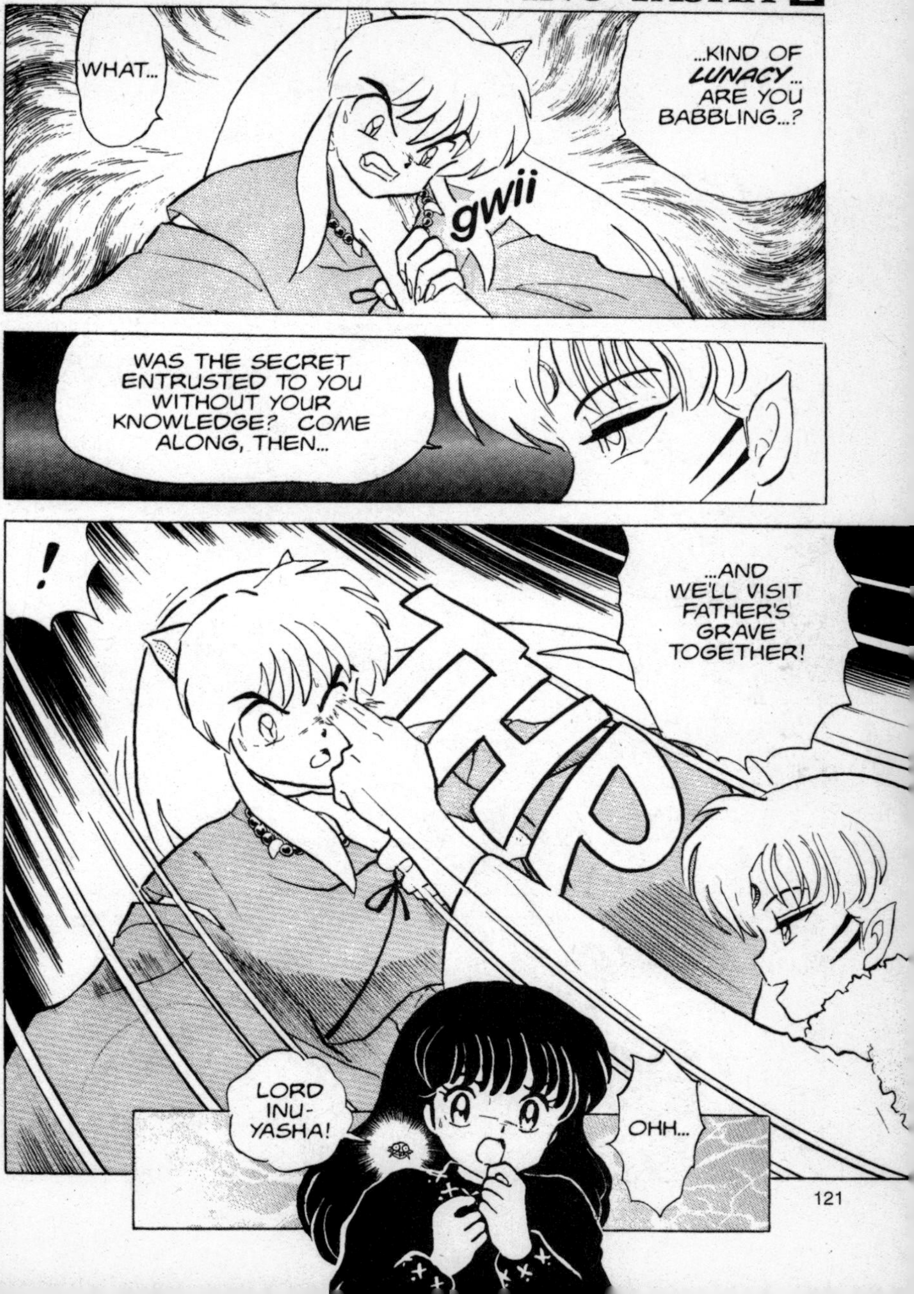
WHAT...
...KIND OF LUNACY... ARE YOU BABBLING...?
gwii
WAS THE SECRET ENTRUSTED TO YOU WITHOUT YOUR KNOWLEDGE? COME ALONG, THEN...
!
THP
...AND WE'LL VISIT FATHER'S GRAVE TOGETHER!
LORD INU-YASHA!
OHH...

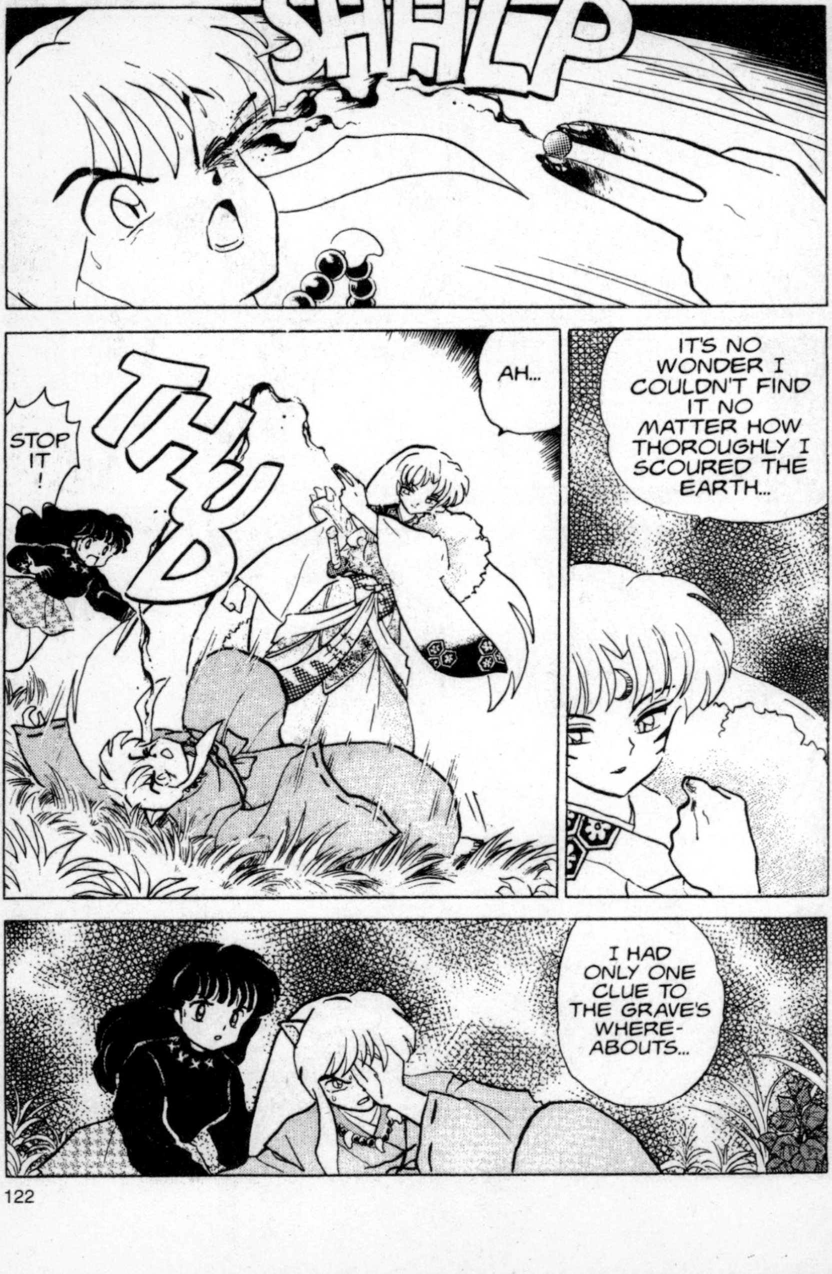
SHHLP
STOP IT!
THUD
AH...
IT'S NO WONDER I COULDN'T FIND IT NO MATTER HOW THOROUGHLY I SCOURED THE EARTH...
I HAD ONLY ONE CLUE TO THE GRAVE'S WHERE-ABOUTS...

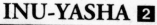

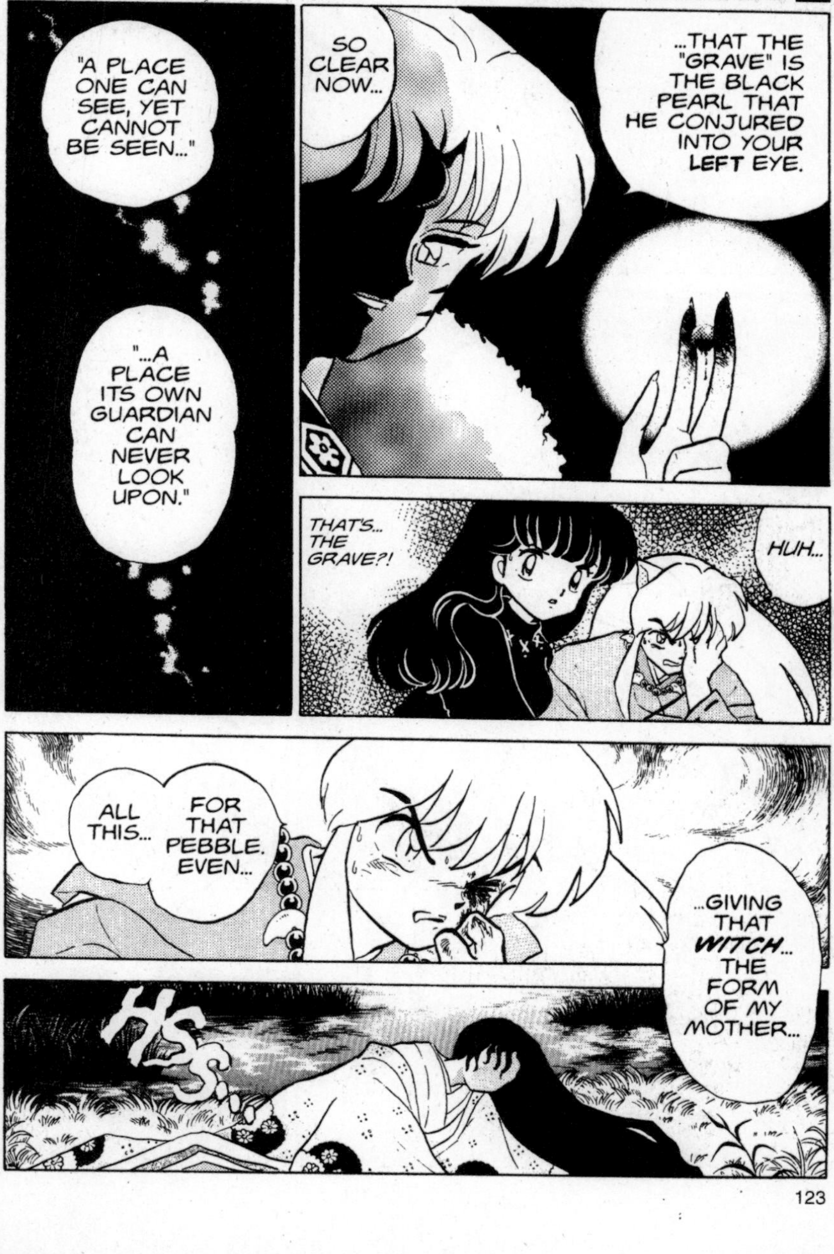
"A PLACE ONE CAN SEE, YET CANNOT BE SEEN..."
"...A PLACE ITS OWN GUARDIAN CAN NEVER LOOK UPON."
SO CLEAR NOW...
...THAT THE "GRAVE" IS THE BLACK PEARL THAT HE CONJURED INTO YOUR LEFT EYE.
THAT'S... THE GRAVE?!
HUH...
ALL THIS... FOR THAT PEBBLE. EVEN...
...GIVING THAT WITCH... THE FORM OF MY MOTHER...
HSSS

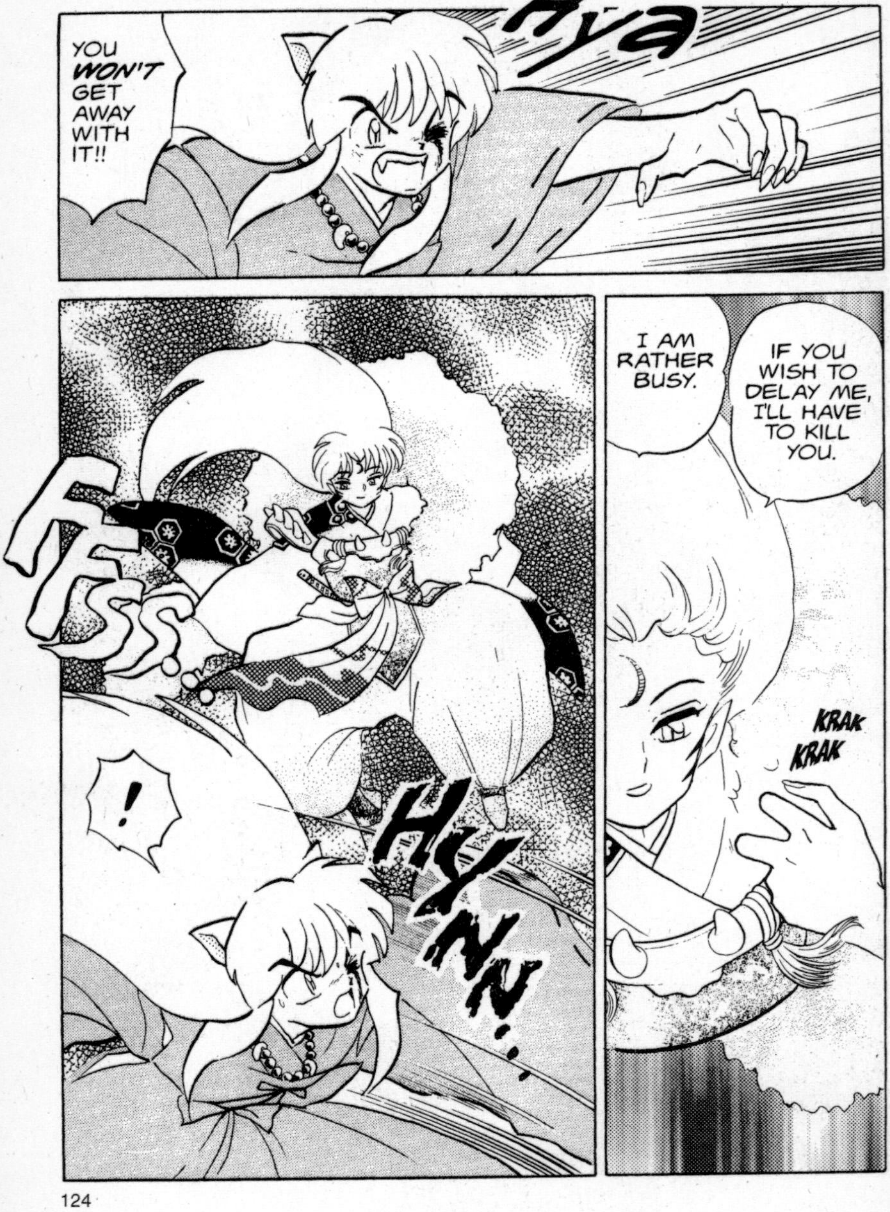
Hya
YOU *WON'T* GET AWAY WITH IT!!
FSSS
!
HYNN...
I AM RATHER BUSY.
IF YOU WISH TO DELAY ME, I'LL HAVE TO KILL YOU.
KRAK KRAK

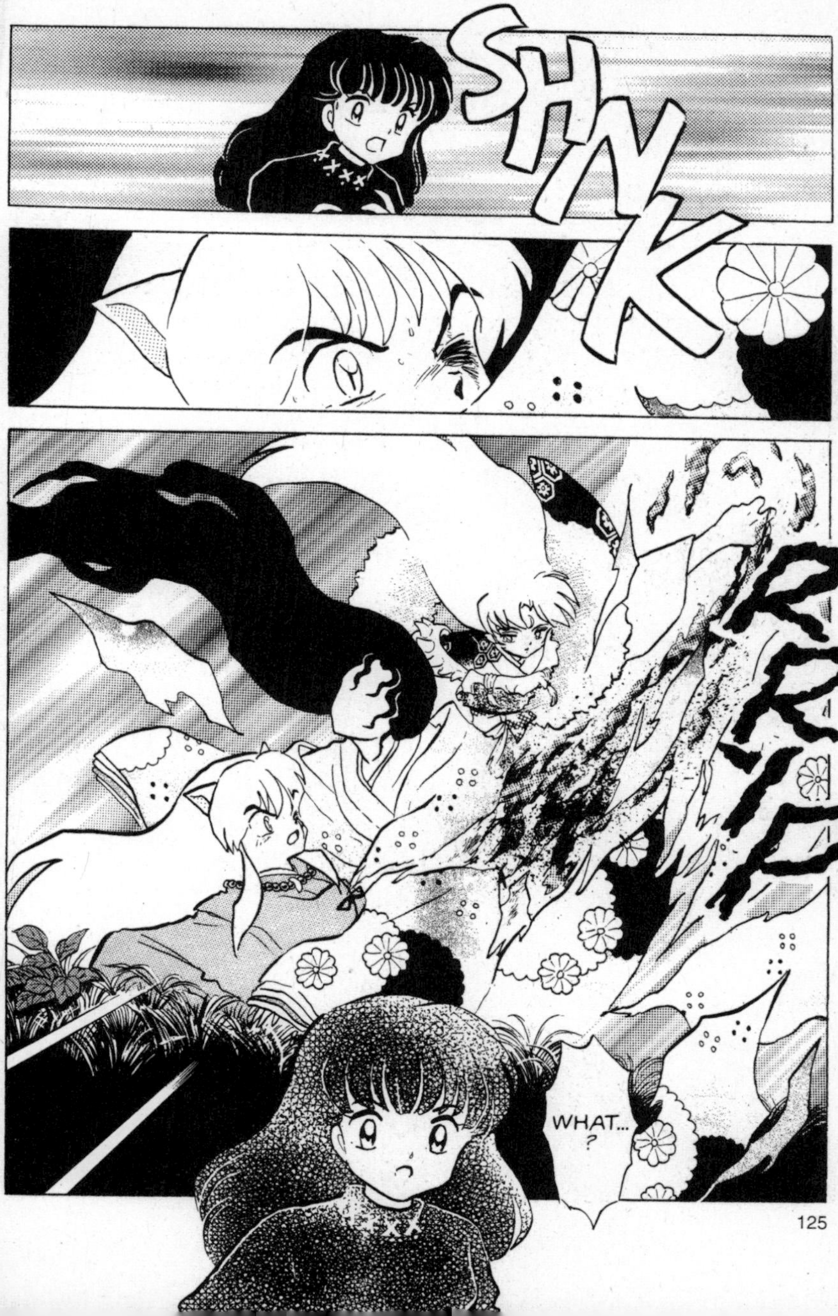
SHNK
RRRIP
WHAT...?

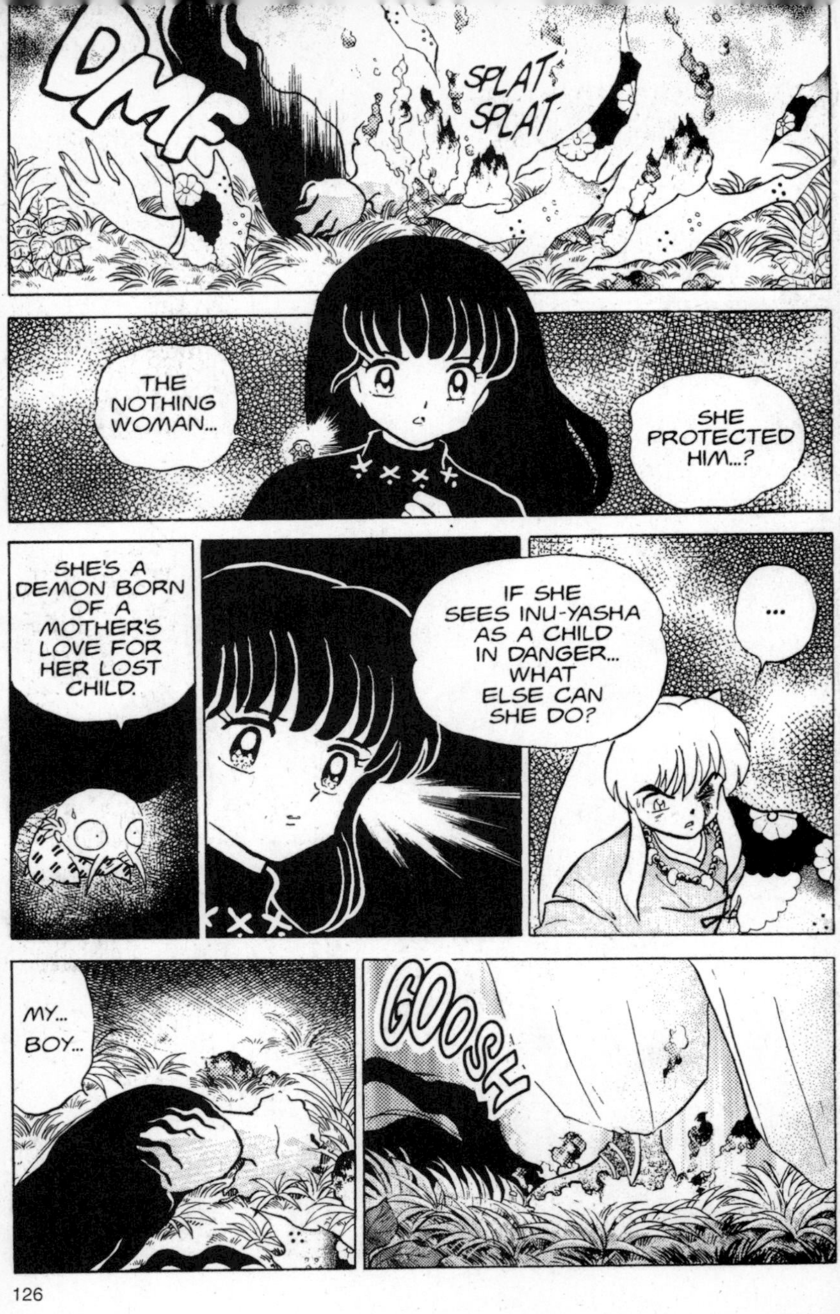
DMF
SPLAT SPLAT
THE NOTHING WOMAN...
SHE PROTECTED HIM...?
SHE'S A DEMON BORN OF A MOTHER'S LOVE FOR HER LOST CHILD.
IF SHE SEES INU-YASHA AS A CHILD IN DANGER... WHAT ELSE CAN SHE DO?
...
MY... BOY...
GOOSH

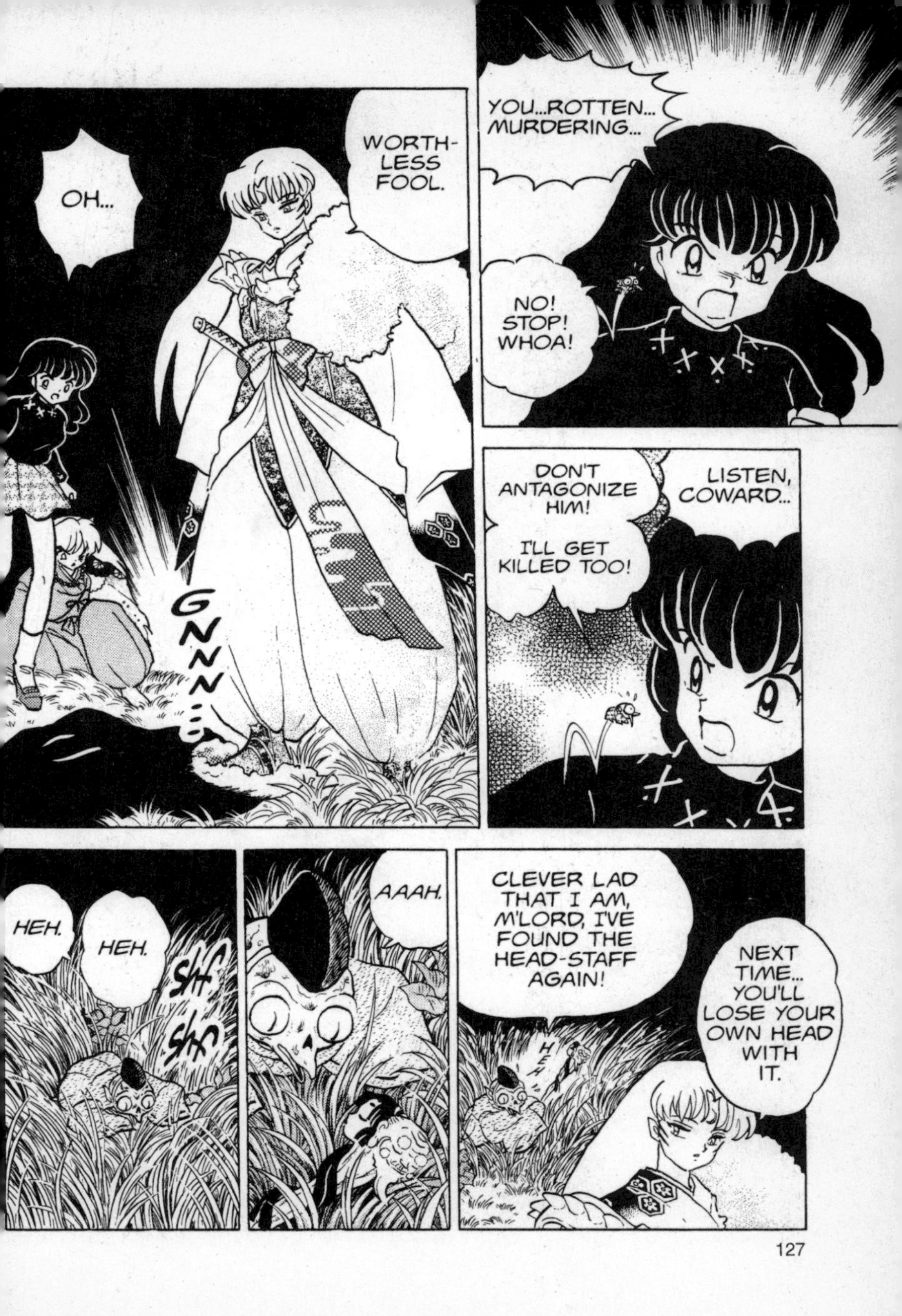
OH...
WORTH-LESS FOOL.
GNNN...
YOU...ROTTEN... MURDERING...
NO! STOP! WHOA!
DON'T ANTAGONIZE HIM!
I'LL GET KILLED TOO!
LISTEN, COWARD...
HEH.
HEH.
SHF
SHF
AAAH.
CLEVER LAD THAT I AM, M'LORD, I'VE FOUND THE HEAD-STAFF AGAIN!
HEH
NEXT TIME... YOU'LL LOSE YOUR OWN HEAD WITH IT.

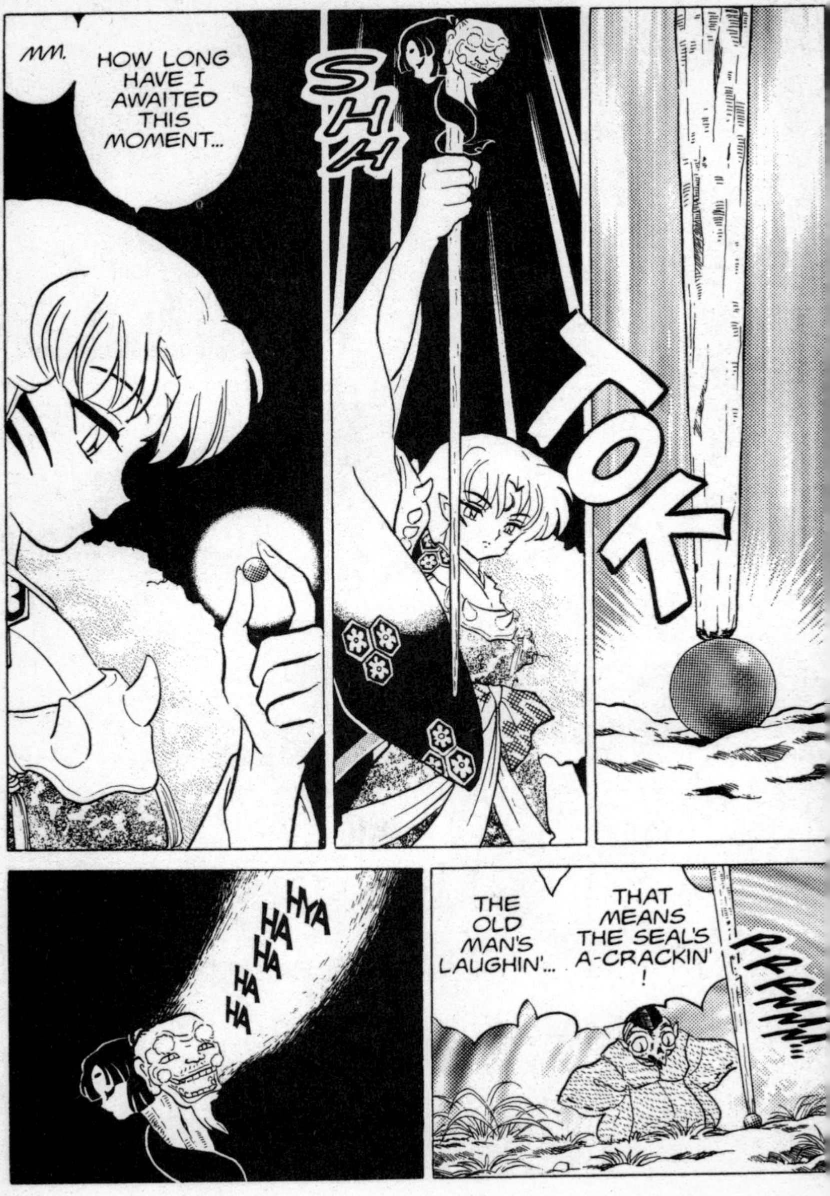
MM.
HOW LONG HAVE I AWAITED THIS MOMENT...
SHH
TOK
HYA HA HA HA HA
THE OLD MAN'S LAUGHIN'...
THAT MEANS THE SEAL'S A-CRACKIN'!
RRRMMM...

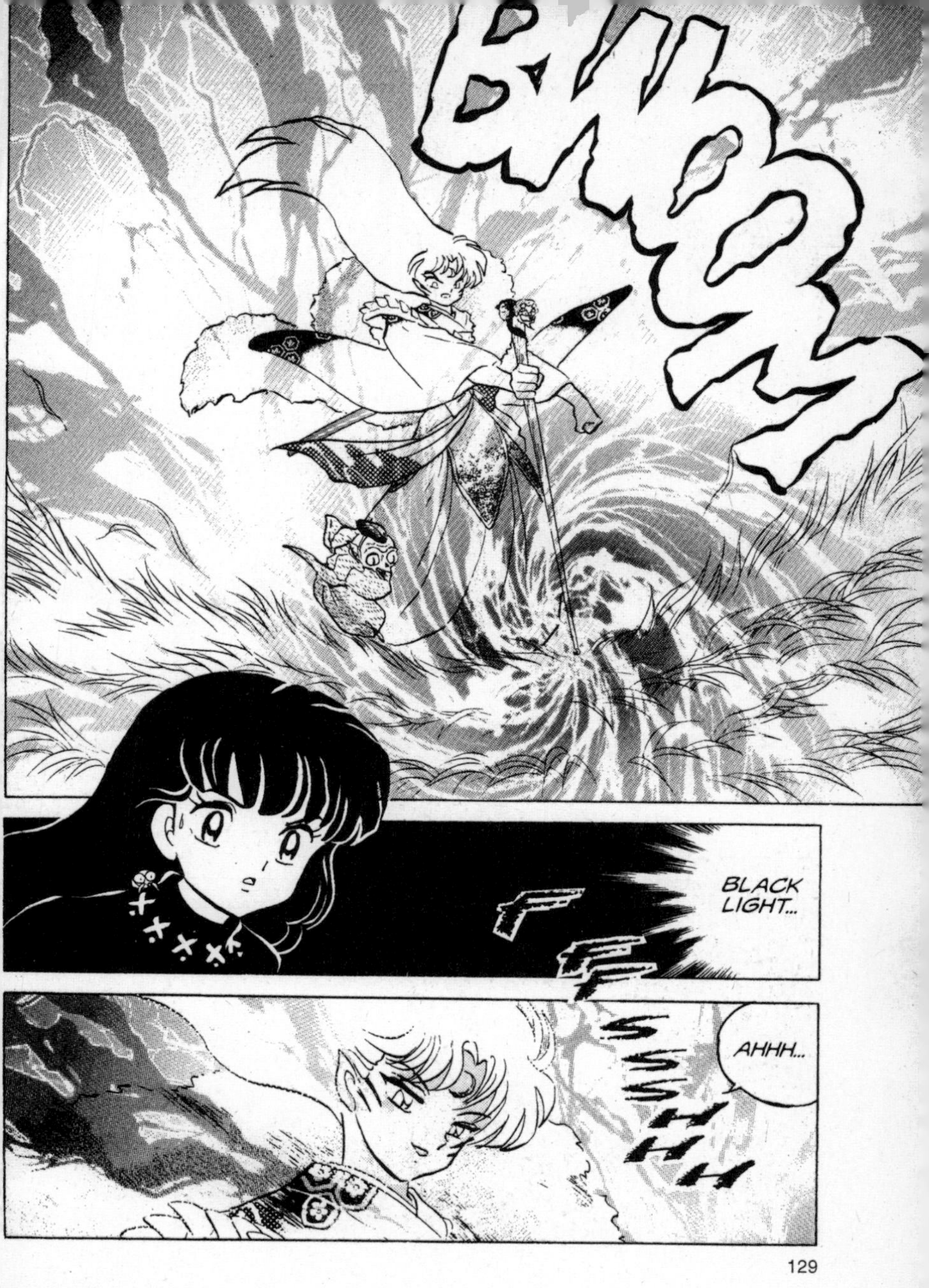
BAOOM
BLACK LIGHT...
FF
AHHH...
SSSHHHH

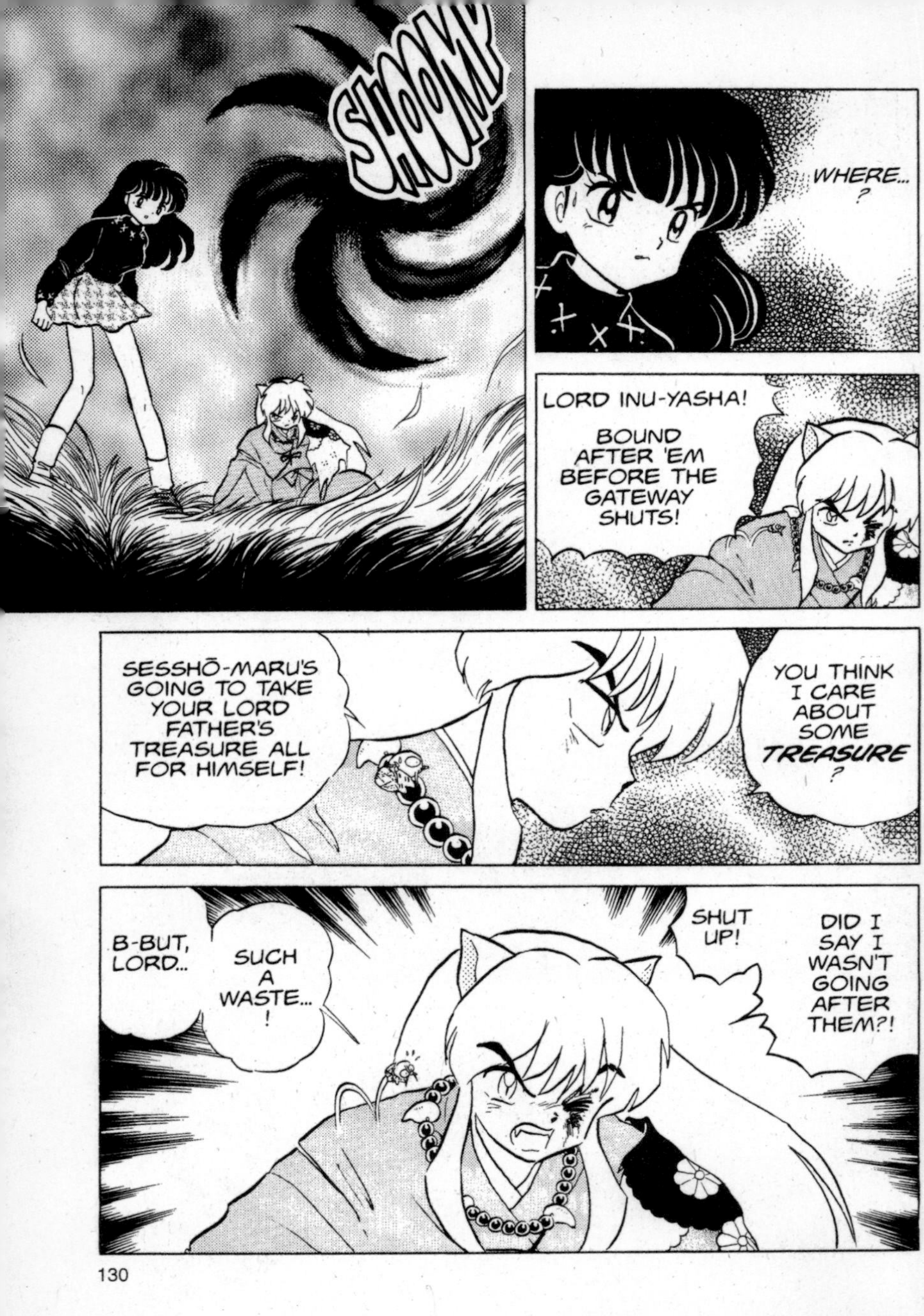
SHOOMP
WHERE... ?
LORD INU-YASHA!
BOUND AFTER 'EM BEFORE THE GATEWAY SHUTS!
SESSHŌ-MARU'S GOING TO TAKE YOUR LORD FATHER'S TREASURE ALL FOR HIMSELF!
YOU THINK I CARE ABOUT SOME *TREASURE* ?
B-BUT, LORD...
SUCH A WASTE... !
SHUT UP!
DID I SAY I WASN'T GOING AFTER THEM?!

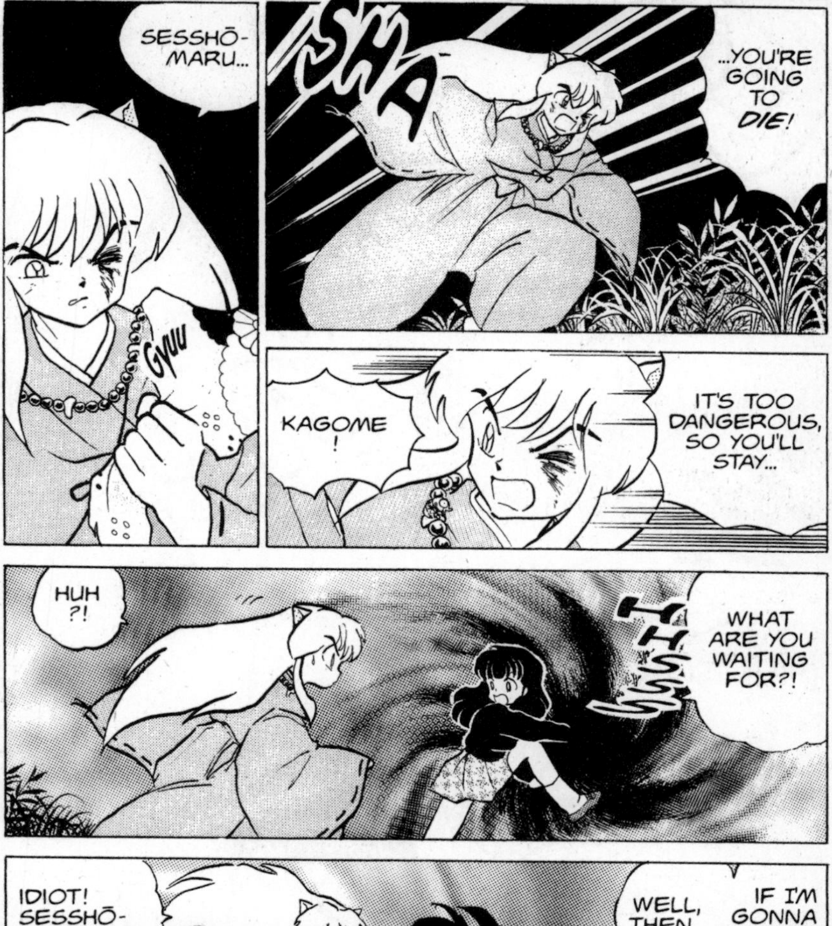
SESSHŌ-MARU...
GYUU
SHA
...YOU'RE GOING TO *DIE*!
KAGOME!
IT'S TOO DANGEROUS, SO YOU'LL STAY...
HUH?!
HISSS
WHAT ARE YOU WAITING FOR?!
IDIOT! SESSHŌ-MARU'S IN THERE!
WELL, THEN...
IF I'M GONNA *POUND* HIM, I BETTER BE THERE TOO!
FWA

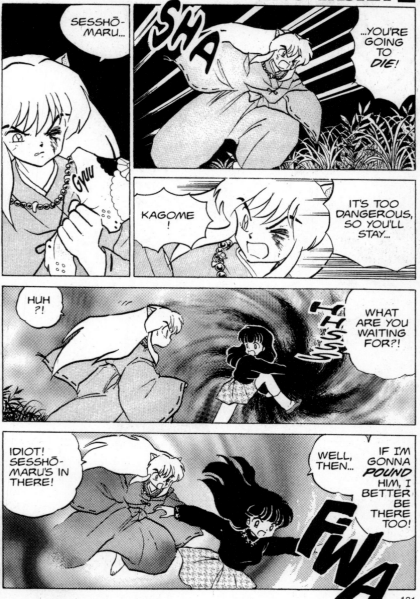

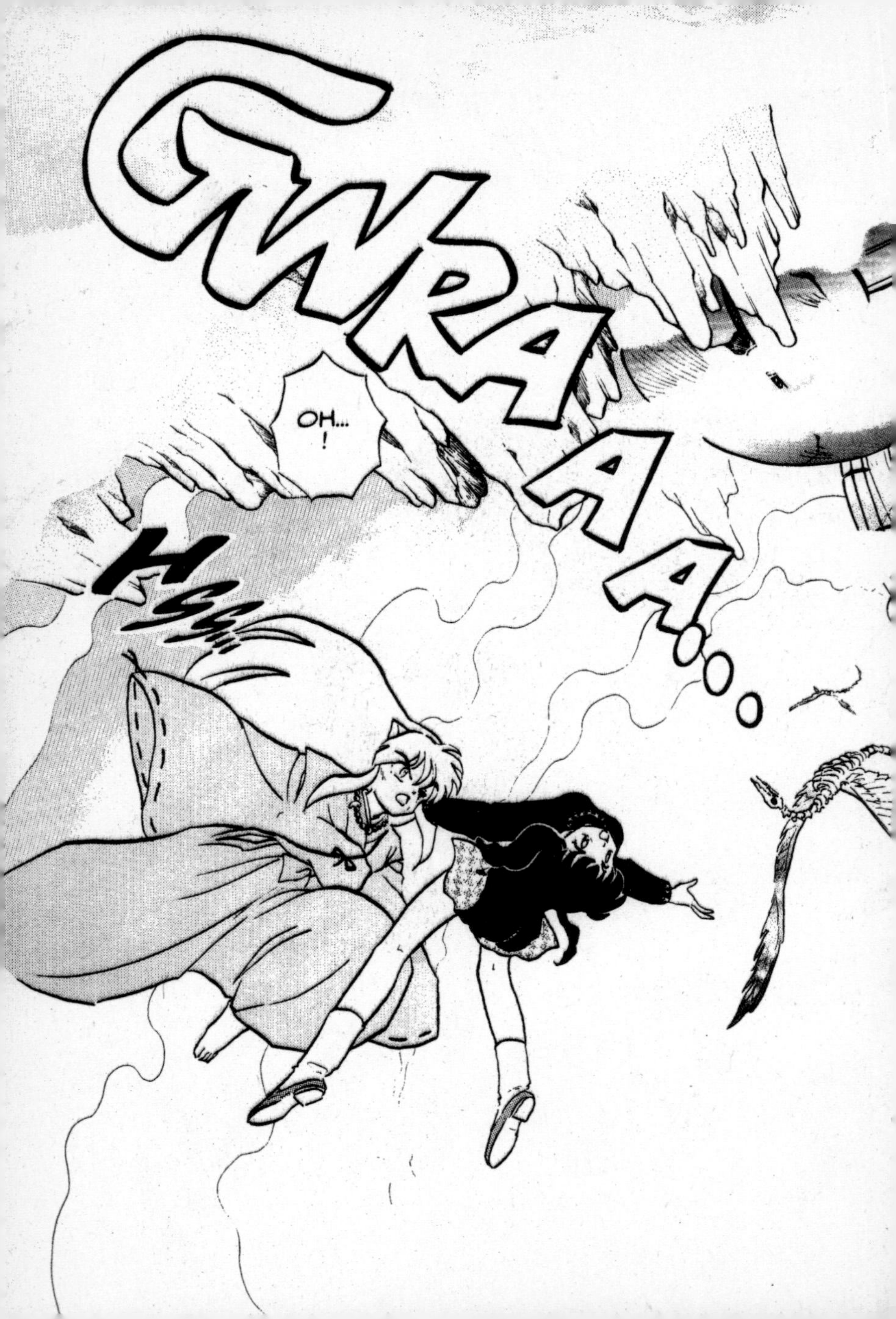
GWRAAAA...
OH... !
HSSS!!

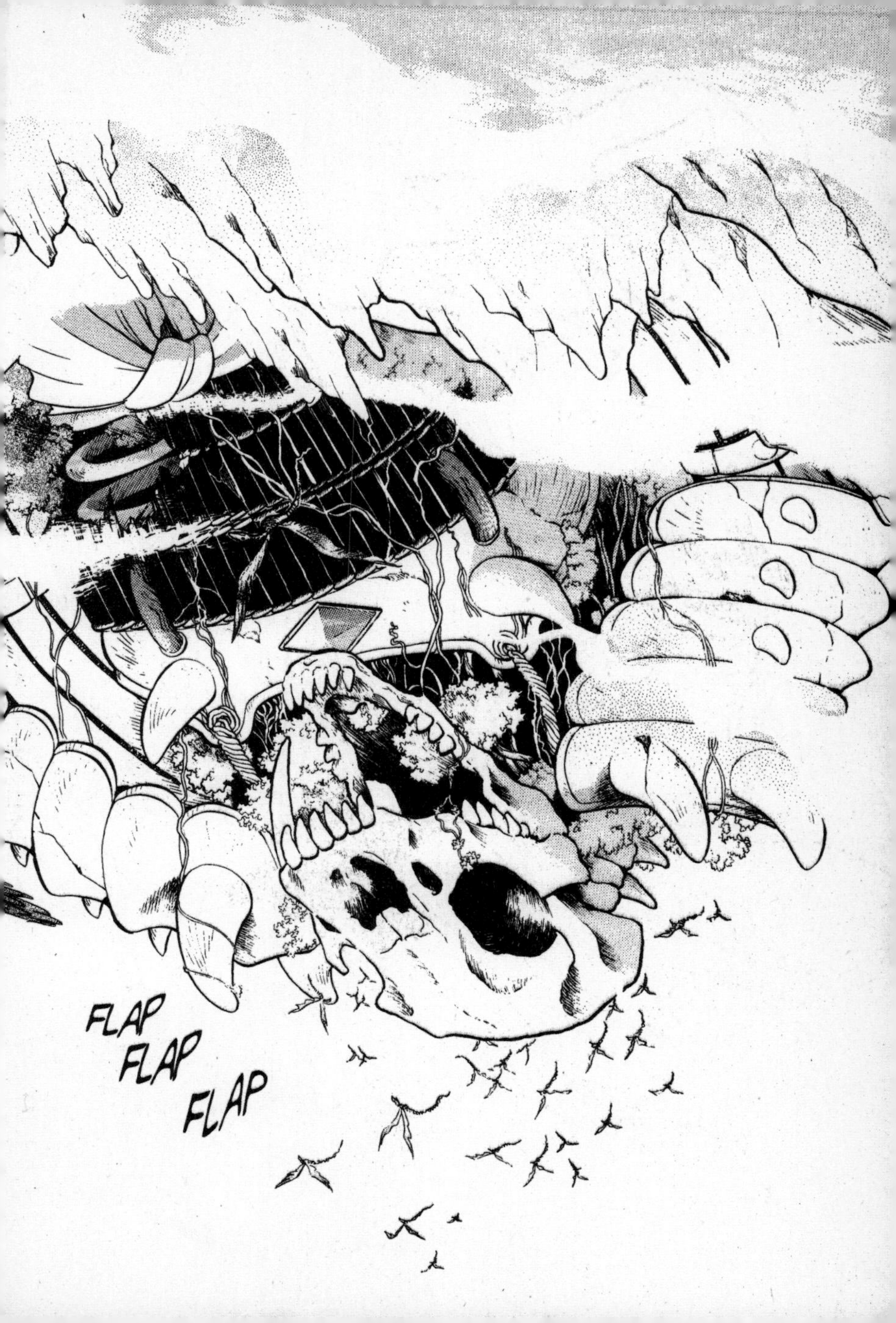
FLAP
FLAP
FLAP

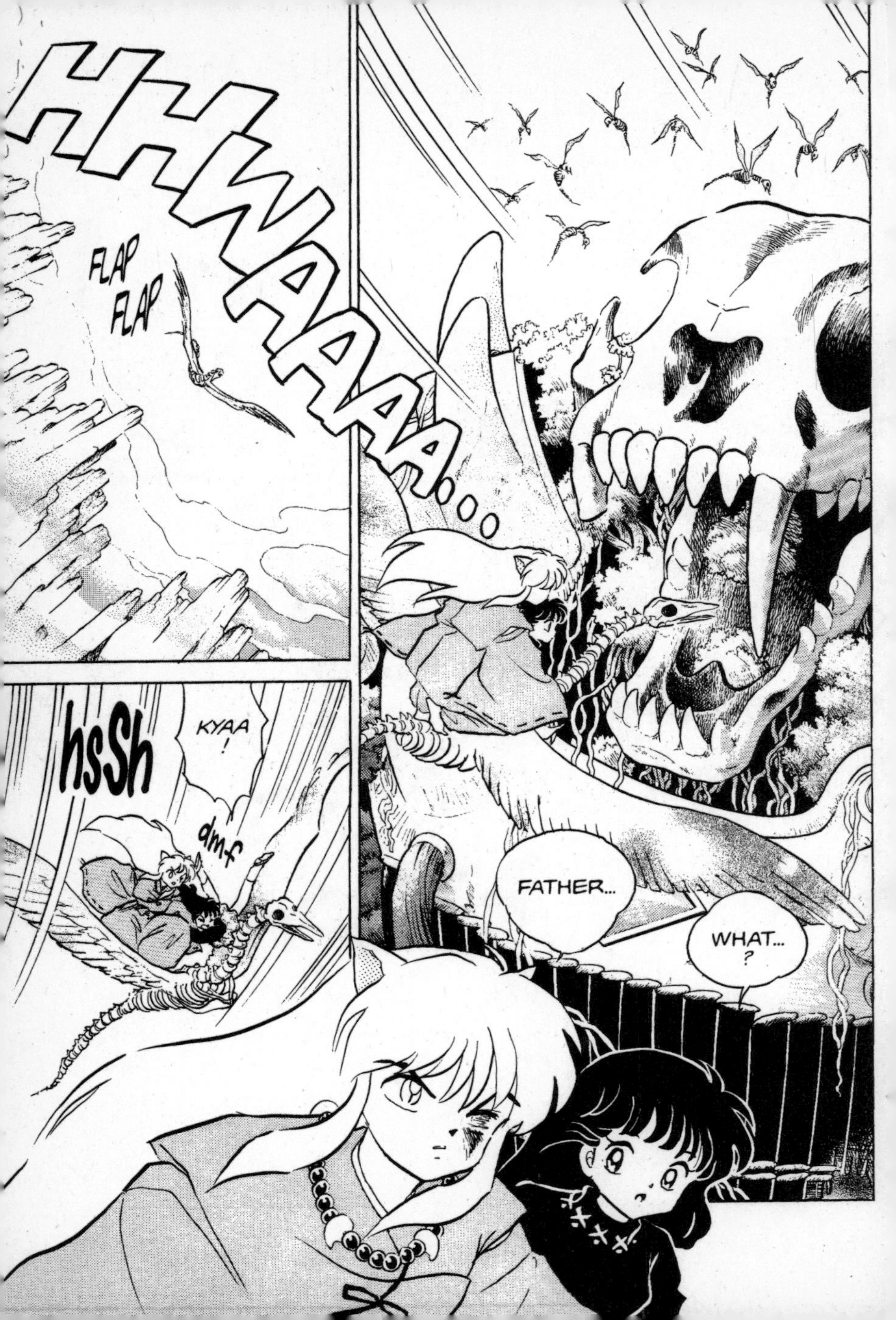
HHWAAAAA...
FLAP FLAP
hsSh
KYAA!
dmf
FATHER...
WHAT...?

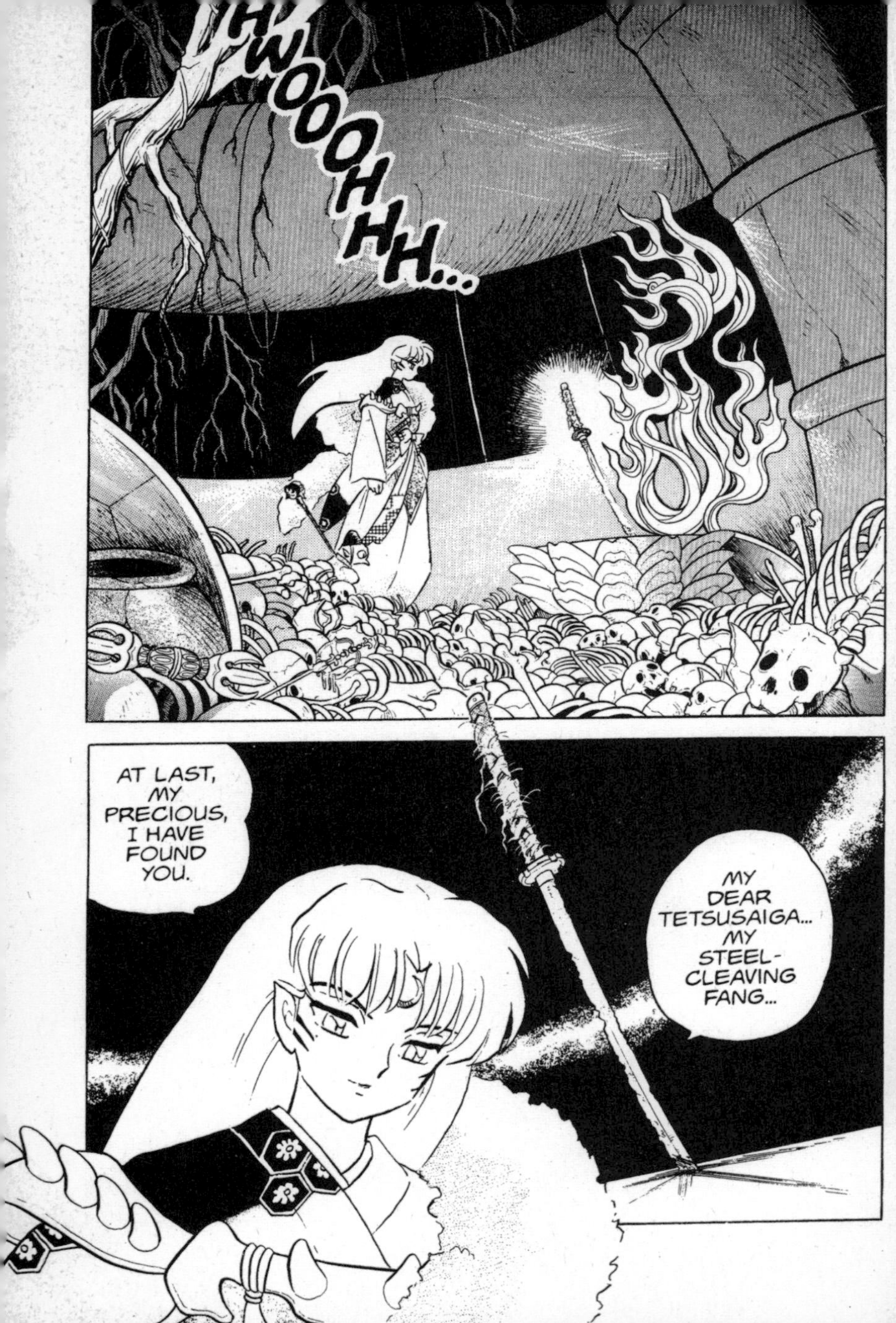
HWOOOHHH...
AT LAST, MY PRECIOUS, I HAVE FOUND YOU.
MY DEAR TETSUSAIGA... MY STEEL-CLEAVING FANG...

THE FANG OF STEEL

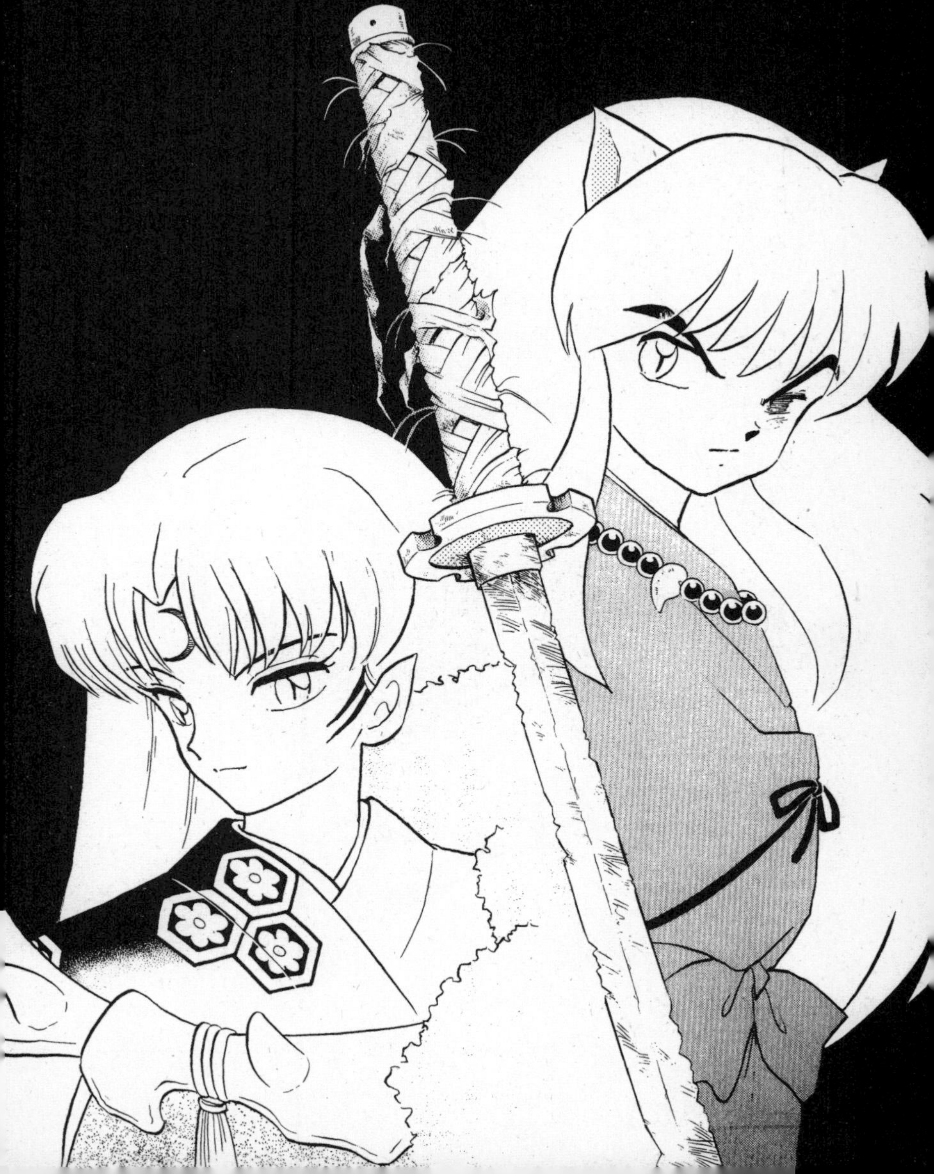

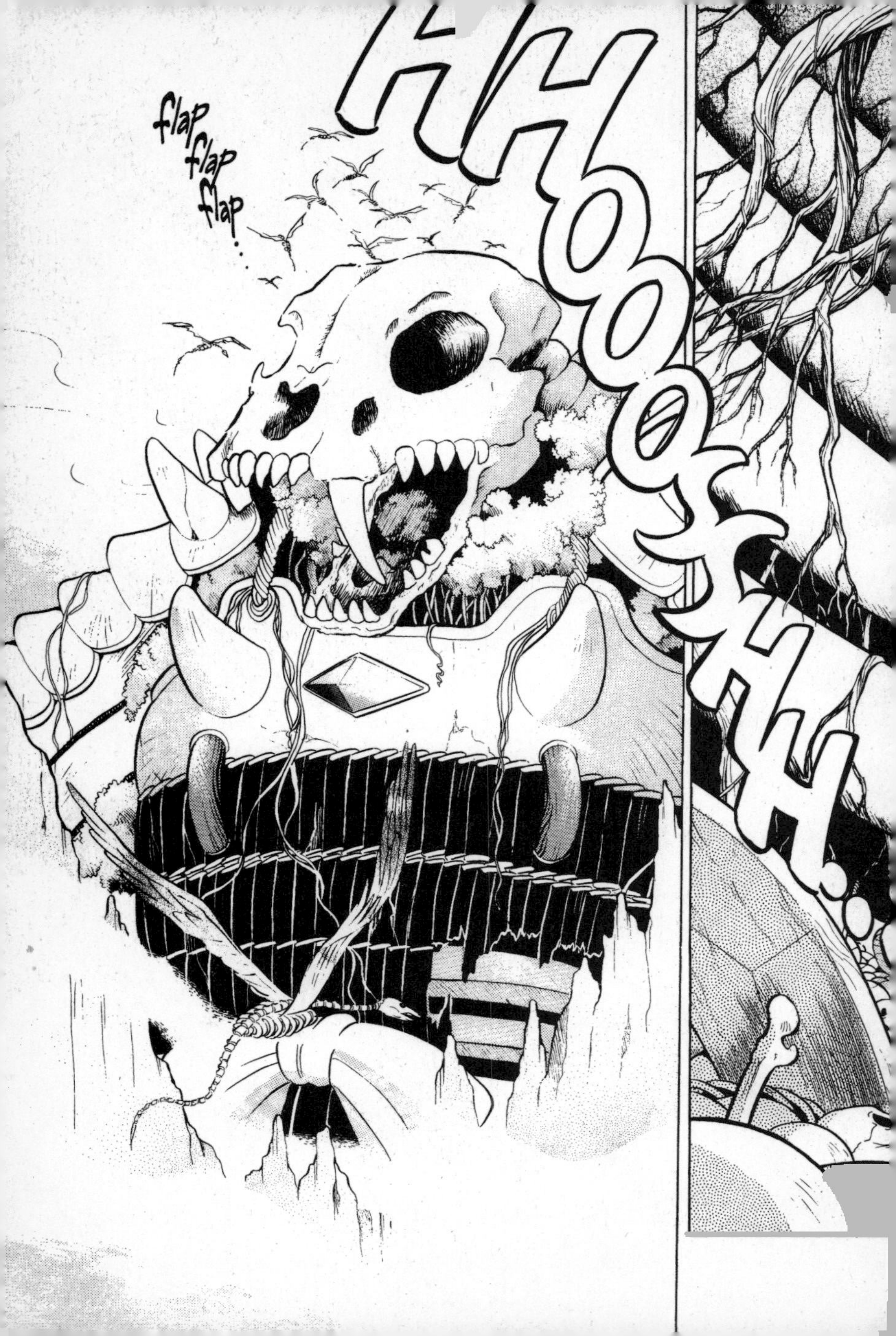
flap flap flap...
HHOOOOOHHH...

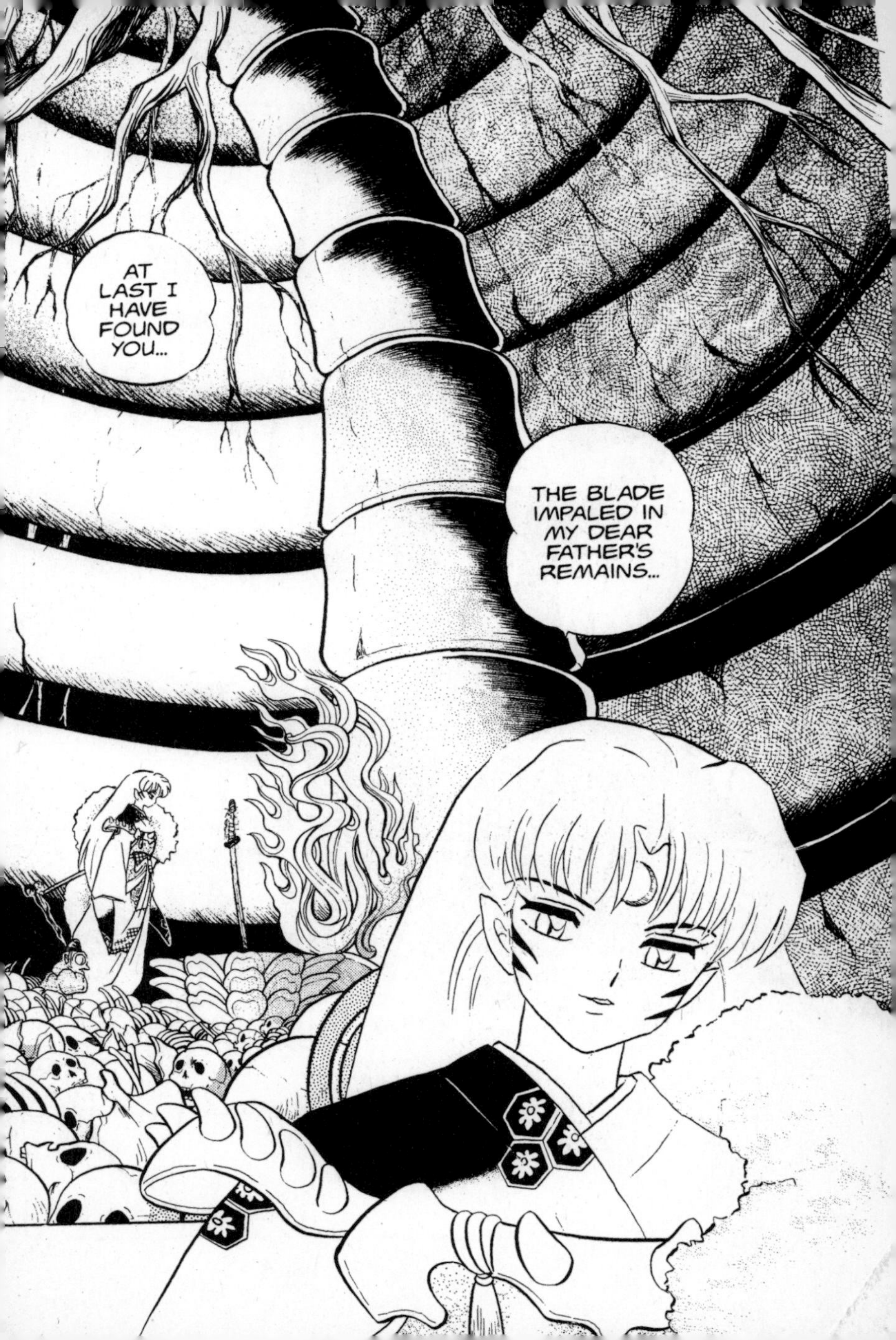
AT LAST I HAVE FOUND YOU...
THE BLADE IMPALED IN MY DEAR FATHER'S REMAINS...

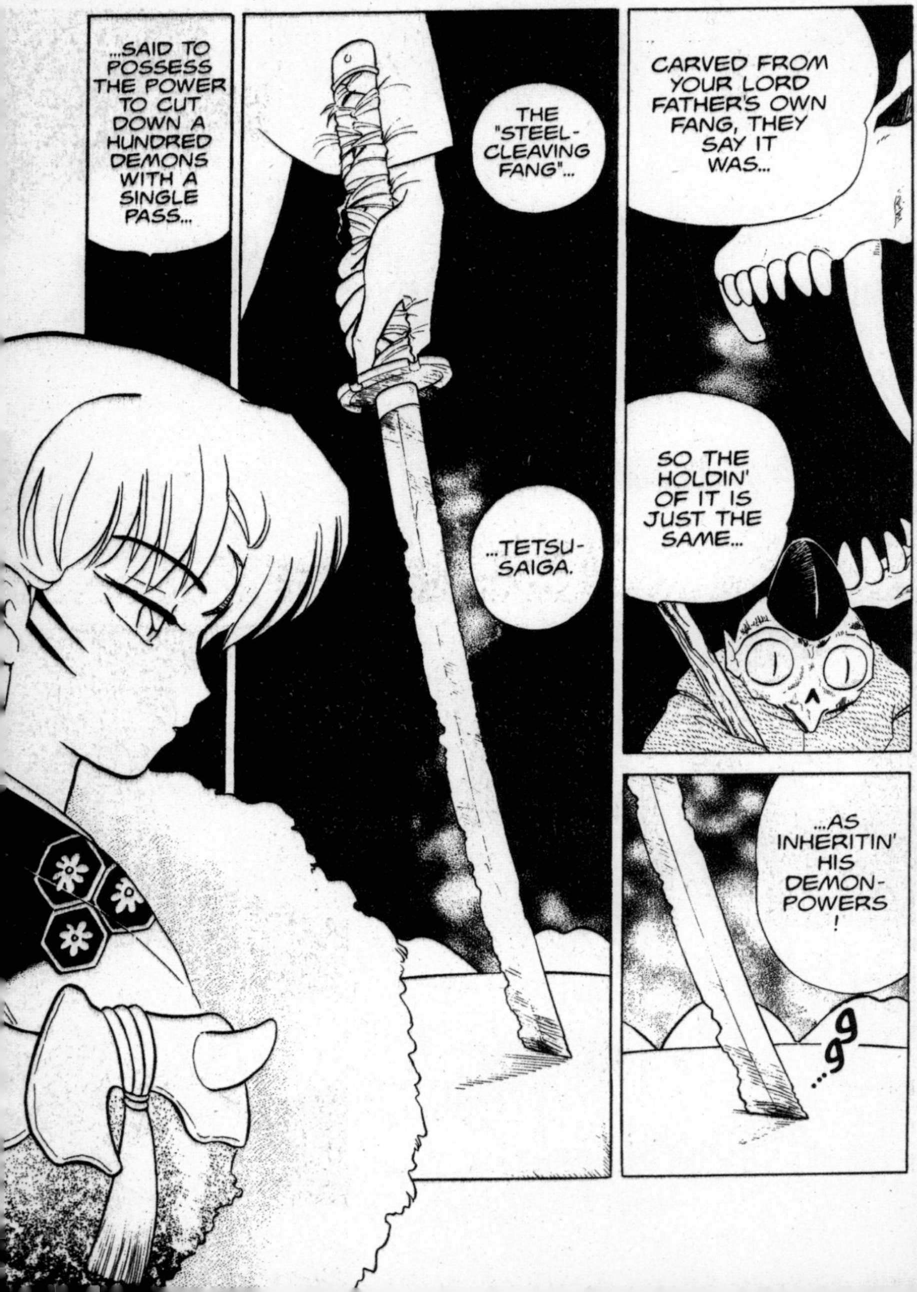

...SAID TO POSSESS THE POWER TO CUT DOWN A HUNDRED DEMONS WITH A SINGLE PASS...
THE "STEEL-CLEAVING FANG"...
...TETSU-SAIGA.
CARVED FROM YOUR LORD FATHER'S OWN FANG, THEY SAY IT WAS...
SO THE HOLDIN' OF IT IS JUST THE SAME...
...AS INHERITIN' HIS DEMON-POWERS!

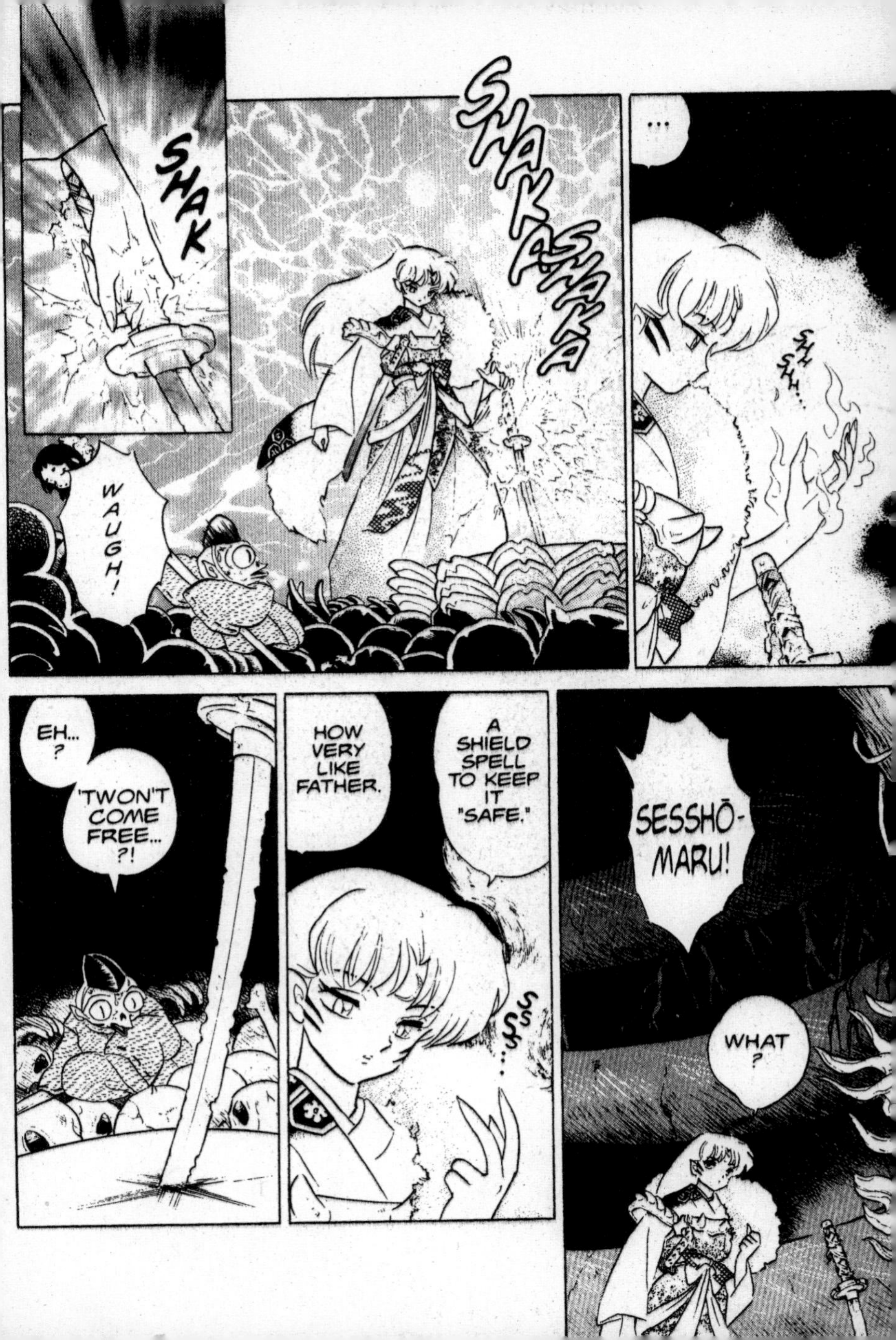
SHAK
SHAKASHAKA
WAUGH!
...
SHH SHH...
EH...?
'TWON'T COME FREE...?!
HOW VERY LIKE FATHER.
A SHIELD SPELL TO KEEP IT "SAFE."
SSS...
SESSHŌ-MARU!
WHAT?

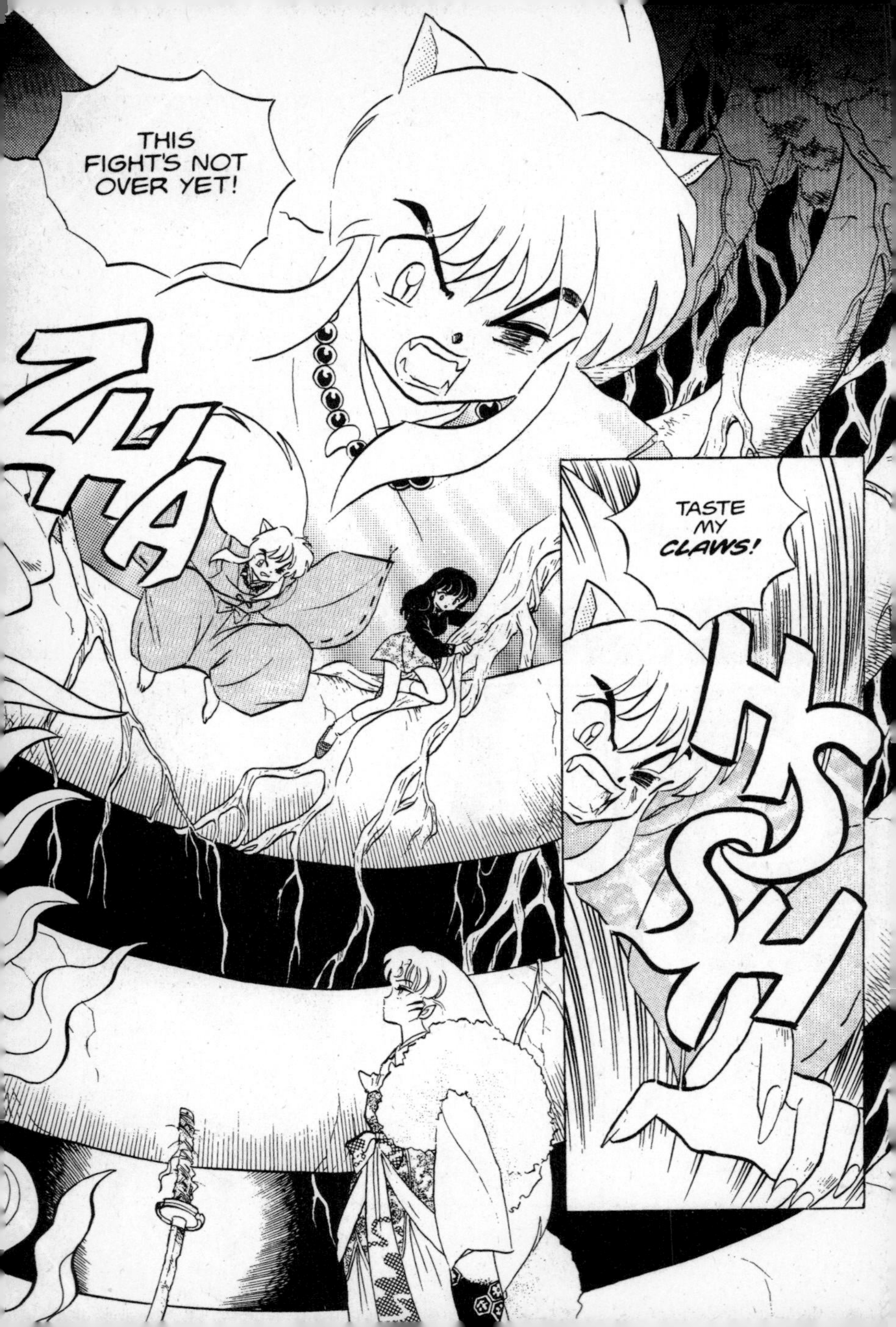
THIS FIGHT'S NOT OVER YET!
ZHA
TASTE MY CLAWS!
HYSSH

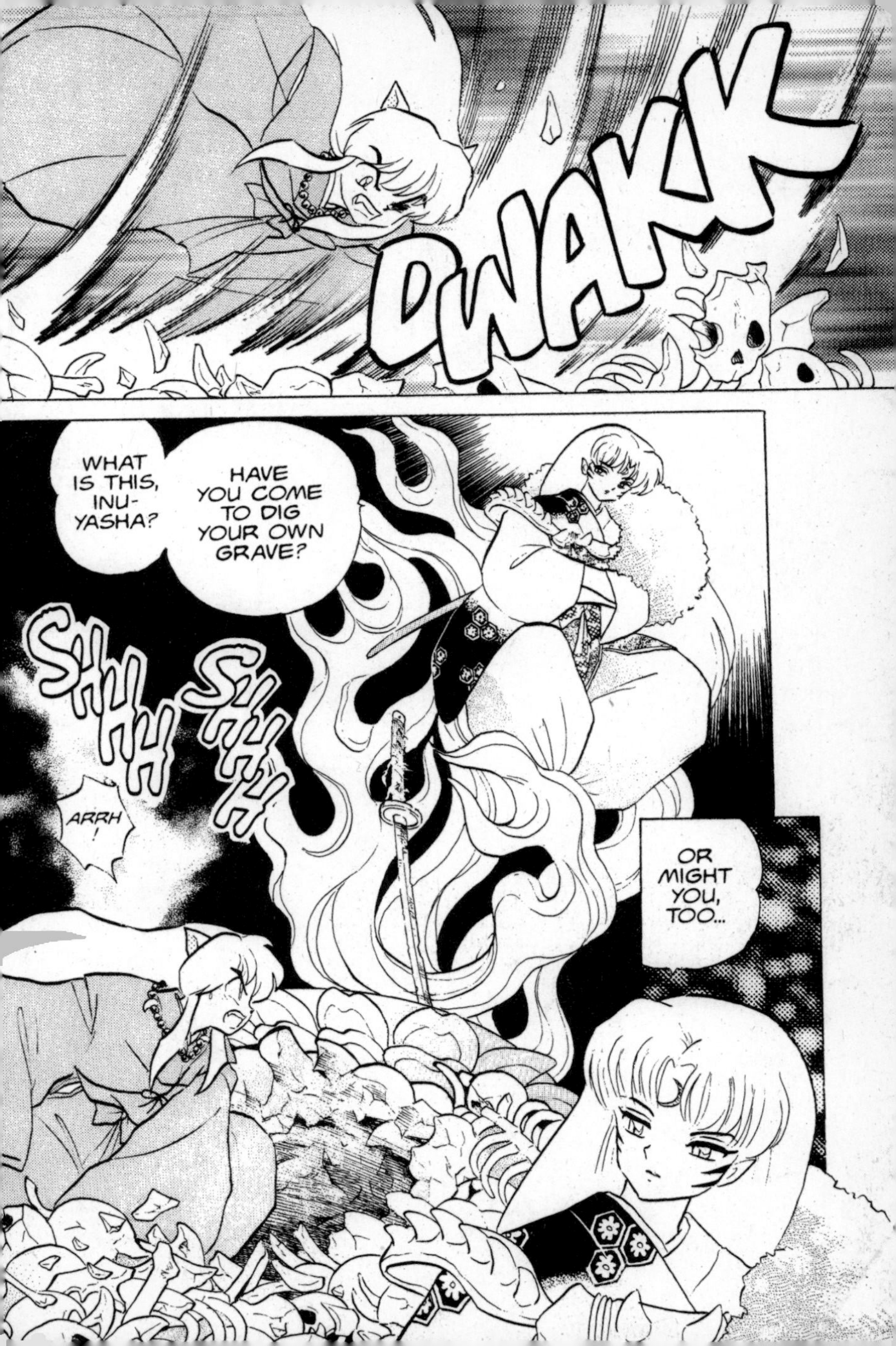
DWAKK
WHAT IS THIS, INU-YASHA?
HAVE YOU COME TO DIG YOUR OWN GRAVE?
SHHH
SHHH
ARRH!
OR MIGHT YOU, TOO...

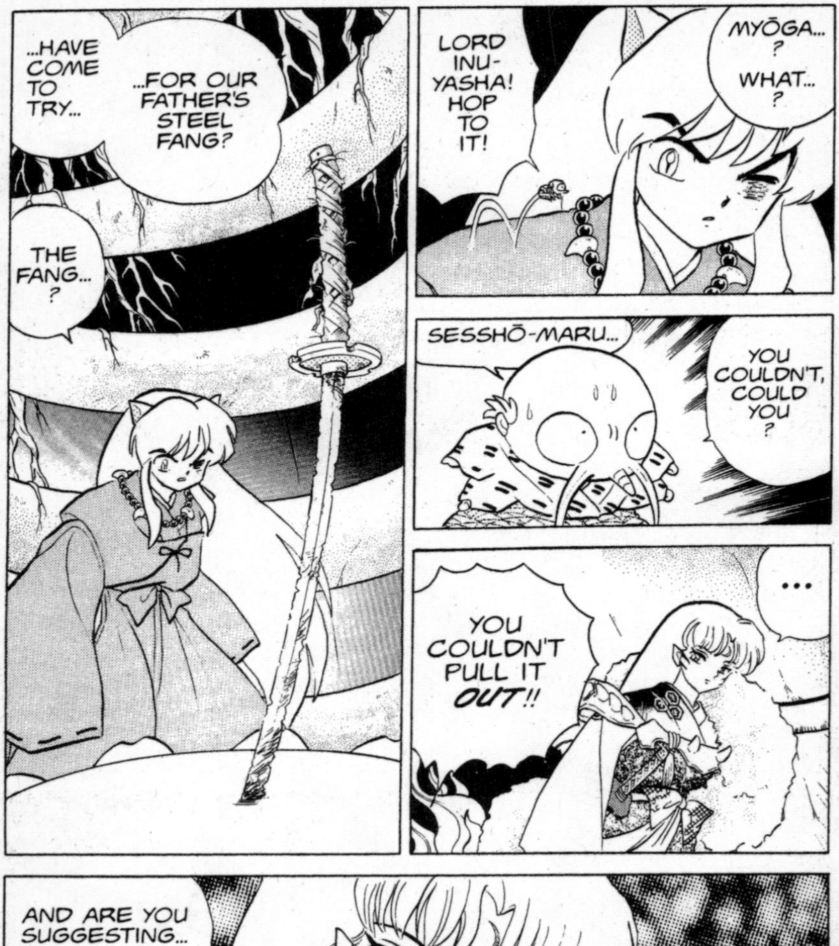
...HAVE COME TO TRY...
...FOR OUR FATHER'S STEEL FANG?
THE FANG... ?
LORD INU-YASHA! HOP TO IT!
MYŌGA... ? WHAT... ?
SESSHŌ-MARU...
YOU COULDN'T, COULD YOU ?
YOU COULDN'T PULL IT *OUT*!!
...
AND ARE YOU SUGGESTING...
...THAT MY BROTHER CAN?

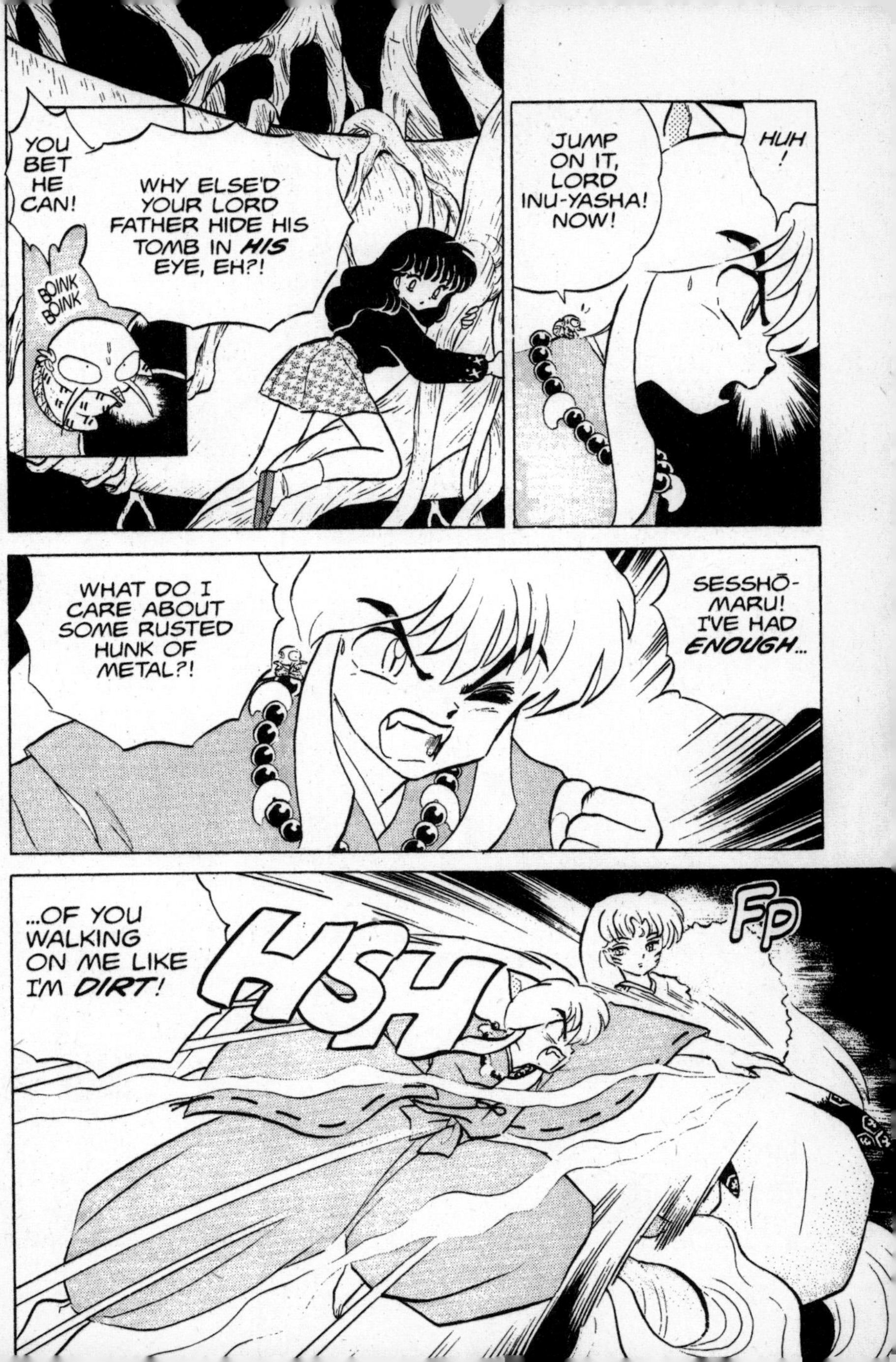
YOU BET HE CAN!
WHY ELSE'D YOUR LORD FATHER HIDE HIS TOMB IN *HIS* EYE, EH?!
BOINK BOINK
JUMP ON IT, LORD INU-YASHA! NOW!
HUH!
WHAT DO I CARE ABOUT SOME RUSTED HUNK OF METAL?!
SESSHŌ-MARU! I'VE HAD *ENOUGH*...
...OF YOU WALKING ON ME LIKE I'M *DIRT*!
HSH
FP

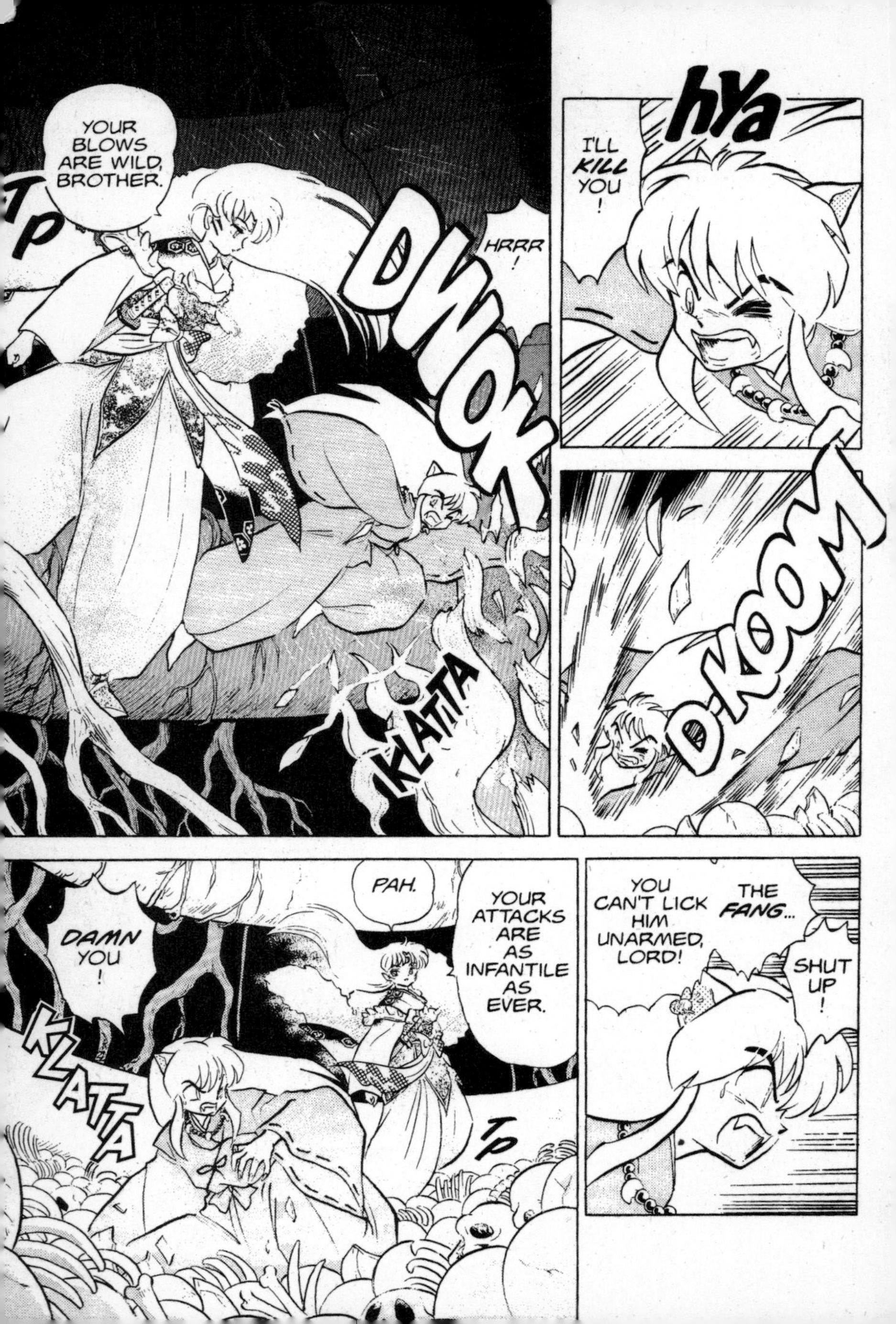
TP
YOUR BLOWS ARE WILD, BROTHER.
DWNOK
HRRR!
KLATTA
hYa
I'LL KILL YOU!
D-KOOM
DAMN YOU!
KLATTA
PAH.
YOUR ATTACKS ARE AS INFANTILE AS EVER.
TP
YOU CAN'T LICK HIM UNARMED, LORD!
THE FANG...
SHUT UP!

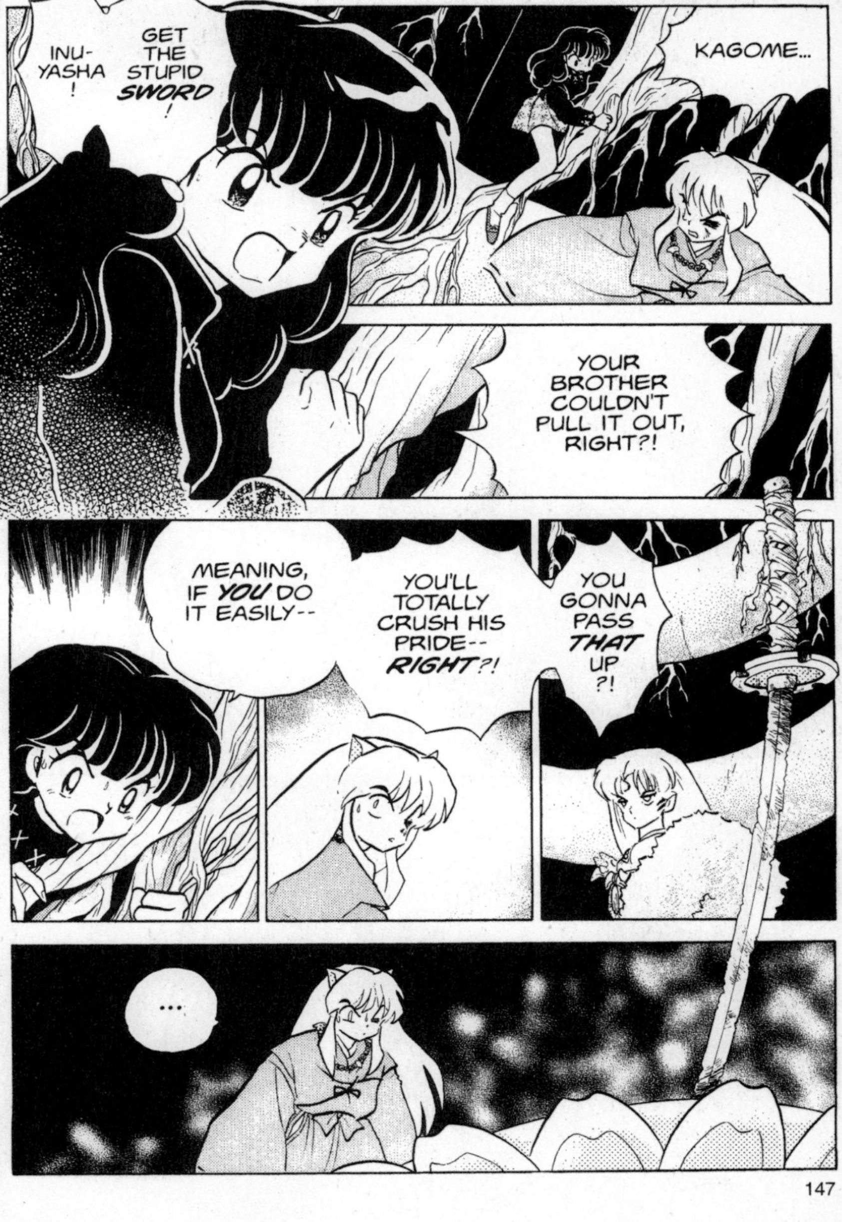
INU-YASHA!
GET THE STUPID SWORD!
KAGOME...
YOUR BROTHER COULDN'T PULL IT OUT, RIGHT?!
MEANING, IF YOU DO IT EASILY--
YOU'LL TOTALLY CRUSH HIS PRIDE--RIGHT?!
YOU GONNA PASS THAT UP?!
...

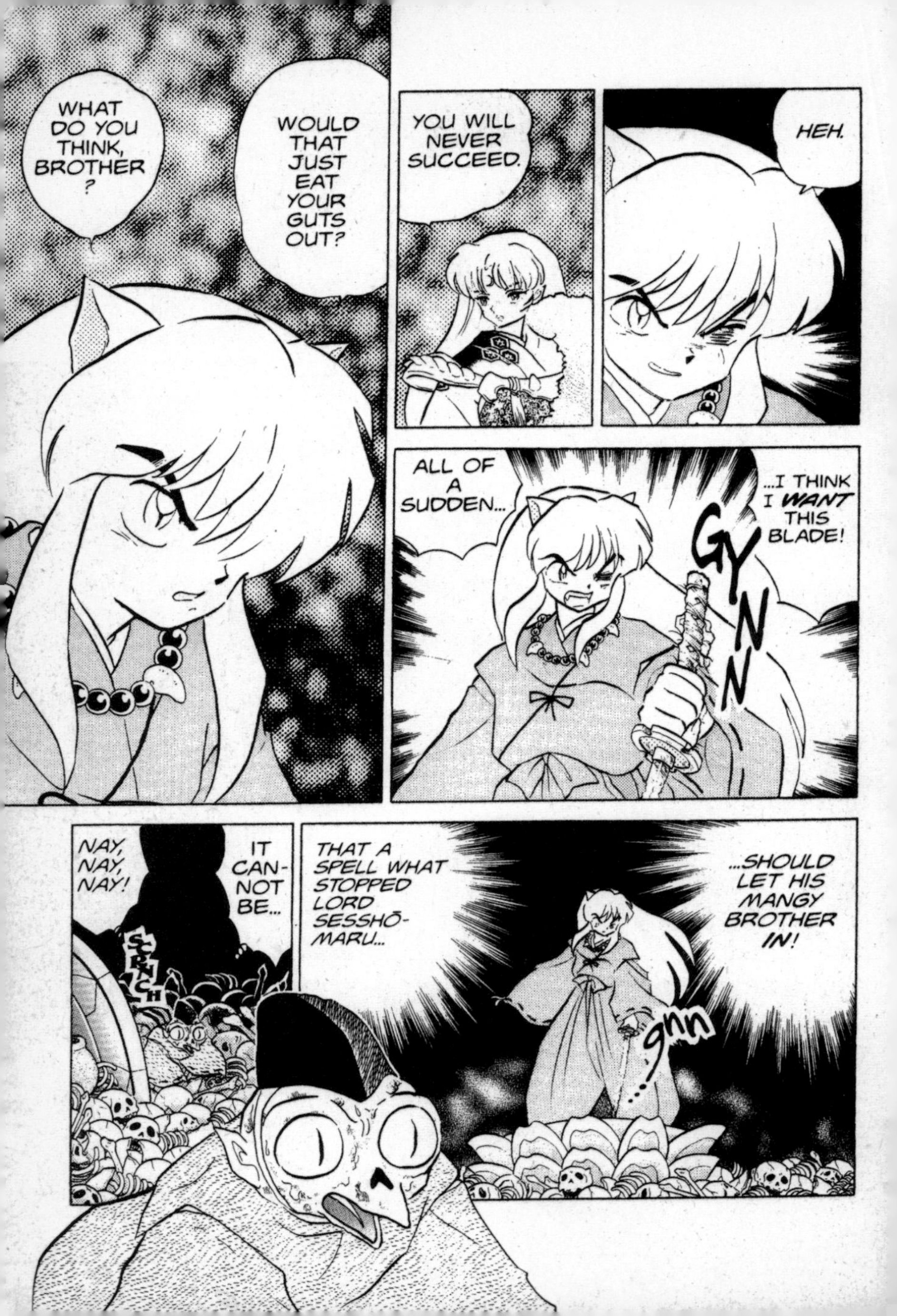
WHAT DO YOU THINK, BROTHER?
WOULD THAT JUST EAT YOUR GUTS OUT?
YOU WILL NEVER SUCCEED.
HEH.
ALL OF A SUDDEN...
...I THINK I *WANT* THIS BLADE!
GYNNN
NAY, NAY, NAY!
IT CAN-NOT BE...
SCRNCH
THAT A SPELL WHAT STOPPED LORD SESSHŌ-MARU...
...SHOULD LET HIS MANGY BROTHER *IN*!
gnn

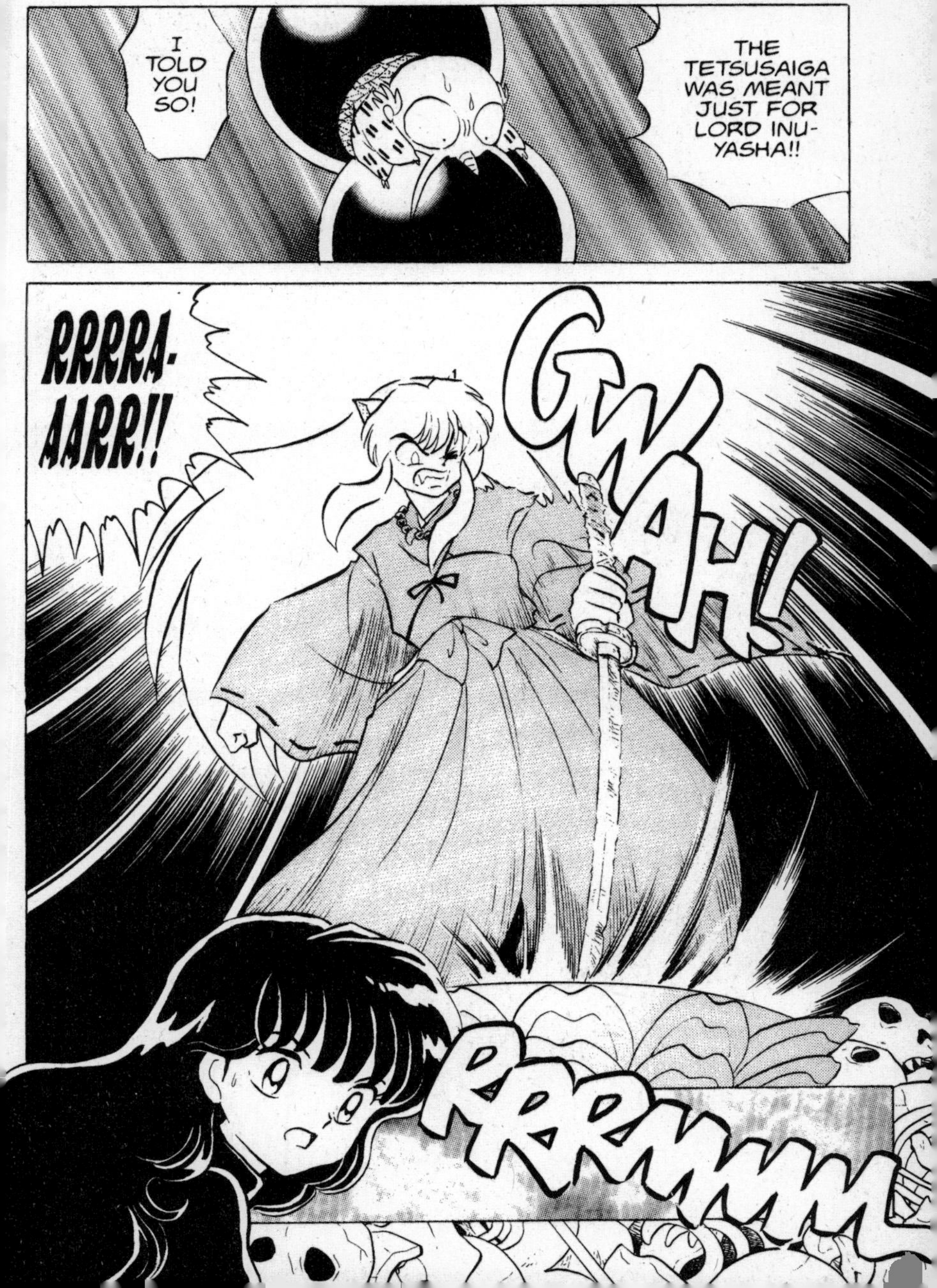
I TOLD YOU SO!
THE TETSUSAIGA WAS MEANT JUST FOR LORD INU-YASHA!!
RRRRA-AARR!!
GWAH!
RRRUMM

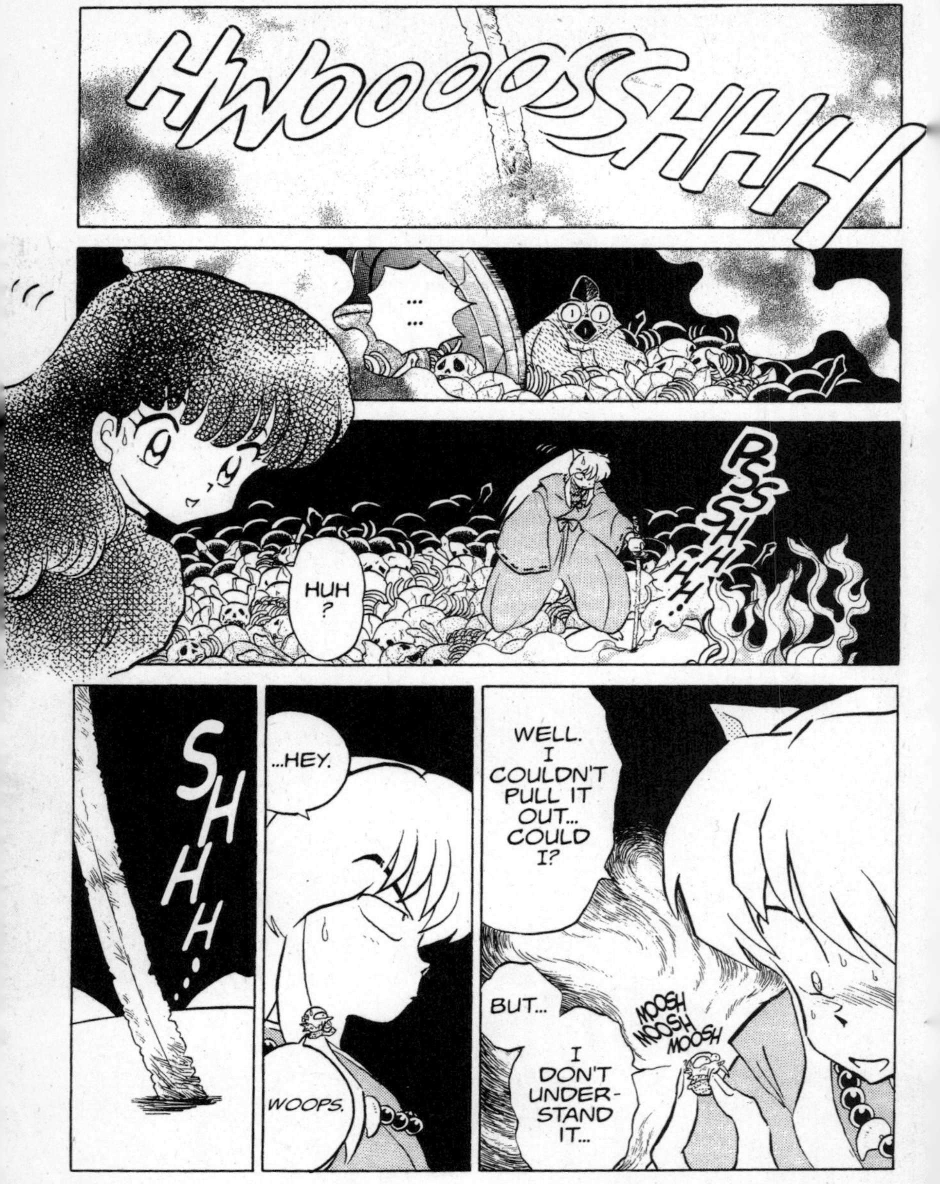
HWOOOOSHHH
...
...
HUH?
PSSSHHHH...
SHHH...
...HEY.
WOOPS.
WELL. I COULDN'T PULL IT OUT... COULD I?
BUT...
MOOSH MOOSH MOOSH
I DON'T UNDER-STAND IT...

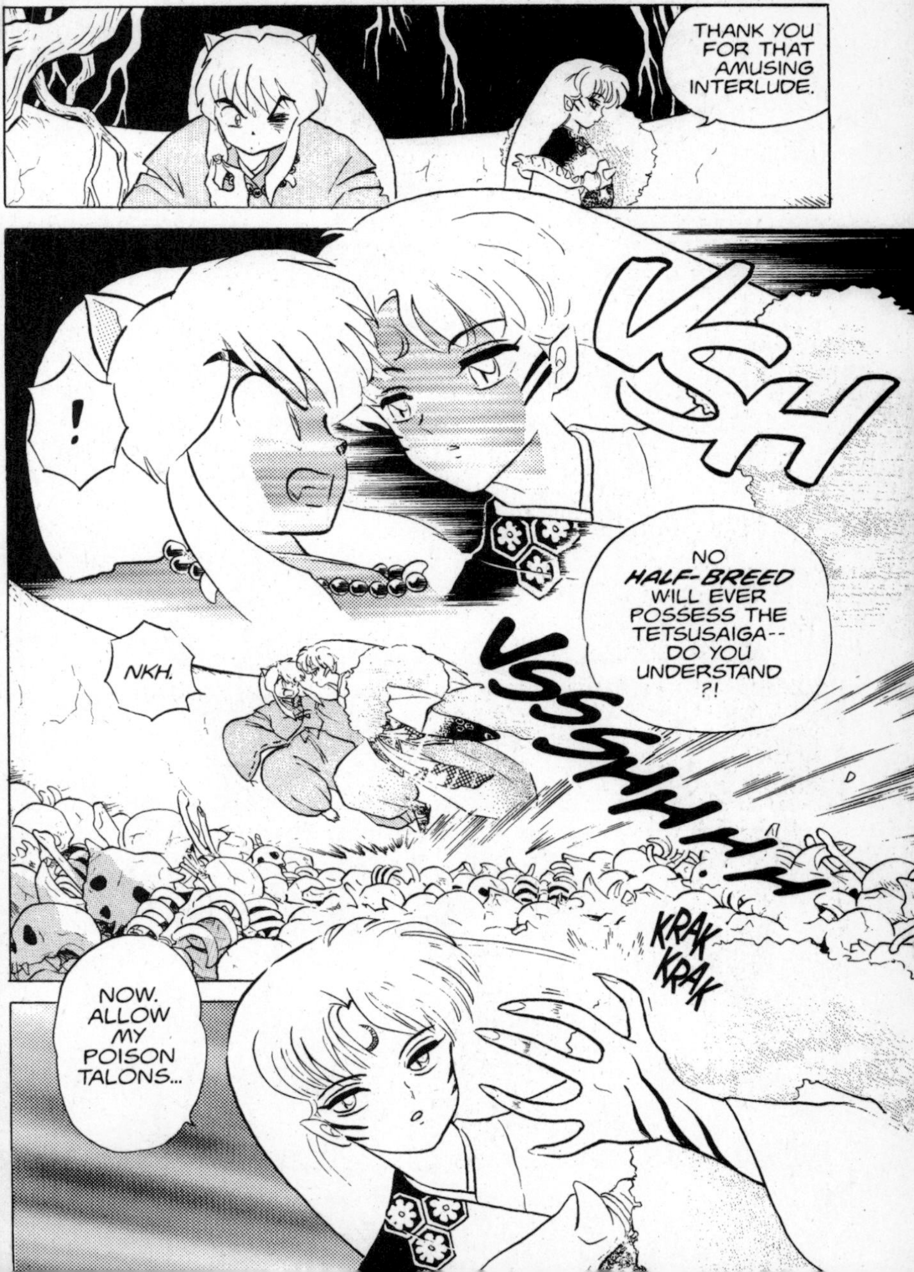
THANK YOU FOR THAT AMUSING INTERLUDE.
VSH
!
NO HALF-BREED WILL EVER POSSESS THE TETSUSAIGA--DO YOU UNDERSTAND?!
NKH.
VSSSHHHH
NOW. ALLOW MY POISON TALONS...
KRAK KRAK

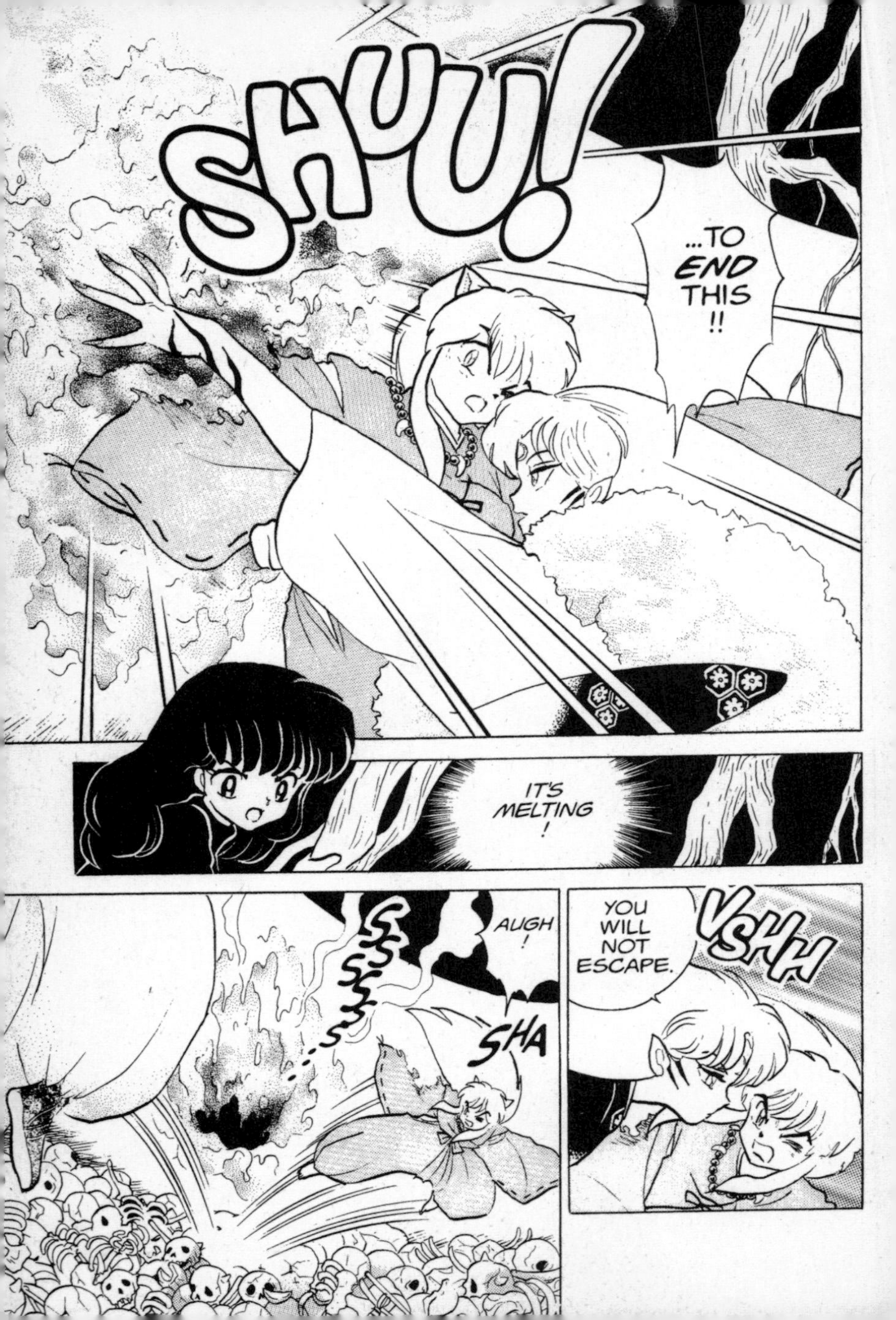
SHYU!
...TO END THIS !!
IT'S MELTING !
YOU WILL NOT ESCAPE.
VSHH
AUGH !
SHA

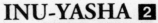

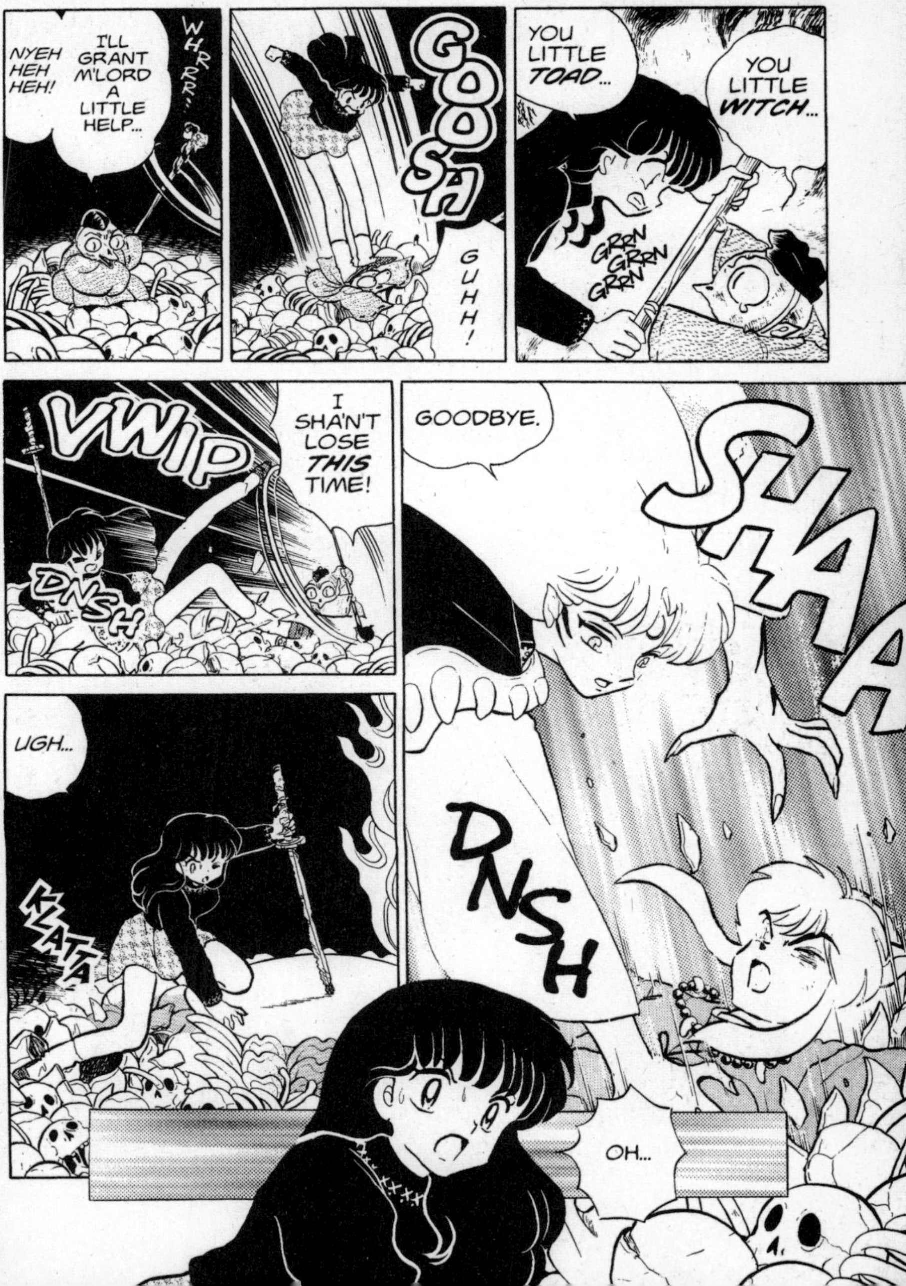
NYEH HEH HEH!
I'LL GRANT M'LORD A LITTLE HELP...
WHRRR...
GOOOSH
GUHH!
YOU LITTLE TOAD...
YOU LITTLE WITCH...
GRRN GRRN GRRN
VWIP
DNSH
I SHA'N'T LOSE THIS TIME!
GOODBYE.
SHAA
UGH...
KLATTA
DNSH
OH...

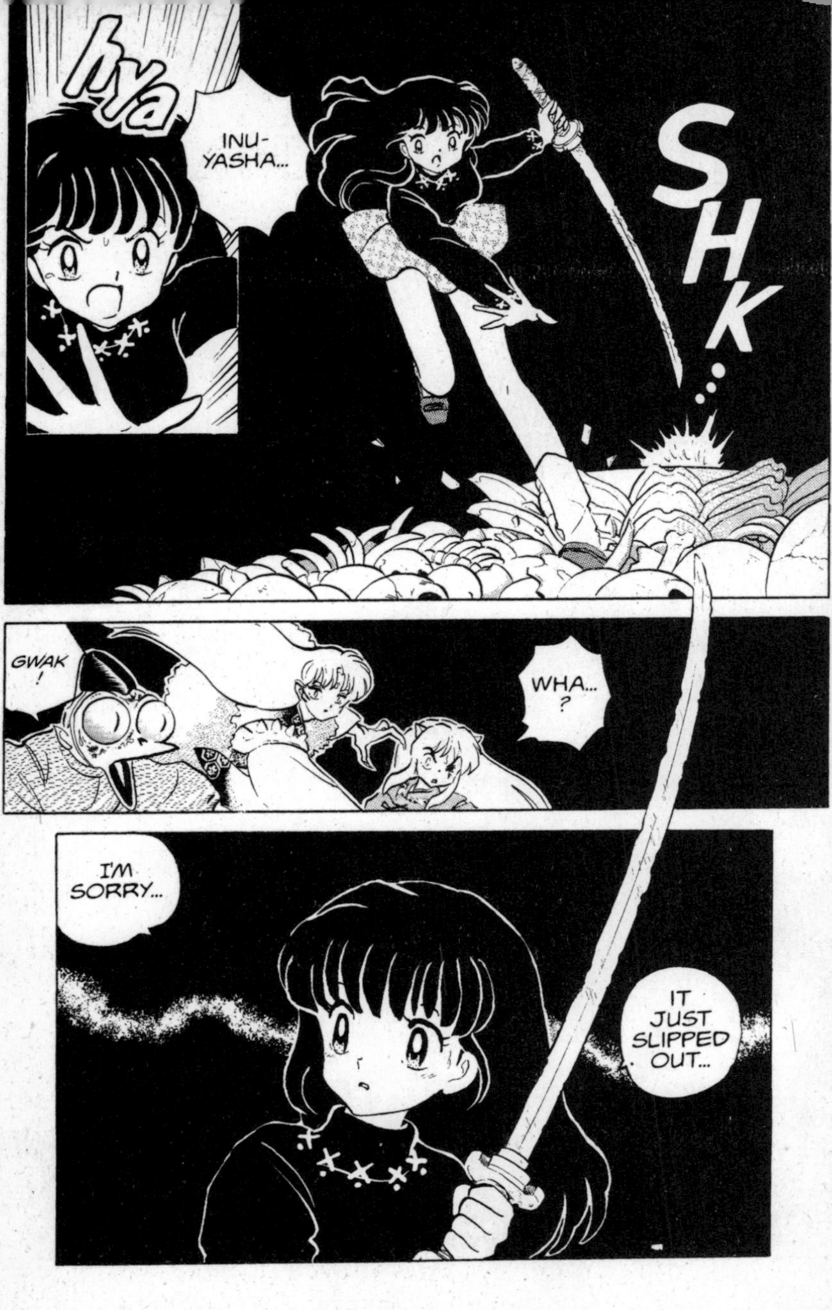
hya
INU-YASHA...
SHK...
GWAK!
WHA...?
I'M SORRY...
IT JUST SLIPPED OUT...

SCROLL NINE

THE TRANSFORMATION

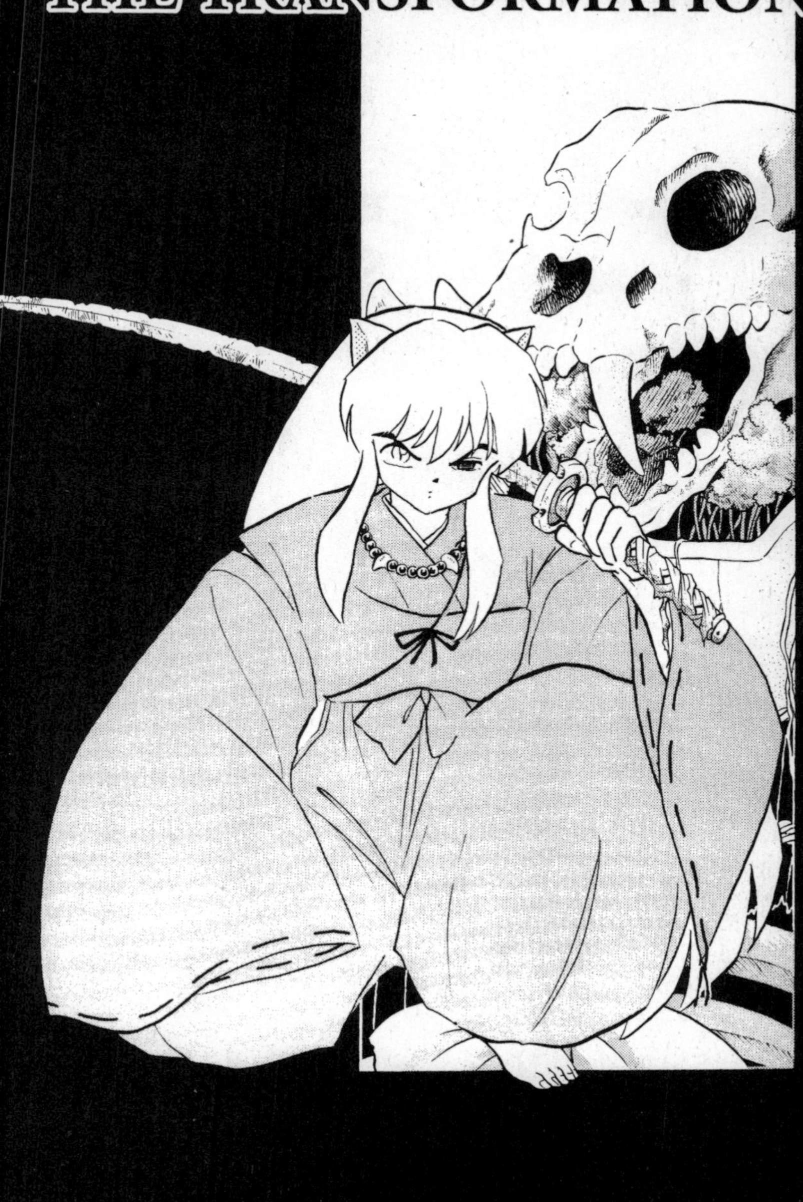

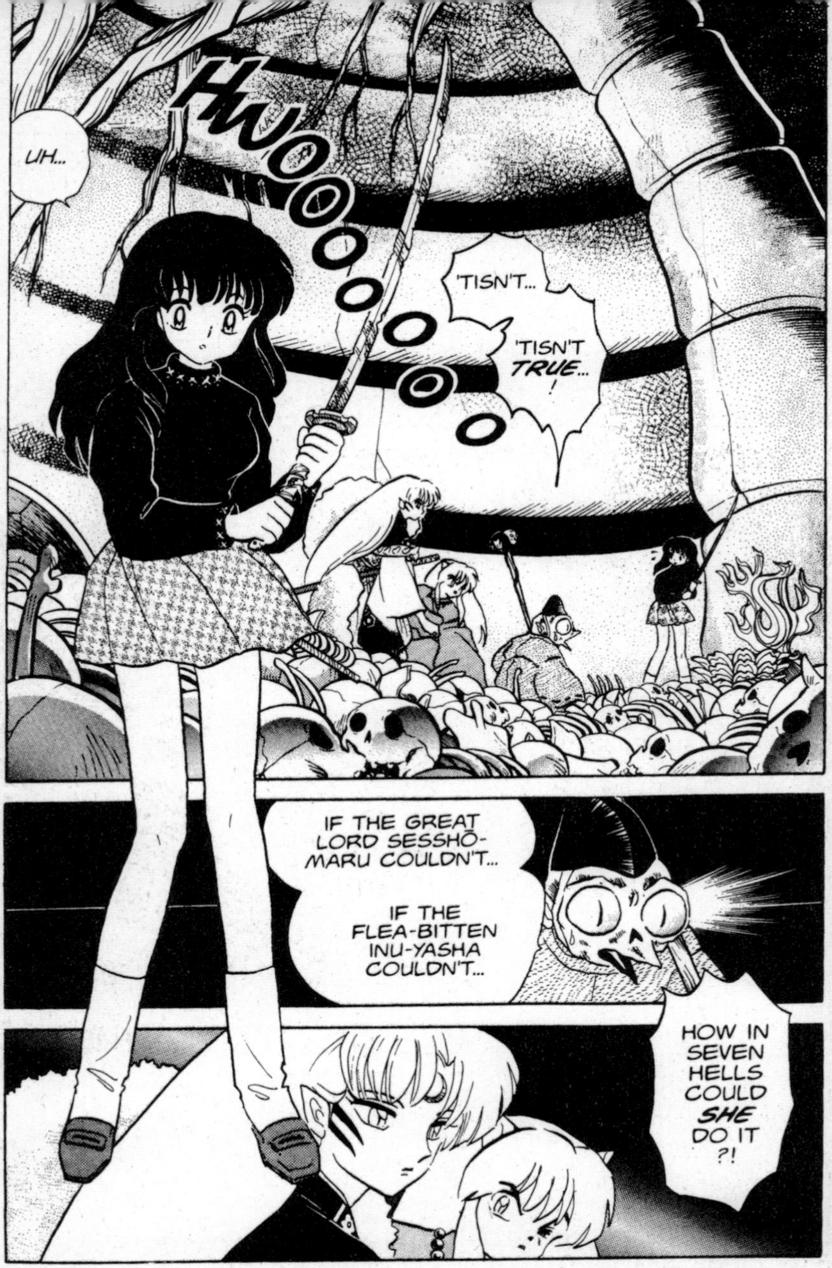
HWOOOOOOOOO
UH...
'TISN'T...
'TISN'T TRUE...!
IF THE GREAT LORD SESSHŌ-MARU COULDN'T...
IF THE FLEA-BITTEN INU-YASHA COULDN'T...
HOW IN SEVEN HELLS COULD SHE DO IT?!

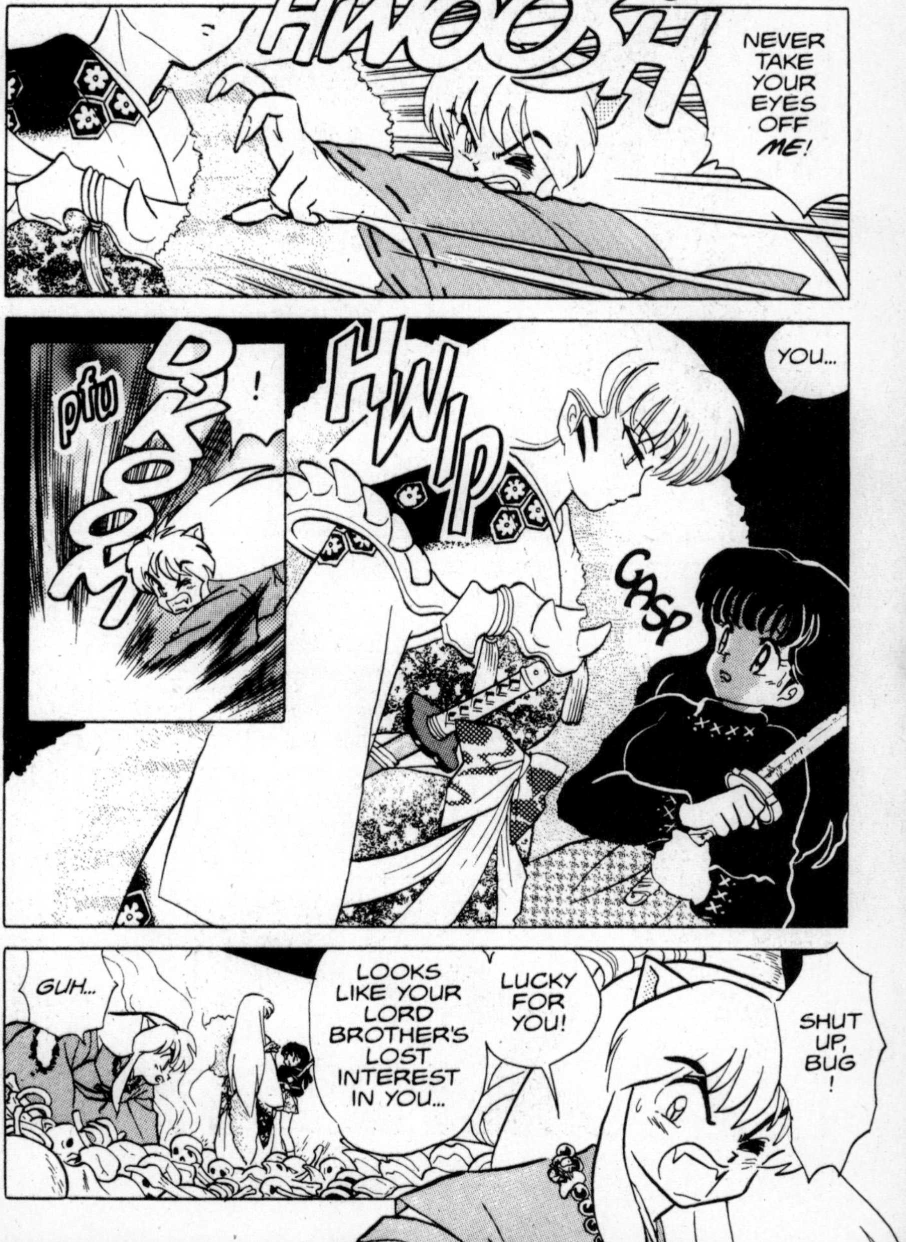
HWOOSH
NEVER TAKE YOUR EYES OFF *ME*!
pfu
DOKOOM
!
HWIP
YOU...
GASP
GUH...
LOOKS LIKE YOUR LORD BROTHER'S LOST INTEREST IN YOU...
LUCKY FOR YOU!
SHUT UP, BUG!

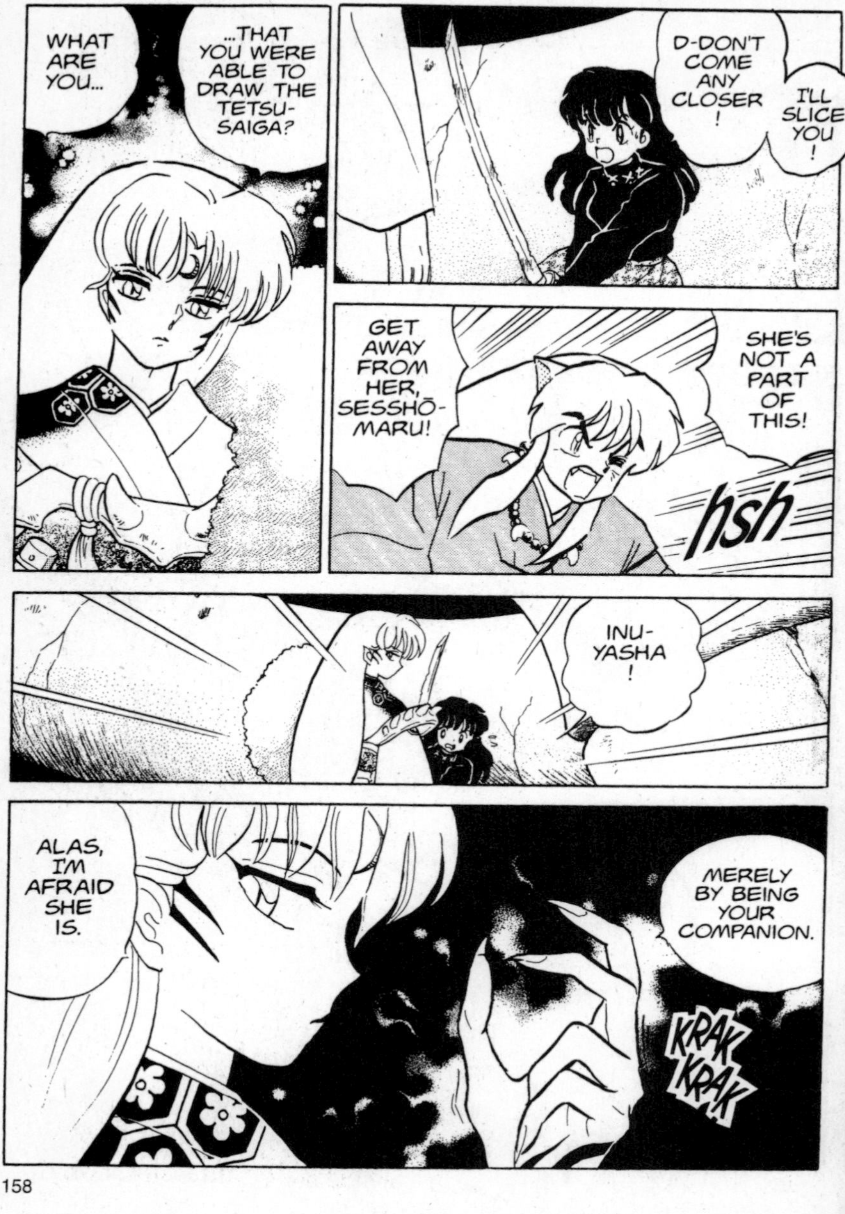
WHAT ARE YOU...
...THAT YOU WERE ABLE TO DRAW THE TETSU-SAIGA?
D-DON'T COME ANY CLOSER!
I'LL SLICE YOU!
GET AWAY FROM HER, SESSHŌ-MARU!
SHE'S NOT A PART OF THIS!
hsh
INU-YASHA!
ALAS, I'M AFRAID SHE IS.
MERELY BY BEING YOUR COMPANION.
KRAK KRAK

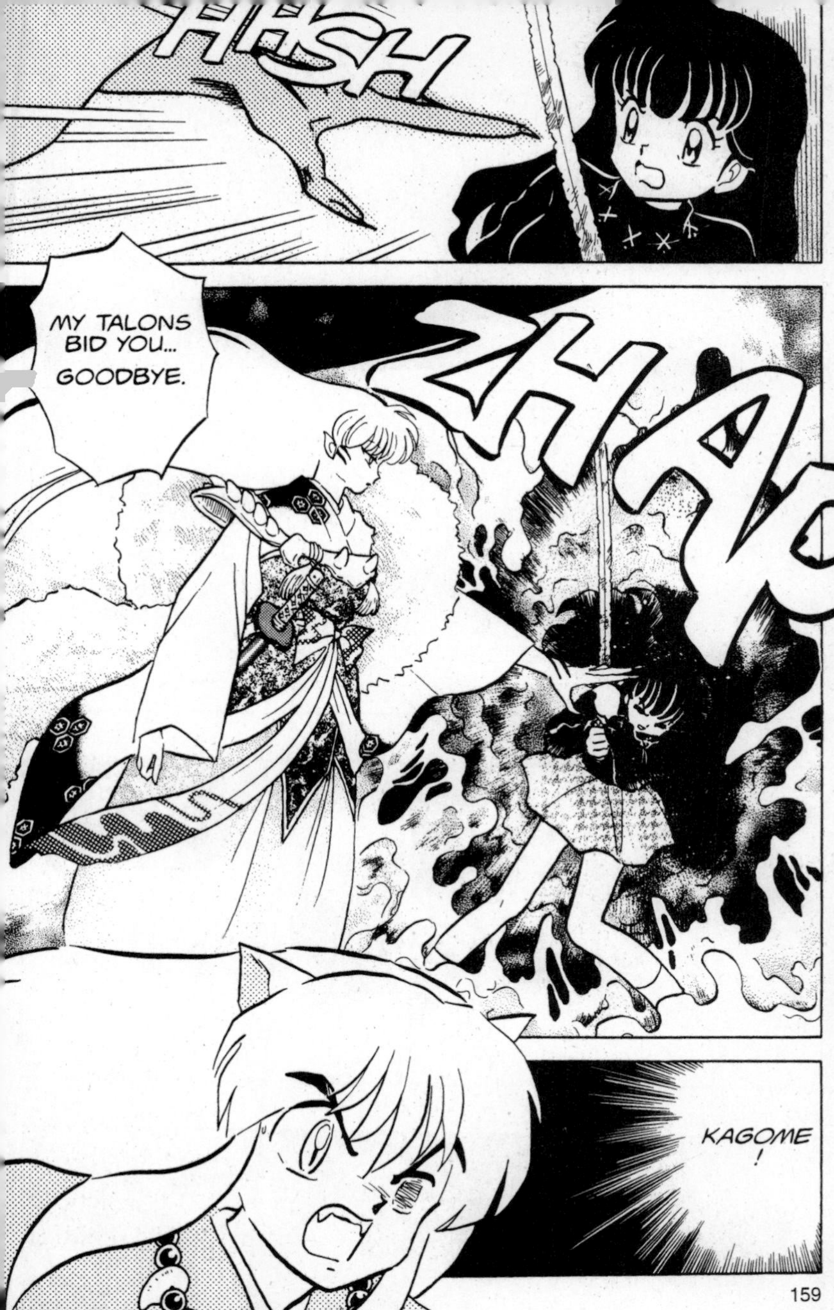
HHSH
MY TALONS BID YOU... GOODBYE.
ZHAP
KAGOME!

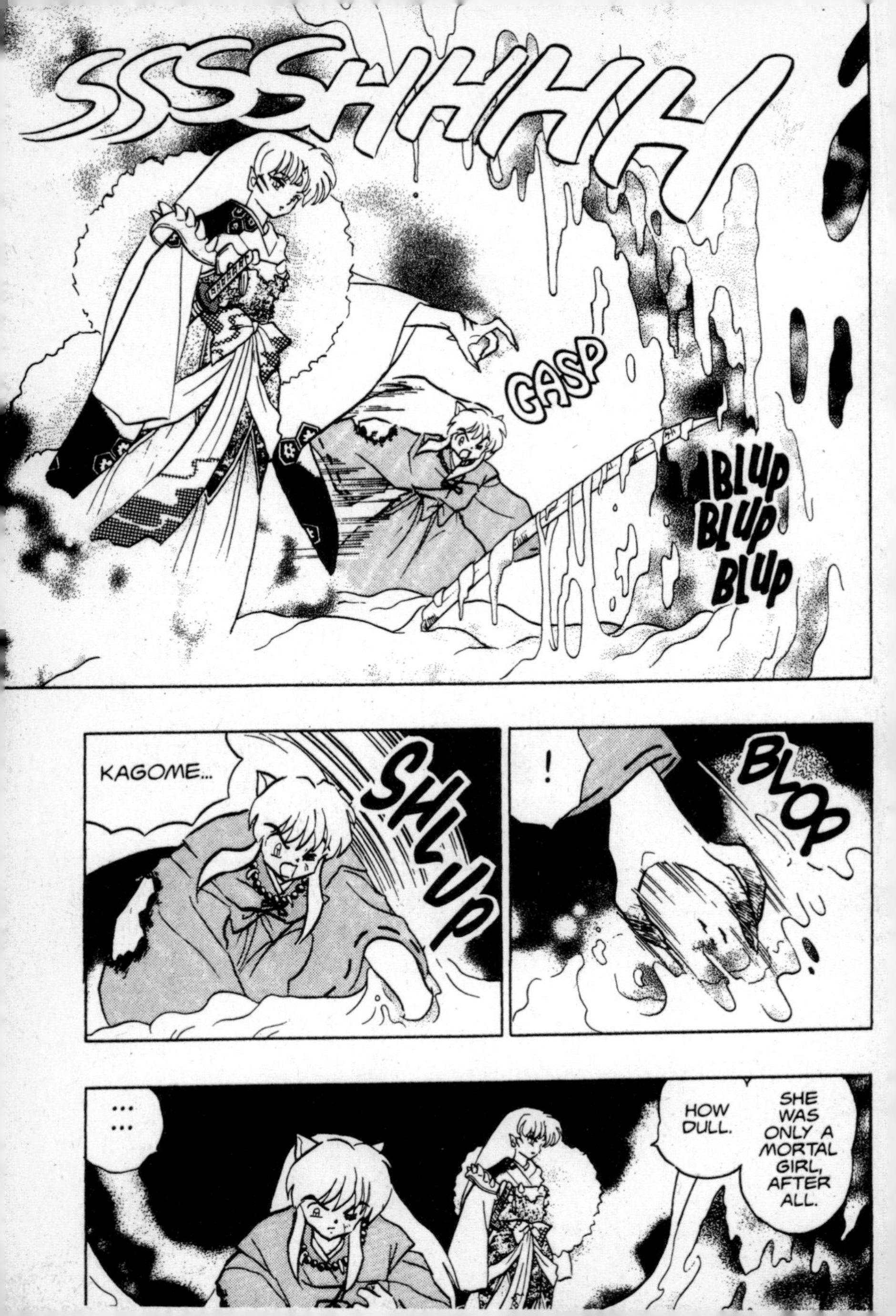
SSSSHHHH
GASP
BLUP
BLUP
BLUP
KAGOME...
SHLUP
!
BLOOP
......
HOW DULL.
SHE WAS ONLY A MORTAL GIRL, AFTER ALL.

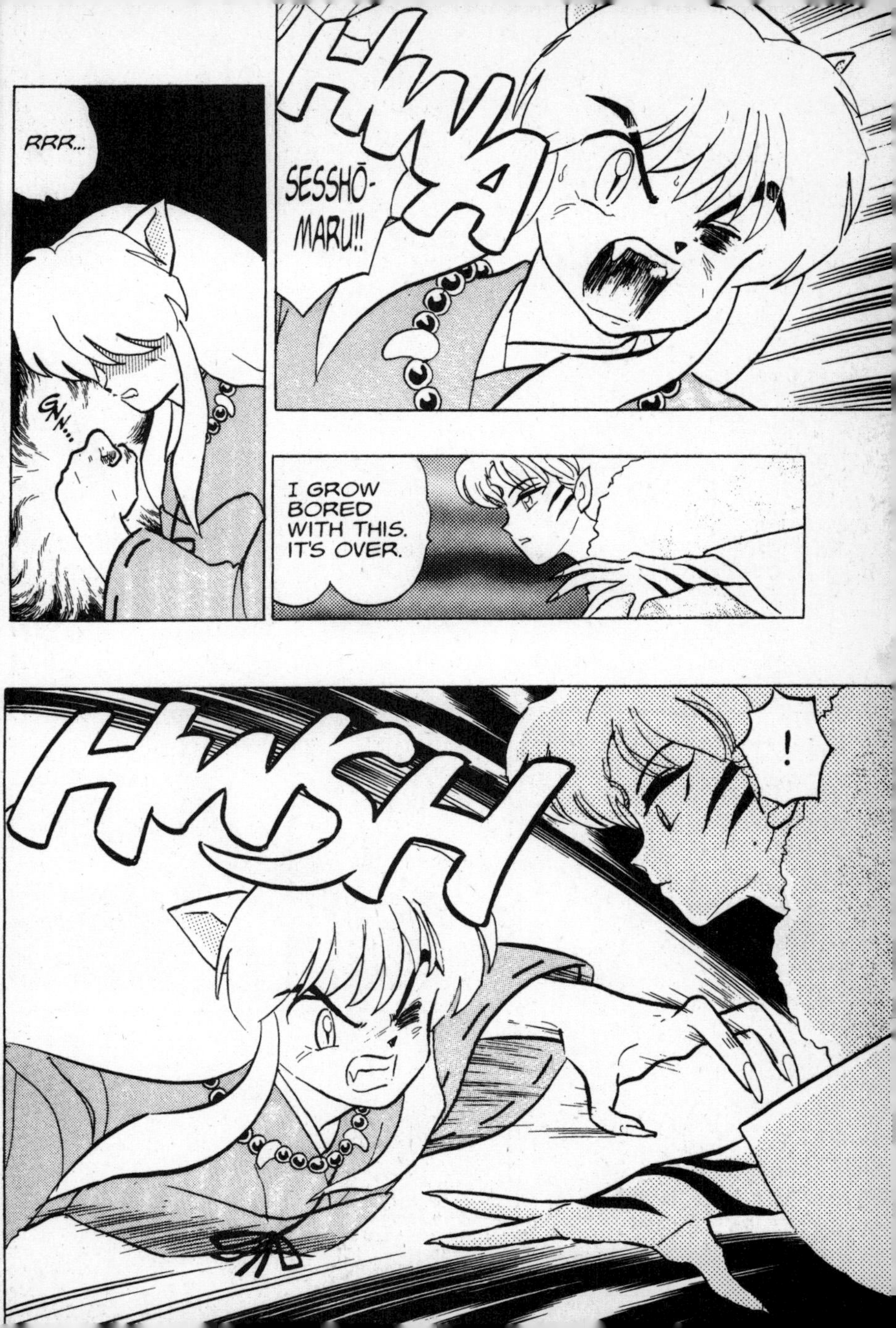
RRR...
GNN...
HWA
SESSHŌ-MARU!!
I GROW BORED WITH THIS. IT'S OVER.
HWSH
!

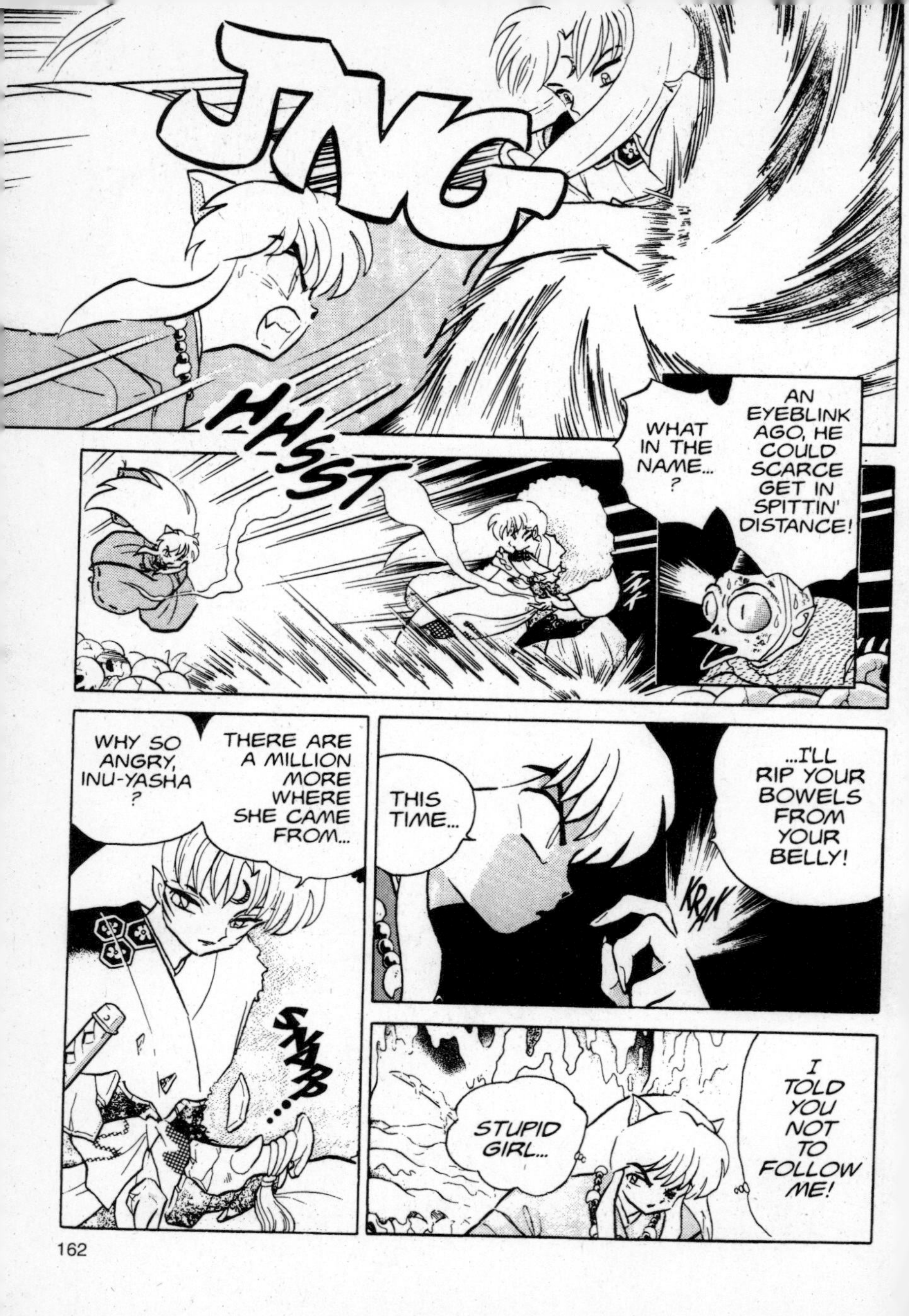
JING
HHSST
WHAT IN THE NAME...?
AN EYEBLINK AGO, HE COULD SCARCE GET IN SPITTIN' DISTANCE!
WHY SO ANGRY, INU-YASHA?
THERE ARE A MILLION MORE WHERE SHE CAME FROM...
SNAP...
THIS TIME...
...I'LL RIP YOUR BOWELS FROM YOUR BELLY!
KRAK
STUPID GIRL...
I TOLD YOU NOT TO FOLLOW ME!

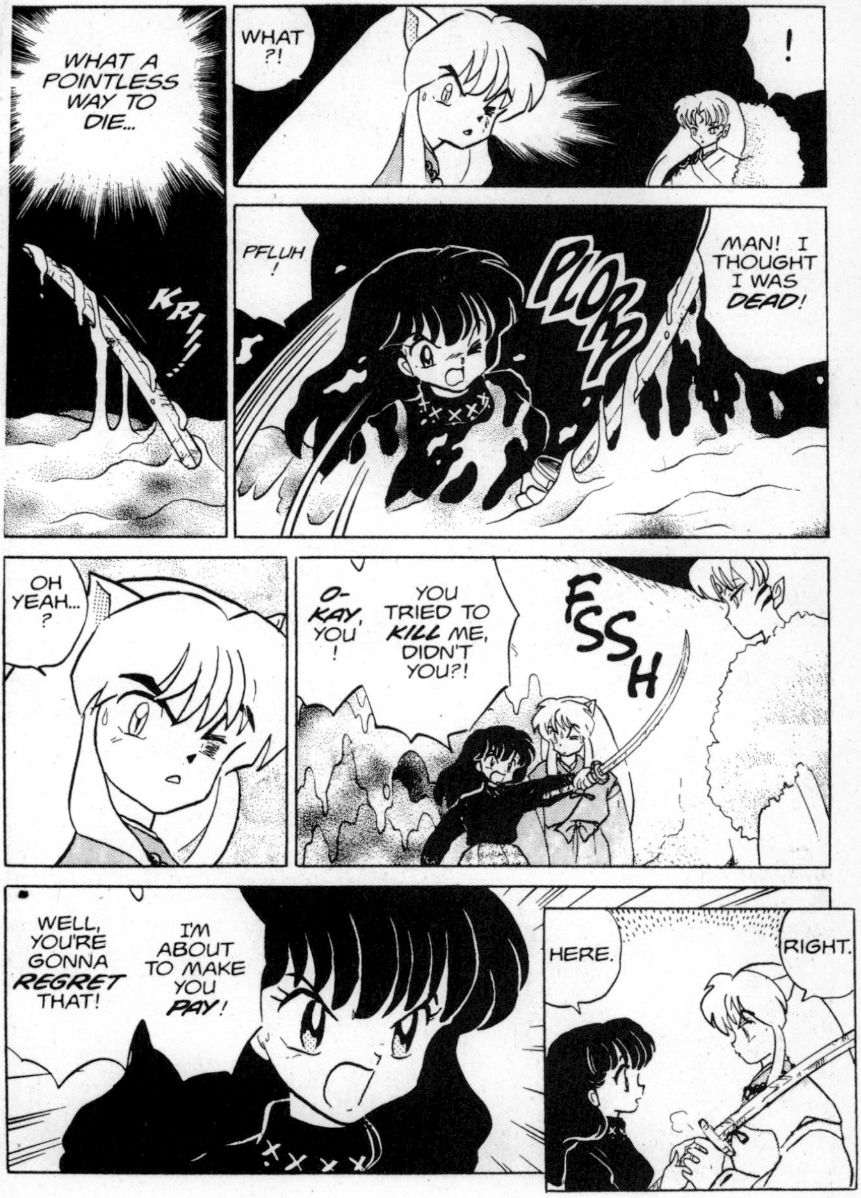
WHAT A POINTLESS WAY TO DIE...
WHAT ?!
!
KRI...
PFLUH !
PLOP
MAN! I THOUGHT I WAS DEAD!
OH YEAH... ?
O-KAY, YOU !
YOU TRIED TO KILL ME, DIDN'T YOU?!
FSSH
WELL, YOU'RE GONNA REGRET THAT!
I'M ABOUT TO MAKE YOU PAY!
HERE.
RIGHT.

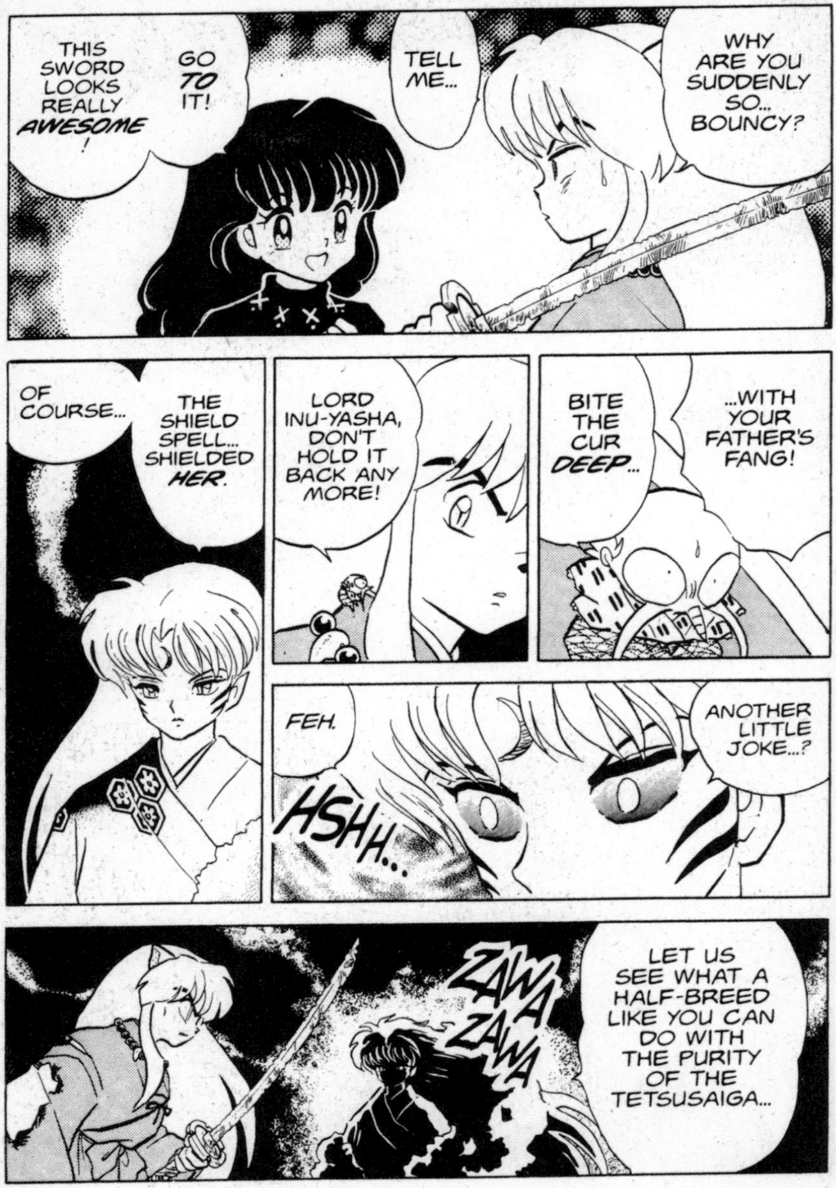
THIS SWORD LOOKS REALLY AWESOME!
GO TO IT!
TELL ME...
WHY ARE YOU SUDDENLY SO... BOUNCY?
OF COURSE...
THE SHIELD SPELL... SHIELDED HER.
LORD INU-YASHA, DON'T HOLD IT BACK ANY MORE!
BITE THE CUR DEEP...
...WITH YOUR FATHER'S FANG!
FEH.
HSHH...
ANOTHER LITTLE JOKE...?
ZAWA ZAWA
LET US SEE WHAT A HALF-BREED LIKE YOU CAN DO WITH THE PURITY OF THE TETSUSAIGA...

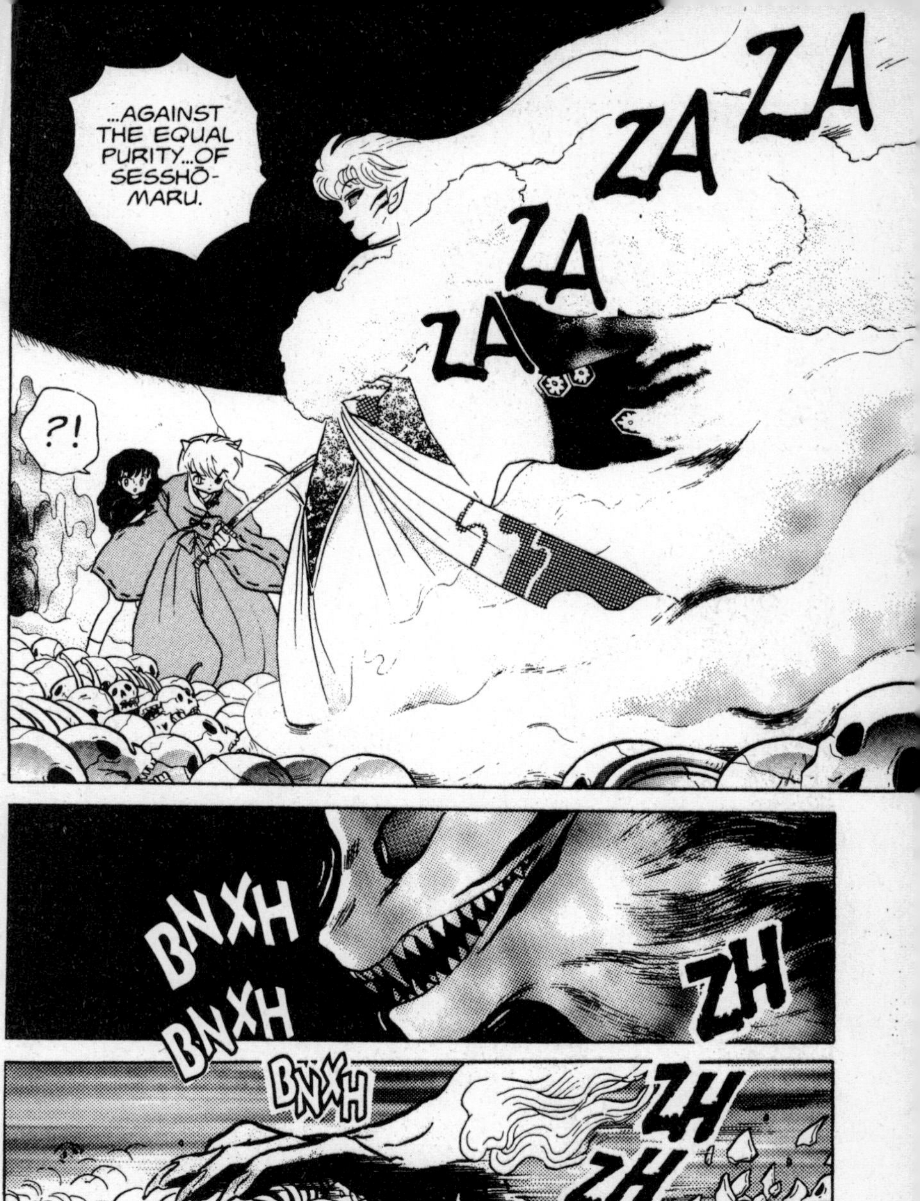
...AGAINST THE EQUAL PURITY...OF SESSHŌ-MARU.
ZA ZA ZA ZA ZA
?!
BNXH BNXH
ZH
BNXH
ZH ZH

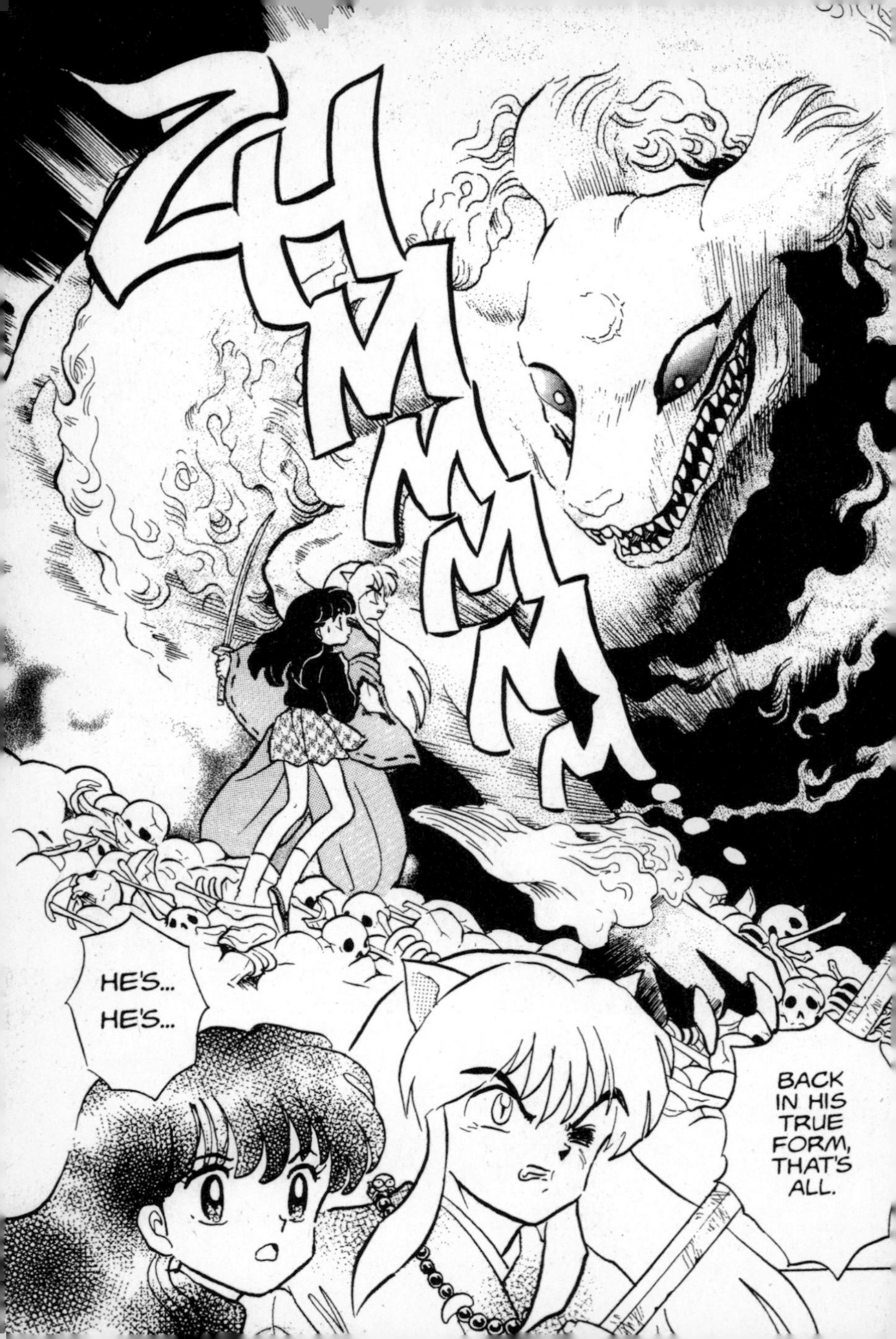
ZHMMMMM
HE'S... HE'S...
BACK IN HIS TRUE FORM, THAT'S ALL.

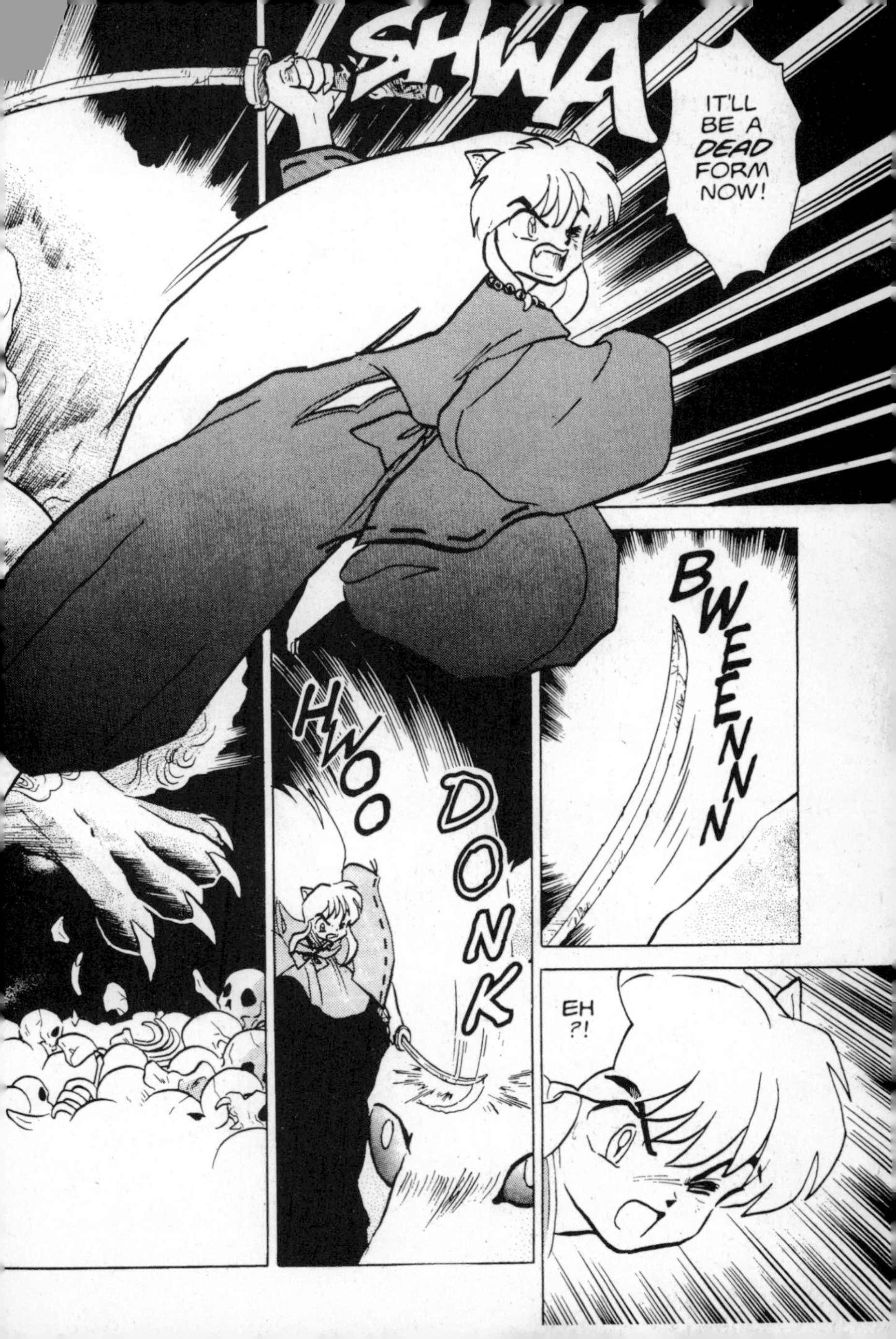
SHWA
IT'LL BE A *DEAD* FORM NOW!
HWOO
DONK
BWEENNN
EH ?!

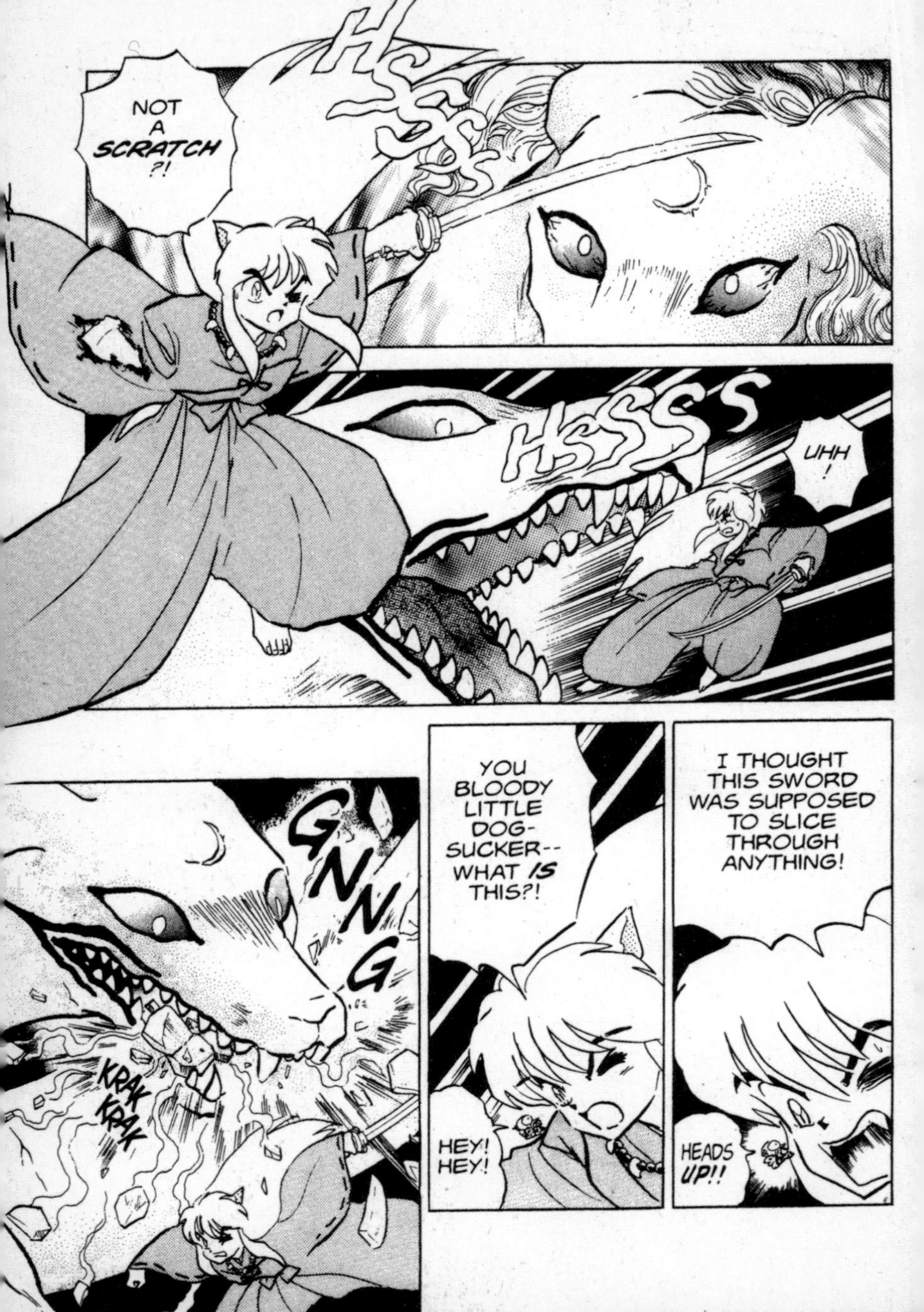
HISSS
NOT A SCRATCH ?!
HISSSS
UHH !
GNNG
KRAK KRAK
YOU BLOODY LITTLE DOG-SUCKER-- WHAT IS THIS?!
HEY! HEY!
I THOUGHT THIS SWORD WAS SUPPOSED TO SLICE THROUGH ANYTHING!
HEADS UP!!

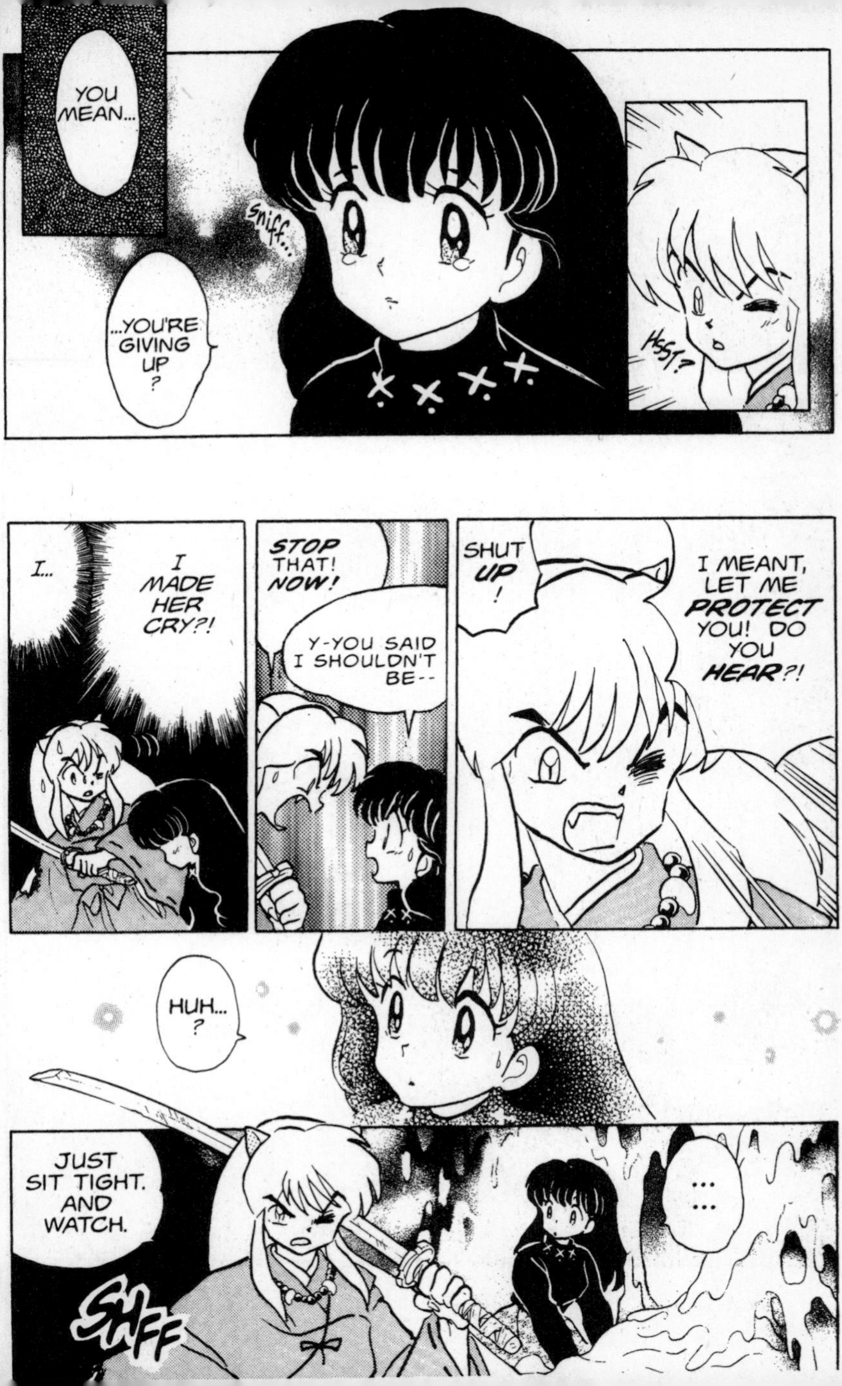
YOU MEAN...
Sniff...
...YOU'RE GIVING UP ?
HSST?
I...
I MADE HER CRY?!
STOP THAT! NOW!
Y-YOU SAID I SHOULDN'T BE--
SHUT UP!
I MEANT, LET ME PROTECT YOU! DO YOU HEAR?!
HUH... ?
JUST SIT TIGHT. AND WATCH.
SHFF
......

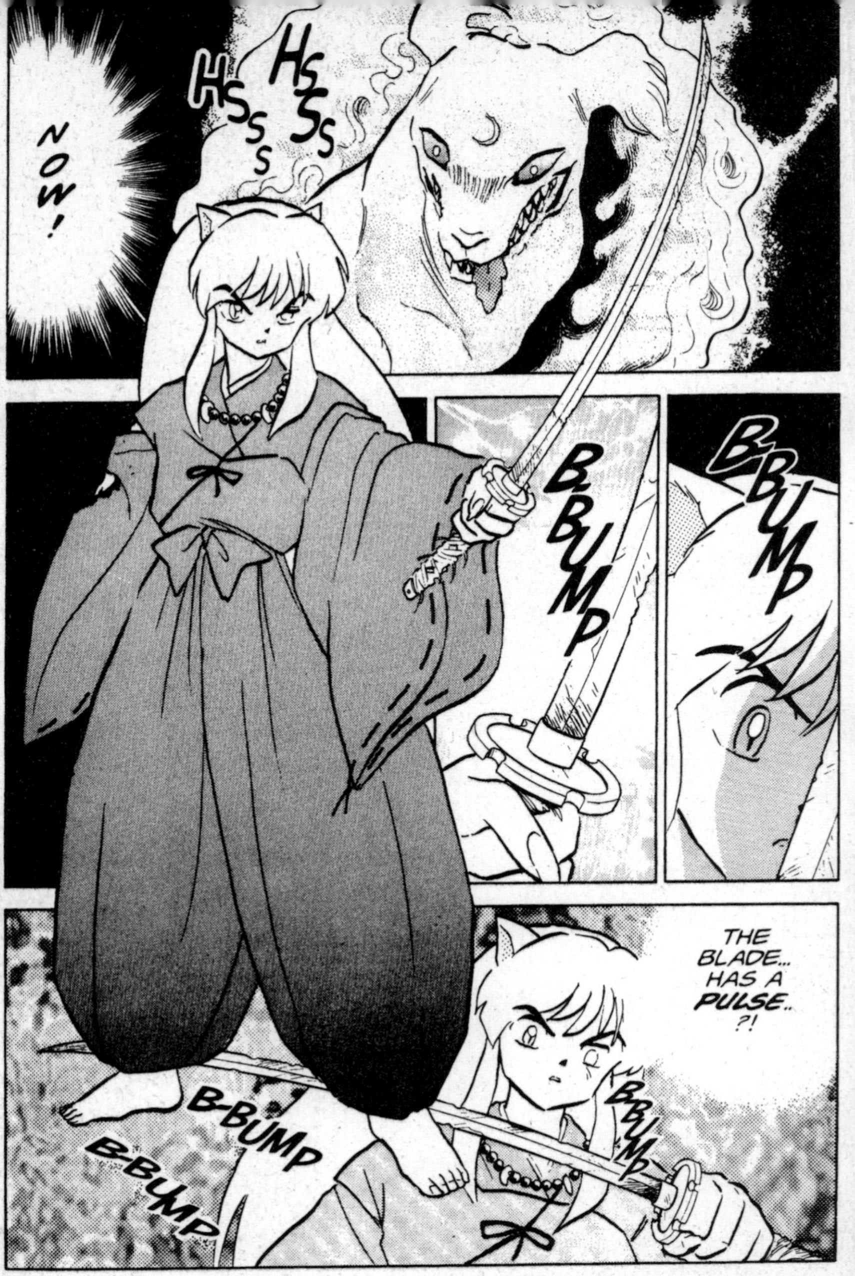
NOW!
HSSSS
HSSSS
BBUMP
BBUMP
THE BLADE... HAS A **PULSE**.. ?!
B-BUMP
B-BUMP
BBUMP

SCROLL TEN

LEGACY

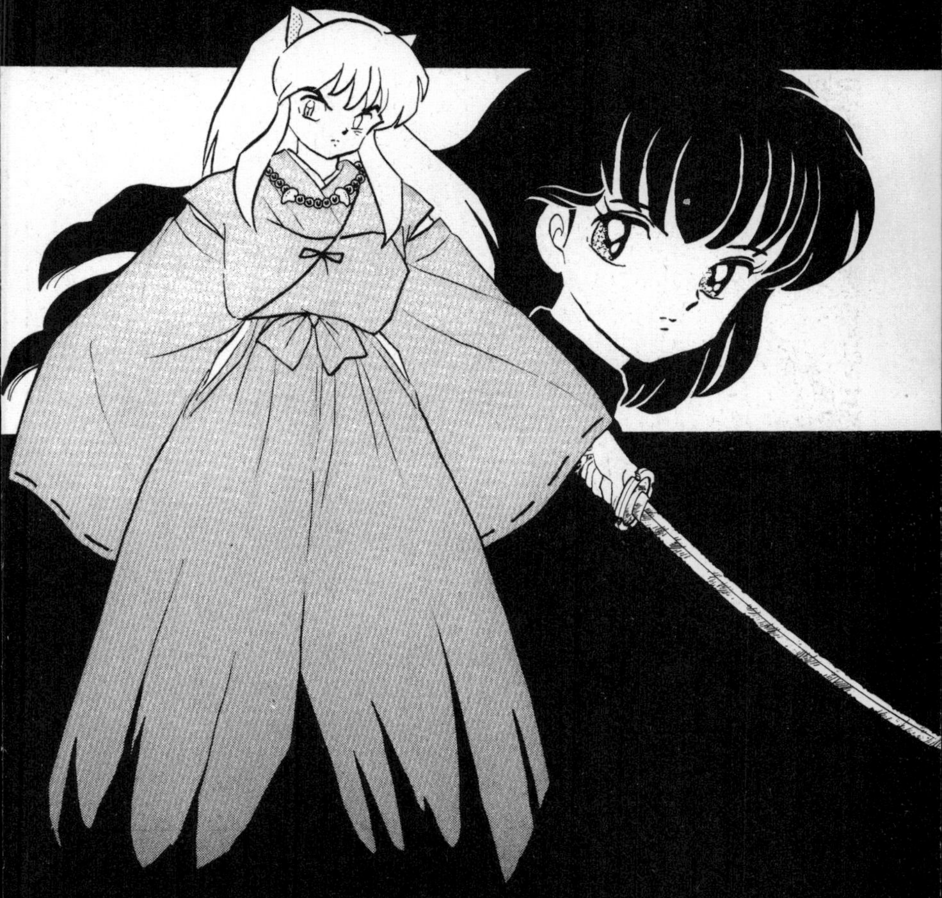

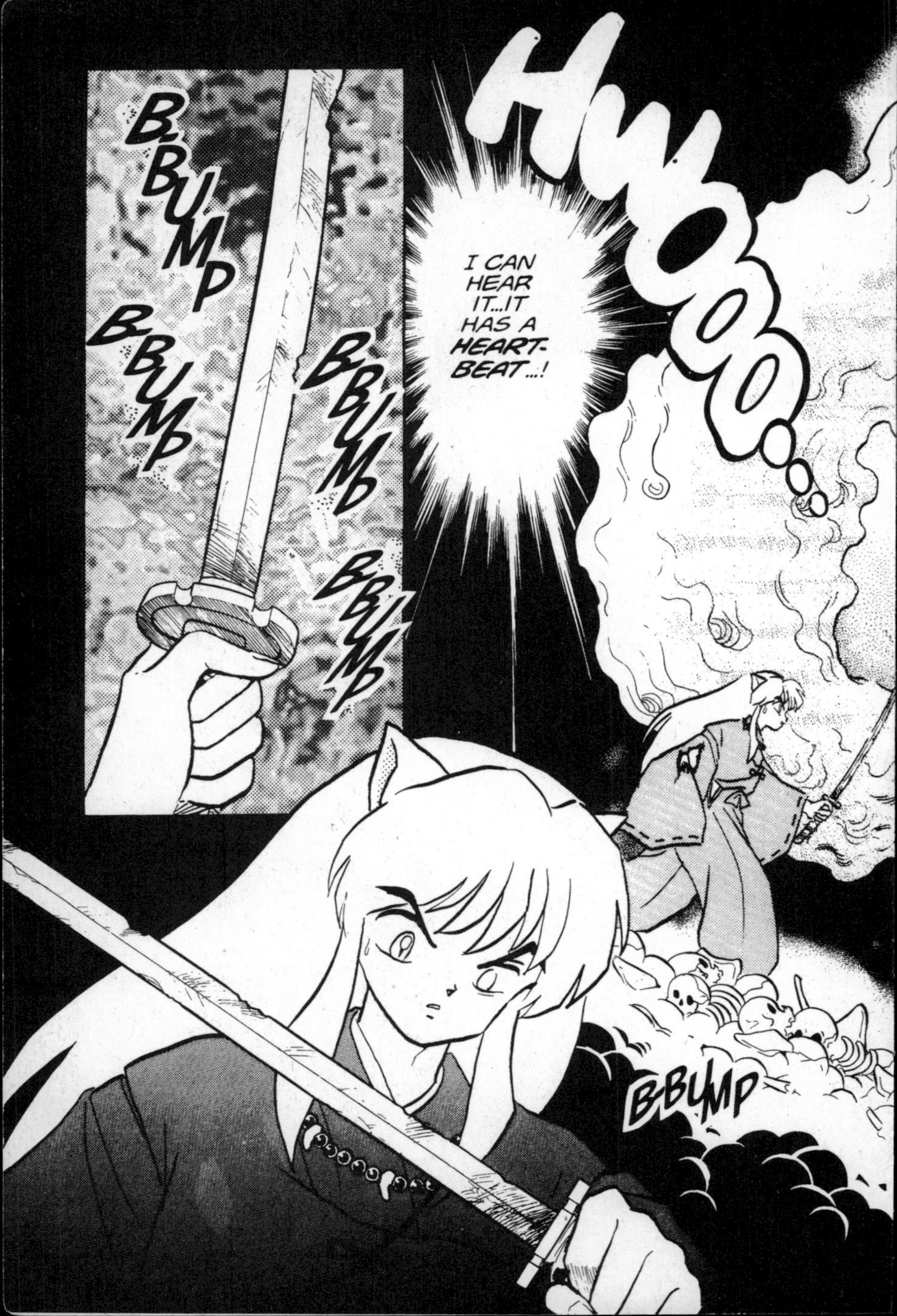
B-BUMP
B-BUMP
B-BUMP
B-BUMP
HWOOOO......
I CAN HEAR IT...IT HAS A HEART-BEAT...!
B-BUMP

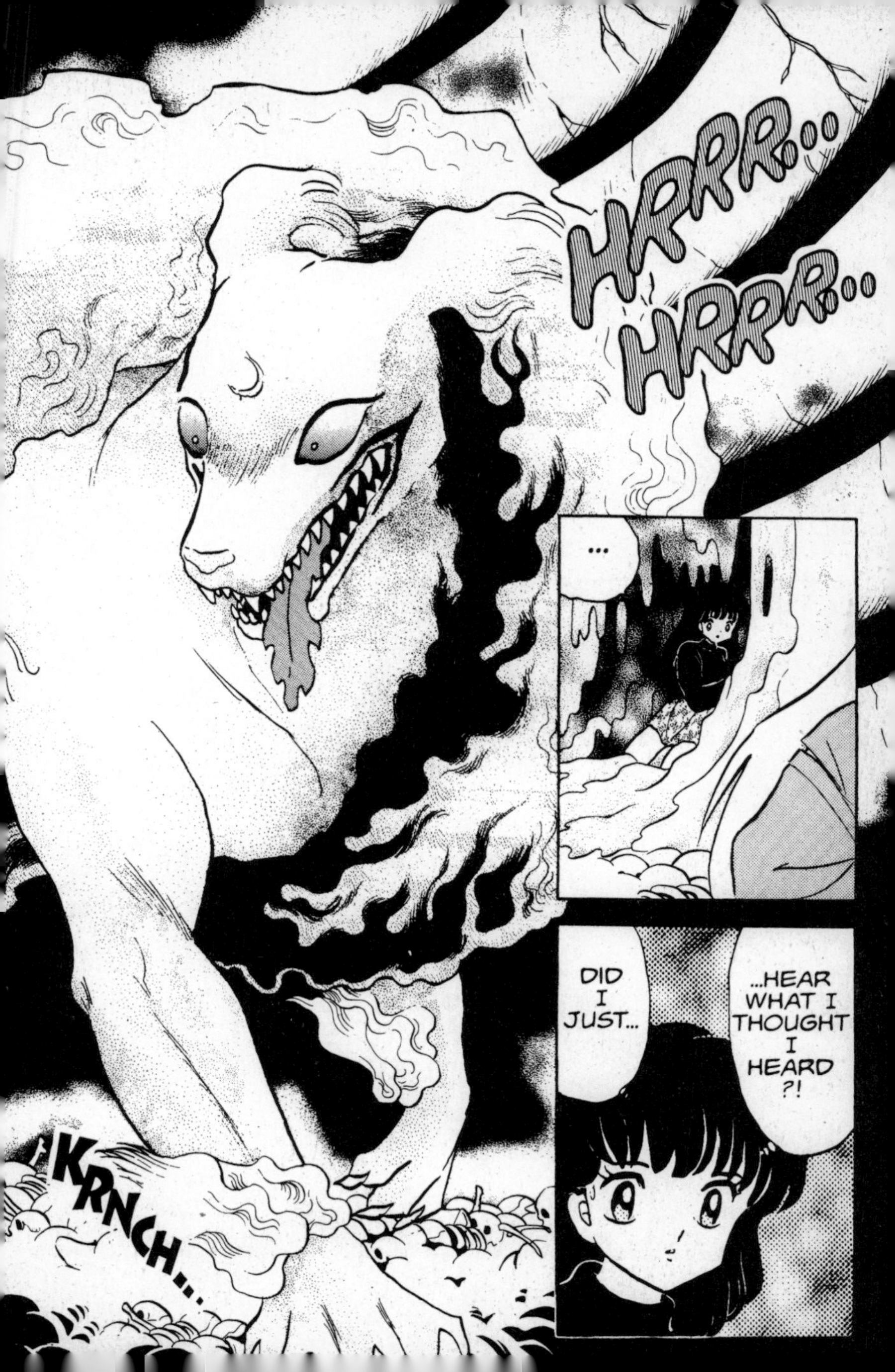
HRRR...
HRRR...
KRNCH...
...
DID I JUST...
...HEAR WHAT I THOUGHT I HEARD ?!

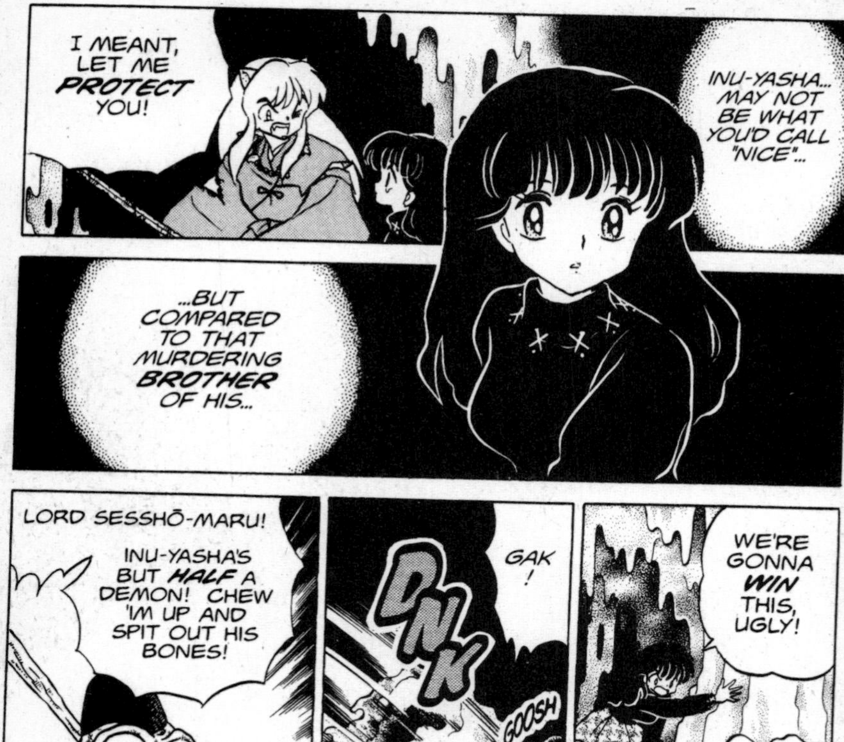
I MEANT, LET ME PROTECT YOU!
INU-YASHA... MAY NOT BE WHAT YOU'D CALL "NICE"...
...BUT COMPARED TO THAT MURDERING BROTHER OF HIS...
LORD SESSHŌ-MARU!
INU-YASHA'S BUT HALF A DEMON! CHEW 'IM UP AND SPIT OUT HIS BONES!
DNK
GAK!
GOOSH
WE'RE GONNA WIN THIS, UGLY!
GOOD LUCK, INU-YASHA!

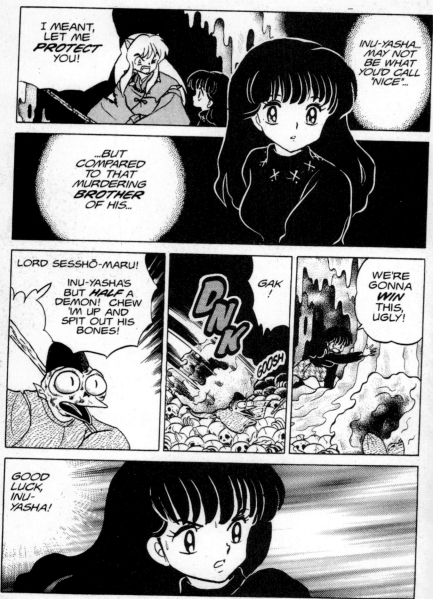

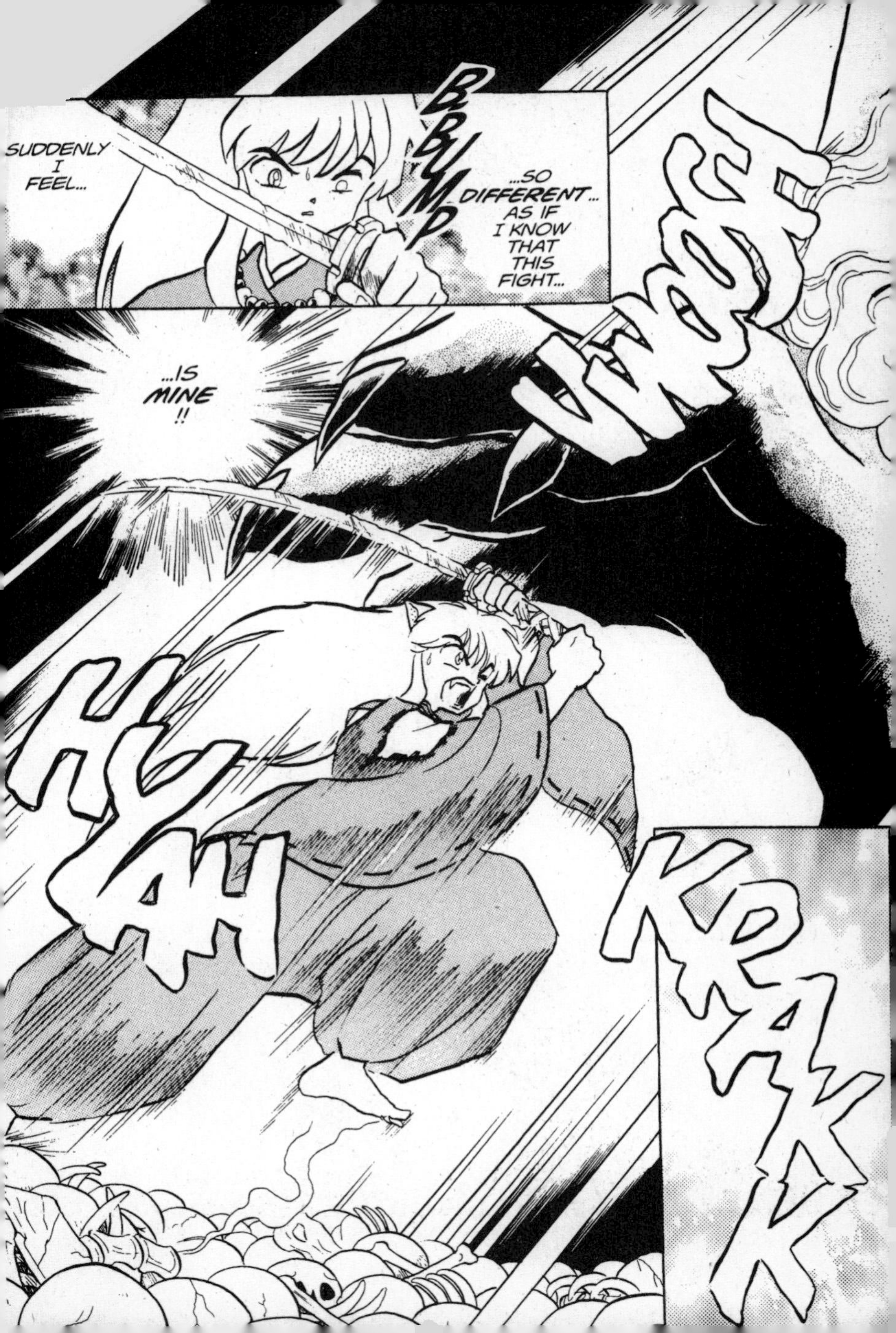
SUDDENLY I FEEL...
BA-BUMP
...SO DIFFERENT... AS IF I KNOW THAT THIS FIGHT...
...IS MINE !!
HAH
KRAKK

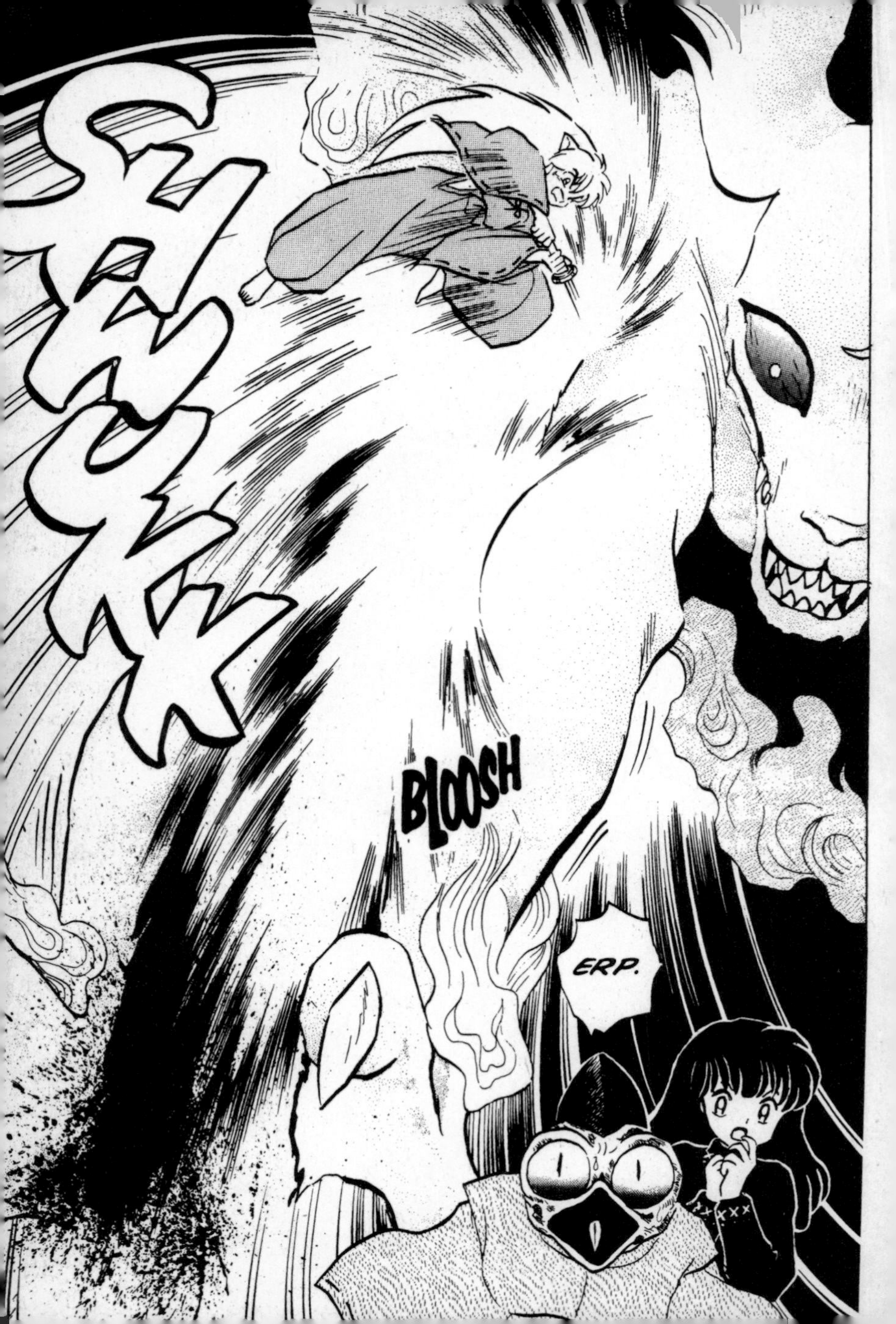
BLOOSH
ERP.

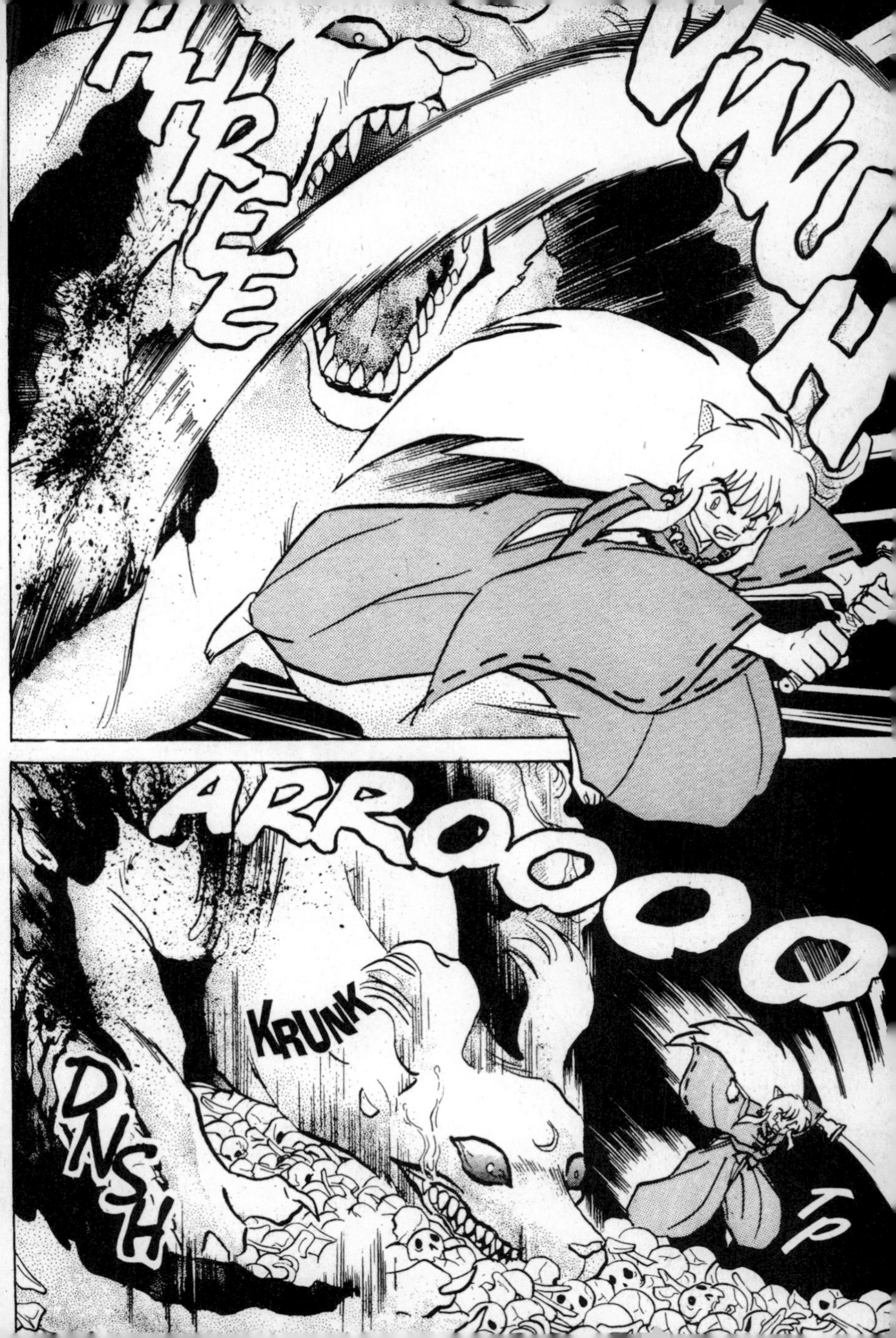
ARROOOOO
KRUNK
DNSH

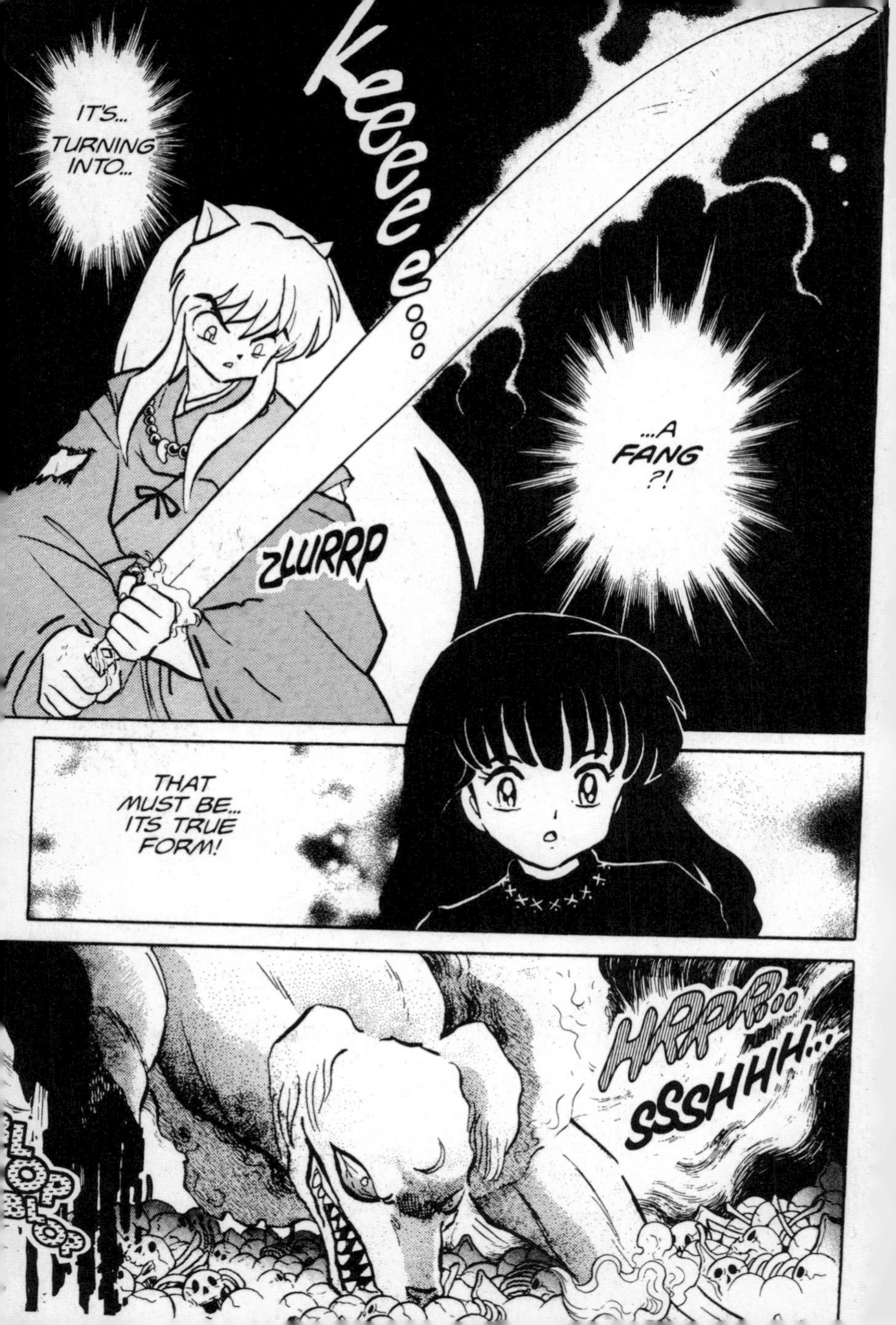
IT'S... TURNING INTO...
Keeeeeeooo
ZLURRP
...A FANG ?!
THAT MUST BE... ITS TRUE FORM!
LOP
BLOP
SSSHHH...

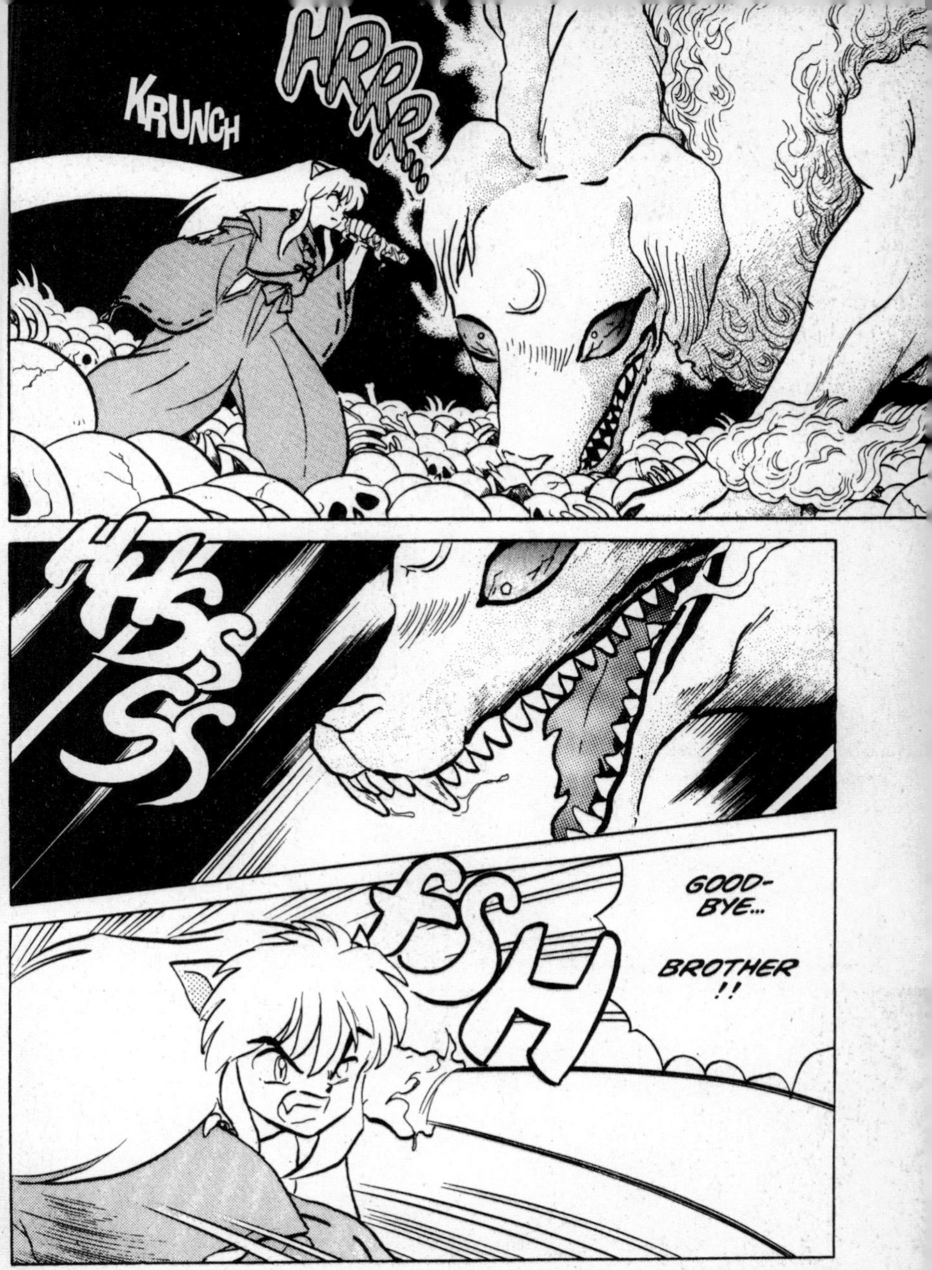
KRUNCH
HRRR...
HISSS
FSH
GOOD-BYE...
BROTHER !!

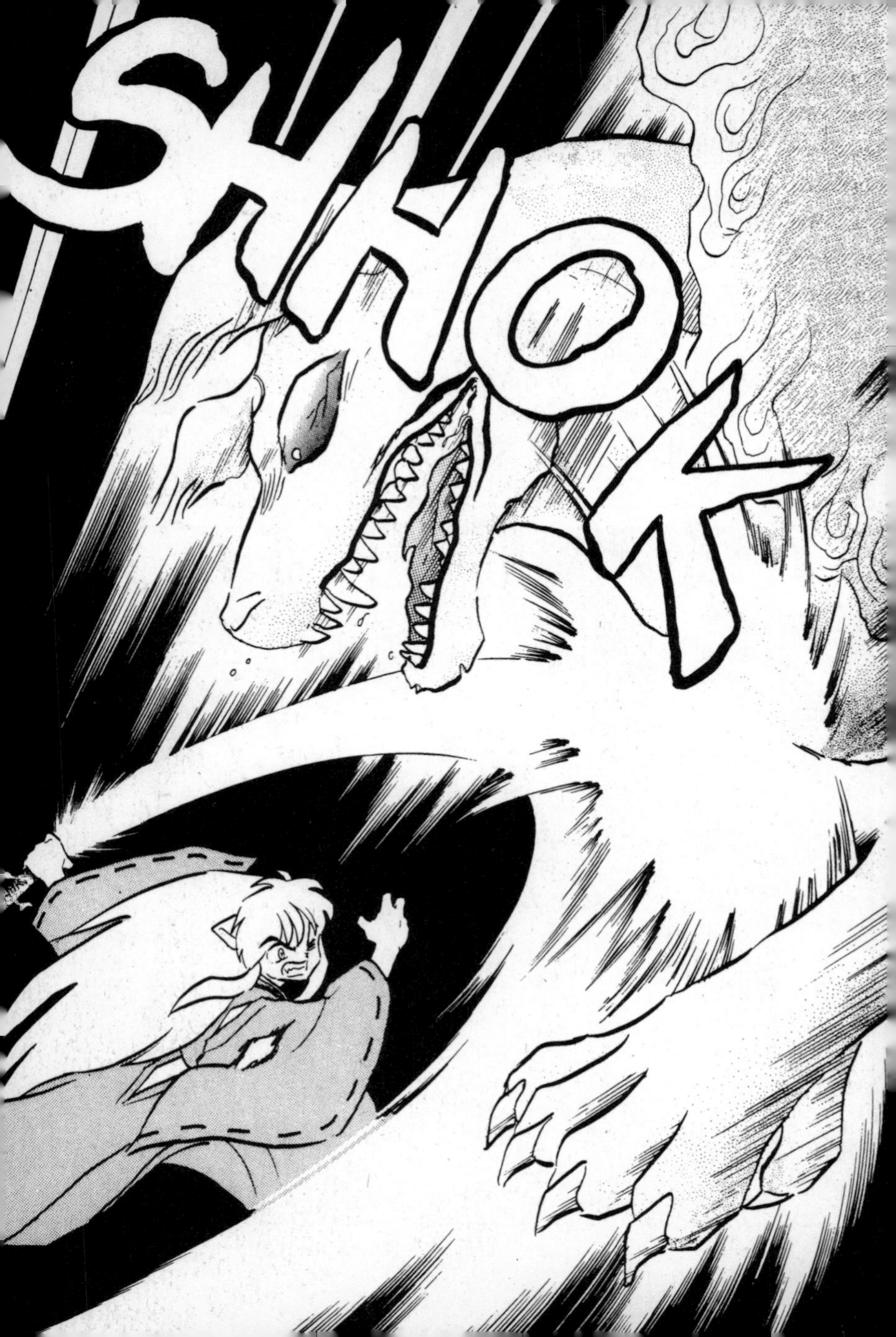
SHHOK

TO BE CONTINUED...

About Rumiko Takahashi

Born in 1957 in Niigata, Japan, Rumiko Takahashi attended women's college in Tokyo, where she began studying comics with Kazuo Koike, author of *CRYING FREEMAN*. She later became an assistant to horror-manga artist Kazuo Umezu (*OROCHI*). In 1978, she won a prize in Shogakukan's annual "New Comic Artist Contest," and in that same year her boy-meets-alien comedy series *URUSEI YATSURA* began appearing in the weekly manga magazine *SHÔNEN SUNDAY*. This phenomenally successful series ran for nine years and sold over 22 million copies. Takahashi's later *RANMA 1/2* series enjoyed even greater popularity.

Takahashi is considered by many to be one of the world's most popular manga artists. With the publication of Volume 34 of her *RANMA 1/2* series in Japan, Takahashi's total sales passed *one hundred million* copies of her compiled works.

Takahashi's serial titles include *URUSEI YATSURA, RANMA 1/2, ONE-POUND GOSPEL, MAISON IKKOKU* and *INUYASHA*. Additionally, Takahashi has drawn many short stories which have been published in America under the title "Rumic Theater," and several installments of a saga known as her "Mermaid" series. Most of Takahashi's major stories have also been animated, and are widely available in translation worldwide. *INUYASHA* is her most recent serial story, first published in *SHÔNEN SUNDAY* in 1996.

LOVE MANGA?
LET US KNOW WHAT YOU THINK!

HELP US MAKE THE MANGA
YOU LOVE BETTER!